YALE PUBLICATIONS IN THE HISTORY OF ART, 36
George L. Hersey, Editor

Frontispiece. Panoramic view of Farfa facing west

The Imperial Abbey of Farfa

ARCHITECTURAL CURRENTS OF THE EARLY MIDDLE AGES

Charles B. McClendon

YALE UNIVERSITY PRESS
New Haven and London

Published with assistance from the Frederick W. Hilles
Publication Fund of Yale University.

Designed by Susan P. Fillion and set in Weiss type by
The Composing Room of Michigan, Inc.
Printed in the United States of America by
Murray Printing Co., Westford, Mass.

Library of Congress Cataloging-in-Publication Data

McClendon, Charles B.
    The imperial abbey of Farfa.

    (Yale publications in the history of art, 36)
    Bibliography: p.
    Includes index.
    1. Abbey of Farfa.   2. Architecture, Carlovingian—
Italy—Farfa.   3. Architecture, Romanesque—Italy—
Farfa.   4. Farfa (Italy)—Buildings, structures, etc.
I. Title.   II. Series.
NA5621.F359M3   1987   726'.7'094525   86-3466
ISBN 0–300–03333–8 (alk. paper)

10   9   8   7   6   5   4   3   2   1

To J. A. C.

Contents

Acknowledgments

This study has been facilitated by many individuals and institutions. First among them is Richard Krautheimer, who has served as my mentor in every sense of the word. He first suggested the topic to me as deserving of detailed investigation and has subsequently provided steadfast support, enthusiastic encouragement, and constructive criticism during every phase of my work. My special thanks go also to the monastic community of Farfa Abbey, especially to Father Stefano Baiocchi and the present abbot, Father Anselmo Bussoni, for the warm hospitality I have enjoyed over the years while working at Farfa. Without such generosity this study could never have been realized.

My initial research and sojourn in Rome during the academic years 1974 to 1976 were made possible by a Samuel H. Kress Art History Fellowship to the Bibliotheca Hertziana. Subsequent grants from the Kress Foundation have helped to cover the costs of fieldwork at the monastery and of the completion of the architectural drawings that form an integral part of this book. In this regard, I wish to express my gratitude to the Foundation's former executive vice-president, the late Mary M. Davis, and to the current president, Dr. Marilyn Perry, for their continued support of my work. While I was a Kress Fellow in Rome, the Bibliotheca Hertziana and its director, the late Wolfgang Lotz, provided the ideal conditions for me to carry out my research. Among the members of the staff, all of whom were most helpful, special mention must go to three resident architects who were instrumental in producing the survey drawings of the medieval abbey church at Farfa. Claus-Christian Willems shared with me the demanding task of measuring and recording the remains of the building. Peter Haas and Gerhard Bergmann were responsible for minor modifications to the survey drawings and for all but one of the axonometric reconstructions. To them go my sincerest thanks for their patient and meticulous work. The resident photographer, Gabriele Fichera, provided several plate-negative photographs of the monumental east end of the abbey church that appear in this publication.

My dream of carrying out excavations of the medieval abbey at Farfa became a reality through the auspices of the British School at Rome and its former director, David Whitehouse, now chief curator of the Corning Museum of Glass in Corning, New York. In a dramatic demonstration of good faith, the British School organized and funded the first year of fieldwork in 1978, and Dr. Whitehouse has remained the driving force behind the excavation project ever since. In subsequent years, this work has received the generous support of a variety of additional funding sources, including the National Endowment for the Humanities, the Samuel H. Kress Foundation, the British Academy, and the Center for Field Research through its Earthwatch program. The permission to excavate was granted to the British School, over several seasons, first by Ing. Giovanni di Geso of the Soprintendenza per i Beni Ambientali ed Architettonici del Lazio and subsequently by Dr. Maria Luisa Veloccia Rinaldi of the Soprintendenza Archeologica del Lazio. The site supervisors, Peter Donaldson and Roberta Magnusson, helped to assure the success of the excavations in innumerable ways. To all the above go my heartfelt thanks.

Over the years, I have enjoyed the valuable advice of countless friends and colleagues, of whom only a few can be singled out for special mention. They are: Walter Cahn, Caecilia Davis-Weyer, Mario D'Onofrio, Judson Emerick, Creighton Gilbert, Katherine Kiefer, Joan Lloyd, John Mitchell, Valentino Pace, Cecil Striker, and Irmgard Voss. Bernhard Bischoff very kindly shared with me his unrivaled expertise on palaeographic matters. And Walter Horn has been a constant source of information and enthusiastic support.

A Morse Fellowship in the Humanities from Yale University, awarded for the academic year 1982–1983, allowed me the time and financial resources to prepare the manuscript for publication. During the same period, a grant-in-aid from the American Council of Learned Societies made it possible for me to inspect manuscripts in various European libraries that were relevant to my study of the Romanesque frescoes at Farfa. Similarly, an A. Whitney Griswold Faculty Research Grant from Yale enabled me to make a final inspection of the excavation site and the recovered artifacts. The architectural historian, Jean Bony, and the historian, Robert Brentano, renowned experts in their respective fields, were kind enough to read portions of an earlier draft of this text and to provide their detailed criticisms that in turn allowed me to avoid many pitfalls in fact and interpretation. Those errors that remain are entirely my own.

My thanks go to those at Yale University Press who have contributed to this publication: to George Hersey, editor of the Yale Publications in the History of Art Series; to Judy Metro, fine arts editor; and to Otto Bohlmann, who carefully edited the text. Also in New Haven, the architect Daniel Cecil prepared the maps and the final versions of the survey and reconstruction drawings of the abbey, the abbey church, and the excavations that appear in this volume. I cannot thank him enough for his expert draughtsmanship and his unwavering good humor. Another young architect, Keith Hudson, added some last-minute touches to these illustrations. And finally, my wife, Judith Calvert, has contributed to the completion of this study in ways beyond measure.

Introduction

The Benedictine abbey of Farfa was without question one of the great monasteries of Central Italy in the Middle Ages. Founded in the late seventh century through Lombard patronage, Farfa passed into Frankish hands with the conquests of Charlemagne and subsequently prospered under the protection and patronage of the Holy Roman Emperor until the Concordat of Worms in 1122. Its land holdings were extensive, and, as an important imperial establishment within a short distance of Rome (Map 1), the monastery often found itself at the center of events involving the empire and the papacy.

The importance of Farfa has long been recognized by historians, who have found its famous Register and Chronicle, both compiled ca. 1100 by the archivist Gregory of Catino, to be indispensable sources for the political, social, and economic history of medieval Italy. In contrast, the physical remains of the monastery itself have received little attention from historians of art and architecture, due in part to the fragmentary nature of the remains. Various archaeological investigations were initiated during the first decades of this century but for one reason or another were never completed. From 1959 to 1962, a restoration campaign by the Superintendency of the Monuments of Lazio (which is now the Soprintendenza per i Beni Ambientali ed Architettonici del Lazio) revealed more of the medieval church, but these discoveries were left

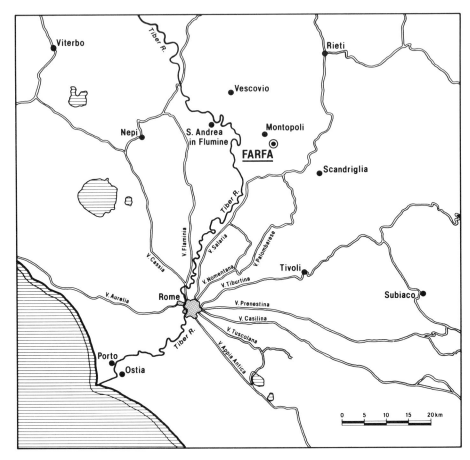

MAP 1. Map of Central Italy showing the locations of Farfa, neighboring sites,
and ancient Roman roads

largely unstudied. The historical significance of Farfa alone seemed to warrant a
new examination of the material, and this study was first conceived to fulfill
that goal.

My work began in 1974–1975 with a detailed examination of the visible
remains of the medieval church, which resulted in a thorough photographic
record and a series of survey drawings, rendered on a scale of 1:50. During this
process, various phases in the building's construction became apparent; once
established, these phases could be reconstructed and dated through historical,
archaeological, and stylistic evidence. These results, in turn, permitted an
assessment of the place of the Farfa abbey church in the overall development of
medieval architecture. The primary purpose, then, has been to record and
analyze this little-known medieval monument; moreover, in spite of the incomplete state of its remains, sufficient information exists to provide a detailed

picture of the medieval abbey church and an understanding of the circumstances under which it was built.

A few words of explanation should be added. The extensive remains of fresco decoration in various parts of the abbey church will be considered here only insofar as they pertain to the building's history. The paintings will be described, their decorative programs reconstructed as much as possible, and an approximate date proposed on the basis of stylistic or historical evidence. A full stylistic and iconographic treatment, however, particularly of the Romanesque wall paintings in the base of the bell tower, goes beyond the scope of this architectural monograph. Such a study would necessarily involve not only a detailed technical examination of the paintings but also an extensive comparative analysis of manuscript illumination and other wall paintings in the region that would take us too far afield. Although I hope to complete such a project in the near future, my primary concern here will be to see how these paintings relate to their architectural setting.

Excavations at Farfa abbey were initiated in 1978, sponsored jointly by the British School at Rome and Yale University, with David Whitehouse, then director of the British School (now chief curator at the Corning Museum of Glass in Corning, New York), and myself serving as directors of the project. The area made available for investigation lay adjacent to the west end of the medieval abbey church and corresponds in size (40×40m.) to almost one-sixth of the monastic site. By 1983, after six seasons of fieldwork, the remains of numerous medieval features had been uncovered, including a courtyard with paved walkways, several contingent structures, a subsidiary chapel, and numerous burials. Substantial evidence of pre- and post-medieval habitation was also found. More limited seasons in 1984 and 1985 have helped to clarify these earlier findings. Preliminary reports of the excavations have appeared in the Italian journals *Archeologia medievale* and *Archivio della società romana di storia patria*. A full analysis of the project together with specialized studies of the pottery, coins, glass, and human, animal, and botanical remains, will appear in the final report, now in preparation. The results of this extensive investigation can only be summarized here insofar as they pertain to the medieval monastic layout, and my analysis of the excavations should be viewed as preliminary while the wealth of archaeological data continues to be evaluated. Nevertheless, the major building phases of the monastery are clear and need to be seen in conjunction with the history of the medieval abbey church. My remarks are therefore addressed to those interested primarily in the history of architecture rather than medieval archaeology per se. In this way, the present volume should be seen both as a separate work, standing on its own merits, and as an eventual complement to the final excavation report.

This study is thus both limited and ambitious in scope. It is limited in that its concerns are predominantly architectural, and it is ambitious in its attempt to evaluate the significance of the various building phases of the abbey in the broader context of the architectural currents of the early Middle Ages. The remains of the medieval abbey at Farfa shed light on obscure yet pivotal moments in the development of medieval architecture as a whole. In addition, an attempt has been made to go beyond the analysis of forms in order to understand the function of various architectural features and the motivations behind their adoption. Here the extensive archaeological evidence, together with the historical record, help to provide the human factor that is all too often missing in studies concerned solely with the development of styles and building technology.

The book has been arranged in a form that as much as possible separates fact from interpretation. Thus the first three chapters provide the historical and archaeological information upon which this study is based, so that the reader can arrive at his or her own conclusions. Chapters 4–6, on the other hand, represent my own ordering of the material in a chronological sequence involving a comparative study of representative buildings in each period. Such a "synthetic approach" is meant to place the achievements of the abbey of Farfa in their proper setting. Above all, I have tried to convey some sense of the creative dynamics involved in the development of architecture in Europe from the eighth through the eleventh centuries and the role Farfa may have played in this process.

1

The Historical Background
and Its Sources

It is not my purpose to recount the ab-
bey's history in full, for in 1921 Ildefonso Schuster published a monumental
history of the abbey of Farfa entitled *L'imperiale abbazia di Farfa*, which in spite of
the need for revision has yet to be superseded.[1] In order to understand the
historical background to the archaeological and art-historical concerns of this
study, however, it is important to review the documentary evidence upon
which present knowledge is based and to outline the major events in the
monastery's history.

THE SOURCES

The most important primary sources for the history of Farfa are provided in the
work of Gregory of Catino, a monk and archivist of the monastery at the end of
the eleventh and the beginning of the twelfth centuries.[2] In 1092, at the age of
thirty-two, Gregory was asked by Abbot Berardus II to compile the charters of
the monastery. This work, entitled *Liber gemniagraphus sive cleronomialis ecclesiae
pharphensis*, is usually referred to as the *Regestum farfense*, or simply the Farfa
Register.[3] By ca. 1100, Gregory had transcribed the documents up to his own
time.[4] The project was taken up again twenty-five years later by Gregory's

1

nephew and pupil, Todinus, who added some seventy folios of contemporary and older texts to the compendium. In all, the collection comprises some 1,300 documents and is preserved today in two large volumes in the Vatican Library (Vat. lat. 8487). [5]

Around 1103, Gregory began to collect transactions in land and other property belonging to the monastery in the *Liber largitorius vel notarius monasterii pharphensis*, now a codex in the Biblioteca Nazionale in Rome under the heading of Ms. Farf. 2. Before completing this task, however, Gregory turned his energies to condensing much of the information contained in the Register and the *Liber largitorius* into an untitled chronicle, known today as the *Chronicon farfense*, or Farfa Chronicle (Bib. Naz. Ms. Farf. 1). [6] Gregory's last work, the *Liber floriger chartarum coenobii pharphensis* (Bib. Naz. Ms. Farf. 3), was begun around 1130, when he had reached his seventieth year, and it contains a topographical list of the monastery's land holdings. Gregory's prolific career as an archivist and historian was not only a high point in the literary achievements of the monastery, but it proved also to be of major consequence for the development of cartularies in medieval Italy. The Farfa Register, in particular, served as a model in the twelfth century for similar undertakings at the neighboring monasteries of Montecassino, S. Sofia at Benevento, and S. Vincenzo al Volturno. [7]

The Farfa Register and Chronicle were not the first times that the history of the monastery had been recorded, however. Two shorter works have come down to us that recount Farfa's earliest years and were therefore among the most important sources for Gregory's own research. The first of these is a history entitled *Libellus constructionis farfensis*, or simply the *Constructio*. It was written by an anonymous monk sometime in the second half of the ninth century and recounts the history of the monastery from its founding in the late seventh century until the death of the fourteenth abbot, Hildericus, in 857. The preserved text is not the original one but a copy forming part of a Farfa lectionary from the eleventh century (Bib. Naz. Ms. Farf. 32). The authenticity of the account has never been questioned, and its reliability was confirmed by the discovery in 1959 of a large portion of the carved epitaph of Abbot Sichardus (ca. 830–842), which is recorded word for word in the *Constructio*. Furthermore, the Latin text of the *Constructio* is less corrupt than other chronicles of the period in Italy, and this high standard of letters at Farfa has been explained as a reflection of the monastery's close relationship to Carolingian centers of learning north of the Alps. [8]

The second chronicle fortunately begins where the *Constructio* breaks off. It is aptly called *Destructio monasterii farfensis*, for its text covers a tragic period in the monastery's history when Saracen raids forced abandonment of the abbey in the late ninth century and a reestablishment in the tenth century fostered a scandalous laxity of morals. This is a very personal work, written by one of Farfa's most influential abbots, Hugo (998–1039), in which the monastery's once glorious past, tragic destruction, and recent depravity are evoked in an apparent attempt to promote the author's program of monastic reform. The text is preserved in a mid-sixteenth-century copy now in the Vatican Library (Vat. lat. 6216).[9]

Fortunately, all of the aforementioned historical sources have been published. The most important of these, the Farfa Register, was edited by Ignazio Giorgi and Ugo Balzani and published in five volumes from 1879 to 1914.[10] Balzani also published the Farfa Chronicle in two volumes in 1903, following an earlier edition by Muratori.[11] At the beginning of the first volume of the Chronicle, Balzani also included an edition of both the *Constructio* and *Destructio* and parts of the *Liber floriger*. The *Liber largitorio* was published by G. Zucchetti in two volumes in 1913 and 1932 respectively.[12] Taken together, these works form the basis for reconstructing the history of the monastery at Farfa in the Middle Ages.

Outside the strict realm of historical compilations, but nonetheless of significance to this study, is a liturgical guide usually referred to as the *Consuetudines farfenses*, or the Farfa Customary. Portions of the text were first published in the eighteenth century by Dom J. Mabillon, who knew only a corrupt version in the library of St. Paul's-outside-the-Walls in Rome.[13] Bruno Albers realized the primacy of a copy in the Vatican Library (Vat. lat. 6808) that was published in 1900 as the first volume in his *Consuetudines monasticae*.[14] In 1980, a new and definitive edition of the Farfa Customary appeared as part of the series *Corpus consuetudinum monasticarum* under the title *Liber tramitis aevi odolonis abbatis*.[15] The reference to Abbot Odilo of Cluny (994–1049) in the title of the new edition takes note of the fact that it is now universally recognized that the contents of the Customary, although written at Farfa, represent the liturgical practices of the great Burgundian abbey of Cluny.

Albers and others before him had accepted the text as a straightforward record of the customs of Farfa and therefore assumed that the famous description of the abbey church and other monastic buildings in chapter 142 referred to Farfa as well.[16] Ildefonso Schuster was among the first to realize that the layout of the monastery described in the Customary did not coincide with the topography at Farfa.[17] In addition, numerous other details, such as lists of relics, names of monks, and dedications of altars have been shown to have no relation to Farfa but are, instead, known from other sources to have been present at Cluny.[18] In retrospect, a Cluniac customary having been brought to Farfa is not surprising, in view of the fact that Farfa was reformed in the first half of the eleventh century under the strong influence of Cluny.

The preface and prologue of the Farfa Customary are in fact specific in explaining the methods and motivations for obtaining a Cluniac customary.[19] Abbot Hugo of Farfa (998–1039), in his desire to reform the abbey, sought first the aid of Romualdus of Ravenna and then Abbot Odilo of Cluny. It was in this spirit that Hugo wished to have a copy of the customs of the renowned

Burgundian abbey. John, a monk and disciple of Romualdus, went to Cluny in order to observe and record its liturgical practices.[20] While there, he combined two written versions of the Cluniac customs,[21] which he then brought back to his own monastery of S. Salvatore in Montopoli, situated only a few miles from Farfa.[22] This composite text was subsequently obtained by Abbot Hugo.

A careful study of the Vatican manuscript shows, however, that several redactions took place before the text reached its present form. The patchwork nature of this process is evident in the erratic order of the contents and several sections that are repetitive.[23] More telling are various chronological indications that contradict one another. For example, the description of the monastery must date to ca. 1040 because there is no mention of the famous marble cloister that Odilo built at Cluny in the last years of his life (d. 1049),[24] yet several individuals that the Customary names in a fragmentary necrology and in connection with a list of books distributed at Lent are known from other sources to have been alive as late as 1050.[25] From these and other indications the following sequence of events can be reconstructed: (1) sometime in the first quarter of the eleventh century, the monk John went to Cluny and brought back his compilation of the Cluniac customs, which was later made available to Abbot Hugo at Farfa; (2) Hugo himself seems to have been at Cluny between 1027 and 1032, at which time he may have obtained additional material, including the description of the abbey; (3) the necrology and booklist may have been brought by a Cluniac monk named Martin, who is known to have been at Farfa between 1050–1060; (4) a firm terminus ante quem for the final compilation is provided by the earliest marginal note in the manuscript, which refers to the translation of the relics of St. Nicholas from Myra in Asia Minor to Bari in South Italy in 1087.[26] Thus it would seem that the Vatican manuscript was written at Farfa sometime during the abbacy of Berardus I (1047–1089). A palaeographical analysis of the text supports a date in the second half of the eleventh century.[27]

The complex history of the Farfa Customary not only demonstrates the liturgical concerns of the abbey in keeping with the ideals of monastic reform but it also documents the continuous contact between Farfa and Cluny that was maintained throughout the first half of the eleventh century. As I shall show, the time of the Customary's compilation corresponds to a period of particular importance for the building history of the Italian abbey.

With the end of Gregory of Catino's scribal activities in the 1130s,[28] information concerning the abbey is far more limited. Papal and imperial decrees, miscellaneous correspondence, and occasional marginal notes in the Farfa Customary serve as the main historical sources during the later Middle Ages.[29] For the post-medieval period, the most detailed record is an unpublished chronicle in the Vatican Library (Barb. Lat. 2350, XXXII–141) written by Archangelus De Alexandris, another archivist at Farfa, who narrates the history of the abbey up to 1627. While the section concerning the Middle Ages is derived from the sources just described,[30] it does provide useful information about the development of the abbey in the Renaissance and early baroque periods. Miscellaneous records in the Archivio di Stato in Rome and the archives of the monastic library at Farfa, dating from the fourteenth century to the present day, supplement these later accounts.[31]

HISTORY

Little is known about the history of the site in antiquity. Its name comes from the nearby Farfa River, a tributary of the Tiber mentioned occasionally by classical authors. In the *Aeneid*, for example, Virgil refers to the Sabine ancestors of the Claudian line as "those who drink from the Tiber and the Farfarus," while in the *Metamorphoses* Ovid writes of "the naiads that dwell . . . in the deeply shaded Farfarus."[32] However, the name of the river was not used to designate the monastery until the late tenth century A.D. Before then it was usually described in documents, such as those compiled in the Farfa Register, as "in territorio sabinensi" or "in fundo Acutiano," referring to its location on the hillside of Monte Acuziano, now called Monte S. Martino.[33]

The monastery attributes its ultimate origin to an obscure figure known as Lawrence of Syria. He is first mentioned as the founder of the monastery in a letter of privilege from Pope John VII (705–707), where he is referred to as "Laurentius . . . episcopus venerandae memoriae."[34] According to the Farfa Chronicle and the *Liber floriger*, Lawrence was an ascetic from Syria who came to Italy on pilgrimage. He was elected a bishop of the Sabina but, because of his extreme piety, renounced his episcopal title in order to follow a more eremitic life. He is said to have performed many miracles (such as killing a dragon atop Monte Acuziano), and by so doing helped to convert the Sabine countryside to Christianity. He is reported to have founded a monastery toward the end of his life in the area of Farfa with a few disciples and his sister Susanna. The dates of Lawrence's activity in Italy are uncertain. Gregory of Catino was unsure but estimated that Lawrence had lived sometime between the end of the fourth and the middle of the fifth centuries.[35] Modern historians suggest a date in the sixth century as more likely, because it would be in keeping with the strong influence of eastern monasticism known to have been current in Central Italy at that time.[36] Recent archaeological evidence, discussed in the next chapters, tends to support the latter view.

Solid historical evidence begins only in the late seventh century with the arrival of Thomas of Maurienne, a priest and pilgrim from the Savoy region of southern Gaul. The mid-ninth-century *Constructio farfensis* recounts in considerable detail his founding of the monastery between 680 and 700. While praying late one night in the church of the Holy Sepulchre on a pilgrimage to the Holy Land, Thomas witnessed a vision of the Virgin Mary, who commanded him to

return to Italy and reopen an abandoned basilica dedicated in her name. Once
in the Sabina, Thomas and a small group of followers, with divine guidance,
came upon the dilapidated sanctuary, overgrown with vines and infested with
vipers, where he established a monastery.[37]

The new foundation soon attracted the attention of the Lombard duke of
Spoleto, Faroaldus II, who was also instructed by the Virgin in a dream to
support and protect her monastery.[38] In 705, Faroaldus II wrote to Pope John
VII requesting a letter of privilege containing the threat of anathema to those
who infringed upon the rights of the monastery. The request was granted in
that the pope recognized the Lombard duke's patronage, while reserving papal
jurisdiction over matters of consecration.[39] This laid the groundwork for a
duality of authority—secular and ecclesiastical, Lombard and Roman—that
would play such a significant role in the monastery's subsequent history. By his
death ca. 720, Thomas left the monastery established with ducal patronage,
papal sanction, and substantial territorial holdings. The stage was thus set for
the monastery's growth into a dominant force in the political and economic
affairs of Central Italy.

Thomas was succeeded as abbot by a series of capable men who came, for
the most part, from southern Gaul. Outstanding among the ten abbots of the
eighth century were Alanus of Aquitaine (ca. 761–769) and Probatus (ca. 770–
781), a Sabine native. Alanus was a pious scholar, famous for a series of
homilies,[40] who spent much of his time in seclusion beside an oratory of St.
Martin atop Monte Acuziano overlooking the monastery. Probatus, on the
other hand, was a practical man of action who in 778 completed construction of
an aqueduct to supply the burgeoning abbey.[41] Probatus also served as papal
emissary to the Lombard king Desiderius. The failure of the abbot's negotia-
tions was followed by Charlemagne's military intervention and seizure of the
Lombard crown in 774, which in turn brought Farfa under Frankish rule. In
775, Charlemagne declared the monastery exempt from civil and episcopal rule
and taxes, placing it on a par with the royal abbeys of northern Europe.[42] In
fact, Farfa was the first Italian abbey to receive such a privilege from the new
Frankish ruler.[43] Whether by chance or by policy, the next three abbots were
Franks: Ragambaldus (ca. 781–786) from Gaul, Altbertus (ca. 786–790) from
Paris, and Mauroaldus (ca. 790–802) from Worms.[44] It was also during this
period that the mixed rule, in practice at the abbey since its foundation by
Thomas of Maurienne, was replaced by the exclusive use of the Rule of St.
Benedict, a move in keeping with Charlemagne's precepts for monastic re-
form.[45]

Thus, by the turn of the ninth century, Farfa was closely linked with the new
imperial court at Aachen and the great ecclesiastical centers of the north. Abbot
Mauroaldus, for example, is known to have corresponded with Alcuin.[46] Abbot
Benedict (ca. 802–815) journeyed twice over the Alps to receive imperial
confirmation of the monastery's privileges, and he died while attending court at
Frankfurt.[47] In Abbot Ingoaldus (ca. 815–830), Farfa enjoyed an interna-

tionally renowned leader who spent much of his time in attendance at synods in the north and at the imperial court.[48] He also seems to have been a friend of Hilduin, abbot of both St.-Denis and St.-Medards at Soissons, and he may well have helped Hilduin obtain permission to transfer the relics of St. Sebastian from Rome to Soissons in 827.[49] In 823, Ingoaldus had to defend the monastery before the emperor Lothar in Rome against the territorial claims of the papacy. The emperor ruled in favor of the monastery, reconfirming Farfa's lands and privileges. In this decision the monastery's imperial protection and its immunity from papal control were clearly stated: "The Apostolic Lord acknowledges that he has no rights of dominion aside from that of consecration."[50] This was neither the first nor the last such dispute with the papacy, but it was a decisive one, explicitly proclaiming the monastery's independence from Rome. At the death of Ingoaldus, Farfa was at the zenith of its wealth and prestige.[51]

From the art-historical point of view, the sources provide little concerning Farfa's first century and a half. Abbot Mauroaldus is said to have "decorated the church lavishly with silver and gold," probably in reference to liturgical furnishings. His successor, Benedict, also enriched the church with liturgical objects and codices.[52] It is only with the abbacy of Sichardus (ca. 830–842) that substantial information is given, for he was an avid builder. Indeed, the *Constructio farfensis* devotes an unusually lengthy and detailed account of his building activities, which deserves to be quoted in full:

> In consequence of the growth of this place and of its inhabitants, he was eager to construct religious buildings, and in like manner he did not neglect to provide temporal ones as well. For example, the oratory which we hold in honor of the Savior, he built joined to the church of the Virgin with a crypt below where he honorifically interred the bodies of the holy martyrs Valentine and Hilarius, translated from Tuscany, together with the body of St. Alexander the son of Felicitas.

A passionary, written at Farfa in the late ninth century, adds that the body of St. Alexander was brought by Pope Gregory IV (827–844) in procession from Rome (presumably following the Via Salaria, along which the saint's tomb was originally located) and that the pope dedicated the new oratory on the third day before the kalends of January.[53] Unfortunately, the year is not given, but the translation of relics from Rome to Farfa may have been an act of reconciliation following the settlement of another territorial dispute between the abbey and the papacy in 829.[54] This would mean that the event may have taken place early in Sichardus' rule, perhaps around 830. Be that as it may, this is the first attested papal visit to the monastery in accordance with the aforementioned limitation of the pope's jurisdiction to matters of consecration. The passage continues:

> In various locations belonging to this same monastery, he strove to rebuild many other old and ruined churches and to build anew even more

which can still be seen today. He also acquired great riches for this place, such as, lands and ecclesiastical and other innumerable ornaments, so that it can be said that none of his predecessors surpassed him in this, as can be learned from the epitaph in his memory. For therein is read about his lifelong residence in the abbey and his acceptance of its leadership as well as about his birth and death:

Here in this tomb lies the venerable abbot Sichardus, / Who governed well the holy work of this monastery. / God claimed him while still in his mother's womb, / So that he could be a colleague of the prophet Jeremiah. / For although the world had not yet known his birth, / Both his parents pledged him to this temple. / These places he constructed with skill and in a marvelous manner, / And he protected his entrusted flock from the savage enemy. / On his behalf, whoever reads this, do not cease, with goodness of mind, / To offer prayers day and night, / So that he may be deemed worthy to be among the angelic hosts, / And with death conquered, to obtain the kingdom of heaven.[55]

The actual epitaph recorded by this passage was discovered in 1959 by the Superintendency of Monuments during a restoration campaign of the present church (plate 84). The inscription is an expression of the full flowering of the revival of classical epigraphy that characterized the Carolingian Renaissance.[56] And its exquisite quality demonstrates the high standard of workmanship under Sichardus, confirming the phrase: HAEC LOCA PRUDENTI CONSTRUXIT ET ORDINE MIRO. The reign of Abbot Sichardus was obviously a high point in the architectural history of the abbey church and the monastery.

The *Destructio* describes the general appearance of the monastery at its height in the ninth century. The abbey church, it says, was roofed with lead, and the interior shone from colorful stone revetment and gem-studded cloths decorating various altars. But there were also five subsidiary churches besides the main abbey church. One basilica dedicated to St. Peter was used for the "canons,"[57] while two others served the infirmary, one for convalescent monks and one for those near death. The fourth church is described as being situated "in the royal palace" (*in palatio regali*) and formed part of the complex built expressly to house the emperor during his visits to the abbey.[58] The fifth and last church was dedicated to the Virgin, as was the main abbey church, but this one stood "outside the walls" (*extra muros*), to be used by women, who were strictly forbidden from entering the monastery.

Aside from the churches, the monastery contained various workrooms (*officinae*) connected by stone-paved walkways. There were also arched porticoes; those innermost (*intus*) within the monastic compound were reserved for the monks as their cloister, while those more on the periphery (*foris*) were accessible to the laity. The entire site was protected by heavy walls and towers, giving the impression of a fortified city. In sum, Farfa's position as one of the great abbeys of Italy seems to have been amply displayed by the layout of the monastery.[59]

Upon the death of Sichardus, the emperor Lothar exerted his authority by placing the monastery under the rule of Bishop Peter of Spoleto. This blatant obstruction of the monastery's recognized right to elect its own abbot did not last. The monks selected from among themselves Hildericus (ca. 842–857), who was then duly confirmed by the emperor. The monastery, however, was required to pay a pension to Peter, and the emperor insisted that the bishop oversee any future election and investiture of an abbot. Thus Lothar's hold on Farfa remained firm and was more obvious than under Hildericus' predecessors.[60] At the same time, Hildericus proved to be a pious man and an effective promoter of Farfa's territorial expansion.

In May 872, the emperor Louis II visited Farfa after having received the imperial crown in Rome. Masses were held in the abbey church, and the emperor with his court was the guest of the monks in their refectory. Soon after, upon his return to Rome, he issued a letter of privilege confirming the rights of the monastery and vowing to protect and defend its possessions.[61] Although Farfa was an imperial abbey and maintained a palace for imperial visits, this is the first documented visit of an emperor to the monastery.

Despite the emperor's promises, the days of the monastery's greatness were numbered. Unquestioned in theory, the imperial presence was nebulous in fact. The Carolingian empire was fast disintegrating, and Louis's successors were virtually powerless in Italy.[62] In the second half of the ninth century, the countryside of Central Italy was being overrun by the Saracens, and Farfa was left to stand alone. St. Peter's in Rome had been sacked in 846; both Montecassino and S. Vincenzo al Volturno fell in 883. In 897, after seven years of resistance to the Saracens, Abbot Peter (890–919) decided to abandon the monastery. The Farfa treasures were divided among three groups of monks. One group left for Rome, another for Rieti, and a third followed Peter with the precious books and archives to the church of St. Hippolytus near Fermo in the Marches.[63] They were soon forced to move again for more security to a *castello* named S. Vittoria, on Monte Matenano. The *Destructio* relates that the "infidels" were so impressed with the magnificence of the monastery at Farfa that they chose not to destroy it but to use it for quartering. Destruction came instead from Christian looters who entered the monastery late one night when it was temporarily empty, which suggests that the Saracen contingent was a small one. The looters lit a fire in one corner that spread accidentally throughout the monastery, leaving it in ruins.[64]

With the beginning of the tenth century, Farfa entered a bleak period, its monastery abandoned and its monastic community dispersed. Abbot Peter died in 919 and was buried in a small church, dedicated to the Virgin, which he had built on Monte Matenano.[65] Between 930 and 933, Abbot Ratfredus was able to reinstate a small group of monks at the site of the monastery in the Sabina. In

936, however, while visiting the abbey's possessions in Rome, Ratfredus was poisoned by two monks, Campo and Hildebrand. This, the most scandalous episode in the monastery's history, underscores the depravity of the times. Campo then became the new abbot, residing at Farfa, while his accomplice Hildebrand was given charge over the abbey's possessions in the area around Fermo.

It was precisely at this time that Alberic, *princeps romanorum*, invited the renowned abbot of Cluny, Odo, to reform the monasteries of Rome. Although Odo's efforts were successful in Rome and Montecassino, he was never allowed to enter the monastery at Farfa.[66] In 947, after his death, a small group of Cluniac monks attempted to introduce reform measures at Farfa but were forced to flee upon threat of their lives. In reprisal, Alberic stormed the monastery with his own troops and installed as abbot a Cluniac, Dagibert of Cuma (947–953).[67] Dagibert's attempts at reform met with resistance, however, and he too was poisoned.[68] The rule of the next abbot, Adam, marked a return to the licentiousness of the past. John III (966–997), on the other hand, seems to have made a major effort to consolidate the monastery and its landholdings. Beginning in 967, Farfa again came under imperial protection, this time from the Ottonian house.[69] But it was not until the arrival of the young abbot Hugo that the fortunes of the abbey truly began to turn for the better.

Hugo was of noble birth and had been a monk at the nearby monastery of S. Quirico. In 997, aged twenty-five, he was able to purchase confirmation to the abbey from Pope Gregory V. Although not an unusual procedure in its day, this act of simony found disfavor with the young, idealistic emperor Otto III. Hugo was subsequently dismissed and replaced by an imperial nominee. However, following a petition on the part of the monks at Farfa, the emperor reinstated Hugo. On February 22, 998, Hugo was invested by Otto III with the abbacy of Farfa. The emperor proclaimed that henceforth the abbot was to be freely elected by the monastic community and subsequently presented first to the emperor for approval and then to the bishop of Rome for consecration.[70] Thus by the year 1000, the traditional bond between the Holy Roman Emperor and the monastery at Farfa had been firmly reestablished.

Hugo proved to be what contemporaries termed a *columna maxima* of the monastery and the Church.[71] Without doubt, his most important and lasting achievement at Farfa was the introduction of monastic reform. A restoration of monastic ideals seems to have been his first priority upon becoming abbot.[72] It may seem ironic that Hugo, who had initially acquired the abbacy through simony, should have been such a fervent reformer, but this stain on his past, which he termed a "most grave crime,"[73] seems in fact to have further motivated his actions in this regard. He sought assistance for his reform first from Subiaco and then from Montecassino, but both efforts were disappointing. He then met St. Romualdus, founder of the order at Camaldoli, who had been elected abbot of S. Apollinare in Classe, outside Ravenna, in 996. Hugo invited a group of

Classinese monks to introduce the teachings and discipline of Romualdus at Farfa. At the same time, either in Ravenna or at Farfa, Hugo came into contact with Abbots Odilo of Cluny and William of Dijon, who persuaded him to use Cluny as the model for his reform.

Sometime around the year 1000, Hugo presented his Constitution, establishing at Farfa the customs of Cluny that served as the rule of monastic life for the next two hundred years.[74] It was probably at this time or not long after that the monk John, mentioned in the prologue of the Farfa Customary, went to Cluny in order to study the customs of the Burgundian monastery. Thus, early in Hugo's abbacy Farfa was not only restored to a primary position in the political affairs of Italy, but it entered into the mainstream of the monastic reform movement.

In spite of favorable omens, the long abbacy of Hugo (998–1039) proved to be a continuous and embittered struggle with the lords of the Sabina and the Marches, above all with the Crescenzi family, over the monastery's territorial rights; it was a dispute that often resulted in armed conflict as well as litigation. The burden of these affairs may in part be responsible for Hugo's having resigned the office of abbot on two occasions: from 1009 to 1014 the monastery was nominally ruled by a nephew, Guido, while Hugo remained in the monastery still exerting considerable influence; in 1027 Hugo again resigned, but this time he chose to leave the monastery because of the animosity felt between himself and the newly elected abbot, another Guido (II). It seems likely that Hugo spent part of his exile at Cluny. In 1036, however, Hugo returned to head the monastery until his death in 1039.

Hugo's elected successor, Suppone, was immediately replaced by Almeric, the candidate favored by the emperor, Henry III. A decade later, however, the same emperor removed Almeric and reinstated his old rival Suppone, who died within a year. In October 1048, the monks of Farfa elected a new abbot, choosing from among themselves a young monk named Berardus. Probably having taken note of the recent past, Berardus set out immediately for the imperial court north of the Alps, where he received confirmation from the emperor on the day after Christmas.[75] Not long after, Berardus was consecrated by Pope Leo IX (1049–1054). He enjoyed a particularly amiable relationship with both emperor and pope, and seems to have started his rule at peace with the Crescenzi as well.

The monastery was again at the height of its power and wealth. In a letter to Pope Leo IX, Berardus speaks of having charge over five hundred monks, a number that must include not only Farfa itself but its dependencies as well. The record of Berardus's election shows that eighty-two individuals participated, categorized as thirteen priests (*presbiteri*), twenty-five priests who were monks (*presbiteri et monachi*), three monastic deacons (*diaconi et monachi*), fifteen monastic subdeacons (*subdiaconi et monachi*), eight monastic clerics (*clerici et monachi*), and fourteen monks (*monachi*).[76] Although we are not informed about those who did not take part in the election, a nucleus of about eighty monks and priests compares closely to the population of Cluny at this time[77] and thus represents a sizable monastery. In September 1050 Berardus was again at the imperial court, this time at Goslar, in order to receive confirmation of the monastery's privileges and possessions from Henry III.[78]

By 1059, the monastery's relationship with the Crescenzi and the counts of the Marches had again deteriorated, and Berardus sought the support of the new pope, Nicholas II (1059–1061). In February 1059 the pope, together with Abbot Desiderius of Montecassino, was received at Farfa. A year later, on July 6, Nicholas II returned in order to consecrate the two main altars of the abbey church, dedicated to the Virgin and to the Savior.[79] On this occasion, the pope was requested by Berardus to examine documents pertaining to the monastery's rights and privileges, after which the pope officially issued his recognition of Farfa's rights under Lombard law, subjugation to the emperor, and immunity from papal authority. In September of the same year, the apogee of Farfa's rapport with the Papal See was formalized by a letter from Nicholas II again confirming the privileges of the monastery.[80] This favorable situation was soon to change, however, for the last years of Berardus's abbacy were clouded by the Investiture Controversy.

In 1065, Berardus was again north of the Alps to receive a confirmation of privileges from Henry IV, who had recently come of age. Signs of the impending conflict are already evident in this document, for the young king strongly reaffirms Farfa's sole responsibility to his own royal authority.[81] Soon after, Henry's mother Agnes visited Farfa and donated numerous precious gifts, among which were richly decorated altar cloths for the two principal altars of the abbey church.[82] In 1082, the emperor Henry IV himself visited the monastery, perhaps accompanied by the antipope Clement III.[83] Berardus attempted to maintain diplomatic ties with Pope Gregory VII, but they were often strained. Already in 1078 Gregory had threatened the abbot with excommunication at a Lateran synod.[84] Thus when Berardus died in 1089, Farfa found itself in a dilemma. The monastery could not abandon the imperial cause in face of threats from the local lords and the ambitions of the papacy. At the same time, Farfa found itself becoming increasingly isolated from the papacy and the monastic communities of Central Italy.

These problems caused factions to appear within the monastery. The monks elected Rainaldus to succeed Berardus, but he soon proved to be inept, and the emperor, Henry IV, installed Berardus II, a nephew of the deceased Berardus, as abbot with the aid of troops in 1091. The new abbot, however, seems to have aggravated the growing dissent by living luxuriously and showing favoritism to a select group of monks. Particularly audacious was his plan to build the monastery anew at the summit of Monte Acuziano, purportedly for strategic reasons and because the old abbey was in need of repair; it may also have reflected the now open schism within the monastic community. In 1097, to realize this scheme, Berardus II called upon all the economic means at his disposal, but construction was aborted by his sudden death in 1099.[85]

Oddo, a Lombard monk, was hurriedly selected to succeed the tyrannical Berardus II, but he too proved incapable and died in shame after having stolen objects from the monastery's treasury. The subsequent election of a young deacon, Beraldus, also called Berardus, as abbot was a fortunate one. The monastery's prime concern in 1100 was to protect itself against the lords of the Sabina and the Marches. Berardus III proved to be an effective military leader, not only restoring much lost territory to the abbey but also staunchly support-ing the emperor Henry V's campaign against Pope Paschal II. It was at this time that the *Orthodoxa defensio imperialis*, a treatise defending the supremacy of the emperor, was composed by an anonymous monk at Farfa.[86] Berardus III's rule until his death in 1119 seems to have been an economically productive one, and the abbot's exploits find particular favor with the author of the Farfa Chronicle.

The period of unity which the monastery enjoyed under Berardus III was broken soon after his death. The monks elected Rainaldus as their new abbot, while the serfs and laity supported a low-born monk named Guido. Emperor Henry V, in turn, preferred Berardus IV, whom he installed as abbot with imperial troops in 1121. Guido fled, taking with him numerous treasures[87] to finance his planned resistance to the usurper, for which he received military support from Pope Calixtus II. As Berardus IV and Guido fought over the abbot's throne, the emperor and the pope negotiated the Concordat of Worms in 1122, ending the Investiture Controversy. For Farfa, the new agreement meant the end of imperial protection, the so-called *defensio imperialis*, that had shielded the abbey from papal encroachments in the past. In effect, the papacy had obtained its long-sought-after goal of being able to influence directly the affairs of the abbey. With time, Farfa would come under complete papal control.[88]

The new situation became apparent almost immediately, for in 1123 Berar-dus IV was deposed as abbot and Guido, the papal candidate, was allowed to return. But by 1125 Guido's acts of revenge against the abbey caused a group of monks, the aged Gregory of Catino among them, to petition the pope for Guido's removal. In the presence of two cardinals representing the pope, Guido was forced to abdicate. The monks then requested that Adenolfus, head of the nearby abbey of S. Salvatore at Scandriglia, a dependency of Farfa, be installed as the new abbot. Their wish was granted, and for the next twenty years, from 1125 to 1144, Adenolfus energetically promoted the interests of Farfa while at the same time strengthening its ties with the papacy. His role has been com-pared to that of Abbot Hugo more than a century before, such was his success in consolidating the abbey and its holdings after a long period of civil strife.[89]

The tenure of Adenolfus as abbot was interrupted by the papal schism of 1130; he sided with Innocent II and was forced into exile along with the pope while Anacletus II held Rome and the surrounding countryside. By the time the schism was finally resolved with the death of Anacletus II in 1138, Farfa was apparently in a ruinous state after years of neglect and the ravages of war. This may explain why in 1142 Adenolfus revived the project of Berardus II to rebuild the abbey atop Monte Acuziano,[90] though little could be accomplished before his death two years later.[91] Nevertheless, Adenolfus left an impressive legacy as a prominent churchman of his day. He had been made a cardinal in 1143 and died in 1144 at Mainz while on a mission for the pope to the imperial court.[92] Moreover, he had been in correspondence with Bernard of Clairvaux, the great spokesman of the Cistercian movement,[93] and had hosted Bernard's student, Bernard of Pisa, who was named abbot of Scandriglia following the death of Adenolfus.

In 1145, Bernard of Pisa was elected pope, and not surprisingly he turned to Farfa in time of need.[94] Driven from Rome by supporters of the new commune, Bernard retreated to Farfa, where he was consecrated pope on March 15, 1145, taking the name Eugenius III (1145–1153).[95] Later in his reign, Eugenius III responded to attempts by the Roman commune to assert its authority in the Sabina by initiating the purchase and consolidation of military strongholds (*castra specialia ecclesiae*) at strategic points in the countryside, a policy that was continued with even greater vigor by his successors.[96] Eugenius III recognized the importance of Farfa in this struggle with the Romans by stating that the monastery was "subject to the Church of Rome and St. Peter in matters of law and defence."[97]

Still, Farfa's links with the empire were never completely severed. Indeed, with the death of Eugenius III and the rise of a vigorous new ruler in the person of Frederick Barbarossa, Farfa's close association with the imperial cause was firmly reestablished. Early in 1155, for example, Frederick sent his chaplain, Heribert, to Farfa in order to collect the so-called *fodrum*, or imperial hospitality tax, even though the monastery had been freed of this obligation by the emperor Henry IV in 1084.[98] Later in the same year, following his imperial coronation in Rome,[99] Frederick Barbarossa visited the abbey himself, and in 1159 Farfa supported the imperial candidate for the papacy, Victor IV (1159–1164), in opposition to Alexander III (1159–1181).[100] Thus, within less than fifteen years, Farfa aligned itself with two seemingly antithetical popes, Eugenius III, promoter of papal hegemony against the Roman commune, and Victor IV, a pawn of imperial policy, reflecting the complexity of the political situation in Central Italy in the middle of the twelfth century.[101]

As late as 1185, the newly elected abbot of Farfa, Pandolfus, obtained a letter of privilege from the emperor,[102] but by the turn of the century the renewal of imperial authority at Farfa had proven ephemeral. Frederick Barbarossa died in Asia Minor in 1190, and his successor, Henry VI, reigned only seven years. More important, Pope Innocent III (1198–1216) saw the reclamation of papal property as a primary goal of his office, and his success in this regard has earned him the name Founder of the Papal State.[103] In 1219 his successor, Honorius III (1216–1227), visited Farfa and instituted a number of administrative reforms intended to stem the monastery's economic decline.[104] Finally, on February 22, 1261, Urban IV (1261–1264) declared that the monastery of Farfa, its possessions, and its inhabitants were outside the jurisdiction of the diocese of the Sabina and subject directly to the Holy See.[105] The papal domination of Farfa was complete.

The monks remained free to elect their own abbot, but their choice had to be confirmed and consecrated by the pope. The abbot of Farfa no longer played a role in international affairs; his influence was restricted to the abbey's shrinking territory, and even then the administration of the abbey was usually handled by a prior. With the possible exception of Abbot Alardus (1355–1363), most of the abbots of the fourteenth century do not seem to have resided at Farfa but in nearby *castelli*.[106] As the Middle Ages drew to a close, Farfa was reduced to a minor establishment of little significance.

The post-medieval history of Farfa lies beyond the scope of this study; nonetheless, one should take note of later events that were of particular importance for both the preservation and the destruction of the medieval monuments. In 1400, Pope Boniface IX introduced the commendatory system at Farfa by naming his nephew, Cardinal Francesco Carbone Tomacelli, the monastery's papal overseer, bringing to an end the monastery's direct line of abbots. Among Tomacelli's first acts was to request that the pope rescind the ancient ban on women entering the monastery, so that he could invite merchants and the general populace of the region to a jubilee celebrated on May 8, 1401. This festival initiated a tradition of fairs that came to be held biannually, on feast days of the Virgin, and developed into a major source of income for the abbey.[107] The revenues from this first venture apparently allowed for a restoration of the abbey church, because a new main altar was consecrated on August 8, 1402.[108]

At about the same time, a group of German monks was brought in from the neighboring abbey of Subiaco to assist in the spiritual reform of the monastic community. By 1420, Giordano Orsini had been named commendatory, and the office remained in the hands of the Orsini family without interruption for the rest of the century. In 1477, Pope Sixtus IV issued a bull recognizing an internal division within the monastery, whereby the palace complex with its stables and servants' quarters was relegated to the commendatory and his court, while the cloister and adjacent buildings were given over exclusively to the monks.[109] Under Giovanni Battista Orsini (1482–1503), a new abbey church was built and consecrated on March 25, 1496.[110] Although the introduction of the commendatory system at Farfa seems to have brought about many physical improvements in the monastic buildings, the office was used by the popes to reward relatives and allies, with little regard for the particular wishes of the monks. Thus the domination of the office by the Orsini family in the fifteenth century was followed in the sixteenth and seventeenth centuries by that of several prominent families in Rome, including the della Rovere, the Farnese, the Perretti, and the Barberini. [111] Each period of familial rule left its own building legacy.

In 1567 the remaining German monks were expelled, [112] and Farfa joined the Cassinese congregation. The monastery was sacked by French troops in 1798 and was secularized briefly during Napoleonic rule. With the restoration of the Papal State, Cardinal Luigi Lambruschini was named commendatory, and in 1836 he began the demolition of the palace complex that had served the commendatories since the fifteenth century. [113] In 1841, the abandoned monastery was given over to the bishop of the Sabina. In 1872, the abbey and its property were confiscated by the new Italian state, and in 1878 part of the monastic site was sold into private hands. [114] In 1919, largely under the auspices of Ildefonso Schuster, Farfa was united with the Benedictine monastery of St. Paul's-outside-the-Walls in Rome. In 1921, monks from the Roman abbey were introduced at Farfa, and in 1928 the abbey was declared a national monument. Today the monastery of Farfa remains an active Benedictine house, although the size of the monastic community is greatly reduced.

2

The State of
the Problem

THE SITE

The abbey and adjoining village of Far-
fa lie approximately fifty km., or thirty miles, northeast of Rome, just off the
Via Salaria in the picturesque Sabine Hills that form the western extent of the
limestone mass of the central Apennine range (Map 1).[1] The monastery oc-
cupies a narrow shelf that runs along the northeastern slope of Monte S.
Martino, formerly known as Monte Acuziano or Monte Mutilla, overlooking
the narrow valley of the Fosse Riano that empties into the Farfa River to the
west (Map 2 and frontispiece). There is evidence to suggest that the site of the
monastery was artificially terraced in antiquity. Near the base of a retaining
wall at the northwest corner of the abbey can still be seen the remnants of *opus
reticulatum* masonry, comparable to examples in Rome and the surrounding area
from the first century B.C. to as late as the third century A.D. Moreover, the
position of the terrace, halfway along the eastern slope of a hillside, follows the
recommendation for the ideal placement of a villa in the famous treatise on
agriculture by Columella, written sometime in the first century A.D. Archaeological data derived from the recent excavations at the abbey, including scattered Arretine pottery, fragments of Roman sculpture, and a grave that contained a coin of the emperor Trajan (98–117) along with a second-century oil
lamp, provide clear evidence of Roman habitation of the site.[2]

The village of Farfa, bordering the monastery to the southwest on sharply

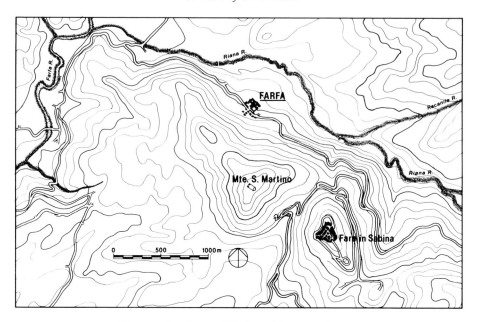

MAP 2. Topographical map of Farfa and the immediate environs

rising terrain, originally provided housing for the influx of merchants and visitors that arrived for the biannual commercial fairs sponsored by the monastery from early in the fifteenth century. Though the individual houses were extensively restored in the 1930s, their basic design incorporating an open storefront on the ground floor with living quarters immediately above conforms to examples from the late Middle Ages and the early Renaissance in Rome and elsewhere in Central Italy.[3] A bird's-eye view of Farfa dated 1686 (Plate 1) shows that the layout of the village has changed very little over the past several centuries. Of the four parallel streets indicated in this view only two are now in use, of which only one is paved with asphalt; the others have become overgrown with weeds among the cobblestones, and the adjoining houses have either been demolished or lie abandoned.

The abbey church in use today was built in the late fifteenth century and was dedicated in 1496; an inscription on the gold coffered ceiling bears the date 1494.[4] The design of the church with polygonal side chapels and a deep choir (Fig. 1) recalls the plan of S. Maria del Popolo in Rome (1472–1480), as does the simple yet well-proportioned façade, divided into three vertical units with a large rose window below the central gable.[5] The Renaissance church was laid out on a north-south axis, perpendicular to the medieval church, with its transept following the foundations of the destroyed medieval nave (Figs. 1–2). The best-preserved parts of the medieval church are, therefore, the eastern and western extremities. The axis of the medieval church actually ran northwest to southeast, following the orientation of the terrain, but for the sake of clarity these directions will be referred to simply as east and west. To the east is a massive bell tower and an adjacent square presbytery (Figs. 2, 5, 6, Plate 19),[6] while to the west are the foundations of a continuous transept, a triumphal arch, and a semicircular apse housing an annular crypt (Fig. 2, Plates 7–13).

The reasons for such a drastic change in the axis of the Renaissance abbey church can only be guessed, but they seem evident enough. First of all, the organization and administration of the abbey had changed radically since the Middle Ages. The monastic community in the fifteenth century was composed of two distinct groups: the cloistered monks and the commendatory with his court. The position of the Renaissance church seems to take this situation into account by splitting the abbey approximately in half, with the monks' cloister positioned to the northeast and the commendatory's palace centered about the square tower to the southwest (Fig. 1, Plate 1). Second, the development of the biannual fairs lent the village new importance, owing to the influx of merchants and their customers. The Renaissance abbey church, therefore, opens onto a public square that links the abbey with the village. As today, the laity entered the church through the portals of the façade, while the monks entered through a door in the elongated choir at the opposite end. Thus in the fifteenth century the abbey church became the focal point of Farfa, reflecting the monastery's new role as both a spiritual and commercial center.

The rest of the monastic buildings date from the sixteenth and seventeenth centuries (Fig. 1). During the last quarter of the sixteenth century, following the reform by the Cassinese congregation, the area to the northwest of the abbey church was developed. In 1577–1578 a simple rectangular structure was erected to serve as the *dogana*, or customs house, for the commercial fairs; today it houses the monastic library. From 1585 to 1590 the so-called "great cloister" was built, composed of a monumental arcaded walkway surmounted by a second storey with individual cells for the monks. The first quarter of the seventeenth century saw the development of the northeast corner of the site, which had been the location of an earlier cloister complex. According to contemporary records, older structures, including a kitchen, refectory, and millhouse, were torn down between 1598 and 1604 to make way for a new refectory and a two-storey dormitory with individual cells connected by vaulted corridors, all built above a vast substructure of vaulted wine cellars. From 1609 to 1611 a smaller refectory and kitchen were added. In 1611 the base of the medieval bell tower and the square presbytery were converted into apartments for the abbot and prior. In 1622 the wall surrounding the garden to the east of the new cloister was rebuilt, and a corridor was constructed to connect the new dormitory to the end of the choir of the abbey church. From 1623 to 1624 a large courtyard with a central fountain was built immediately to the south of the abbot's residence and the garden that today serves as the main entrance to the monastery.[7]

The major building periods of the present monastic complex can be categorized as follows: (1) 1492–1496, the abbey church; (2) 1577–1590, the customs house and the "great cloister;" (3) 1598–1624, two refectories, the kitchen, a two-storey dormitory, the abbot's apartments, the garden walls, and the courtyard with a central fountain. The first phase was carried out under the patronage of the commendatory Cardinal Giovanni Battista Orsini; the second was sponsored by Cardinal Alessandro Farnese; and the last spanned the commendatory reigns of members of the Perretti, Orsini, and Barberini families. In the course of these extensive building campaigns much, if not all, of the medieval abbey was destroyed. Only the bell tower remained as visible evidence of the abbey's medieval origins. Other medieval remains either lay buried or were incorporated into the later monastic structures, until recent excavations and restoration campaigns brought them to light.

PREVIOUS RESEARCH

Modern interest in the site came as a result of the studies of Ildefonso Schuster at the beginning of this century. Although Farfa's numerous historical sources had long been a subject of scholarly research, Schuster was the first to attempt to relate the historical record of the monastery to the physical remains. His findings initially appeared in a series of articles that were subsequently summarized and incorporated into the aforementioned *L'imperiale abbazia di Farfa* of 1921. Schuster correctly recognized the bell tower as a vestige of the medieval church, and he was the first to note traces of a fresco decoration in its ground floor (Plates 1–2). His approach, however, was not an archaeological one, and he mistakenly assumed later modifications of the medieval fabric to be original, such as a second floor division in the ground floor of the campanile. He interpreted the base of the campanile with these added upper and lower levels to be the famous oratory "with a crypt below" (*cum cripta deorsum*), built by Abbot Sichardus (830–842),[8] and assumed that the accompanying frescoes were also Carolingian.[9]

   Schuster's work deserves great credit for stimulating further research, but his preliminary dating of the bell tower, based upon incomplete information, was accepted virtually without question in subsequent studies. His interpretation of the campanile, for example, was followed by Alberto Serafini in his study of the medieval towers of Lazio.[10] Using the terms *oratorii superiore* and *inferiore*, Serafini accepts the base of the tower as Sichardan, and he further proposes the upper five storeys to be additions of the eleventh century.

   The first systematic investigation of the site was begun by a young German archaeologist, Paul Markthaler, in 1925. Quite naturally, Markthaler began with the bell tower, stripping away the interior and exterior plaster coating of the ground floor and critically examining the masonry. Markthaler proved that the floor division in the base of the campanile, which both Schuster and Serafini had thought original, was in fact a later addition because it cut across the medieval fresco decoration. Markthaler also realized that these frescoes were not Carolingian but Romanesque. He began excavations of the entire site and planned a complete monograph on the medieval church, but both undertakings were aborted by his premature death. Nevertheless, his findings on the bell tower were published posthumously in 1928, in an article of the *Rivista di archeologia cristiana* that still warrants our close attention today.[11]

Markthaler's archaeological approach to the monument is commendable, and the information in his article is, for the most part, quite reliable. Markthaler seems to have been reluctant to contradict the theories of his predecessors, however, and goes to considerable lengths to show that in spite of conflicting evidence the base of the bell tower is still to be interpreted as Carolingian. In his view, the base was not vaulted until the eleventh century, at which time the interior was relined with approximately 30 cm. of reinforcing masonry and corner piers to support a groined vault and a new second storey. The last three storeys, he suggests, were added later, in the twelfth or thirteenth century.[12] Crucial to his argument is a wall with a round-arched doorway abutting the northwest corner of the tower base (Fig. 6, Plate 46). For Markthaler, this is the nave wall of the pre-Carolingian church, fitting with the description of the Sichardan oratory as having been built "joined to the basilica of the Virgin" (*adiunctum ecclesiae Sanctae Mariae*).[13] How he reconciled an oratory "with a crypt below" with a single unvaulted structure (as he envisioned the tower to have been in the ninth century), he does not specify. Yet, in spite of its preliminary nature, Markthaler's work was a major advance in the understanding of the medieval church at Farfa.

Markthaler made several other important discoveries, which had to wait another ten years before their publication by Don Giuseppe Croquison in the *Rivista di archeologia cristiana* of 1938.[14] Markthaler had left an unfinished plan of his excavations, which Croquison published for the first time in this article (Fig. 16). Croquison also reopened the excavations begun by Markthaler in order to clarify two significant findings that Markthaler had indicated on his plan: (1) the substantial remains of the walls of a square presbytery adjoining the bell tower to the southeast and (2) the traces of an apse and annular crypt at the opposite end of the church. Croquison sensed the difficulties these discoveries posed to previous theories about the medieval church. In his discussion he compares the Farfa annular crypt to ninth-century examples in Rome and realizes that such an annular crypt would correspond to the "crypt below" for the martyrs' relics of the Sichardan oratory. But again, like Markthaler, Croquison could not bring himself to disagree with previous opinion. Since from his point of view the bell tower had already been shown to be from the Sichardan phase, he decided that the west end must therefore be pre-

Carolingian. He was struck by the sills of lamp niches in the crypt passage that seem to slope like those of windows and he observes that the outsides of these niches have been closed with brick unlike the stone masonry of the rest of the crypt wall. This brings him to the conclusion that the niches originally served as windows for an apse above ground and that only later, at some unspecified time, was the apse transformed into a crypt. [15]

Croquison is similarly perplexing in his analysis of the east end (which he persistently calls the west end). He accepts Markthaler's interpretation of the campanile base as the Sichardan oratory with an eleventh-century remodeling, i.e., vaulting, frescoes, and second storey, and points, with good reason, to the consecration of the two principal altars of the abbey church by Pope Nicholas II in 1060 as the most likely period for the completion of the remodeling. The discovery of the square presbytery, however, leaves Croquison in a quandary. It does not fit well with the interpretation of the bell-tower base as part of a ninth-century westwork and in style seems similar to eleventh-century square presbyteries in the Rhine and Mosan region. He therefore suggests three possibilities: (1) the square presbytery is contemporary with the campanile base and is thus ninth-century, which he admits is unlikely; (2) the square presbytery is the literal rebuilding of an earlier structure; or (3) it constitutes an original addition of the eleventh century. He prefers the last alternative. To Croquison, the base of the bell tower was built in the ninth century by Abbot Sichardus as part of a western transept or westwork. In the eleventh century, he proposes, this westwork was transformed into two bell towers with a central square presbytery. He also speculates about the strong architectural influence that ecclesiastical centers of the Holy Roman Empire north of the Alps would have exerted on an imperial abbey in Italy in the ninth and eleventh centuries. [16]

In the end, the reader is left confused more than convinced. Yet Croquison's study, however self-contradictory, marked the last serious examination of the site for some time. His publication of Markthaler's unfinished work, together with precious on-the-spot observations, makes the information contained in this article invaluable. With the advent of World War II, the excavation trenches were filled in, and the medieval church at Farfa was left unstudied for another twenty years. [17]

Between 1959 and 1962, the Superintendency of the Monuments of Lazio (now the Soprintendenza per i Beni Ambientali ed Architettonici del Lazio) carried out a restoration campaign of the Renaissance church and its decoration. At the same time, they reopened the excavations of the annular crypt. Below the pavement of the Renaissance transept they discovered foundations of the nave and a large medieval pavement in situ. When they dismantled the baroque main altar, they found encased within it the fragment of a wall bearing frescoes on both sides. Unfortunately, record-keeping was not systematic, and there exist only a few unlabeled photographs, one published plan without scale

(Fig. 17), and three brief published reports with which to evaluate this work.[18] Although the restoration work was sometimes careless, the Superintendency brought to light important remains of the medieval church, which they left, for the most part, accessible for future study.

Subsequent studies of Farfa are of more limited value. In 1964, an architect, Nicola Franciosa, published a booklet with survey drawings of the eastern complex.[19] But this survey was made before the restoration of the bell tower that revealed the original appearance of the upper storeys. Furthermore, the drawings are cursory at best and inaccurate in numerous important details. Without concern for archaeological evidence, Franciosa uses his imagination in reconstructing the east end, and he makes no attempt to compare the church to contemporary monuments in Italy or elsewhere in Europe. Nor does he discuss the annular crypt or other findings of the Superintendency, although the western apse and transept are shown on a schematic ground plan. In a large volume entitled *Abbazie del Lazio*, published in 1970, a chapter on Farfa written by Carlo Pietrangeli provides a useful summary of what had been said before, but it adds little that is new.[20]

In the meantime, in 1968, the private construction firm of Studio Pouchain was contracted by the Superintendency of Monuments to restore and consolidate the bell tower and square presbytery. The remaining exterior plaster was stripped away, exposing the medieval masonry, window openings were restored to their original form, and the base of the bell tower was shored up with reinforced concrete. The only report of this work at Farfa appears in a handbook published by the Pouchain company that summarizes the various restoration projects it carried out in many parts of Italy between 1968 and 1978.[21]

In the mid-1970s, two articles appeared on the medieval abbey church at Farfa. The first was originally presented by Adriano Prandi as a paper at a conference on Carolingian Rome sponsored by the University of Rome and was subsequently published in the acts of the conference.[22] On that occasion, however, Prandi basically voiced the opinions already expressed by Croquison forty years earlier. The second article is a study by Beatrice Premoli that is primarily concerned with the Romanesque fresco cycle preserved in the base of the bell tower, although she expresses opinions on other aspects of the abbey church as well.[23] She dates these frescoes to the end of the tenth or the first quarter of the eleventh century upon what would appear to be the most superficial of stylistic grounds. Nevertheless, Prandi and Premoli agree on one important point, and that is to question the traditional Carolingian dating of the east end. Prandi suggests it was built sometime during the abbacy of the famous Hugo (998–1039). Premoli is less specific, saying only that it was built during the course of the first half of the eleventh century, begun perhaps under Hugo and finished before the consecration of 1060. How this is reconciled with her earlier dating of the frescoes, she does not explain.

Where my analysis of the building agrees or disagrees with specific points raised by these articles will be discussed in greater detail in subsequent sections of this study. Suffice it to say that the comprehensive investigation proposed by Markthaler was never achieved by subsequent researchers. The following discussion attempts to correct that situation.

3

Architectural Analysis
and Reconstruction

$\mathbf{A}$s I pointed out in the previous chapter, the remains of the medieval abbey church are fragmentary. The nave and west end of the church were torn down to make way for the late quattrocento church, while the east end, including the bell tower, was left standing and was incorporated into later monastic structures. This means that the east end is preserved almost in its entirety above ground, the apse and transept of the west end are preserved only as foundations, and the remains of the nave are, for the most part, covered by the Renaissance church. It will be necessary, therefore, to examine each section separately before attempting to reconstruct the history of the medieval abbey church as a whole.

NAVE

Analysis

Little remains of the medieval nave, its walls having been pulled down to make way for the Renaissance transept. Portions of the foundations were uncovered by Markthaler and later re-excavated by the Superintendency, as shown in their published plans, which provide the outline of the nave (Figs. 16–17).[1] These foundations are no longer visible, but the Superintendency left their

outline in the newly restored pavement of the present church. They are approximately 0.60 m. thick and seem to be composed of small irregular stones.
Unfortunately, the photographs taken by the Superintendency lack a measured
scale and show the foundations still partially covered with earth, making a
detailed description of the masonry impossible.

In his plan, Markthaler indicates parallel foundations to the north and south
of the nave. The Superintendency did not investigate to the north of the nave,
but to the south they found fourteen stone-lined graves, some of which Markthaler had apparently mistaken for traces of foundation walls.[2] Their position,
extending 7.00 m. to the south, would seem to negate the presence of a side
aisle along the southern flank of the nave.

The most substantial vestige of the medieval nave was discovered by the
Superintendency encased within the baroque high altar. This wall, measuring
1.95 m. long by 0.59 m. thick and with a maximum height of 1.98 m., is visible
today below a modern altar and ciborium (Plate 3). The wall appears to be built
primarily of brick interspersed with irregular stonework; bricks projecting from
the west end of the wall fragment average 4 cm. in thickness, with mortar beds
of 1.0–1.5 cm. A detailed analysis of the masonry is impossible because the
wall is frescoed on both sides and capped with modern cement. The south, or
interior, side of the wall is brightly painted with simulated curtains, a common
mural decoration in the early Middle Ages. Photographs from the Superintendency archives show that upon discovery there were traces of a second painted
layer showing only a bejeweled band of decoration (Plate 4). Against this wall
was found the base of a large triglyph, apparently reused as an altar. The upper
half of the triglyph has been completely restored, and the distance between it
and the wall, ca. 30 cm., has been filled with concrete to a height of more than
0.50 m.

The opposite side of this same wall bears a fresco decoration that is recognizable as the remains of the right half of a painted lunette (Plate 5). As preserved
today, this fresco measures 0.95 m. high by 1.06 m. wide, outlined along the
bottom and right side by a double-banded border of red and black. The
fragmentary inscription makes it clear that one is dealing with the funerary
portrait of an abbot: VIR VEN[e]R[abilis] ABB[as] / . . . S[an]C[t]O COENOBIO
ANN[os] / . . . [obi]IT IN PACE XVIII. The last line is only faintly legible today,
but it can be seen clearly in earlier photographs. There is one colorless preparatory layer below the fresco, and the total thickness of the fresco coating is
1.65 cm. The elegant capital letters of the inscription are painted in black on a
white ground, and their height has been ruled in by thin red guidelines. The
image of the deceased is represented as a frontal half-length figure, 0.74 m.
high, with his hands upraised in an orant, or praying, gesture. The cowl is
sleeveless and ends diagonally just below the extremely broad shoulders, revealing the sleeves of a dark-red tunic. The face of the abbot is only partially
preserved, but one can discern the outline of an elongated neck and narrow oval

head framed by a tall rectilinear halo that is yellow-cream in color and outlined in dark red.[3] Immediately below and to the right of the *arcosolium* frame are patches of painted imitation marble revetment and a porphyry disc. In a photograph taken at the time of discovery, one can make out the lower left-hand corner and the bottom horizontal band of a second *arcosolium* frame to the right of the present one (Plate 5). In other words, there may have been more than one funerary portrait on the outer face of this wall.

In the middle of the former medieval nave, now the Renaissance transept, the Superintendency uncovered a medieval pavement in situ (Fig. 2, Plates 6a–b). The pavement is centered about a square panel measuring 1.60×1.70 m., consisting of a green granite disc (0.81 m. in diameter) framed by a checkerboard pattern of green porphyry and various colored marbles. To either side of the panel, following the east-west axis of the medieval nave, are continuations of the checkerboard pattern criss-crossed by marble bands with small red porphyry discs at their intersections. It is not known how far these flanking panels extended to the east and west, although they have been restored to match the dimensions of the central panel and are framed by red and green porphyry strips. Contingent to the porphyry frame of the east alignment of the checkerboard design is an area, approximately 1.56 by 1.86 m., of similar material cut into triangles and squares, 14–17 cm. on each side, to form geometric patterns (Plate 6a). Some 7 m. to the east and on the same axis as the green roundel, a smaller but clearly related panel was discovered, with a checkerboard pattern about a red porphyry oval. To either side and following the axis of the medieval nave a series of porphyry strips was also found, framing alternating square panels of plain white marble plaques and intricate geometric patterns (Plate 6b). Taken together, the extensive remains of this pavement indicate that at one time almost the entire medieval nave was covered by an *opus sectile* floor, with the central axis accentuated by roundels and ovals.

Reconstruction

Although the remnants of the medieval nave are admittedly meager, they are sufficient to arrive at its basic dimensions. The parallel foundation walls indicate an interior width of ca. 8.30 m. and a total width of ca. 9.50 m. when one includes the thickness of the walls. The distance between the remains of the transept to the west and the base of the bell tower to the east is ca. 22 m., giving a width-to-length ratio of 1:2.5 (Fig. 2). As I have already mentioned, the series of tombs extending far to the south of the nave would seem to rule out the presence of side aisles. The fragment of the north nave wall, however, is painted on both sides. The funerary portrait of the abbot is on the north or exterior face and may have been one among several other such memorials. This would suggest that the area north of the nave was a location favored for the burial of abbots. This area could have been an adjoining part of the monastery, such as a cloister walkway, or it may have formed a funerary chapel of some kind set parallel to the nave. Markthaler in fact found traces of a sloping roofline, corresponding to this area, on the west face of the bell tower within a later floor abutting the tower.[4] His plan also indicates parallel foundations, ca. 1.25 and 5.00 m. respectively, under the present choir north of the nave (Fig. 16). Both are no longer visible and cannot be verified.

The height of the nave, though, can be calculated. Between the first and second storeys of the same west face of the bell tower, there is a distinct vertical scar in the masonry that aligns with the nave wall fragment below the present main altar (Figs. 2, 7). This scar is approximately 0.60 m. wide and is composed of irregular stonework immersed in thick mortar. The sawtooth frieze of the bell tower stops abruptly at this vertical line, at which point six wavering courses of brick can be seen (Fig. 7, Plates 25–26). The scar continues upward for another 0.70 m., turning sharply to the left and back again to form a 45-degree angle. Just below the eave of the modern roofing there is a break between the outer corner of the bell tower and masonry fill. The implications are clear. These elements represent the juncture of the nave with the tower, which left a scar when the nave was torn down in the late fifteenth century. Irregular stone masonry, used for the partition walls of the new monastic rooms, fills the void left by the eave of the timbered roof. The width of the nave is already known, and its original floor level is given by the medieval pavement in situ. Following the roof outline, it is not difficult to calculate the approximate height of the nave to have been 10.20 m. to the beamline and 15.10 m. to the ridge (Fig. 7). Although we can reconstruct the silhouette of the nave, there are no indications for the placement of doors or windows.

WEST END

Analysis

Adjoining the remains of the medieval nave to the west are foundations excavated by the Superintendency of a continuous transept, a triumphal arch, and a semicircular apse housing an annular crypt (Fig. 2). The Renaissance church literally cuts these foundations in half from north to south. Thus the east wall and southeast corner of the transept are below the present church and no longer visible. As with the nave foundations, the Superintendency left the outline of the south transept arm in the restored pavement of the west aisle of the present church. These foundations are also clearly marked on the Superintendency plan (Fig. 17), and are further documented by photographs, however difficult to read, taken during the excavations (Plates 7–9). Beyond the confines of the Renaissance church, the Superintendency left the western half of the transept and the annular crypt accessible for inspection today, protected by a modern, reinforced-concrete roof. The exterior facing of these foundations is, however, no longer visible, and its analysis must depend upon secondary information.

Nevertheless, enough is either visible or sufficiently recorded to allow for a detailed analysis.

The Transept and Apse Foundations. The foundations of the transept and apse are approximately 0.69 m. thick, except for the east foundation wall, which increases to more than one meter (Figs. 2, 17). The transept was clearly separated from the nave by the jambs of a triumphal arch that projected ca. 1.20 m. from the south and ca. 1.55 m. from the north (a difference of 35 cm.), thus placing the triumphal arch slightly off the central axis of the nave. The arch rested on massive ashlars, probably Roman spoils (Plate 7). The tip of one block from the east foundation wall of the north transept arm is still visible above the present floor level, formerly incorporated into stairs leading to the Renaissance sacristy, and its size (0.94×0.27 m.) concurs with the dimensions of the ashlars seen in the Superintendency plan and photographs. Large rough-hewn blocks of the same foundation wall are visible below the sacristy. At the northeast corner is a reused block from a classical entablature, identifiable as such by its curved profile (Plate 9).

The primary masonry of the apse and transept foundations is a crude, irregular stonework held together by an abundant amount of fine-grained, yellow-brown mortar. At the juncture of the transept and annular crypt are reused ashlars varying in dimension from 1.10×0.40 m. to 0.30×0.20 m., with single bricks occasionally inserted as fill (Fig. 9B). In the north transept is a small patch of three courses of brickwork 0.19 m. high by 0.60 m. wide. The bricks average 3 cm. in thickness, with mortar beds of 2.0–2.5 cm., giving a module of 34 cm. for five bricks and five mortar beds. There is a similar patch of brickwork just inside the crypt passage. Bricks in different parts of the masonry are of various sizes (ranging in thickness from 2.5 to 4.5 cm.) and are sometimes broken, indicating that they were reused. The upper courses of the south end wall of the transept and its southwest corner are composed of small cut limestone blocks, ranging in size from 20×15 cm. to 30×40 cm., that rest on top of the rubble foundations (Plate 10). This finely cut stone is distinct from the masonry elsewhere in the transept and crypt, and it probably represents a later medieval modification to the complex. Approximately one meter in front of the end wall of the south transept arm is an irregular pile of rubble masonry (ca. 0.50 m. thick) that abuts, but does not bond with, the transept foundations. This line of masonry corresponds to the faint gray line shown on the Superintendency's plan that subdivides the south transept arm (Fig. 17). It most likely formed part of the platform for the crypt stairs, which are discussed in the next section.

The end wall of the north transept arm was later used as a foundation for the southeast corner of the sixteenth-century cloister, and it is preserved to a height of less than 0.80 m. It appears to bond with the west transept arm, and the same type of rubble masonry is present, although the mortar is of a slightly softer consistency. This being the case, the north transept arm appears to have been more than one meter shorter than the south arm (4.36 m. in length as opposed to 5.72 m.).

At the apex of the annular passage are rudiments, ca. 0.80 m. high, of the perpendicular corridor that once led to the venerated relics (Figs. 2, 3, 4, 9B, Plates 13, 15). Again, ashlars were used with several inserted brick courses (bricks 2.5–4.0 cm. thick and mortarbeds 1.75–3.00 cm. thick). Although varied, the masonry of the foundations has a basic coherence—a crude, irregular stone masonry is framed at points of maximum support by large reused ashlars, with bricks casually inserted throughout.

The Crypt. The walls of the semicircular crypt are preserved to an average height of 1.50 m., including the sills of five lamp niches (Figs. 3, 4, 9B, Plate 13). The best preserved of these niches has the dimensions of 31 cm. outer width by 40 cm. deep by 19 cm. inner width. Today it stands to a height of 0.59 m., but the capping lintel indicating its original height is missing. The present height of 2.70 m. as restored by the Superintendency is without any archaeological basis. The other niches are less well preserved, but they have almost identical sill dimensions. The sills slope at an angle averaging 23 degrees, and each has a circular depression (12 cm. in diameter by 5 cm. deep) to hold a lamp. A photograph taken before restoration demonstrates that the depression is an original feature (Plate 16). In the foundations of the south transept arm there is the lower left-hand corner of another lamp niche.

The crypt wall is covered by a layer of intonaco, 1.00–2.00 cm. thick, with traces of painted decoration. Although the surface is at times extremely irregular, there is no sign of a previous decorative layer in the annular passage. The masonry is visible at a few points where there are holes in the plaster, and it resembles the irregular stonework of other parts of the foundations. There are occasional single bricks visible, sometimes used to frame the lamp niches.

The original paving of the annular passage is lost. At the juncture of the crypt and the foundation wall of the south transept arm, however, are three stone slabs (1.43 m. wide), marking the threshold of the subterranean doorway (Plate 17). At the end of the first plaque, opposite the foundation wall, a fragment of a delicately carved door jamb is still embedded in the Renaissance foundations (Plate 18). The stairs leading to the crypt have long since disappeared, but the outline of each individual step (20×30 cm.) is clearly discernible in the original plaster coating of the south transept arm foundation wall (Plates 10–11). The stair profiles begin precisely where the threshold slabs end. There are two distinct layers of plaster on this wall, but both layers follow the stairs, showing that the stairs were in place when the first decoration of this wall was applied. The right side of the plaster layers ends abruptly in a vertical line, probably marking the location of a matching door jamb. Moreover, the slab closest to the curved crypt passage has three holes, one to either side and one in the center, that indicate the position of swivel hinges for door panels (Plate 17).

The foundations of the north transept are not so well preserved, but one step is still in situ, incorporated by the Superintendency into a makeshift base for a pagan sarcophagus on display in the crypt. Significantly, the dimensions of this step correspond exactly to those indicated in the south transept arm (0.20× 0.30×1.55 m.). It will, therefore, be possible to reconstruct the annular crypt and its entrances with considerable precision.

The painted decoration of the crypt is divided horizontally by a broad tripartite band of red and black just below the sills of the lamp niches (Plates 13–14). The bottom half of the frescoed surface shows traces of simulated curtains, typical of early medieval dado decoration. The upper half of the fresco decoration, above the middle border, originally contained figural scenes, which are unfortunately now too fragmentary to be identified conclusively. There are a few delicately modeled feet on a wavering red ground line, but no heads or torsos. Croquison claims to have seen the tonsured head of an old man somewhere on the crypt wall.[5] The scenes were divided by a red-and-black frame that formed a continuation of the horizontal border.

The northern, or right, half of the crypt decoration is better preserved, and two scenes are readable with patience (Plates 12, 14). The most striking is a male figure to the far right, nude but for a loin cloth, in a contorted, reclining position, leaning on his left arm with his right hand upraised in a gesture of defense, recognition, or address. His right knee is up, and the left leg is bent back so that his left foot extends beyond the bottom frame. His head is now missing, but photographs of the Superintendency show that upon discovery a clean-shaven chin was still to be seen (Plate 12). The scene immediately to the left is more difficult to decipher, but one can make out the lower half of a robed figure, turned to the right, seated on a throne with a red cushion, his feet resting on a bejeweled footstool. To the right of the central figure are the feet and hemline of another standing figure, facing left (Plate 14). This composition brings to mind scenes of a pagan emperor ordering the execution of Christian martyrs, as depicted in various frescoes preserved in Rome from the mid-eighth through the mid-ninth centuries, such as those found in the Theodotus Chapel of S. Maria Antiqua, S. Maria in Via Lata, and S. Prassede.[6] I would suggest that these figural scenes represented episodes from the life and martyrdom of the saints whose relics were buried in the crypt.

The first plaster layer of the south transept foundation wall, discussed above, imitates marble revetment and porphyry discs, with the incised lines of the compass still distinct (Plate 11). This first layer is 1.0 cm. thick and pinkish in color, containing a sizable amount of brick particles. The second layer is very thin, fine-grained, and all white, with two simple, reddish-orange horizontal lines. It is difficult to determine which, if either, of these plaster layers is contemporary with the decoration of the annular passage, which exhibits only one plaster layer, because the intonaco surface is not preserved at the junctures of the foundations of the transept arms and the crypt. Two plaster layers are also preserved on a piece of wall abutting the door-jamb fragment.

Reconstruction

Although little can be said about the elevation of the west end, the plan can be reconstructed in detail (Fig. 9A). It consisted of a continuous transept (15.5 m. long by 7 m. wide) separated from the nave by a triumphal arch (5.50 m. wide) resting on ashlar foundations. There is no evidence of any segmentation of the transept, nor are the foundations sufficient to have sustained a central tower. Curiously enough, the north transept arm seems to have been more than one meter shorter than the south arm. The reason for this discrepancy is not known; it may be that a neighboring structure blocked the extension of the transept to the north. Whatever the reason, the entire complex seems to have been ad-justed slightly to fit this irregular situation. The stairs in the north transept arm, for example, were set ca. 50 cm. closer to the annular crypt passage than those in the south arm, while the center of the triumphal arch stood ca. 35 cm. to the south of the central axis of the nave.

In the center of the west wall stood a semicircular apse (5.52 m. in diameter), with an annular crypt below that averaged 1.49 m. wide. The perpendicular corridor was 1.30 m. wide, but its length remains unknown. The crypt seems to have been ca. 2 m. high. Photographs taken by the Superintendency before the restoration show that the fresco decoration on the crypt wall continued another 15–20 cm. below the present modern pavement (Plate 12). By extending the nave floor level, as given by the medieval pavement in situ, the total crypt height would be 1.95–2.00 m. (Plate 11). The horizontal band of the annular passage fresco would also then be exactly in the middle of the crypt height. There were two flights of stairs, one in each transept arm, with approximately nine steps, each measuring 20×30 cm., necessary to connect the nave and crypt floor levels. The step in situ in the north transept arm and the fragment of a door jamb on the south crypt entrance show the stairways to have been 1.55 m. wide (Fig. 9).

Croquison suggests that the semicircular wall of the crypt originally served as an apse above ground, and that only later, at some undetermined date, was it transformed into a crypt. He bases this theory upon the fact that the sills of the lamp niches slope like those of windows and that the exterior closing masonry is brick.[7] The exterior face of the crypt is no longer available for inspection,[8] but various considerations make this theory unlikely. First of all, the presence of windows does not in any way contradict the function of this area as a crypt— as witness, for example, the annular crypt at St.-Denis, consecrated in 775, where such windows are present (Plate 99E).[9] Indeed, the dimensions of the niches indicate that the window openings would have been not more than 5.0 cm. wide, which would be unusually narrow for the fenestration of an apse above ground but would be perfectly in keeping with windows for a crypt. Second, if indeed the niches were originally designed as windows, they were transformed into receptacles for lamps before the fresco decoration was applied, because the uniform plaster surface and red painted border lines follow the contours of the niches inside and out.

Once they were made to serve as lamp niches, they conformed in size to examples in Rome, such as those of the crypt of S. Prassede (817–824). Each niche varies slightly, but the measurements of 31 cm. wide in the front, 40 cm. deep, and 19 cm. wide at the back compare to 36×40×15 cm. at S. Prassede. The niches at S. Prassede are ca. 55 cm. in height; at Farfa, the tallest niche is broken off at a height of 59 cm., so that we cannot be certain of their original height. If they were originally designed as windows, we could expect them to have been approximately one meter high. The most likely reason for their conversion into lamp niches would be a rise in ground level immediately outside the crypt; the possible causes of this change in ground level will be discussed in the next chapter in connection with evidence for the monastic layout. Suffice it to reiterate here that the presence of narrow windows in the crypt does not require acceptance of Croquison's theory that it originally served as an apse above ground.

Prandi, however, agrees with Croquison's conclusions and points to other evidence as well. [10] He notes that the stairs leading to the crypt did not bond with the masonry of the transept and cites the annular crypt of Old St. Peter's in Rome as an example where such bonding does occur. Yet the final report of the excavations below St. Peter's that examined the evidence for the crypt states that no specific indication of the placement of the stairs was ever found. [11] Nevertheless, this cannot be used as a criterion for relative chronology, because the crypt of Old St. Peter's, where Prandi says that bonding occurs, was inserted ca. A.D. 590, some three hundred years after the original construction of the basilica, [12] whereas at S. Prassede, for example, where the crypt is contemporary with the construction of the church as a whole, there is no bonding of the stairs. [13]

Prandi claims also that only the second layer of the two fresco layers preserved along the south transept foundation wall follows the outline of the stairs. As I have shown (Plate 11), this statement is clearly incorrect. Finally, Prandi suggests that a chemical analysis of the mortar from the curved passage of the crypt and the perpendicular corridor proves that these two features were built at different times. Yet the chemical components are identical in both samples, and the variation in their amounts ranges from zero to 4 percent. [14] In short, rather than proving a difference in building campaigns, the composition of the two samples merely indicates that two batches of mortar were measured by hand and mixed at different times, which could have been days or only hours apart. Above all, it is difficult, if not impossible, to accept Prandi's theory that the crypt was created by filling in an already existing church two meters high with earth.[15] Such a procedure is illogical in the extreme. Thus, in spite of Croquison's observations about the lamp niches, the crypt should be seen as part of the overall design of the west end of the church, with the apse, transept, and annular crypt forming an integral whole.

EAST END

Analysis

The bell tower and square presbytery at the east end of the church are the best preserved and most complex remains of the medieval abbey church (Plate 19). In plan, they form two tangential squares on a decidedly different axis from the rest of the medieval church (Fig. 2). They have remained relatively intact, since they were not razed to make way for the quattrocento church but were gradually absorbed into the newly developing monastic complex. Markthaler, in his initial investigation of the bell tower, found the archaeological and documentary evidence for many of these modifications, such as stairways, adjoining corridors, and doorways.[16] Most important, by the early seventeenth century, the square presbytery and campanile were remodeled to accommodate the abbot's residence.[17] Additional floors were added and rooms subdivided vertically, doors and windows punched through walls, and a stairwell added to the east façade of the square presbytery. Until recently, most of the east end of the medieval church lay hidden by these later structures or under subsequent layers of plaster.

The systematic removal of these later walls and plaster coatings began with the work of Markthaler, whose efforts concentrated on the bell tower. He removed the secondary floor in the bell-tower base that cut across the medieval frescoes. He found the original openings in the upper four storeys of the bell tower blocked with colonnettes and capitals still embedded in the later brickwork. But a full restoration of the exterior did not take place until the 1968–1970 campaign sponsored by the Superintendency, at which time the stairwell on the east façade of the presbytery and a lean-to roof obscuring the base of the campanile were also taken down. Corridors and storage rooms on the ground floor, however, were left untouched. Aspects of this restoration were over severe, such as the repointing of the masonry in the upper storeys of the bell tower and a relatively haphazard treatment of the frescoes. Yet in spite of these negative aspects, the east end of the medieval abbey church was made available for a thorough examination for the first time.

The Bell Tower: Exterior.   The campanile dominates the entire monastery, rising in six storeys to a full height of ca. 25 m. (Plate 19). The base of the tower is approximately equal in height to the adjoining square presbytery (13 m.) and is 7.20 m. wide on its east side and 8.04 m. on the north flank. The base, which forms a single vaulted space on the interior, is further subdivided on the exterior into two storeys by a crude sawtooth frieze composed of one row of stone teeth framed by two or three courses of brick. Below this frieze on the east, north, and west sides are pilaster strips and blind arches forming a series of shallow grooves 11 to 12 cm. deep. Above the frieze are blind gabled arches in groups of threes and fours, ca. 1.21 m. wide by 3.75 m. high. There are only three windows: one small round-arched window, 0.45×1.53 m., with stilted jambs between gabled niches in the east, and two larger windows to the north (actually the northeast) in the first storey, measuring 0.85×2.04 m., whose larger size and placement were perhaps designed to take advantage of the morning sun.

Each side of the bell-tower base repeats the same features, but always in different numbers and proportions (Figs. 5–7). The first storey of the east side has four tall, narrow blind arches, 0.67 m. wide by 7.50 m. high, and the second storey has three gabled niches as well as a small central round-arched window (Fig. 5, Plate 20). In the first storey of the north side, in order to make room for the two large windows, the blind arches begin at a considerably lower level and are therefore squatter, measuring ca. 0.83 m. wide by 2.96 m. high (Fig. 6, Plate 22). This side of the campanile being wider, there is room above the frieze for four rather than three blind gabled arches (Plate 23). The west side, on the other hand, has three blind arches below the frieze and three gabled arches above it (Fig. 7, Plates 24–25). The central and right-hand blind arches end only 2 m. below their archivolts. The full length of the left blind arch cannot be determined, for today the entire lower half of this storey forms part of a sacristy, and this wall has been covered by later plaster and by modern cement. A small cupboard-like niche built into the base of this wall bears the date 1546 across its lintel (Plate 27).[18] The south side of the bell tower is not visible from the outside.

The upper storeys of the bell tower are uniform. Each storey has a triple-arched opening, with single recessed surrounds, resting on two colonnettes with broad, triangular capitals (Figs. 5–6, Plates 19, 23). The top three storeys are separated by a brick double cornice made up of two rows of brick sawteeth and vertical bricks as corbels. Between the second and third storeys there is, in place of a cornice, a shallow ledge capped with three courses of brick. The surface around the triple-arched opening of the third storey is recessed with pilaster strips at the corners. On the south side, there is no cornice between the third and fourth storeys, only a horizontal ridge 0.70 m. below where the cornice line should be (Plate 28). There is also no triple-arched opening in the third storey here. Instead, there is the outline of an arch with roughly hewn voussoirs. The soffit of the arch continues through the one-meter thickness of the campanile and can be seen on the inside of the tower, though obscured in large part by modern cement (Plate 29). The outline of this blocked opening is 1.10 m. wide by 2.00 m. high (Fig. 3).

The masonry of the first storey of the bell tower usually shows one course of stone alternating with one course of brick, but not always (Figs. 5–6). Single courses of brick stop and start unpredictably at various points, eventually terminating at different heights in a staggered pattern on each side. In view of its erratic nature, I prefer to call this masonry *opus mixtum*, to differentiate it from the regularity of *opus listatum*, where two or three courses of brick alternate uniformly with one or two courses of stone. The rest of the campanile is a homogenous rough-hewn masonry of porous, calcareous tufa, except at two points in the base of the west side where marble fragments of a column and a base have been casually inserted (Plate 25). In the ground floor of the east side, there is a break forming the outline of a round archway 3.10 m. high by 1.70 m. wide. The masonry fill repeats the familiar *opus mixtum*, but the brick and stone courses do not align with the surrounding masonry (Plate 30). The round and gabled arches of each storey are outlined by single brick courses. In the spandrels of the blind arches, bricks have been set flat so as to form a diamond pattern (Plate 31). On the west side, these brick spandrels are framed by red and green porphyry strips (Plate 32). On the south side of the tower at the third-storey level, cut-stone blocks are set at the corner and immediately surround the round-arched opening noted above, but in between is a very irregular masonry with numerous brick fragments (Plate 28).

A modulus is difficult to determine owing to the irregularity of the masonry. The bricks average 4 cm. in thickness, sometimes 3 cm. and occasionally 5 cm., while the tufa blocks vary from 11 to 24 cm. thick, averaging 17–18 cm.

The Bell Tower: Interior. The ground floor of the bell tower is a tall rectangular space (5.61 × 4.83 m.), covered by a groin vault supported in the corners by engaged square piers (Figs. 2, 8). The apex of the vault is 10.60 m. high, roughly corresponding to the second-storey division of the exterior. The vault itself was rebuilt during the restoration campaign, but Markthaler had already uncovered the corner piers and the juncture of the arches of the vault (Plate 33).[19]

The small round-arched window in the east side of the campanile base pierces the interior off-axis and below the arc of the vault (Fig. 8, Plate 34). Centered at the base of the east wall is a round-arched niche (0.60 m. deep) corresponding in location and size to the masonry break noted on the exterior (Plate 35). The north wall is interrupted only by the two large round-headed windows, at which point the wall is 1.19 m. thick; a modern doorway pierces the base of the same wall (Fig. 8). At the base of the west wall, in line with the niche of the opposite wall, is the outline of a blocked doorway (1.70 × 7.20 m.) capped by a monolithic lintel (Fig. 8, Plate 36). Supporting the irregular masonry fill of the doorway is a brick relieving arch, a technique common in later modifications to the medieval fabric. Above the lintel is a small rectangular niche lined with brick, still blackened with soot from the lamp it once contained. On the south side, a monumental arch (10 m. high by 3.71 m. wide, with jambs ca. 1 m. thick) stands blocked by rubble fill and modern brick (Fig. 8, Plate 37). In the southeast corner is a patch of the original pavement, composed of pieces of porphyry, marble, and serpentine, providing the medieval floor level of the bell-tower interior (Plate 38).

The masonry is uniform rough-hewn blocks of tufa and occasionally of limestone, similar to that of the exterior but without any brick courses (though the voussoirs of the large niche in the east wall are outlined by a single course of brick). The middle elevation of each wall is scarred by the vault of the secondary floor removed by Markthaler.[20] When this floor was added in the sixteenth century, the bottom halves of three of the corner piers were removed, but their footings remain in situ. At several points, especially along the north wall, the excess mortar has been crudely pointed, forming coarse horizontal striations of a *falsa cortina* across the inner face of the tower (Plate 39a–b). This pointing may have been particularly useful for the application of plaster for the fresco decoration.

The Bell Tower: Fresco Decoration.   Although portions of the fresco decoration in the base of the bell tower were visible to Ildefonso Schuster at the beginning of this century,[21] the full extent of the program was first revealed by Markthaler in the late 1920s. In 1980–1981, the frescoes were cleaned and consolidated.[22] The paintings were found to be true fresco, comprising a single layer of intonaco applied directly to the masonry surface without a preparatory layer and without sinopia drawings; such a procedure is the norm for medieval wall paintings in Central Italy. There is no evidence of an earlier fresco layer anywhere in the tower's interior. There were several hands involved, however, as evidenced by the varying styles of the program, and there is one clear *pontata*, or horizontal plaster joint, in the upper half of the north wall. In short, the paintings of the bell-tower base are the result of a single decorative campaign. Unfortunately, no funds were available for chemical analyses of the pigments.

Although less than 50 percent of the original painted surface is preserved, Markthaler was able to show that the frescoes depicted an interrelated Old and New Testament cycle, dominated by the representation of the Ascension of Christ that covered the entire north wall (Fig. 8). Immediately below the vault, Christ is shown in profile carrying a cross over his left shoulder and reaching for the hand of God with his right hand, as flanking angels look on. Bust-length angels emerging from a thin layer of clouds gesture to the semicircle of attendant apostles below. In between, at the level of the two large windows, the apostles Peter and Paul holding scrolls appear in the right and left corners respectively (Plates 40–42). Decoration in the lowest zone is now lost, but Markthaler saw two large medallions bearing half-length portraits of saints, one male and one female, with simulated curtains in the area below.[23]

The east wall has three preserved scenes. Just below the arch of the vault and to the right of the window is a half-length, white-bearded figure that Mark-thaler identified as God the Father, but it more likely represents an Old Testa-ment prophet (Plate 34). The next zone was framed top and bottom by a painted cornice composed of two mouldings with egg-like patterns. To the upper right are the heads of a group of three men and two women and the torso of a sixth figure. One of the women is haloed and may represent the Virgin Mary. In the center of the next register is the representation of a large earthen water vessel that suggests the scene is the Marriage of Cana. Immediately above the apex of the altar niche in the east wall is the enigmatic representation of the Adoration of the Phoenix that Markthaler likened to the Vision of Ezekiel and the Resurrection of Christ (Fig. 8, Plate 35). The phoenix is shown standing upright, in profile with a cross nimbus about its head and a partial inscription that reads: [pho]ENIX. The mythical bird is framed by an arch from which emerge two angels blowing trumpets, while two groups of figures approach from the left and right, identified as laity and monks respectively.[24] Again, medallions of saints seen by Markthaler in the lowest zone are now lost.

The west wall is crowned by a representation of Christ in Majesty, with Christ seated on a globe and surrounded by a host of angels (Plate 43). Because of the presence of a black demon with wings and a tail at the feet of the angels to Christ's right, Markthaler interprets this scene as the Temptation in the Desert, a depiction of Matthew 4:11 where Christ, having scorned Satan, is adminis-tered by angels. The representation of Christ on a globe with a book in his left hand, however, indicates that the demon in question, which is now barely visible, represents instead the Devil in the form of a chained dragon as de-scribed in Revelation 20:2–3.

As is the case with the east wall, a central register of the west wall is framed top and bottom by a painted double moulding. In the upper left-hand corner is a seated male figure, dressed only in a loin cloth and covered with sores (Plate 44), who gestures to three figures standing in front of him. A woman stands behind him, her head framed by the archway of a building. Rather than the representation of Job, which first comes to mind, Markthaler suggests that the scene portrayed is the story of Naaman, who in the Book of Kings is cured of leprosy by washing in the Jordan River.[25] According to Markthaler, the signifi-cance of this scene for the Farfa monastery would be the reference in the biblical text to the Pharphar River (2 Kings 5:12–13): "Are not the Abana and Pharphar, rivers of Damascus, better than all waters of Israel so that I may wash in them and be clean?" If this is the case, it should be noted that the scene seems to be without parallel in Christian art, and most likely the iconography of the story of Job has been adapted to fit a new meaning.[26] In the middle of this same zone are traces of a painted spiral colonnette, to the left of which are a pair of feet. Directly below are four male figures with arms outstretched toward a white block-like object (Plate 44). Markthaler and Schuster identify this scene as the Sacrifice of Noah (Genesis 8:20–21).

The inner faces of the jambs of the monumental arch in the south wall each bear three registers. The top level contains standing saints in ecclesiastical robes and the middle one shows equestrian saints. The lowest level is only partially preserved on the western jamb, but one can make out the shoulder and left arm of a standing figure holding a gold crown. An accompanying vertical inscription reads: S. CONSTANTIUS. Schuster was the first to suggest that the figure represented is the martyr Constantius, bishop of Perugia.[27] Particularly striking about the fresco decoration from an overall point of view is the emphatic architectural frame. The corner square piers are decorated by two tiers of painted columns with leafy capitals and shafts with either spiral or vertical fluting. The east and west walls are divided into three horizontal registers by elaborate mouldings, sometimes with their own spiral colonnettes. As I have already noted, the dado zone was composed of portrait medallions and simulated curtains. Only the Ascension scene was uninterrupted and would have been clearly visible from the crossing through the monumental arch of the south wall.

Although the entire program exhibits many common characteristics, such as heavy outlining of the figures, at least two styles may be distinguished. The first is best represented by the west wall in the Story of Naaman and Christ in Majesty (Plates 43, 44). Clearly, the individual responsible for the latter scene was the superior artist, but both scenes exhibit the same buildup of flesh tones and drapery through broad areas of flat color. The drapery was then highlighted by streaks of pure white, much of which has since worn off. A very different approach is represented by the bust-length angels and the apostles of the Ascension (Plates 41–42). Here the palette is far more varied, with a wide range of colors applied in broad parallel strokes, giving the painting an impressionistic quality that is also very expressive in the combination of the contorted postures of the figures and their swirling drapery.

On occasion, both styles appear on the same wall. In the Ascension (Plate 40), the flatter first style is evident in the figure of Christ and the full-length attendant angels and the second style in the lower two-thirds of the scene. There is a clear horizontal break, or *pontata*, between these two sections of the north wall. The joint has been plastered over, and the tips of the wings of the half-length angels (the "men in white" referred to in Acts) have been painted over the juncture. It would seem that the artist or artists using the first, more linear, style were responsible for the entire cycle except for the lower two-thirds of the Ascension scene. While this could simply represent a division in labor, it could also represent a chronological gap, albeit a short one, caused by a break in the work or at least a transition from one atelier to another. Be that as it may, both styles are represented in manuscript illumination produced at the abbey at approximately the same time.

Walls below and adjoining the Bell Tower.   Below the floor level of the campanile are the rudiments of a wall, with a maximum height of 1.20 m., traversing the middle of the tower plan on an east–west axis (Figs. 2, 8, Plates 45a–c). The

wall is broken in the middle, but both halves seem to align, although the
eastern half is ca. 1 m. thick and the western half narrows to 0.50 m. The entire
wall is composed of massive unhewn limestone blocks with a minimum of
mortar (Plate 45a). On the northern face are remains of a primitive fresco
decoration, imitating marble revetment in the dado and crude floral forms
above (Plate 45b). Only the north face is frescoed. The other side shows no
sign of decoration and was probably the exterior face. The western half of the
wall is met at a right angle by another wall, 0.50 m. thick, and west of this
junction is a second, more sophisticated fresco decoration. The dado below
shows the upper parts of a curtain decoration, while above are another curtain
and the tail of a peacock framed by a broad rainbow band (Plate 45c). Unfortunately, the wall cannot be followed any farther, for the tower foundations have
been set in reinforced concrete with a brick facing. Markthaler, however, saw it
continue several meters beyond the tower to the east and west (Fig. 16). The
wall has no direct relationship to other remains of the medieval church. Markthaler's plan labels it a late Roman wall,[28] but a more likely explanation is that it
represents the remnants of an early medieval monastic room, decorated a
second time upon the addition of a perpendicular wall, that was later leveled
when the bell tower was built.

Adjoining the northwest corner of the bell tower, Markthaler discovered the
upper half of an arch, 1.70 m. wide and with voussoirs 0.30 m. thick (Plate 46).
This wall is crucial to his identification of the bell tower as the Sichardan
oratory, because he interprets it as the remains of the pre-Carolingian church.
Certainly, it is the remains of a blocked opening with a threshold ca. 0.50 m.
below the seventeenth-century corridor level. But the surrounding masonry is
extremely crude rubble work, characteristic of sixteenth- and seventeenth-
century modifications to the east end.[29] In this same rubble wall are the outlines
of the stilted jambs of two windows, ca. 0.90 m. above the apex of the arch
(Fig. 6). Rather than being a relic of the medieval church, this wall forms the
north flank of the sacristy abutting the west side of the tower, with an inscription of 1546 (Plate 27).[30] The voussoirs of the arch are partially broken and
filled with this rubble masonry; thus, although the arch itself may be medieval,
the wall is not.

The Square Presbytery: Exterior.   In plan, the presbytery adjoining the bell
tower forms a perfect square 8×8 m. on the inside and roughly 9.60×9.60 m.
on the outside (Fig. 2). The thickness of the walls varies: the north and south
walls average 0.90 m., and the east wall tapers to only 0.60 m. Curiously, each
side of the presbytery was restored in a different manner. The south side was
almost completely restored, supposedly to its original appearance, whereas the
north side was rebuilt partly in stucco and partly with recessed brickwork. On
the east side, the later stairwell was removed and the fragmented wall was
stabilized with recessed brickwork.

The north and south sides of the square presbytery are the best preserved and echo one another (Plates 48–49). Each is articulated by seven narrow and extremely elongated blind arches (11.30 m. tall, an average of 0.52–0.53 m. wide, and 0.12 m. deep). Though the bottom half of the north side is obscured by adjoining rooms, the bases of five pilaster strips are still visible in an abandoned washroom (Fig. 6, Plate 52). The arches and one sill of two small windows (Fig. 6, Plate 50) are also preserved on the north side. The south side has been completely rebuilt and must therefore be treated with caution in any reconstruction; a photograph taken during restoration, however, makes it relatively easy to recognize the original masonry (Plates 47–48). Here one can see the arcades of the blind arches directly below the later cornice, as well as the segments of arches of two smaller windows corresponding in position to those noted on the south side.

The east façade of the presbytery stands as a gigantic jigsaw puzzle, with only small portions of its original masonry preserved (Plate 53). The recessed modern brickwork of the restorers is immediately recognizable. At the center of the bottom of the wall are the bases of seven pilaster strips, framed by broader pilaster strips at each corner and terminating at the same level as those on the north and south sides. Here the same number of blind arches was repeated, but the greater width of the façade, due to the fact that it does not abut the bell tower, necessitated an alteration in proportions. The widths of the central five niches correspond to those on the sides, although the blind arches to the far left and right are considerably wider, i.e., ca. 1 m. The arcading of these blind arches is not preserved, but the springing of the first arch to the right is indicated by a segment of its brick outline, which is on the same level as the blind arcades on the north and south sides.

The square presbytery is built of *opus mixtum* similar to that of the adjoining bell tower. Unlike the campanile, however, where this masonry is found only in the base, the square presbytery has *opus mixtum* throughout (Figs. 5–6). It is not possible to tell if the square presbytery and the bell tower actually bond, because at the crucial point of their juncture the masonry of the square presbytery has been obliterated through later modifications. The lower section of the northwest corner of the square presbytery was destroyed to make way for the seventeenth-century corridor that passes along the base of the bell tower. Directly above, in the corner formed by the joining of the presbytery and the bell tower, a stairway was added to give access to the tower's third storey. Either in the process of its construction or in its subsequent removal by Markthaler, the original masonry was lost, but the courses of the *opus mixtum* do align between the presbytery and the tower. As in the bell tower, bricks in the square presbytery average 4 cm. in thickness, and the rough-hewn tufa blocks 17–18 cm.

While there would appear to be a more consistent alternation of brick and stone courses in the square presbytery, on the north side—which is the best preserved—the brick courses stop and start in a manner reminiscent of the bell tower. The arcades of the blind arches are outlined by a single course of brick, but there are no bricks set flat in their spandrels. The arcade on the north side is capped by a simple row of square cut blocks framed top and bottom by a single row of bricks (Plate 51). In the gable of the east façade there is a horizontal break, above which is pure limestone construction (Plate 53). The spaces between the pilaster strips at the base of the east side are mostly filled with irregular stone work, but the middle four are blocked with *opus mixtum* similar to, but not aligned with, the masonry courses of the pilaster strips themselves (Plate 54).

The Square Presbytery: Interior.   The interior of the square presbytery is in far worse condition than the exterior. It has been divided in half vertically and horizontally by rubble walls, to accommodate the abbot's quarters above and the entrance corridor and an adjacent storeroom below (Figs. 3–5). In the south wall, the two narrow windows have been extensively restored, but the right half of the left window is original to a point 0.80 m. below the archivolt (Fig. 4, Plate 55). In the north wall, corresponding to the window arch and sill noted on the exterior, is a niche with splayed jambs measuring 1.74 m. high by 0.45 m. wide (Fig. 3, Plate 58a). In the left half of the same wall, more than two meters higher, is a small blocked round-arched window 0.80 m. high by 0.51 m. wide (Fig. 3, Plate 56).

In the corners and middle of the north, south, and east walls are remains of engaged columns. The columns in the center of the north and south walls are preserved to their full height (8.00 m.), with their capitals and bases embedded in the vertical dividing wall (Figs. 3–4). Their bases and plinths (10 cm. high) are of stone, and the shafts and capitals are primarily of brick (Plates 57b, 58b). Even though the upper halves of the columns are covered by intonaco, the corners of simple block capitals are discernible (Plates 57a, 58a). The columns in the corners and middle of the east walls are preserved only within the thickness of the horizontal, secondary floor. The restorers left a trench with the stubs of these columns in place (Plate 59a–c). In the northeast corner at ground level, the column and its base are gone, but the scar of broken bricks is still visible. The southwest column shaft, covered with later plaster, is embedded in the ground-floor corridor wall (Fig. 5). Although there is no trace of the northwest column, the scar of a broad arch (0.45 m. high) curves from this corner to the capital of the column in the center of the north wall (Fig. 3, Plate 56).

The upper half of the west wall reveals a single massive archway 6.43 m. wide, which has original voussoirs ca. 1 m. high and which has been relined with a second set of smaller voussoirs 0.60 m. high (Fig. 5, Plate 60). Each arch must represent a different building phase, for the soffit of the first arch is decorated with a frescoed meander pattern (Plate 61). The outline of the jambs of this second phase are partially visible at ground level. Above the arch are two lunettes (1.75 m. high by ca. 2.80 m. wide), now blocked and their soffits painted with Renaissance frescoes. Between the lunettes is the faint outline of another arched scar, terminating in a patch of brickwork, most likely the original placement of a corbel.

Much of the interior of the square presbytery is still covered with modern plaster or littered with patching and restoration masonry. Basically, the visible masonry falls into three categories: (1) original masonry of rough-hewn tufa blocks similar to the interior of the campanile; (2) the vertical dividing wall of rubble masonry with a brick relieving arch that is definitely not original because it envelops the engaged columns;[31] (3) the modern restoration masonry, usually composed of cut tufa and easily identifiable by its unworn texture and dark-gray cement. Similar to the second type is the patchwork in the northwest corner, where presumably another engaged column once stood. Doorways, on the other hand, in the east and north walls have been filled with modern brick. The only exception to this scheme is the base of the east wall, which is only partially visible. It will be remembered that this wall is extremely thin, and here patches of brick courses of the *opus mixtum* are discernible. The bricks of the columns average 3.5 cm. in thickness, with mortarbeds of 1.5 cm. Related to these are the shafts of two other engaged columns of brick, one inserted in the inner corner between the square presbytery and the bell tower and another matching it on the other side of the archway in the south wall of the bell-tower base (Fig. 3, Plate 63). These shafts are covered by a layer of intonaco, but the mortarbeds are pointed like those of the interior of the bell tower base and have the same modulus, i.e., five bricks and five mortarbeds to 27 cm., as the engaged columns in the square presbytery.

The Square Presbytery: Fresco Decoration. As in the case of the bell tower, the interior of the square presbytery was covered by a fresco cycle, although it is far less well preserved. In fact, there appear to have been three distinct fresco layers. On the shafts of the two completely preserved engaged columns there are two discernible layers (Plates 57a, 58a). The first is a medieval imitation of fluting and geometric patterns, whereas the top layer clearly dates from the Renaissance and has white floral patterns on a pink ground. In the lower left (or north) corner of the east wall of the presbytery, however, next to the scar of the brick engaged column, there are two medieval fresco layers. These remains are too fragmentary to identify the subject matter, but the layers are clear nonetheless. The first layer has a bright yellow oval outlined in black on a green ground, painted very briskly. Overlapping this is a second, thin layer (0.35 cm. thick) with a yellow border and white lettering on a blue ground. This second layer seems to relate to the frescoes preserved above the horizontal dividing floor. Visible in the trench with the column stubs are fragments of a Last Judgment scene; one can make out the middle torso of Christ, who wears a purple robe with a gold cross in front and who stretches out his pierced hands (Plate 64a). He is flanked by standing angels, each holding an orb and a scroll, and by a retinue of seated apostles (Plate 64a–b). Along the north wall at the same level are fragments of the bejeweled walls of the Heavenly Jerusalem. Above were standing figures, and below, no longer extant but visible in an old photograph, there were the heads of tonsured and hooded monks. On the east and north walls are the faded figures of standing angels.

On the north wall, between a modern doorway and the middle engaged column, is the vestige of a fresco showing a winged angel with veiled hands approaching another figure to the right, whose arms are outstretched toward the angel. At the very bottom on the lower left, a cupped hand indicates that the latter figure is seated in the left hand of yet another figure. The scene has been identified as a representation of the Assumption of the Virgin. The soul of the Virgin is depicted as a diminutive figure being lifted to heaven by Christ to a host of awaiting angels, similar to a detail of the so-called Farfa Casket, an ivory box presented to the abbey by a merchant from Amalfi named Maurus in the second half of the eleventh century.[32]

As I have already mentioned, there is a meander pattern of red, yellow, blue, and green on the soffit of the first triumphal arch in the west wall. The second soffit had two layers. The first represented busts of apostles and Christ in a style that corresponds to the documented reconsecration of the main altar in 1401. On top of this layer was painted a second series of busts from the late quattro-cento (Plate 62). This coincides with the second layer of the painted decoration on the engaged columns and the surrounds of the blocked window of the north wall, which bears the monogram of the commendatory Giovanni Orsini, 1435–1476 (Plate 58a). At this same time, the busts of prophets and evangelists were presumably painted in the soffits of the lunettes above the triumphal arch (Plate 65), and the medieval Last Judgment on the east wall was painted over with the same figures but in a more "modern" style (Plate 66). Thus, the square presbytery must have gone through at least four decorative campaigns during the Middle Ages and the early Renaissance.

Reconstruction

The campanile is preserved in its entirety, except for the loss of a seventh storey that was dismantled at the end of the last century as a precautionary measure following an earthquake tremor.[33] Otherwise, but for small details, there is little evidence to question its present appearance. A lintel doorway at the base of the west wall communicated with the church or neighboring monastic buildings. The niche at the base of the east wall, on the other hand, was used for the placement of an altar. This is shown by the frescoed cross in the apex of its soffit, which was positioned to be seen directly from below by a viewer facing east—the celebrant before an altar.

The square presbytery is a different matter, but its reconstruction becomes equally clear. The exterior north and south sides mirrored one another with their seven slender blind arches. The east wall used the same number of blind arches, but with different proportions. Though the inner five arches followed the width of those on the north and south sides, they were framed by considerably wider ones. The height of the blind arch on the far right was on a level with the arcades of the sides. The other arches may have stopped on the same level or, as in my reconstruction drawing, they may have been stilted (Fig. 10), following the outline of the gabled roof. There may have been small windows in this east façade, but it cannot be proven. The two windows on the south side have been rebuilt too long; originally, they must have followed the dimensions of the preserved window on the north side (Fig. 6, Plates 50, 58a). There is another smaller window in the upper left half of the north wall (Plate 56), but there is no evidence that it was matched by another one on the south side. The eave line of the square presbytery seems to have been raised ca. 0.50 m., and the pediment of the east façade has been rebuilt. A baroque cornice is still in place on the south side, while on the north there is a simple stone-and-brick frieze, identical to that of the fifteenth-century church (Plate 51). Above this frieze the additional 0.30 m. is irregular fill.

The original interior roofing system is more problematic. Franciosa, for example, reconstructs it with groin vaulting as in the bell tower.[34] In comparison to the thick walls and square piers used to sustain the groin vault of the bell-tower base, however, the walls of the larger square presbytery are extremely thin. The walls of the campanile range in thickness from 1.00 m. to 1.62 m., whereas the east wall of the square presbytery narrows to less than 0.60 m.! Furthermore, it is extremely difficult, as Franciosa discovered, to accommodate the engaged column in the middle of the east wall into a normal system of vaulting without a central support of some kind, which would illogically break up the interior square space of the presbytery. The obvious solution is that the engaged columns and blind arcading played more of a decorative role than a structural one, defining the interior space and supporting a timber roof (Fig. 11). On the west side, the blind arches were probably supported by a corbel set between the two lunettes.

The Crossing. In plan and elevation, the bell tower and square presbytery are integral, and they both originally opened onto a common crossing through massive archways. This is also clear from the two engaged columns visible in the northeast and northwest corners of the area of the crossing. The height of the crossing is indicated by the blocked round-arched opening on the south side of the bell tower's third storey (Fig. 3, Plate 28); presumably, the horizontal ridge marks where the eave of a low lantern met the bell tower. The opening compares in size to the windows on the north side of the bell tower's first floor and allowed light from the ample fenestration of the campanile's upper storeys to pass into the crossing (Fig. 11). This would also explain the presence of the lunettes above the triumphal arch in the square presbytery as a means of bringing light into an otherwise gloomy space.[35]

It is impossible to say with certainty how the crossing was roofed. It may have been vaulted, but I have preferred to reconstruct it with a timber roof and the engaged columns supporting blind arches, as in the square presbytery. From the exterior, the crossing would not have been prominent—low, with approximately equal height to the apex of the presbytery's pitched roof (Fig. 10). The crossing probably had a pyramidal or hipped roof, for there is no scar where a gable would have met the bell tower. There may have been small round-arched windows or *oculi* between the presbytery roof and the eave of the crossing. Two on the west side above the nave roof would coordinate with the two lunettes in the west wall of the presbytery.

Original Plan and the Second Bell Tower.   There is little doubt that the east end of the abbey church originally possessed two towers. The presence of a crossing, as just described, necessitates a symmetrical plan. Thus, a matching campanile or, at least, a projecting transept arm should be expected to the south. Markthaler in fact discovered the foundation of just such a structure, as indicated on his plan (Fig. 16). The fact that these foundations supported a second tower is confirmed by the papal bull issued by Sixtus IV in 1477, which describes the abbey church as "the church with the towers" (*ecclesiam cum turribus*).[36] This document was written while the medieval church was still standing, some fifteen years before the Renaissance church was begun. Furthermore, a painting from about this same time, now in the monastery's museum, represents Thomas of Maurienne holding a model of the church with two towers flanking the apse at the east end (Plate 67). Even after the Renaissance church was built, the official insignia of the abbey remained a two-towered silhouette, usually shown in a frontal view.

The second tower and crossing were apparently torn down in the early seventeenth century to make way for the granary and bakery that formed the west wing of the 1624 courtyard. In this regard, it is interesting to note that the arches of the groin vaults in the 1622 corridor, which passes through the ground floor of the square presbytery and alongside the east face of the bell tower, are supported by corbels of reused medieval capitals. Several of these capitals are comparable in shape, size, and decoration to those in the extant bell tower (Plates 68–69). Others have been collected in the abbey museum (Plate 70a–b).

Thus, the plan of the east end consisted of a rectangular crossing flanked by roughly square compartments that were groin-vaulted with shallow altar niches in their east walls (Figs. 2, 11, 15). The arches of the crossing into the transept arms were considerably higher and narrower than the triumphal arch into the presbytery. The floor level of the crossing, as indicated by the preserved pavement in the bell tower, was ca. 20 cm. higher than the nave, requiring one step. The level of the column bases in the square presbytery suggests that there were two more steps between the crossing and the presbytery (Fig. 11).

Comments on Construction.   In terms of construction, the east end is both cautious and experimental. The dearth of fenestration in the square presbytery is a conservative aspect, as if the designers were afraid to pierce the wall. Only in the bell tower's upper storeys and in the north side of its massive base were many openings allowed. The vaulting of the campanile base was reinforced by thick walls and square corner piers, although there seems to have been a lack of ability or desire to vault the larger square presbytery. In general, the forms and profiles are primitive. Pilaster strips and blind arches, for example, have a long tradition and are among the simplest means of exterior buttressing, but at Farfa there is an element of play in the use of these forms. The proportions and combinations of the blind arches are forever changing, expressing an apparent enjoyment in the pliability of the wall surface for its own sake. On the interior the masonry is rough-hewn with a crude, wavering *falsa cortina*. On the exterior there is an attempt at regularity through the use of *opus mixtum*, yet the brick courses stop and start abruptly, almost to the point of whimsy. Bricks were appreciated for their decorative, not structural, potential, except perhaps for the engaged columns in the presbytery. Bricks are never used for archivolts, as one might expect, but for outlining voussoirs and creating diamond patterns in the spandrels. Consequently, the erratic *opus mixtum* forms a quiltlike pattern of striations across the entire ground floor (Figs. 5–6).

Consistent with these seemingly contradictory qualities are indications of changes in the midst of building. The similarity between the masonry of the bell tower and the fill of the arched break on the exterior of its east wall suggests that the break was intended originally as a doorway or an apse (since it was ultimately used to house an altar), but that it was blocked up while the tower was still under construction. The same thing happens at the base of the exterior east wall of the presbytery, where the spacings between several pilaster strips have been filled in with identical *opus mixtum*. The wall is particularly thin at this point, and it may have proven structurally unsound, requiring an immediate refilling. This verges on incompetence, evident at first on the plan, which shows the marked curvature of the north wall of the square presbytery (Fig. 2).

This provides a clue to discovering the building procedure, a speculative venture, admittedly, but an instructive one. The south and east walls of the presbytery meet at a good right angle. The problem arose when the north wall was to meet the bell tower. The campanile has an axis close to that of the nave, probably because it physically abutted it. The square presbytery, on the other hand, was built a considerable distance away from the nave, and any attempt to align it with the nave's central axis may have been obstructed by an intervening apse, if, as I believe, the presbytery was an addition to an older church.[37]

Apparently, the masons at Farfa had a limited cache of bricks, most likely taken from an ancient Roman ruin. Either the construction of the elevation of the presbytery progressed ahead of that of the bell tower, or bricks were held in reserve for it. In sum, the east end of the medieval church at Farfa does not exhibit a great display of technical expertise; rather, it seems to represent a piecemeal and experimental process.

THE MONASTIC LAYOUT

In 1978, the British School at Rome together with Yale University initiated excavations of the monastic site at Farfa. An open field was made available that lay alongside the western flank of the Renaissance church and thus immediately outside the medieval semicircular apse and transept (Fig. 1). The area measures approximately 40×40 m., bordered to the north by the cloister built in 1585–90, to the west by the monastic library, originally built in 1577 as the customs-house for the biannual fairs, and to the southwest by a massive square tower, approximately 14×11 m. (Plate 71). By the end of the 1983 season, the entire area had been opened to a depth of almost three meters, revealing a series of interlocking structures dating from the early Middle Ages to the Renaissance, with evidence of extensive modifications in subsequent periods. For a full analysis of this material, including coins, pottery, and human and animal remains, the reader should consult the final report now in preparation. My purpose here will be to discuss the architectural remains as they pertain to the history of the medieval abbey.

As in the abbey church, portions of walls and foundations elsewhere in the medieval monastery were rebuilt, sometimes reused and more often destroyed to make way for later structures. Therefore, in order to recognize and to reconstruct aspects of the medieval layout, we need first to get some idea of the disposition of the buildings in the area in more recent times. The seventeenth-century bird's-eye view of Farfa (Plate 1) identifies the excavation area as the "palace of the . . . Cardinal Abbot Commendatory with the prisons and piazza in front of the stables."[38] The 1686 print shows that the palace complex was composed of the tower at the corner of the excavation site with adjoining structures to the east—a rectangular unit projecting at a right angle followed by a square courtyard formed by low interlocking, boxlike units. These subsidiary structures presumably represent the prisons and stables referred to in the engraving. This is not to suggest that the print should be taken as accurate in every detail. We need only look to the representation of the Renaissance church façade to see that the rose window is missing, or to the sixteenth-century cloister (labeled no. 10) to see that the piers and arcades are not included. Still, the engraving is useful in recognizing the general arrangement and function of various sections of the monastic complex.

A literary description of the palace complex is found in an eighteenth-century manuscript, preserved in the Farfa archives, which records that the annex to the tower was multi-storeyed, with the ground floor occupied by the prison on one side and the stables on the other. Immediately above were the living quarters of the constable and his assistants. [39] The earliest description of the complex comes in the aforementioned papal bull of 1477, which refers to a kitchen, servants' quarters, cellars, stables, and a garden. In addition, the palace is described as having stood "outside the cloister" and near the entrance of the monastery, occupying the space from "the main gate to the abbey church."[40] The gate in question probably refers to the large archway, now walled up but surrounded by finely cut stone masonry and adjoining the square tower at its northwest corner (Plate 73). This information is essential for understanding the excavated remains.

Much of the commendatory's palace was demolished in 1836 and again in 1893,[41] but remnants of the complex were still visible at the beginning of this century. The tower appears in early photographs as a hollow shell, with only its two southern and western walls standing (Plate 72); the rest of the area was used as a garden. In distant panoramic views of the abbey, ruins of the annex are also discernible, although just barely, and a photograph from 1935 (Plate 74) shows a detail of one of its walls. But, as I shall demonstrate, even though this wall formed part of the commendatory's palace, its ultimate origin is medieval. The same may be true of the tower itself. The southwest corner of the tower displays reused ashlars and interspersed bricks in a manner similar to portions of the medieval crypt. But this technique was used in later periods as well, as seen for example in the corners of the arched gateway of the piazza in front of the Renaissance church and in several houses of the village. Still, it is tempting to see the tower as part of the "palace of the abbot" documented as early as the fourteenth century, [42] which in turn may have originated as part of the imperial palace mentioned by Abbot Hugo in his description of the Carolingian abbey. Although the date of the massive tower remains uncertain, the excavations have revealed the plan of the annex with its stables, as well as important indications of the medieval use of the area.

In a general view of the excavation site taken at the end of the 1982 season, the stables are recognizable by their lateral manger shelves and cobblestone paving that slopes toward a series of brick-lined drains (Fig. 12, Plates 75–76). Instead of an open courtyard as seen in the print, the central compartment of the stables (10.8 × 8.0 m.) was found to contain a massive cylindrical pier that presumably supported the upper storeys of the annex (Fig. 12, No. 7). To either side, small doorways open onto two narrower rooms with cobble floors. The room to the south, measuring 9.5 m. long by 4.0 m. wide, terminates at the east end in a semicircular apse that has been unevenly broken through to make way for a crude set of stairs (Fig. 12, No. 10). The room adjoining the central compartment to the north measures 14.9 m. long by only 3.6 m. wide, with a manger shelf along its inner north wall (Fig. 12, No. 2); its cobblestone flooring was removed in the course of the 1979–1980 excavation campaigns. Between the stables and the square tower was found a number of small cubicles, one of which was used as a cesspit that provided fragments of broken pottery and glass together with a damaged metal crucifix, all dating from the seventeenth and eighteenth centuries (Fig. 12, No. 13). Thus, the remains of this area agree with the documentary information concerning the commendatory's palace.

It soon became apparent, however, that in the construction of the stables several earlier walls had been reused. For example, the apsed room to the south was originally built as a chapel. The right side of the opening in the apex of the apse displays the smooth outward splay of the jamb of a window set slightly off axis (Fig. 12, No. 10), and the inside of the apse itself still bears faint traces of what was once brightly colored fresco decoration. More specifically, the masonry and mortar used, made up of hewn tufa and limestone blocks (varying in size from 26×12 cm. to 11×10 cm.) and horizontal pointing, are identical to those in the interior of the medieval bell tower (Plate 77). But it is clear that the chapel was built up against an even earlier wall of decidedly different construction: a rubble masonry with deep pilaster strips, one of which is walled up behind the left half of the chapel apse (Fig. 12, No. 9). This wall, too, bears traces of fresco decoration (Plate 78), which I shall discuss later. For now, it will suffice to recognize that this section of the excavation site displays at least two medieval phases.

The central room of the stables also utilized remains of medieval structures. The mangers to the south are built against the medieval wall with pilasters (Fig. 12, No. 9), while the western wall (Fig. 12, No. 12), with its cut-stone masonry, is an extension of the end wall of the chapel that cuts through the earlier rubble wall. On a line with the cylindrical pier to the north and south are thick piers of cut stone. The pier to the south (0.89 m. high by 1.46 m. wide by 0.55 m. deep) covers an earlier plastered surface on the rubble wall (Fig. 12, No. 8). To the north, the matching pier bonds with a masonry bench (0.51 m. high by 2.04 m. long by 0.50 m. deep) that had been enveloped by the crude rubble masonry of the stable manger (Fig. 12, No. 6). These piers must have supported an arch or massive beam that spanned the width of the room. It may be that the room was already vaulted in a pre-stable phase; certainly the placement of the mangers seems to have been determined by an earlier arrangement of stone benches.

The north wall of the central room exhibits an even more complex history, involving at least five phases (Fig. 12, No. 5, Plate 79). The earliest stage, represented by the base of the wall, is preserved to a maximum height of approximately 2.30 m. and is characterized by the use of unhewn stones, with abundant amounts of a light yellowish mortar with white inclusions that has been measured in irregular patches over the exposed northern face. The wall extends to a length of ca. 14 m., at which point it ends abruptly with the scar of another wall that met it at a right angle. Phases two, three, and four, using a grayish, pebbly mortar and no surface smearing, involved patching and rebuilding of the wall at different points to a preserved height of one additional meter. The fifth and last phase seems to have occured during the period when the area was converted into a stable, and it is represented by more rubbly masonry with a whitish mortar and a vertical line of bricks for a doorway. The general alignment of this wall in all of its phases corresponds to that of a spur wall that Markthaler indicates on his plan as projecting from the northwest corner of the transept (Fig. 16). It could not be verified if the wall actually bonded with the end of the transept, because the Superintendency would not permit the protective masonry lining, capped with cement and asphalt, that they had placed along the outside of the crypt and transept to be disturbed.

The parallel wall to the north (Fig. 12, No. 2), on the other hand, was clearly built *ex novo* for the stables, for it rests on a trench foundation more than 2.5 m. deep that cuts through all earlier features. The cobblestone paving between these two walls (Fig. 12, Nos. 2, 5) served to seal and protect all earlier features below it from future disturbance, which allows us to date these features to before the fifteenth century. The manger along the inner face of the north wall, resting on the trench foundation, was found to override a line of shallow rubble masonry footings, 55 cm. wide by 55 cm. deep (Fig. 12, No. 3). Up against these footings three rubble masonry piers were uncovered, averaging 0.90 m. high by 0.70 m. wide by 1.20 m. long and set at regular intervals of 2.5 m. Numerous burials (Plate 81) were found throughout the area. Most were constructed of brick and mortar, the others of cut stone. The contents of these tombs had been ransacked, but, as I shall discuss in the next chapter, sufficient archaeological information was retrieved to provide a series of dates in the early Middle Ages.

Few architectural remains were found between the stables and the sixteenth-century cloister, an area labeled in the 1686 view as the "piazza in front of the stables" (Plate 1). Level with the top of the trench foundation of the north stable wall (Fig. 12, No. 2) a series of compact earth-and-gravel strata was discovered, each no more than 2 to 3 cm. in thickness, which yielded numerous coins ranging in date from the fifteenth to the eighteenth centuries. The large quantity of coins may be explained by the fact that space in the stables is known to have been leased to merchants during the biannual fairs.[43] Beginning approximately one meter below this level were found more burials, differentiated from those below the cobble floor of the neighboring stable only by the fact that several inhumations were recovered undisturbed and that most of the graves were crudely constructed, without any sophisticated masonry lining. Within the lowest stratum of burials, a short stretch of rubble masonry (72 cm. wide by 1.05 m. long by 55 cm. high) on a north-south axis was found emerging from the base of the Renaissance trench foundation, corresponding roughly to the position of the masonry break at the end of the first phase of the wall projecting from the end of the transept (Fig. 12, No. 11).

The only substantial architectural feature in this area is a low wall (0.80 m. high by 0.58 m. wide) set 2.70 m. outside and concentric to the medieval apse (Fig. 12, No. 1, Plate 80). The fabric of the wall exhibits several periods of building. The first phase of the wall, preserved to a height of only 50 cm., is composed of unhewn stones set in a fine yellowish mortar, a type of masonry similar to that of the apse. The outer, or western, surface has several fragments of a thin white plaster coating. The apex of the curved wall seems to have had an opening 2.30 m. wide, lined with large cut blocks of tufa. At a later date, this opening was filled in, and the wall was rebuilt with unhewn blocks in a whiter and coarser mortar, preserved to a height of ca. 30 cm. This second phase shows no signs of a plaster coating. Later still, the northern end of the curved wall was extended ca. 2.5 m., using a much cruder construction of very irregular blocks with no attempt at coarsing.

Immediately in front of the curved wall a series of stone drains composed of monolithic blocks was found, 45 cm. wide by 20 cm. thick, with a shallow concave channel (12 cm. deep) cut down the center (Plate 82). The drains belong to the first phase, because they are set at the same level as the beginning of the plaster layer at the base of the wall. The curved wall, though not the drains, is included in Markthaler's plan (Figs. 12, 16); the southern extension of the curved wall, however, does not join the church, as he indicates, but was found to end ca. 3 m. in front of it. The Renaissance trench foundations (Fig. 12, No. 2) cut across the curved wall at this point, with a single ashlar having been allowed to protrude, which was then incorporated into the rubble masonry of the manger. Space for excavation between the curved wall and the apse was restricted, but one tomb of finely cut stone was found along with three others outlined in loose rubble similar to several examples below the cobble floor of the stable's north room.

Before summarizing the results of the 1978–1983 excavations, I should mention other evidence for the monastic layout discovered by the Superintendency in 1959. Immediately inside and below the entrance of the Renaissance church was found a wall, set roughly parallel to the façade. The wall is no longer visible, but it is shown on the Superintendency's plan (Fig. 17), and its outline is indicated in the restored floor of the church. Photographs taken at the time of discovery show a stretch of masonry more than one meter thick (no exact scale is given), with a series of shallow pilasters along its northern face (Plate 83a). This must have been the exterior side, because two walls project from it to the south. One of these projections forms a rectangular block (ca. 6×5 m.), with a hollow core that presumably housed a spiral staircase and square recesses serving as lamp niches (Plate 83b). The east-west alignment of this wall appears to link up with the southern wall of the apsed chapel in the excavation zone. The finely cut stone masonry of the two structures is also comparable.

The definitive analysis of the construction phases uncovered by the 1978–1983 excavations must await the final report. For present purposes, it is important to recognize that the Renaissance palace complex replaced earlier medieval structures on the site and that among these medieval remains one can discern at least four different phases, which may be listed as follows (Fig. 12): (1) the lowest courses of the straight wall in line with the end of the transept (Fig. 12, No. 5), a wall which predates or is at least coeval with the earliest burials, together with the fragment of another wall meeting it at right angles (Fig. 12, No. 11); (2) the curved wall, the shallow footings below the manger and cobble floor of the northernmost section of the stables, and perhaps the rubble masonry wall with pilaster strips (Fig. 12, Nos. 1, 3, 9); (3) a series of rectangular piers replacing the aforementioned shallow footings; and (4) the apsed chapel and the structure with a spiral staircase below the entrance of the Renaissance church (Fig. 12, No. 10, Plates 77, 83a–b). The cut-stone piers and masonry bench in the central room of the stables may be later still (Fig. 12, Nos. 6, 8). It should be noted that the position of these features generally follows the east-west alignment of the medieval abbey church. In order to determine the date and possible function of these subsidiary structures, I shall now return to my analysis of the abbey church.

4

The Pre-Carolingian and Carolingian Phases

THE EIGHTH-CENTURY CHURCH

Little is known about the original church at Farfa. The *Constructio* states only that at the end of the seventh century Thomas of Maurienne "reopened" an abandoned "basilica" dedicated to the Virgin.[1] Presumably in the course of the eighth century this church was either greatly modified or completely rebuilt to satisfy the needs of a growing monastic community. Unfortunately, the *Constructio* is silent on this point—aside from vague references to aspects of decoration carried out under abbots, mostly in the early ninth century.[2]

The oldest remnant of the medieval abbey church that can be dated with any confidence is the fragment of the nave wall discovered by the Superintendency encased within the baroque high altar (Plate 3). One recalls that this wall fragment is painted on both sides. The south side is brightly painted with simulated curtains, a common mural decoration throughout the Middle Ages. This side obviously formed part of the interior of the medieval church, because it faces the remains of the *opus sectile* pavement that lay along the central axis of the medieval nave. The opposite side of the same wall, however, bears the remains of the painted lunette framing the funerary portrait of an abbot (Plate 5).

The form of the funerary portrait, including the *orans* gesture and the lunette frame, derives ultimately from painted funerary portraits found in the early

Christian catacombs of Rome.[3] Such funerary monuments continued to be used in the early Middle Ages as well. For example, in the Hypogeum at Poitiers, the tomb chamber for an Abbot Mellebaudus dated ca. 700, a broad lunette was set up on the north wall without any figural decoration, but with a lengthy inscription composed of bold capital letters and red guidelines painted on a white ground.[4] In the Roman catacombs and at Poitiers the lunette shape resulted from an *arcosolium* over the recessed tomb, whereas at Farfa there is no trace of a scar from a masonry arch, although the fragmentary nature of the wall makes the evidence far from conclusive. A similar observation can be made for a funerary lunette in the lower church of S. Clemente in Rome, reliably dated on stylistic grounds to the third quarter of the ninth century.[5] In both cases, at Farfa and in Rome, an arch of carved stone or some other material may have framed the lunette by abutting the wall rather than being bonded with it. One is reminded of the description of the burial of Charlemagne in Einhard's biography that refers to a golden arch (*arcus*) with a likeness (*imago*) and an inscription having surmounted the Emperor's tomb.[6] A similar, though less elaborate, arrangement may have existed for the abbot at Farfa as well.

The representation of the abbot is too fragmentary to date on the basis of style alone, and the left half of the accompanying inscription that presumably contained the name of the abbot has been lost. But the preserved section of the inscription does refer to the day of the abbot's death: [obi]IT IN PACE XVIII. The *Constructio* provides the date of death for twelve of the fourteen abbots who ruled the monastery from its foundation to the mid-ninth century. Of this group, only Abbot Altbertus is recorded as having died on the eighteenth, i.e., the eighteenth day before the kalends of January. The year is not given, but it may be calculated as ca. 790 from additional information in the chronicle.[7]

Palaeographic aspects of the inscription are in keeping with this date. In particular, the use of curled serifs places the funerary inscription within the tradition of decorative initials found in numerous manuscripts from the early Middle Ages, for exaggerated serifs were particularly favored in the initials and title pages of Merovingian and Lombard manuscripts from the seventh and eighth centuries.[8] The Carolingian reformers eventually rejected this tradition, but not before experimenting with curly serifs in such early manuscripts as the Godescalc Evangelistary from between 781 and 783 and the Dagulf Psalter produced for Pope Hadrian I (772–795).[9] That the abbey of Farfa, newly come under Frankish rule, should have participated in this development is not surprising. It should be noted also that Abbot Altbertus originally came from Paris, whereas his successor, Mauroaldus, came from Worms and was in correspondence with Alcuin, the head of the school at the imperial palace in Aachen. The abbot's funerary portrait would therefore seem to provide a terminus ante quem for the nave wall fragment of ca. A.D. 790–800.[10] If this dating is correct, it provides evidence for the reconstruction of the eighth-century church.

A closer examination of photographs of the frescoed wall taken at the time of its discovery suggests that originally there may have been more than one funerary portrait (Plate 5). In the lower right of the wall fragment, to the right and slightly below the portrait frame, one can discern the lower left-hand corner of a second lunette, made up of a broken curved line meeting a straight horizontal border. Between the two lunettes, the photographs show portions of imitation marble revetment and a porphyry disk that can still be seen today. The presence of a second lunette or funerary portrait would suggest that the north side of the wall formed part of an area reserved for the burial of abbots, further explaining why the nave wall had been painted on both sides. In this context, one should also note that the vertical distance between the bottom horizontal of the lunette frame and the floor level of the medieval nave, given by the *opus sectile* pavement in situ, is approximately one meter, which would be more than enough room to accommodate a sarcophagus. [11]

As I have already pointed out, the abbey church appears to have been aisleless; the Superintendency found no evidence of an aisle in its limited excavations of the area south of the nave (Fig. 17). Instead, this area was found to be filled with numerous burials that, unfortunately, were left poorly documented by the excavators. They did not investigate beyond the north wall of the nave, which sustains the funerary portrait, but the very existence of this stretch of masonry would seem to negate the presence of a colonnade. And the wall is too long (1.95 m.) to have served as a pier. One must assume, therefore, that the church also had no aisle to the north. This being the case, the exterior fresco may have decorated the inside of a cloister walkway. Another possibility would be a chapel that adjoined the abbey church on a parallel axis along its north side, as found, for example, at St. Martin at Angers from the early eighth century or at St. John at Müstair in Switzerland from ca. 800 (Plates 92–93). [12] Markthaler in fact found traces of a sloping roofline, corresponding to this area, on the west face of the bell tower within a later floor abutting the tower. [13] His plan also indicates that under the present choir he uncovered foundations of walls set parallel to the nave at a distance of ca. 1.25 and 5.00 m. respectively (Fig. 16). Both foundations are no longer visible, and until further archaeological evidence is available, the question of a funerary chapel must remain conjectural.

Although the evidence is meager, the available information suggests that in the eighth century the abbey church was a modest, single-aisled structure with a narrow chapel or cloister walkway immediately to the north that was used primarily, if not exclusively, for the burial of abbots. Such a design would be in keeping with other examples elsewhere in Europe, especially within the Frankish realm. The question of the position of an apse will be addressed in the next section.

It should be pointed out, however, that if one is to assign the nave walls of the abbey church to sometime before the end of the eighth century, the remains of the luxurious *opus sectile* pavement, preserved along the nave's central axis, must belong to a somewhat later period (Plates 6a–b). More specifically, the design of a central roundel surrounded by a dense checkerboard pattern may be compared to a series of floors found in churches in Rome built during the Carolingian period: S. Maria in Cosmedin (Pope Hadrian I, 772–795), the S. Zeno Chapel of S. Prassede (Pope Paschal I, 817–824), S. Giorgio in Velabro (Pope Gregory IV, 827–844) and SS. Quattro Coronati (Pope Leo IV, 847–855). In general terms, these pavements represent a revival of the *opus sectile* technique not seen in Rome since the early Christian period; it also seems likely that their material was taken from ancient Roman floors and reused.[14] If the marble and porphyry in the floor at Farfa could be shown to have come originally from the site, it would suggest that the earlier Roman villa was a lavish affair. Be that as it may, the overall size and character of the Farfa pavement are closest to the floors laid out during the reigns of Popes Paschal I and Gregory IV, between 817 and 844. I would suggest, therefore, that the *opus sectile* pavement at Farfa should be seen in the context of a documented building program at the abbey in the first half of the ninth century, a subject to which I shall now turn my attention.

THE NINTH-CENTURY CHURCH

Since its discovery by Markthaler in the late 1920s and its further excavation by the Superintendency of Monuments in 1959–1962, the western complex of transept, semicircular apse, and annular crypt has generally been considered to belong to the eighth-century church. Markthaler was never able to complete his analysis of the structure, but all subsequent scholars, from Croquison to Prandi and Premoli, have been unanimous in their assignment of this part of the church to the abbacy of Thomas of Maurienne (ca. 680–720). There are, however, several factors that argue against this interpretation.

From a purely structural point of view, it seems unlikely that the nave, as represented by the foundations uncovered by the Superintendency and the wall fragment bearing the abbot's funerary portrait, belongs to the same building campaign as the transept. First of all, there is a significant difference in the thickness of the foundations: 0.59 m. for the nave and 0.69 m. for the apse and transept. Second, the foundations of the east wall of the transept increase to a thickness of one meter and must have supported an equally substantial wall. The motive for reinforcing the transept at this point is difficult to explain, unless the thickened wall served as a buttressing element at the juncture of the nave and the west end. Third, the foundations of the triumphal arch, as well as the rest of the western complex, are slightly off-center (ca. 35 cm) in relation to the axis of the nave. Taken together, these technical observations suggest that the nave and the transept are the result of two different periods of building.

The design of the west end also speaks for a date later than the eighth century. The form and dimensions of the annular crypt correspond to several examples in Rome, beginning with the insertion of an annular crypt in the apse of Old St. Peter's ca. 590 under Pope Gregory the Great (Plate 94).[15] The annular crypt was particularly popular in Rome during the first half of the ninth century, as is seen at S. Cecilia (817–824), S. Marco (827–844), and SS. Quattro Coronati (847–855).[16] More important, the combination of an annular crypt with a continuous transept as it exists at Farfa appears in Rome only in the ninth century, as represented by S. Prassede (Pope Paschal I, 817–824) and S. Stefano degli Abissini (Pope Leo IV, 847–855) (Plates 95, 99D).[17] Both churches are prime examples of the conscious revival of the plan of Old St. Peter's in Rome in the ninth century and relate to the Carolingian Renaissance, in general, by their predilection for early Christian models.[18] On this basis alone, it seems more reasonable to suggest that the west end at Farfa dates to the ninth century rather than to the eighth.

This same design also appears at the church of S. Maria di Vescovio, the ancient site of Forum Novum just north of Farfa, that served as the cathedral of the diocese of the Sabine region in the early Middle Ages.[19] Moreover, the church at Vescovio helps us to envision the elevation of the west end at Farfa, because it is comparable in size, and its transept, apse, and annular crypt are preserved almost totally intact (Plates 96–97, 99B). The transept, attached to an aisleless nave, forms a continuous rectangular block measuring on the interior 17.52 m. long, 5.56 m. wide, and ca. 11 m. high. The central apse, pierced by three large round-arched windows now walled up, measures 6.38 m. in diameter. The annular passage, 1.30 m. wide and 2.15 m. high, is roofed by large rectangular travertine slabs. The perpendicular corridor at the head of the annular passage is ca. 2 m. long and terminates in an arched recess where the relics were placed (Plate 97). The horizontal altar slab is a later addition and bears a fifteenth-century inscription, but the lower boxlike receptacle and the fresco decoration on the arch, representing the Lamb of God flanked by John the Baptist and John the Evangelist, are original.[20] Immediately above this area stands a masonry altar with traces of fresco decoration, and a small window, or fenestella, at its base that allowed the congregation in the nave to have visual contact with the relics in the crypt while the celebrant officiated at mass behind the altar (Plate 98). The desire to unify the tomb and the altar had been a prime motivation for the development of the annular crypt at Old St. Peter's, and the church at Vescovio closely follows that model (Plate 94).[21]

There are also remains of stone chancel screens, carved with interlace ornament, in situ to the left and right of the stairs that ascend to the altar platform, demonstrating that the area immediately in front of the apse was screened off from the nave. All of these features, with only slight variations, were presumably present in the western complex at Farfa. In addition, numerous other details at Vescovio, such as the masonry of the crypt with irregular stonework framed by large ashlars and intermittent bricks and the vestiges of painted curtains, or vela, preserved along the lower portions of the right transept arm, are so close to the methods of construction and decoration at Farfa that there seems little doubt that the two structures were built at about the same time.

Bruno Apollonj-Ghetti has studied the church at Vescovio in considerable detail, and he dates the annular crypt to the ninth century on the basis of its close affinity to the aforementioned examples in Rome.[22] This date is further supported by the style of the fresco on the end wall of the central corridor of the crypt (Plate 97). The squat proportions of the figures of the two saints, the linear treatment of their drapery, and the broad areas of flat color find an almost exact parallel in the frescoes of the lower church at S. Clemente in Rome, particularly the Ascension panel, dated by an inscription to the reign of Pope Leo IV (847–855).[23]

Documentary evidence for the construction of the crypt at Vescovio is lacking,[24] but this is not the case at Farfa. The *Constructio*, after all, gives prominent mention to the building activities of Abbot Sichardus (830–842). More specifically, it states that Sichardus built an oratory in honor of the Savior "attached to the church of the Virgin with a crypt below" to house the relics of SS. Valentine and Hilarius as well as the body of St. Alexander, son of Felicitas, brought from Rome by Pope Gregory IV (827–844).[25] How should this passage be interpreted? The term *oratorium*, derived from the verb *orare*, "to pray," was used loosely in the Middle Ages, often interchangeably with the term *capella*. It did not designate a specific architectural form but merely indicated any place of prayer that was smaller than a church (*ecclesia*) and did not serve the needs of a parish. In a monastic context, it was often used to denote where relics were kept and the daily office was performed. An oratory could be free-standing, incorporated within a larger structure, or, as in the case at Farfa, attached to a church.[26] The term *cripta* or *crypta* in the Carolingian period normally referred either to a subterranean passage or to the vaulted ground floor of a multi-storey westwork.[27] The *Constructio* is precise, however, in describing the crypt at Farfa as situated "below" the oratory; if the oratory had been a multi-storey affair, we would expect to find the term *turris* or "tower" used at some point in the text.[28] I would suggest, therefore, that the description of the Sichardan oratory refers to the complex of the apse, transept, and annular crypt that was added to the west end of the eighth-century church.

Yet this same passage in the *Constructio* has often been cited as evidence for a westwork at Farfa, which would make it the only known example in Italy.[29] It is true that altars dedicated to the Savior often formed part of a westwork, but they were not restricted to them. Likewise, the cult of the Savior was especially popular in the eighth and ninth centuries, above all among the Franks, and it was used for both primary and secondary dedications in a wide variety of churches.[30] The altar to the Savior in a westwork, though, was usually situated in the *cripta* or ground floor, whereas the altar at Farfa was clearly positioned above the crypt. The upper storeys of westworks usually contained altars dedicated instead to one or more archangels.[31]

But is there any physical evidence at Farfa to support the theory of a west-work? Although the origins and function of the Carolingian westwork are still vigorously debated (in spite of the extensive literature on the subject), its general typology is well known.[32] The two best-preserved examples, at Char-lemagne's royal chapel at Aachen, from ca. 800, and at the abbey church of Corvey, from ca. 875–80, demonstrate that a westwork served as a monu-mental entranceway composed of a massive central unit of two or more storeys flanked by smaller stair towers. Schuster's initial identification of the bell tower at Farfa as the Sichardan oratory seemed to make the theory of a westwork all the more plausible. Markthaler, however, proved that the interior floor divi-sions of the bell tower were not original, and subsequent investigations have shown that stair towers, or any flight of stairs for that matter, were never present in this part of the abbey church in the Middle Ages. As I shall argue in the next chapter, the bell tower is best understood as part of a larger complex that was built in the eleventh century. As for the western complex, the founda-tions of the transept and triumphal arch show no sign of a crossing, and they are too insubstantial to have supported a massive tower. In short, there is no basis whatsoever for the theory that the Sichardan oratory took the form of a westwork.

On the other hand, the use of a continuous transept and annular crypt would have been particularly fitting for the veneration of relics brought from Rome by the Pope, because it paralleled developments in Rome itself. The annular crypts of the various ninth-century churches in Rome were built not only to enhance traditional cult sites but to receive large numbers of additional relics that were being transferred into the city from the outlying catacombs, which had long been abandoned and were in a state of disrepair. The *Liber pontificalis*, or Book of the Popes, explains that the church of S. Prassede, for example, was built to shelter "the remains of many saints lying in ruined cemeteries so as to save them from neglect."[33] I would argue, therefore, that the model of Old St. Peter's was revived in Rome not only because it referred to the "Golden Age" of Christian antiquity, as Richard Krautheimer has so clearly demonstrated,[34] but also because it fulfilled a deep-seated desire to place these relics in a setting that was considered appropriate to their venerated status.

North of the Alps, a similar sense of "propriety" with regard to the treatment of relics was combined with the drive toward a romanization of the Frankish church in matters of liturgy and architecture, expressed in contemporary sources as the desire to follow "Roman custom" (*morem romanorum*). Already in the second half of the eighth century, the royal abbey church of St.-Denis was rebuilt with a transept and annular crypt to honor the tomb of the apostle of the Gauls (Plate 99E). It is not mere coincidence that this work was initiated at a time when the Frankish realm entered into a new alliance with Rome, enhanced by the visit of Pope Stephan II to Paris in 754. Similarly, in the first quarter of the ninth century, the great abbey church of Fulda was rebuilt with a western transept in direct imitation of Old St. Peter's in Rome to house the body of St. Boniface, the apostle of the Germans (Plate 99A). In both cases, at Fulda and at St.-Denis, the design of the abbey church expressed the strong ties with Rome by placing the tomb of the local martyr in a setting that emulated both the basilica of St. Peter and that of St. Paul, which also had a continuous transept, providing a reference to the two apostles of the Romans.[35]

Not only Roman architectural designs but also Roman relics were transmitted to the north, often surreptitiously.[36] A case in point is the famous account by Einhard, the great scholar of the Carolingian court and biographer of Charlemagne, that describes how he obtained the relics of SS. Marcellinus and Peter from the Roman catacombs off the Via Labicana in 827.[37] Einhard tells us that he first placed the bodies of the two martyrs in the corridor crypt of the church he had newly built on his country estate at Steinbach. The saints, however, appeared to Einhard to express their displeasure with their new surroundings and to instruct him to move them elsewhere. They guided Einhard to his other estate at Seligenstadt, where he built another church, between 830 and 840, this time following the lines of Old St. Peter's, with a projecting transept, semicircular apse, and annular crypt (Plate 99F).[38] No doubt a variety of factors prompted Einhard's actions, as was the case with most translations of relics, but in his written account Einhard credits the martyrs with having influenced the disposition of their resting place.[39] It is worth noting, too, that the construction of Einhard's church at Seligenstadt coincided with the abbacy of Sichardus (830–842). This is not to suggest that Einhard was in any way responsible for the design of the church at Farfa, but I would propose that Einhard's story concerning the translation of the remains of SS. Marcellinus and Peter may be seen as representative of the attitude toward Roman relics at the time. In other words, as the relics of Marcellinus and Peter "felt at home" in the annular crypt at Seligenstadt, so too the body of St. Alexander would have found an appropriate setting in the western complex at Farfa.

Einhard built the church at Seligenstadt *ex novo*,[40] whereas Sichardus added his oratory to a pre-existing church. But such an additive or piecemeal approach toward church architecture was not uncommon at the time. At St. Maurice-d'Agaune, for example, apses were added both to the east end and to the west end of the abbey church at different times in the course of the later eighth century (Plate 100A).[41] Similarly, excavations at Cologne Cathedral have revealed that the Merovingian church with its apse to the east was enlarged, ca. 800, by the addition of a second apse at the west end, which was circumscribed by a semicircular atrium corridor (Plate 100B).[42] At the great abbey of Fulda, the *sapiens architectus* Abbot Ratger (802–817) added an apse and continuous transept to the west end of the basilica that had been built under his predecessor Baugulf (779–802) with its apse to the east (Plate 99A). Significantly, the two phases of the abbey church at Fulda were considered by contemporaries to be distinct not only in time but also in terminology: one section was known as the eastern sanctuary, or *templum orientale*, and the other as the western sanctuary, or *templum occidentale*. As one source explains, Ratger, "joining the western sanctuary with the other, . . . made one church" (*ecclesiam*).[43]

This brings me to another important issue. If the western apse at Farfa was the oratory to the Savior, then the original, main altar dedicated to the Virgin must have stood elsewhere. This raises the possibility of a double-apse plan: one apse to the west dedicated to the Savior and another to the east, whether semicircular or square, dedicated to the Virgin. Unfortunately, the most likely area for the location of such an eastern apse is below the present sacristy, which is inaccessible to excavations. To be sure, a double-apse plan would be without precedent in Italy in the ninth century, but it would correspond to the Carolingian churches at Cologne, Fulda, and St.-Maurice. Other examples from the ninth century are the Cathedral of St.-Jean at Besançon (consecrated in 814), St. Salvator at Paderborn (ca. 850; Plate 100C), and St. Georg at Reichenau-Oberzell (888–896).[44] Moreover, the use of a double-apse scheme for the abbey church on the famous Plan of St. Gall, drawn up sometime between 820 and 830, indicates that the design was prevalent in monastic circles in the first half of the ninth century (Plate 101).[45]

In spite of numerous attempts to explain them, the meaning, function, and origin of the double-apse plan in Carolingian architecture remain obscure. Presumably Charlemagne's efforts to have the liturgy of the Frankish church closely follow Roman usage played a major role. Certainly the growing importance of the cult of relics was a factor as well.[46] In this regard, it is interesting to note that the two apses of the abbey church on the Plan of St. Gall contain altars dedicated to St. Peter and to St. Paul, which is an obvious allusion to Rome. Furthermore, the locations of the two apses, St. Peter's in the west and St. Paul's in the east, correspond to the placement of the main apses of the early Christian basilicas of the martyrs in Rome; i.e., the apse of Old St. Peter's stood in the west, while the apse of St. Paul's-outside-the-Walls faced east.[47] Regardless of the reasons for the development of the double-apse plan, it is fair to say that if the arrangement appeared at Farfa it could only have been due to influence from northern centers of the Carolingian empire. The presence of a second, eastern apse at Farfa in the ninth century must remain conjectural; however, the identification of the western complex as the Sichardan oratory is supported by the results of the 1978–1983 excavations that are discussed in the next section.

THE MONASTIC LAYOUT

The Pre-Carolingian Abbey

As with the abbey church, there is little evidence concerning the arrangement of the monastery before the Carolingian period. The only mention of subsidiary structures in the *Constructio* is a reference to an atrium that stood in front of the church when Thomas of Maurienne founded the abbey. The reference appears in an episode where, from the front doors of the church, a disciple of Thomas watches the envoys of Duke Faroaldus II depositing supplies in the "atrium."[48]

Archaeological information from the 1978–1983 excavations is somewhat more telling and suggests, for several different reasons, a Christian settlement of the site before that of Thomas of Maurienne. First of all, two graves in the lowest stratum of burials below the narrow corridor of the Renaissance stables were found to have tegulated coverings *a cappucina*, ceramic tiles set in the form of a gabled roof, which is characteristic of burial practice in Italy and Gaul from the early Christian period through the seventh century.[49] Second, at approximately the same level as the tegulated graves but in the open area between the stable and the sixteenth-century cloister, fragments of an African red slip ware plate were found, bearing the stamped designs of a bejeweled cross flanked by chalices and stylized peacocks, that may be securely dated to the middle of the sixth century.[50] Third, a layer of ash covering this same stratum provided a carbon-14 date of A.D. 610 ± 80 years.[51] To this may be added the unstratified find of a coin issued under the emperor Justin II (565–578). Taken together, this evidence points to a sixth-century Christian settlement of the site that may well correspond to the legendary foundation of Farfa by Lawrence.[52] The layer of burnt material, moreover, may represent a destruction of the site by the Lombards, who invaded Italy in the second half of the sixth century, destroying many of the religious establishments in their path, such as Montecassino in 589.[53]

The base of the wall in line with the south end of the transept of the abbey church (Fig. 12, No. 5) predates, or is at least contemporary with, the earliest burials on the site, for it does not override them at any point. This wall also met another rubble wall (Fig. 12, No. 11), now only partially preserved, at a right angle indicated by a visible masonry scar. It seems reasonable to suggest that these two walls represent the outline of the atrium mentioned in the *Constructio*. In addition, a block of rubble masonry (1.05 m. long by 0.50 m. wide, at which point it is covered by later masonry) embedded within the easternmost rectangular pier may have served as the base of a column forming part of an interior arcade (Fig. 12, No. 4). It also seems likely that the sixth-century settlement merely used the courtyard of an earlier Roman villa or farmhouse (Fig. 13), as evidenced by the tomb containing a Trajanic coin and by the vestige of the *opus reticulatum* wall, as well as by the abundance of Arretine sherds and reused Roman building materials that have been found at all levels of the site.[54]

While the exact form of the Laurentian and Thomasine foundations remain highly speculative (Fig. 13), it is important to note that the area proposed for the atrium seems to have remained open throughout the subsequent history of the site. It corresponds, for example, to the "piazza in front of the stables" in the

1686 view. It is known to have served as the entrance to the church in the fifteenth century, and, as I shall indicate in the next section, the area was occupied by an atrium in the Carolingian period. It would not be surprising to find that this continuity in function began with the founding of the abbey itself.

The Carolingian Abbey

The Documentary Evidence.   Discussion of the monastic layout at Farfa in the ninth century would best begin with the description of the Carolingian abbey by Abbot Hugo, written at the end of the tenth century. The passage deserves to be quoted in full:

> There were five other basilicas besides the main one, of which one was constructed in honor of St. Peter and used by the canons. The second and third were for the needs of sick monks. Of these two, one was for the infirm who were convalescing, while the other was for those approaching death. Likewise, both had adjoining living quarters and bath facilities for ordinary use. The fourth basilica formed part of the royal palace [*palatium regale*] which had been built to house the emperors during their visits to the monastery. The fifth church, small but marvelously built, was set up outside the walls of the monastery in honor of the Virgin Mary, where women gathered for prayer and visitations in accordance with an old rule prohibiting women from entering the monastery. . . . . There were workrooms [*officinae*] roofed with tiles and walkways paved with squared stones, some of which may still be seen today. It had arched walkways all about both inside and outside [*intus et foris*], those inside for the use of the monks as their cloister, while those outside were used by the laity. The enclosure of the entire monastery was strengthened by towers, giving the impression of a fortified city.

In reading Hugo's description, one thinks immediately of the great abbeys of the Carolingian realm north of the Alps, which may have been his intention, for he concludes by stating, "In the whole kingdom of Italy, none compared to this monastery [Farfa] in wealth, except that of Nonantola." Unfortunately, nothing is known about the architectural layout of the monastery of Nonantola, situated just outside Modena in North Italy, during this period.[55] Instead, references to subsidiary churches and paved walkways bring to mind the famous representation of the abbey of St.-Riquier, built between 790 and 799 by the lay abbot Angilbertus, friend and associate of Charlemagne (Plate 102).[56] Here the two smaller churches of St. Benedict and of the Virgin are shown connected to the main abbey church by a series of covered walkways arranged in a trapezoidal scheme. The general topography of the site indicates that the longest side of the courtyard at St.-Riquier measured almost nine hundred feet,[57] a size that would have been impossible at Farfa. Nevertheless, it is interesting to note that the church of the Virgin is shown with its entrance situated outside the porticoed enclosure, which may provide some idea of the arrangement of the fifth church at Farfa that was also dedicated to the Virgin and stood "outside the walls" in order to serve women. Yet the subsidiary church at Farfa was presumably situated outside the fortification walls and not outside an inner courtyard as depicted for St.-Riquier.

It should be emphasized that the representation of St.-Riquier must be approached with great caution. It is, after all, an early seventeenth-century engraving (Petau, 1612) purportedly derived from a miniature in a late eleventh-century chronicle, making it several times removed from its subject. Medieval renderings of architectural elevations, at least before the late Gothic period, are generalized at best and unreliable in most details. It is also difficult to distinguish with any certainty between features in the engraving that pertain to the Carolingian period and those that may have resulted from a Romanesque rebuilding.[58] Although the writings of Angilbertus testify to the existence of the two subsidiary churches and the triangular disposition of the courtyard, which for him symbolized the Holy Trinity, recent excavations have un-covered a square cloister on the same side of the abbey church that does not appear in the engraving at all.[59] Similarly, partial excavations of the church of the Virgin, preserved only in its foundations, show that the church was originally octagonal and that the nave seen in the engraving is in fact an eleventh-century addition.[60] In short, the famous view of the monastery of St.-Riquier may be used for the reconstruction of the layout at Farfa only in the most general sense.

A far more reliable record of monastic building in the Carolingian period is the Plan of St. Gall, which was drawn up for Abbot Gozbertus (816–836) as he prepared to rebuild his abbey around 830 (Plate 101). Here are the vital components of a Benedictine abbey rendered in the most intricate detail—from chapels to chicken coops, as it were—providing a visual lexicon of the architectural forms available to builders in the ninth century, in that virtually every feature is clearly labeled with a Latin inscription. For example, the word *officina*, or "workshop," is applied to the structure immediately to the right of the cloister, which is labeled "the house and workshop of the chamberlain" (*domus et officina camerarii*). The core of the building is a rectangular space divided in half to serve as working and living quarters, surrounded in turn by cubicles for various craftsmen (leatherworkers, metalworkers, and woodworkers), as explained by the accompanying inscriptions.

Although the Plan gives no indication of the elevation, Walter Horn and Ernest Born, following the example of houses and barns that are preserved in northern Europe from the late Middle Ages, have reconstructed this building entirely of wood, with elaborately trussed ceilings.[61] Acquaintance with the building techniques at Farfa suggests that such buildings would have been built of irregular stone masonry walls with wooden-beam ceilings. Still, this detail of the Plan of St. Gall offers some idea of what Hugo means by "workshops," keeping in mind, too, that he states explicitly that at Farfa they were "roofed with tiles." Hugo, however, may also be using the term *officinae* in a more general sense to mean all the buildings within the monastic enclosure. Walter Horn points out that the note accompanying the Plan of St. Gall refers to the drawing in its entirety as representing *de posicione officinarum.*[62] Similarly, the description of the layout of the monastery, in this case Cluny, in the Farfa Customary is entitled "*de positione seu mensuratione officinarum.*"[63] Such a broad meaning may have been derived from the Rule of St. Benedict (cap. IV), which states that "the workshop [*officina*] is the enclosure of the monastery and the stability of the community."[64] Hugo, on the other hand, clearly differentiates between the churches, which he describes first, using the term *basilica*, and the "workshops," which are mentioned only later. It would seem, then, that for Hugo the term *officinae* referred to all the buildings within the monastic enclosure aside from the churches.

The term *arcus* is used on the Plan to label a series of arches shown along the inside of the monks' cloister, presumably analogous in form to the "arches of covered walkways" (*arcus deambulatorii*) mentioned in Hugo's description. The Plan can also be used to reconstruct the two infirmary chapels, one for the sick and the other for the dying, with adjoining living quarters and bath facilities. At the top of the Plan is a double-apsed chapel (simply labeled *ecclesia*) with an intermittent dividing wall. The lower half of the chapel opens onto the courtyard of the infirmary on the left, while the upper half of the chapel is connected to an identical cloister for the novitiates on the right. There is no evidence that the two chapels at Farfa were arranged in this manner with opposing apses, but the Plan provides one possible solution. One would, however, expect more direct access between the two chapels, in order to serve both the sick and the dying, than is shown on the Plan. Perhaps, instead of being connected end to end, the chapels were set to either side of a common courtyard. But such a reconstruction remains purely conjectural.

Instead of a "royal palace" (*palatium regale*), the Plan of St. Gall has a "house [*domus*] for distinguished guests" situated immediately to the left of the entrance to the main abbey church. There is a central hall with peripheral sleeping quarters and private lavatories for the nobility. The servants are relegated to a long narrow hall in the front, and the horses are stabled at the back, which would require that the mounts be led through the central hall. Unlike the case with the "palace" at Farfa, there is no indication of a private chapel belonging to the guest house.[65] The Plan of St. Gall, therefore, allows us to envision some aspects of Hugo's description but not others. For more precise information, we must turn to the results of the latest excavations—though the Plan of St. Gall is also useful for a discussion of these results.

The Archaeological Evidence.   Among the initial results of the 1978–1983 excavation project was the verification of the existence of the curved wall shown circumscribing the western apse of the abbey church on Markthaler's plan (Fig. 16). In its first phase, the wall stood only 0.50 m. high, with a central opening 2.30 m. wide, and was covered on the exterior by a layer of white plaster. The stone drains following the outer curve of the wall presumably served to catch the runoff from a slanted roof that covered the area (2.70 m. wide) between the apse and the curved wall (Fig. 12, Plate 82). The modest height and thickness of the wall suggest that it served primarily as a partition wall, with a series of colonnettes or other vertical supports to hold up the lean-to roof (Fig. 14).

Directly on top of the drains and filling their channels was found a thick layer of charcoal, also containing charred and broken roof tiles, that has been dated by carbon-14 analysis to A.D. 780 ± 80 years. The date, of course, refers to the time the wood was cut and not when it was used or when it burned. It is tempting to assign this burnt layer to the fire reported in the *Destructio* that was caused by looters after the abbey was abandoned in A.D. 897. Undoubtedly, this was not the only fire to have taken place at Farfa in the course of the Middle Ages, but it is the only one mentioned specifically in the documentary sources. Too, the long period of abandonment of the site following the 897 fire would explain why the drains were not repaired and cleared of debris. Ceramic sherds found in the same stratum as the drains agree with a late-eighth- or ninth-century date.[66]

The use of stone drains is still common in Italy today along sidewalks and in courtyards. Their use in the early Middle Ages is confirmed by a passage in the Chronicle of Montecassino that describes the subsidiary church of S. Salvatore built by an abbot of Montecassino, Gisulf (796–817). The pertinent section reads:

> He [Abbot Gisulf] also built an atrium in front of the same church [S. Salvatore] with a length of forty cubits [17.1 m.] and similar in width, with sixteen columns all around on each side, while he placed alongside the pavement, stone drains [*lapideos canales*] in which the water might always run.[67]

Thus, both archaeological and historical factors, together with the curved wall's obvious association with the western apse, indicate that we are dealing with a portion of the Carolingian abbey.

Construction of the curved wall may well have necessitated blocking up the narrow windows in the newly completed crypt, for the floor of the passageway immediately outside the apse, as indicated by the level of the stone drains, was little more than 40 cm. below the exterior sills of the crypt windows. Moreover, the curved wall and its roof would have cut off all direct light to the crypt, making the presence of windows useless. This sequence of events suggests that the western complex of the abbey church was built first, in order to receive the relics brought from Rome and Viterbo, perhaps as early as 830, and that shortly thereafter it was decided to add the curved wall.

Before discussing the motivations behind this new arrangement, it should be noted that the addition of the curved wall brought about modifications to other features in the area as well. The wall projecting from the end of the south transept arm (Fig. 12, No. 5) was substantially rebuilt, and a shallow foundation was set parallel to it at a distance of ca. 3 m., joining the south end of the curved wall (Fig. 12, No. 3). This line of masonry presumably served as the footings for a series of upright supports of wood or stone. Any evidence of stone drains matching those along the curved wall was destroyed with the construction of the deep trench foundations of the north wall of the Renaissance stables (Fig. 12, No. 2). Nevertheless, it seems evident that these two parallel lines of masonry joined with the curved wall about the western apse of the abbey church to form a set of interlocking porticoes (Figs. 13, 14). The extent of this courtyard to the west and north cannot be determined, owing to the obstruction of later monastic buildings, but the archaeological evidence clearly indicates that in the ninth century a porticoed courtyard or atrium was built at the west end of the abbey church, involving an extensive remodeling and perhaps an enlargement of an earlier enclosure. This new arrangement did not preclude the use of the area as a site for burial. Indeed, it seems to have enhanced the process.

Within the area defined by these porticoes were found numerous burials, arranged in at least three distinct layers above the sixth-century tegulated tombs. We have no evidence to date these burials conclusively. Most were found severely disturbed, with the tombs either empty or containing the partial remains of one or more individuals. Only those in the lowest strata and farthest from the church were found intact. The burials were modest indeed; the body was usually found fully articulated, with no objects of personal adornment.

Since early Christian times, atria had been popular sites for burial, and the most prominent example, the courtyard in front of the basilica of Old St. Peter's, is known to have been used for the placement of tombs well into the Middle Ages.[68] The close proximity, however, of the western apse of the abbey church at Farfa offered the additional advantage of permitting burial near the relics of the crypt, or *depositio ad sanctos*, to use the medieval term.[69] This concept was perhaps expressed most vividly by John Chrysostom in the fifth century when he wrote, "Where the martyrs are buried, demons are scourged, while men are chastened and delivered."[70] At Farfa, not only were the tombs situated near the crypt, but there seems also to have been a hierarchy in the types of burial. If one may generalize, the burials farthest from the church tend to be simpler, occasionally outlined with mortared rubble or a few unhewn stones, whereas those nearest the church, and especially inside the curved wall and within the adjacent portico, are usually constructed of brick and mortar or dressed stone.

In 1959, during the excavations of the crypt, the Superintendency came upon an elegant Roman battle sarcophagus immediately outside the juncture of the apse and the north arm of the transept of the abbey church. No strat-igraphic records were kept, but a photograph taken at the time of its discovery verifies the location of the find (Plate 85). Pagan sarcophagi are known to have been reused at Farfa in medieval times for the burial of abbots. One example, now in the Archaeological Museum in Perugia, which dates to ca. A.D. 200 on the basis of its style, bears a medieval inscription that identifies it as the tomb of Abbot Berardus, who died in A.D. 1089: ABBA BERARDUS SEMPER VENERANDUS PRIMA DIES MENSIS TULIT HUNC LUGENDA NOVEMBRIS. In the context of the demonstrated funerary function of the area, it seems reasonable to suppose that the battle sarcophagus, too, was reused for the burial of an abbot, even though it bears no inscription to that effect. I would further suggest that the position of the battle sarcophagus, together with the numerous masonry tombs, indicates that the area between the apse and the curved wall, protected by a lean-to roof, was reserved for the burial of abbots.

The elaborate arrangement for monastic burial at Farfa may have been due, at least in part, to the new and more restrictive regulations concerning burial customs issued by the Synods of Aachen in 809 and of Mainz in 813. On both occasions, burial in a church was prohibited to everyone except bishops, abbots, priests, and nobility. In other words, monks who were not priests—the majority in this period—could not be buried in a church.[71] This same legisla-tion has been cited as a primary cause for the development of the so-called outer crypt, such as the subterranean burial chapel appended to the apse of St.-Denis by Abbot Hildiun in 832 or the more elaborate arrangement of vaulted passages surrounding the apse of St.-Philibert-de-Grandlieu from approximately the same time.[72] The sources for Farfa, however, must be sought elsewhere.

The arrangement of the atrium at Farfa with its eastern portico circumscrib-ing a western apse has yet to be found elsewhere in Italy, but it does closely resemble a series of important Carolingian monuments north of the Alps. For example, concentric walls framing an apse appear at both the eastern and western ends of the abbey church on the Plan of St. Gall (Plate 101). To the west, a semicircular entranceway is represented by a single curved line and an inner row of square supports. The accompanying inscription reads: "Here a roof extends supported by a wall and by columns" (HIC MURO TECTUM IM-POSITUM PATET ATQUE COLUMNIS).[73] Thus, the portico was meant to be covered by a lean-to roof similar to the one reconstructed for Farfa. The intermittent space between the portico and the apse was to be left open: "Here stretch out a parklike space without a roof" (HIC PARADISIACUM SINE TECTO STERNITO CAP[t]UM).[74] The same is true at the east end, where a single wall is shown about the apse with the intervening space labelled: "Here the plains of a parklike space extend without a roof" (HIC SINE DOMATIB[us] PARADISI PLANA PARANTUR).[75]

The term "paradise" comes from the Greek *paradeisos*, referring to an enclosed garden, and early Christian writers used the term to describe the Garden of

Eden in the Book of Genesis.[76] By the middle of the eighth century, however, the word "paradise" was also used to refer to the atrium in front of Old St. Peter's, owing to the mosaic representation of the Apocalypse on its façade. Following the Roman precedent, the name was applied to the atrium in front of the Carolingian abbey of St.-Riquier.[77] It would seem that the semicircular *paradisi* on the Plan of St. Gall represent an adaptation of the traditional rectilinear scheme of an atrium in order to fit the double-apse plan of the abbey church.[78] As I mentioned previously, an identical arrangement was used ca. 800 for the western entrance of Cologne Cathedral (Plate 100B).[79]

So far as I know, the term "paradise" does not appear in the Farfa documents. Moreover, the "paradise" spaces of the Plan of St. Gall were meant to be left uncovered, whereas at Farfa the area around the western apse was, in all likelihood, roofed. But one should not forget the original purpose of the Plan as expressed in the accompanying note addressed to Abbot Gozbertus: "Please do not imagine that I have undertaken this task . . . supposing you . . . in need of our instruction," it reads, "I have drawn this for you alone to scrutinize."[80] In other words, the Plan was meant to be adapted to the needs of the particular site according to the wishes of the abbot and the monastic community.

Just such a disputation did take place at the abbey of Fulda at about the same time as the Plan of St. Gall was being drawn up. *The Life of Abbot Eigil* of Fulda relates that following the consecration of the new and monumental abbey church in 819, a council of the brethren was called to discuss the appropriate location for a new cloister. Should it be built to the south of the abbey, they were asked, following the previous arrangement? Or should the new cloister be placed to the west of the church, "according to Roman custom" (*romano more*)? Not surprisingly, the latter proposal was adopted, "because of the vicinity of the martyr's relics [those of St. Boniface] that rested in that part of the basilica [i.e., the west end]."[81] Here both the desire for a location *ad sanctos* and the desire to follow Roman custom are expressed.[82]

There is little information about the specific design of the cloister at Fulda, although it seems to have stood virtually intact until the early seventeenth century, when a new cloister was built. Between 1908 and 1910, however, Joseph Vonderau excavated just outside the western end of the baroque church that had replaced the Carolingian one.[83] He found the remains of two curved walls, built one against the other (with a total thickness of 2.35 m.), that circumscribed the main apse at a distance of ca. 5 meters (Plates 99A, 103). A projecting spur wall more than one meter long to either end of the curved wall presumably indicates where the curved wall joined the porticoed walkways of the cloister. Unfortunately, Vonderau did not extend his excavations further to the west in order to reveal the rest of the cloister.

Just inside the curved wall, however, Vonderau found twelve burials, ranging in date from the twelfth to the fourteenth centuries. One of the tombs was built of stone and mortar, six others showed traces of wooden coffins, and five involved plain stone sarcophagi. The contents of these tombs were poorly preserved, but one of the stone sarcophagi contained the remnants of elaborate liturgical vestments, datable to the twelfth century, that left little doubt that the deceased had been an abbot. [84] Owing to the limited nature of the excavations, it is not clear when this area was first used for burial, but Vonderau suggests that the practice began under Abbot Thioto (856–869), who is known to have decorated the cloister and to have deposited the relics of SS. Antonius and Eonius in it. [85] According to Vonderau, the inner of the two curved walls (1.25 m. thick) was added to support a vault or roof of some kind that covered the space between the outer curved wall and the western apse, thus protecting the tombs. Certainly the placement of the burials, like the location of the cloister itself, was due to the proximity of the relics in the western end of the abbey church.

The arrangement at Fulda, therefore, has several points of comparison to the layout at Farfa: (1) Both abbey churches followed the scheme of Old St. Peter's, with a western apse and transept (Fulda had a hall crypt instead of an annular crypt); (2) both monasteries had porticoed courtyards appended to the west end of the abbey church; (3) these courtyards included a curved wall that was concentric to the western apse; (4) the space between the curved wall and the apse was used for burial—it is known that at Fulda abbots were buried in this space, at least by the twelfth century if not earlier, and the same seems to have been the case at Farfa as well. The Plan of St. Gall also shows a curved wall around its eastern and western apses, although there is no indication that the intervening space was meant to be used for burial. [86]

I would suggest, therefore, that the arrangement at Farfa is best understood in the context of the building of the church and cloister at Fulda and of the formulation of the Plan of St. Gall. All three projects were carried out at roughly the same time, i.e., between 820 and 840. Also, all three establishments were imperial abbeys. It thus seems unlikely that the similarities in architectural forms on the Plan of St. Gall, at the abbey of Fulda, and at Farfa could be purely accidental. This is not to suggest that they are derived from a common model; [87] rather, they must reflect a process of communication and exchange between major monastic centers in the first half of the ninth century, a process that was used to address common architectural concerns. The Plan of St. Gall represents one method by which architectural forms could be transmitted from one monastic center to another. On the other hand, the extensive travels of the abbots of Farfa, especially to the imperial court and church synods in the north, would have provided ample opportunity for contact with the leaders of other monastic centers in the Carolingian realm.

The reconstruction of the rest of the monastic layout is far less clear. Among the other medieval features uncovered by the excavations, the rubble masonry wall wedged between the central room of the stables and the apsed chapel is undoubtedly the oldest (Fig. 12, No. 9). Even though there is no firm evidence for assigning a date to this wall, other than the fact that it must predate the chapel, fragments of its fresco decoration do provide an approximate chronology. The best-preserved portions of the painting are to be found behind the right half of the chapel apse, where courses of the apse vault of the chapel have fallen away. Although these are extremely fragmentary and faded, one can make out the left thigh of a standing, draped figure measuring 0.13 m. high, which means that the figure was originally only slightly smaller than lifesize (Plate 78). All traces of the highlights have worn away. Visible now is only the black underpainting, applied in lively, broad strokes representing the stylized drapery folds of an unengaged left leg and parallel V-folds to the right.

The painting is self-assured in its execution and retains a sound understanding of ponderation in a standing human figure as seen in examples of early medieval art under strong Byzantine influence. The only evidence for a more precise dating is the presence of a thick horizontal band, or *clavus*, across the middle of the thigh. Meyer Schapiro has shown that the *clavus* is an element of dress that is characteristic of Lombard and Carolingian painting in the eighth and ninth centuries.[88] In North Italy, it appears on the figures of the angels and of Joseph in the fresco cycle of Castelseprio, generally dated to the eighth century, and on various figures in the frescoes of St. John at Müstair, dated to the ninth century. In Central and South Italy, the *clavus* appears on the thigh of the Annunciation Angel in the mosaics of SS. Nereo ed Achilleo (795–816) and in the figure of the executioner in the crypt frescoes of S. Vincenzo al Volturno (824–842), a monastery closely affiliated with Farfa. After the middle of the ninth century, this detail of costume seems to disappear from Italian mural decoration. To the right of the remains of the standing figure is an incised circle (0.23 m. in diameter) with a patch of flesh-colored pigment in the center that resembles the profile of a human face. Although the evidence is meager, the fresco may have represented a standing saint with a kneeling figure (a donor?) immediately to the right and bearing a halo. At the very least, it is clear that the upper zone of this wall was decorated with figural representations.

At a slightly lower level, on one of the pilasters that bonds with the rubble wall, the dark stain of a horizontal band (0.06 m. high) can be seen, framed top and bottom by two parallel snap lines, guidelines created by plucking a string drawn across the wet plaster coating of the fresco. A series of capital letters has been incised across the dark band; an R, N, and L are particularly legible. Traces of snap lines and lettering are found elsewhere on the same plastered surface, demonstrating that several inscriptions accompanied the figural decoration. Inscriptions of comparable size and palaeographic details, including several incised letters, can be seen in the aforementioned crypt frescoes at S. Vincenzo al Volturno (824–842). While far from conclusive, the convergence of several elements—the classicizing elements of the draped standing figure, the presence of the *clavus* in the middle of the thigh, and the palaeographic characteristics of the partial inscription—would fit in well with a date sometime between the middle of the eighth century and the middle of the ninth.

The original dimensions of this room are not known; to the west the frescoed wall is broken off by later masonry, and to the east the wall continues under the Renaissance church (Fig. 12, No. 9). And no remains of a matching wall to the south have yet been found. However, the buttressing elements of the two pilasters (10 cm. thick) and the elevated position of the figural zone of decoration indicate that the building was originally of considerable height. In addition, the presence of fresco decoration would suggest that the room served as a chapel or meeting hall for the monastic community or important guests. It seems highly unlikely that such elaborate decoration would have been applied to a simple working space or dormitory. Thus, there were at least two rooms of considerable size situated to the south and on a parallel axis to the cemetery and the abbey church, even though their exact function and reconstruction remain unclear.

The massive tower, cubic in plan, at the southwest corner of the site may also have formed part of the monastic layout during this period. The structure has been heavily restored on many different occasions. At the beginning of this century, it was only a ruined shell. The south and west sides of the base were shored up with modern brick, but the southeast corner was left exposed and exhibits massive ashlars with occasional interspersed bricks, similar to sections of the apse and transept foundations of the west end of the abbey church. In the Renaissance, the tower formed part of the palace of the commendatory housing the cardinal's apartments, which may have involved a remodeling of the abbot's palace, mentioned in documents of the fourteenth century. It is tempting, though it is far from proven, to see this structure as having originally formed part of the imperial palace referred to in Hugo's description of the abbey. Could the adjoining frescoed room have been the aforementioned chapel of the "royal palace" in the early Middle Ages?

SUMMARY

The preceding discussion of the archaeological and documentary evidence for the architectural history of the abbey from its foundation through the ninth century allows us to reconstruct the following sequence of events: (1) The first Christian settlement of the site took place toward the middle of the sixth century, most likely through the instigation of the legendary figure known as Lawrence of Syria, at which time tegulated graves were set in what may have been the courtyard of an abandoned Roman villa. The site was subsequently overrun by the Lombards in the second half of the sixth century. (2) At the end of the seventh century, Thomas of Maurienne came upon the ruins of a basilica and atrium in which he established a small monastic community. In the course of the eighth century, the monastery was presumably enlarged with a funerary chapel, possibly built along the northern flank of the aisleless church. (3) The abbey was extensively rebuilt under Abbot Sichardus (830–842). In the abbey

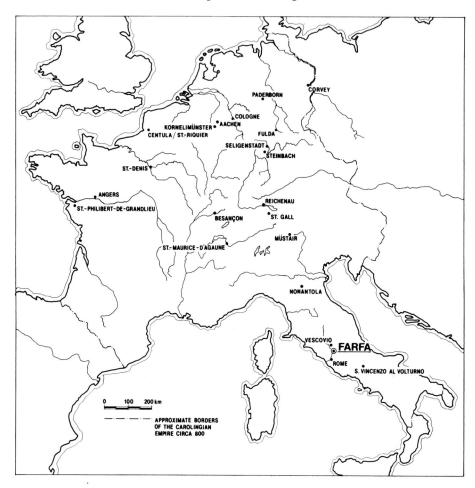

MAP 3. Western Europe at the beginning of the ninth century, with locations of
comparative monuments for the Carolingian abbey and abbey church

church, a luxurious *opus sectile* pavement was placed along the central axis of the
old nave. Most important, a transept and an apse with an annular crypt were
added to the west end of the church in order to receive relics brought from
Rome and Viterbo. The construction of this western complex necessitated a
remodeling of the atrium so that its eastern portico circumscribed the new apse
(Fig. 13). The atrium's proximity to the relics in the crypt made it a favored
place for burial, with the area immediately surrounding the apse reserved for
the tombs of abbots. In short, the phrase from Sichardus's epitaph—HAEC
LOCA PRUDENTI CONSTRUXIT ET ORDINE MIRO—seems to have been fully
justified. (4) By the end of the ninth century, the monastery contained five
subsidiary chapels in addition to the main abbey church, a palace for visits by
the emperor, a cloister for the monks, and an atrium open to the laity, all
surrounded by massive fortification walls.

The designs of the abbey church and the atrium in the ninth century were in keeping with the latest architectural developments both in Rome and in major ecclesiastical centers north of the Alps (Map 3). Above all, the transept, apse, and annular crypt followed the Carolingian revival of the plan of Old St. Peter's. The adaptation of the eastern wing of the atrium so that it curved about the western apse of the church is a feature otherwise unknown in Italy, but it finds close analogies to arrangements from the first half of the ninth century in the north at the abbey of Fulda, at the cathedral of Cologne, and on the Plan of St. Gall. To be sure, Farfa was built on a much smaller scale than many of its northern counterparts, but it should be noted that the abbey church at Fulda was of extraordinary size, which must have taxed the technological limits of the day. In fact, it is well known that the monks of Fulda complained to Charlemagne about the "enormous and superfluous buildings . . . by which the brethren are unduly tired and the serfs are ruined." They suggested instead that "all things should be done in moderation."[89] Charlemagne turned a deaf ear to such complaints, but his successor, Louis the Pious, did not hesitate to remove the architect-abbot, Ratgar, from his post. Indeed, Werner Jacobsen has pointed ed out that, on the whole, churches built during the reign of Louis the Pious were considerably smaller than the grandiose projects of the preceding generation under Charlemagne.[90] Moreover, it is not surprising to find that the dimensions of the abbey church at Farfa are similar to those of the neighboring churches of Rome and Vescovio (Plate 99).

Farfa, then, adapted the architectural currents of the day to its own needs, making the monastery impressive not because of its size but because of the sophistication of its design. Our information is far from complete, but it is clear nonetheless that the buildings at Farfa eloquently expressed the abbey's position as an important imperial establishment within a short distance from Rome.

5

The Early
Romanesque Phase

THE ELEVENTH-CENTURY CHURCH

The east end of the medieval abbey church presents an imposing complex of a design strikingly different from its Carolingian counterpart: heavy, thick walls to sustain vaulting; exterior pilaster strips; interior engaged columns and square piers; Romanesque fresco decoration; and no traces of any earlier construction. Moreover, my survey shows the presbytery to be noticeably off the axis of the rest of the church. All these elements point to a date considerably later than the ninth century.

It is obvious from the previous chapter that this study disagrees with the traditional view that the Sichardan oratory is to be identified with the base of the bell tower. This theory goes back to the preliminary work of Ildefonso Schuster and has been accepted almost without question ever since. But it was based on erroneous assumptions and, above all, on the simple fact that at the beginning of this century the bell tower was the only recognizable remnant of the medieval church. If this a priori assumption is put aside, one is able to see the eastern complex, of which the bell tower is only a part, with new eyes.

In an apparent desire to correlate his examination of the bell tower with the identification of its base as the Sichardan oratory, Markthaler develops an elaborate theory. Because the narrow, tall, and vaulted interior of the bell-tower base, as first uncovered by Markthaler, does not agree with a ninth-century date, he conjectures that the vaulting was an addition of the eleventh century, involving a 30-cm.-thick masonry relining with corner piers; he infers this on the basis of the vertical break of the fresco decoration along the inner jambs and soffits of the two windows in the north wall (Plate 39a). The three upper storeys he assigns to the twelfth and thirteenth centuries. [1]

My survey of the bell tower shows no evidence for any such phases. The masonry is uniform throughout. On the interior, the corner piers bond with the wall and there is no sign of a masonry break in the soffits of the windows. On the contrary, the mortar pointing, or *falsa cortina*, found throughout the interior of the campanile base running below the fresco decoration continues along the full thickness of the inner jambs of the windows (Plate 39a–b). Therefore, the vertical break in the fresco layer in the jambs of the windows probably indicates the position of lattice screens. Moreover, the contractors hired by the Superintendency in 1968 to stabilize the tower found that its masonry consisted of a rubble core faced inside and out by cut stone. [2] Clearly, the inner stone facing was integral to the structure from the beginning. On the exterior, the corner pilaster strips of the third storey are a simple adjustment from the closed, vaulted ground floor to the open, fenestrated upper storeys (Figs. 5–6, Plates 19, 23). Certainly construction of the upper storeys may have proceeded gradually, but there is no reason to see them as substantially later. Furthermore, in spite of what one might at first think, there is no stylistic discrepancy between the exterior wall articulation of the bell-tower base and its open upper storeys.

This last point is demonstrated by a comparison with the bell tower of the church of S. Scolastica at Subiaco. The tower has undergone two restoration campaigns (1935–1937 and 1962–1964), but prerestoration photographs show that the restored areas were based on preserved features. [3] The similarity to the tower at Farfa is immediately apparent (Plate 104). It is built of similar rough-hewn tufa blocks and rises in seven storeys to a height of ca. 31 m. The upper five storeys are pierced by triple-arched openings, resting on colonnettes. Each storey is surmounted by a brick cornice with three rows of saw-teeth and simple stone corbels. The cornices of the last two storeys, with their intersecting blind arches, are presumably later additions. [4]

S. Scolastica's link with Farfa is unmistakable in the bottom two storeys (Plate 105a). As at Farfa, the ground floor corresponds to a tall, groin-vaulted interior with square corner piers. On the exterior of the second storey there is a series of Lombard bands, outlined in brick with individual bricks set flat in the spandrels. The center of the wall is recessed and bears traces of three brick gables resembling the cornice, perhaps used as votive niches. In 1962–1964, the Superintendency of Monuments freed the base of the tower from accumulated obstructions and discovered, on the west façade, a round-arched window surrounded by five blind arches, which are repeated on the sides (Plate 105a–b). [5] Again, the voussoirs are outlined in brick with bricks set flat in the spandrels. This is the same motif, here with squatter proportions, seen on the exterior of the ground floor of the Farfa tower. The two towers are so similar in terms of design, decoration, and construction that one must conclude that they are contemporaneous, if not built by the same team of masons. Such a close relationship is not difficult to explain, since from the Middle Ages to the present day the two great monasteries of the Sabina have maintained close artistic and spiritual ties.[6]

Most important, the tower of S. Scolastica is securely dated by an inscription that states it was consecrated "in the fourth year of the pontificate of Leo IX," i.e., the year 1053.[7] On this basis alone one could assume a mid-eleventh century date for the bell tower at Farfa, but there is also documentary evidence to support this supposition. First is an undated letter from Pope Leo IX (1049–1054) to Abbot Berardus of Farfa (1048–1089), allowing the abbot to select a bishop from wherever he wished to consecrate "your church."[8] Admittedly, the phrase *tuam ecclesiam* need not refer to the abbey church, but the importance of the church is implied by the need for papal sanction, and consecration was, after all, the sole privilege allowed the Pope in this imperial monastery. However, that this letter does, in all probability, concern the abbey church at Farfa can be seen in the fact that on July 6, 1060, Pope Nicholas II, the immediate successor to Leo IX, accompanied by an entourage of cardinals, consecrated its two main altars to the Savior and to the Virgin Mary (*Domini Salvatoris et Sanctae Mariae*).[9] Afterwards, on a visit to the monastery in 1065, Queen Agnes, mother of Henry IV, donated vestments for the two new principal altars.[10]

This dual dedication goes back to the ninth century, when Sichardus added his oratory of the Savior to the west end of the church of the Virgin. Then, with the consecration by Pope Gregory IV, as now with a consecration by Nicholas II, one may be dealing with the construction and rebuilding of a double-apse church: the east end dedicated to the Virgin and the west end dedicated to the Savior. On the other hand, it is equally possible that the two main altars were now both placed in the east end of the church, as the combined Marian and Christological iconography of the Romanesque frescoes would suggest. Medieval documents are always difficult to interpret and must be treated with caution, but together with the comparison to the 1053 tower at S. Scolastica, it can safely be assumed that the east end of the abbey church was well under construction when Abbot Berardus inquired from Pope Leo IX about consecration protocol, and that it was substantially complete by 1060 when consecrated by Pope Nicholas II.

It would seem that only the east end of the abbey church was rebuilt at this time. Further excavations of the church would be necessary to confirm this suggestion; it would be helpful, for example, to be able to identify the various parallel foundations indicated on Markthaler's plan. Nevertheless, two points suggest that this was in fact the case. The first is that the masonry scar on the west side of the campanile and the nave wall fragment below the present main altar both indicate the thickness of the nave wall to have been 0.59 m., decidedly less than any part of the east end. The second is the desire of Abbot Berardus II in 1097 to renovate the abbey church. [11] Admittedly, this seems to have been part of his campaign to build a new monastery atop Monte Acuziano, because of the schism within the monastic community discussed in chapter I of this study. If only the east end of the abbey church had been rebuilt under his predecessor, however, the need to renovate the same church would be easily understandable. At the same time, the passage of thirty or forty years alone could have necessitated repairs. It is a fact, nonetheless, that the evidence for an eleventh-century building campaign of the abbey church is restricted to the east end. This, though, does not minimize the importance of the design of this eastern complex. On the contrary, it is one of the most interesting and significant monuments of church architecture preserved from this period in Central Italy.

The Fresco Decoration

As I stated at the outset, a definitive analysis of the Romanesque wall paintings at Farfa cannot be attempted in this study. Nevertheless, one needs to consider how the basic aspects of the style and iconography of these paintings relate to an understanding of their architectural setting. This task is made all the more urgent by the aforementioned article by Beatrice Premoli, in which the frescoes of the bell tower are dated to the end of the tenth century or the beginning of the eleventh, which is a generation or more before the date she seems to propose for the building itself. [12] Clearly, the issue needs to be resolved.

The difficulty confronting Premoli and any student of the paintings at Farfa is the relative dearth of comparable frescoes in the region. Rome, for example, has few preserved wall paintings from the tenth and eleventh centuries. The frescoes of S. Maria in Pallara on the Palatine, now S. Sebastiano alla Polveriera, usually dated to the late tenth century, and those of S. Urbano alla Caffarella, dated by a dubious inscription to 1011 and probably somewhat later, exhibit little in their style or composition that is comparable to Farfa. [13] Nor does the delicate linear style of the paintings from the end of the eleventh century at Castel Sant'Elia near Nepi or S. Pudenziana and the lower church at San Clemente in Rome have much, if anything, to do with our frescoes. [14]

C. A. Isermeyer considered the style of the figures in the Ascension scene at Farfa to be similar to the apse fresco of S. Pietro in Tuscania, which he dated to 1099 on the basis of an inscription on the ciborium. [15] He also compared details of the paintings at Farfa to those of S. Angelo in Formis (1072–1085) sponsored by Abbot Desiderius of Montecassino. As to his first point, the apse fresco at Tuscania, which was tragically destroyed in a recent earthquake, is now generally dated to the second quarter of the twelfth century. [16] Although some general comparisons could be made between the painterly quality of both monuments, the work at Tuscania is far more advanced and self-assured. The gestures are graceful, the figures robust, and the myriad tones delicately blended together, covered by surface highlights forming complex cellular patterns. Farfa seems awkward and crude by comparison. This difference could, of course, simply be one of quality, but I think there is sufficient evidence to suggest that it is instead an indication of an earlier date at Farfa. The relation of the Farfa frescoes to those of S. Angelo in Formis is even less specific. The sharp angular folds and elaborate comb patterns of the highlights of the Cassinese church are completely lacking at Farfa. Also, the proportions of the human body and the construction of the head are totally different. The artist at S. Angelo in Formis attempts to build up the planes of the face through greenish underpainting; even when this procedure is not followed, the hollows of the cheeks and neck are strongly emphasized or sometimes reduced to dotlike patterns.[17] The faces and bodies at Farfa are flat by comparison.

Premoli, on the other hand, compares the Farfa frescoes to wall paintings in North Italy from the early eleventh century (S. Vincenzo at Galliano, S. Orso in Aosta, and the Novara baptistery) and to a series of Ottonian manuscripts from the Reichenau school.[18] Here we have the opposite extreme. In the North Italian frescoes and the Ottonian miniatures, the limbs are modeled by a series of parallel white bands giving them the look of cylindrical or tubelike forms. At Farfa, in spite of the presence of two distinct hands, there is in both styles a concerted attempt to model the figure through a complex pattern of highlights. In the first, more linear style, the highlights tend to coalesce in geometric patterns (Plates 40, 43), whereas in the second, more painterly style, they are created by swirling lines of pigment (Plates 41, 42). Similarly, the Farfa frescoes lack the simple stratified backgrounds of the Ottonian works. Even in the *Maiestas Domini* at Farfa there is an attempt to render, albeit schematically, the colorful clouds of a sunrise (Plate 43).[19]

Markthaler suggests that the frescoes at Farfa were executed shortly before the 1060 consecration, based on a stylistic comparison with a fragmentary wall painting at S. Salvatore Maggiore, a nearby Farfa dependency. He identifies the fresco at S. Salvatore as a portrait of the emperor Henry II and his wife Kunigunda, which allows him to date the painting to before the latter's death in 1039. But this identification is tenuous at best, and the painting is now lost.[20] Regardless of the identity of the individuals represented, there is no reason why the portraits could not be posthumous. An artistic relationship may well have existed between the two abbeys. Indeed, one would expect it, but this cannot be used as a criterion for dating the frescoes at Farfa. In sum, it seems to me that previous attempts to relate the Farfa frescoes to known works of wall painting, whether in Central Italy or the north, have been unsuccessful.

It is far more reasonable to begin an investigation of the frescoes at Farfa by looking first at dated examples of artistic production in the abbey itself. E. B. Garrison, in particular, has been able to attribute a number of illustrated manuscripts to the Farfa scriptorium, or ones related closely to it, based on a careful analysis of the palaeography and other internal evidence. Of these examples, two in particular stand out as relevant to this discussion. The first is a *Collectio canonum* (Vat. lat. 1339), which Garrison dates to the second quarter of the eleventh century; a more recent study by Theo Kölzer suggests a slightly later date.[21] The illustrations are gathered at the beginning of the manuscript, but their accompanying labels are identical to the main text, showing that they belonged to the original assemblage. Most of the illustrations are relatively crude outline drawings with thin washes that are of limited importance to this study. The first illustration (fol. 7r), however, is a full-page representation of the Ascension of Christ that has several analogies to our frescoes.[22] First of all, there is an elaborate architectural frame of superimposed spiral columns, comparable to the columns painted on the square piers of the bell tower. Second, the figures in the manuscript have the same heavy outlines and drapery highlights as in the first, more linear style of the frescoes. A particularly close comparison could be made, for example, between the angels in the manuscript and the angels flanking Christ in the *Maiestas Domini* and the Ascension frescoes (Plates 40, 43). They even share the same square-jawed facial types. Thus, I would suggest that this illustration in the *Collectio* is related to what I have classified as Style I of the frescoes. At the same time, there are also elements in the illumination that recall Style II, such as the agitated gestures of the apostles.

The second, more painterly style of the frescoes is best represented by another, closely related manuscript from Farfa, the so-called Madrid Evangelistary (Biblioteca Nacional, Vitr. 20–6). There is no question that this manuscript was produced at Farfa, as the palaeography and various other details prove. Moreover, the manuscript in Madrid contains numerous full-page illustrations, the style of which Garrison considers to be "exceedingly like" that of the Ascension scene in the *Collectio*.[23] He points to the use of architectural framings and settings, as well as to the similar schematization of highlights on the drapery. My own close examination of the illustrations in each manuscript, however, shows that the application of the pigment is decidedly different. Whereas in the *Collectio* highlights and shadowlines are applied to a thin flat wash of color, the drapery of the Madrid manuscript is built up through thick applications of paint in parallel strokes of contrasting color, so that the surface texture has a thick, "pasty" quality (Plate 106). In short, the impressionistic, painterly style of the Madrid manuscript is strikingly similar to Style II of the frescoes, as represented by the lower two-thirds of the Ascension scene at Farfa (Plates 41–42).

The connection between the Madrid manuscript and the wall paintings can be seen also in the iconography of the scenes. For example, if we look to the representation of the Ascension in the Evangelistary, we see that the figure of Peter in the lower right holds a scroll that seems to float in front of his face, much in the manner of the corresponding figure of Peter in the fresco (Plates 41, 106). In the wall painting, part of the inscription of the scroll is preserved

(DOMINUS LEGEM DAD PACEM MEAM DO VOBIS), which shows that the figure of Peter has been taken from a scene of the Handing of the Law, the so-called *Traditio Legis*.[24] Likewise, the agitated posture of Paul in the lower left of the scene in the manuscript, with lines of drapery that swirl about his abdomen, appears in the corresponding figure in the wall painting. The bust-length angels emerging from clouds, too, are like those in the fresco. Even details of the heads of the apostles find their parallels in the wall painting.

The general composition of the two works is more closely related than it may at first appear. The full-page miniature is divided into two zones, one celestial and the other terrestrial, with two angels serving as intermediaries between the two spheres. The apostles are shown at the bottom of the page crowded behind the more prominent figures of Peter and Paul, who flank the Virgin standing orant on a footstool. At Farfa, Peter and Paul have been elevated to the level of the windows and set in the right- and left-hand corners respectively. The central figure of Mary in the illustration may also have been present in the fresco. The painted surface is obliterated between the two windows, but just below the bust-length angels one can discern portions of the curved red outline of a yellow nimbus. In other words, a haloed figure of some kind originally stood at this level, and no figure other than the Virgin Mary would be appropriate in this scene. Although not mentioned in the biblical text, the Virgin was included in the earliest representations of the Ascension, as in the Rabbula Gospels from the sixth century, in order to emphasize Christ's humanity.[25] At Farfa, of course, the presence of the Virgin would also allude to the main dedication of the church. The only major difference between the manuscript and the wall painting comes in the upper third of the illustration, where Christ is represented in the form of a medallion portrait carried by angels, instead of full-length and in profile as in the fresco. But this section of the mural painting can be attributed to the artists of Style I, as I have already suggested, and they must have used a different model for its composition.

Garrison dates the Madrid Evangelistary to the third quarter of the eleventh century, owing, on the one hand, to its close relation to the *Collectio* and, on the other, to its more advanced palaeography. I would suggest that the two styles of the frescoes at Farfa are similarly interrelated, with one style following the other in rapid succession, Style II being derived from Style I but adding a new and more dynamic concept of the use of color and modeling for the human figure, probably derived from recent developments in Byzantine art.[26] Be that as it may, I submit that these two manuscripts establish an approximate date for the frescoes of the bell tower in the third quarter of the eleventh century.[27] This would mean, of course, that the fresco decoration dates to approximately the same time or, more likely, not long after the construction of the eastern complex as a whole. In addition, the manuscripts show that the stylistic changes apparent in the frescoes were part of an internal artistic development at Farfa.

COMPARATIVE ANALYSIS

We have already seen that the securely dated bell tower of S. Scolastica at Subiaco (1053) is extremely pertinent for dating the east end at Farfa. The bell towers of these two neighboring abbeys share such similarities in design, detailing, and mode of construction that they can be regarded as being the work of the same team of masons. The church of S. Scolastica, however, was completely rebuilt in the thirteenth century and extensively remodeled in the eighteenth, leaving the campanile as the only relic of the early medieval fabric.[28] It can be assumed that, as today, the campanile adjoined the west façade of the church in the eleventh century, for the niches prominent on three sides of the tower are conspicuously lacking on the east side. Furthermore, the round-arched doorways on all four sides of the ground floor indicate that it served as part of the entranceway. Little else can be said about the medieval church of S. Scolastica,[29] and one must, therefore, look elsewhere for comparative monuments to help explain the source and function of the elaborate eastern complex at Farfa.

Local Precedents

The familiar masterpieces of Romanesque architecture to be found in Central Italy, for example the cathedral at Pisa, the baptistery in Florence, S. Pietro in Tuscania and the abbey church of St. Benedict at Montecassino, form part of a later generation of buildings that were not begun until after the church at Farfa was consecrated, and presumably complete, in 1060.[30] Even building in Rome remains an enigma until the beginning of the twelfth century.[31]

Two important churches do survive, however, from the first half of the eleventh century to illustrate building programs contemporary with or immediately preceding that of Farfa: S. Pietro near Ferentillo in Umbria and the abbey church of S. Salvatore on Monte Amiata, the highest mountain in Tuscany. Their relationship to Farfa is more in plan than elevation. Each has a single nave with a tripartite east end that is centered about a rectangular crossing (Plate 107A–B). This tripartite division of the east end may derive from the Lombard tradition established by S. Ambrogio in Milan as rebuilt in the late tenth century and subsequently reflected, ca. 1000, by S. Pietro at Agliate (Plate 107C).[32] There groin-vaulted chapels terminate the side aisles and do not communicate with the central barrel-vaulted forechoir. At Ferentillo and Monte Amiata, this design seems to have been adjusted to fit a single nave plan, so that the side apses and their vaulted forechoirs now form the arms of a projecting transept. The deep barrel vault has been retained for the forechoir, but a crossing has become necessary to permit communication between each unit (presbytery, side chapels, and nave) without the use of side aisles.

S. Pietro in Ferentillo is the less elaborate and probably the earlier of the two, although its date is far from certain (Plate 107A).[33] The rectangular crossing is groin-vaulted and framed by four arches, almost equal in height but not in width. The crossing, in turn, supports a low, transverse tower projecting only slightly higher than the ridge of the nave roof. The transept arms are barrel-vaulted on an east-west axis, while the barrel vault of the forechoir runs transversely north-south. Attached to the end of the north transept arm is a five-storey bell tower of crude unhewn stone masonry and primitive decorative details (Plate 108). Although the construction is simple, the design of the church is highly developed. The segmentation of each spatial compartment is clear and deliberate in both plan and elevation and is presumably related to different liturgical functions. In fact, an influence from the so-called echelon scheme of the east end of the abbey church of Cluny II (dedicated 980) has been suggested to explain the plan of Ferentillo.[34] S. Pietro, however, lacks the monumental transept and side corridors, or *cryptae*, of Cluny II,[35] so that the influence from Cluny, if present, would seem to have been either indirect or greatly simplified. The link with Lombardy seems stronger, as evidenced in particular by the characteristic vaulted forechoir.

Far grander in scale and conception is the abbey church of S. Salvatore on Monte Amiata. S. Salvatore, like Farfa, was an imperial abbey and lay off the *ruga francigena*, now the Via Cassia, which was one of the principal routes linking Rome and northern Europe by way of North Italy and the Alpine passes. The political importance and economic wealth of the monastery, as well as its close contacts with northern Europe, are reflected in the two-tower façade (Plate 109) and a spacious hall crypt that runs below the entire east end. The terminals of the towers and the whole central bay have been restored, but the date of the consecration of the crypt, 1036, may be taken as an approximate terminus ad quem for the construction of the entire building.[36]

In spite of numerous modifications, the basic elements of the medieval church seem to be preserved. The single nave is timber roofed, with no indication of its ever having been vaulted, while its flat walls are interrupted only by a series of recessed, round-arched clerestory windows. The masonry of rough-hewn limestone blocks, recently exposed below Renaissance and baroque plaster and fresco decoration by a restoration campaign, seems to be in keeping with a mid-eleventh-century date. The groin-vaulted crossing is low and broad, without a tower above, and flows into the lower barrel vault of the forechoir. The groin-vaulted transept arms are entered through arches considerably lower and narrower than those on the principal axis. Of the overall plan, only the flat terminations of the central and side apses are suspect, for recent soundings have conclusively proven that the flat east end of the crypt is the result of walling up a series of three semicircular apses.[37] The most likely time for these modifications would have been in 1229,[38] when the abbey came under Cistercian rule.

As an important imperial abbey in Central Italy, S. Salvatore must have been a significant precedent for the Farfa design, but the most that can be said about either of the churches of Monte Amiata and Ferentillo is that they may have served as the starting point from which the Farfa plan developed. In comparison with these two churches, the distinguishing features of the design of the east end at Farfa become more apparent and can be listed as follows: a square presbytery; twin bell towers surmounting projecting side chapels (or transept arms) that flank a rectangular crossing; the exterior and interior articulation of the wall by tall pilaster strips and engaged columns; and the decorative *opus mixtum* masonry. In order to explain the use of these features at Farfa, I shall turn now to an account of their origins, categorized under the two major headings of design and construction.

Design

The Square Presbytery.   Before its importation by the Cistercians in the twelfth century and its subsequent adoption by the Mendicant Orders, the square presbytery as found at Farfa seems to have been extremely rare for church building in Italy. I have already noted this phenomenon in the later Middle Ages with the walling up of the east end of the abbey church of Monte Amiata. Croquison recognized the close similarity of the Farfa scheme to square and rectangular presbyteries common in the Rhine and Mosan Valleys throughout the eleventh century.[39] But he was at a loss to reconcile this observation with his staunch advocacy of a Carolingian date for the base of the Farfa bell tower, to which the square presbytery is integrally related. This is not to say that Carolingian precedents are lacking. On the contrary, numerous examples of square east ends are documented for both the Carolingian and Merovingian periods north of the Alps. Suffice it to mention two important abbey churches from the beginning and the end of the Carolingian era respectively: S. Nazarius at Lorsch (ca. 774) and St. Georg at Reichenau-Oberzell (888–896).[40] Known Italian examples, however, are few and seem to have been used for unusual plans, such as the small, vaulted cruciform church of S. Zeno at Bardolino near Verona from the late ninth century.[41]

In the context of the eleventh century, Croquison was right to look to the Rhine and the Meuse, for this region does seem to have had a marked predilection for the square presbytery. Among the first examples may have been St. Cecilia in Cologne (mid-tenth century), which is often considered as a revival of the Lorsch scheme.[42] It should be remembered, too, that at approximately the same time, the monastery of Lorsch was reformed and had begun a rebuilding campaign of its own. In the early eleventh century, the square presbytery was used for the modest parish church of St. Martin at Zyfflich (perhaps as early as 1000–1020, but more likely somewhat later), interesting for Farfa because they share similar dimensions in plan (Plate 110A).[43] Thereafter follows a long series of abbey churches with either square or rectangular presbyteries in the lowlands of the upper Meuse and Rhine. Among these are St.

Vincent, Soignies (early eleventh century), Ste.-Gertrude in Nivelles (consecrated in 1046), St. Servatius in Maastricht (consecrated in 1039), St. Willi-
brord at Echternach (Phase III, 1016–1031), and St. Nicholas at Messines
(second half of the eleventh century).[44] From here the feature may have spread
to Saxony by mid-century for the remodeling of the Abdinghofkirche, St.
Salvator at Paderborn (1016–1031), and the building of St. Luidger, Helmstedt (mid-eleventh century).[45] More important, the square presbytery was
considered appropriate for the great Salian imperial monastic foundation of
Limburg an der Haardt (1025–1042), west of the middle Rhine, not far from
Lorsch (Plate 110B).[46]

Probably because of their prevalence within monastic architecture of the
empire, the flat termination and square presbytery were adopted a generation
later by the Hirsau monastic reform movement, used first at SS. Peter and Paul
at Hirsau (1083–1091)[47] and thence becoming part of the vocabulary of the so-
called *Hirsauer Bauschule* (Plate 110C–D).[48] In sum, the appearance of a square
presbytery at Farfa in the mid-eleventh century would seem to be in keeping
with the latest developments of monastic architecture within the imperial
sphere.

Twin Bell Towers.   Perhaps the most striking feature of the eastern complex at
Farfa, as I have reconstructed it, is the placement of twin *campanili* above
projecting side chapels. It should be emphasized that we are dealing here with
bell towers surmounting groin-vaulted side chapels; in other words, they are
not the attached stair towers so familiar in Carolingian and Ottonian architecture. Therefore, in spite of an external resemblance to stair towers, the ground
floors of the *campanili* at Farfa were fully integrated with the east end and
presumably, as side chapels, played a significant liturgical role. In this regard, a
recent case has been made for the addition of twin towers in the late tenth
century to the east end of the cathedral of Florence, S. Reparata.[49] Plausible as
this suggestion may be, it is based almost exclusively on the evidence of massive
foundations wedged between the remains of the central and side apses, as
revealed below the present duomo. Nothing is known about the elevation or
interior spatial relationship of the towers to the sanctuary. S. Reparata may well
have been an important contemporary example of the twin-bell-tower scheme,
but one cannot be sure. It is best, therefore, only to consider preserved examples of this design, which are to be found primarily in North Italy.

Two important examples of the use of twin bell towers in the first half of the
eleventh century are only a few kilometers apart in the Val d'Aosta: the cathedrals of Aosta and Ivrea. In each case, the upper storeys of the towers may have
been completed at different times, but their placement undoubtedly formed
part of the initial design. At Aosta, the two *campanili* rise above the vaulted
terminal bays of what was originally a monumental projecting transept (Plate
111A).[50] Consequently, the towers are pushed out from the main body of the

church and stand in majestic isolation. The same solution was used for the contemporary remodeling of St.-Michel at Cuxa (before 1040), in the French Pyrenees bordering Catalonia (Plate 111B).[51] A close kinship between these two distant monuments is not surprising, in view of the common cultural bond enjoyed since antiquity by Catalonia, southern France, and northern Italy, all linked by the Mediterranean Sea. This is, after all, the heartland of *le premier art roman*, as defined and examined by Puig i Cadafalch.[52]

The cathedral at Ivrea presents a very different design (Plate 112).[53] The bell towers are set over the vaulted bays terminating the inner aisles and immediately flanking the central apse, so that their vaulted ground floors serve as intermediary spaces between the aisles and the curious annular passage circumscribing the apse. This concept seems to have been adopted later for the abbey church of S. Abbondio at Como, consecrated in 1095 (Plate 113). There the choir has been elongated, presumably owing to an elaboration of the liturgy. Thümmler in fact considers the bell towers at Como to have been directly inspired by Cluny.[54] I shall return to this problem later. For now, let it suffice to point out that, contrary to those at Ivrea, the bases of the *campanili* at Como are no longer passageways but distinct chapels with individual apsidioles, which are entered from the inner aisles through a tall broad arch and are linked to the choir by a low, arched doorway (Plate 114).

The distinction just made between the use of bell towers at Aosta and Cuxa, on the one hand, and at Ivrea and Como, on the other, may be more apparent than real, for the position of the bell towers depends primarily upon the presence or absence of a projecting transept. Thus, the *campanili* may have been considered appropriate for different church plans, either episcopal or monastic. This suggestion is substantiated by two further variations on this theme in an adjacent geographic area, the Tarentaise of Savoy in the upper valley of the Isère River, linked to North Italy by the mountain passes of the Petit St.-Bernard and the Val di Susa.

The basilica of St.-Martin at Aime (ca. 1020) is a seemingly modest building, but one whose detailing evokes a more sophisticated model. The plan is derived from the previously described Lombard type of nave, side aisles, and tripartite east end with triple apses. Subtle changes have taken place, however, so that both the central and the side forechoirs are groin-vaulted. Remarkably, these vaults are carried by colonnettes wedged between the corner piers. More important, however, are the bell towers that stood above the side chapels, recorded in the nineteenth century but of which only the restored north tower is visible today.[55] More grandiose in scale is the cathedral of Moûtiers-en-Tarentaise, built under Archbishop Amisus (996–1044). In spite of numerous later modifications, the original plan is evident: nave, side aisles, two-towered west façade, and a quadratic segmentation of the east crossing, transept arms, and choir. Wedged between the choir and transept are square, groin-vaulted chapels opening onto the choir but not the transept, and surmounted by bell towers, of which the north one is still preserved.[56] Bell towers above vaulted chapels flanking the choir, then, had ample precedent in the first half of the eleventh century in North Italy—more precisely, in the valleys of the Piedmont and Savoy that served as travel corridors through the Alps to northern Europe.

Thus, it is not surprising that a tradition predating that of Italy should have existed north of the Alps, concentrated within the Alsace-Lorraine region, formerly the heartland of the enigmatic Middle Kingdom of Lotharingia. One of the first and most important uses of double eastern towers may have been at the abbey church of St. Maximin at Trier. Although destroyed in 1674, leaving only its famous frescoed crypt, the general layout of the east end of St. Maximin is described in the dedicatory document of 942, which refers to towers above the side chapels.[57] This arrangement may be visualized by looking at St. Lucius at Werden, an abbey church founded in the mid-tenth century, with close connections to St. Maximin at Trier, and rebuilt in the middle of the eleventh century (consecrated in 1063) with bell towers over the eastern-end bays of the side aisles that unexpectedly broke the continuous silhouette of the aisle roofline (Plate 115). The main evidence for the presence of towers on the plan is a noticeable thickening of the outer wall of the tower bays to sustain the added weight.[58] Derived in turn from the abbey church at Werden is that of St. Luidger at Helmstedt, also dated to the mid-eleventh century on the basis of its architectural sculpture. Again, bell towers stood above the square bays preceding the side chapels, with the only difference being the main apse, which has taken on a square plan analogous to that at Farfa.[59] What emerges, therefore, is a closely related family of monastic churches sharing what Louis Grodecki terms the "chevet harmonique, . . . une des plus belles créations de l'architecture ottonienne," which perhaps originated at St. Maximin at Trier.[60]

Equally problematic is the appearance of bell towers flanking the choir of the Lorraine cathedrals of Metz, Toul, and Verdun. In spite of their poor state of preservation and a relative lack of specific documentation, a local tradition seems apparent in which bell towers with vaulted chapels in the ground floor (and often a chapel in a second floor above) are set between the apse and transept, not dissimilar from the arrangement already described for Moûtiers-en-Tarentaise. The first in this series may have been the cathedral at Metz of Bishop Theodorich II (1005–1046), a building known only partially from excavations. A segmented transept has been found with side apsidioles and traces of the central apse, to either side of which may have been inserted the towers known before the church's destruction in the early sixteenth century and called "les tours de Charlemagne."[61] If so, it would be an interesting precedent for the placement of the two towers at Florence Cathedral, noted above.

Much of the present cathedral of Verdun is the result of building campaigns in the first half of the eleventh century, including a western complex with a quadratic scheme of segmented transept and projecting square apse, between which are wedged two bell towers whose vaulted ground floors serve as entranceways. The same design was used for a rebuilding of the east end of Verdun from 1144–1147 and for that of Notre Dame de Mont-Devant-Sassy a few years later (1150–1170).[62] The layout of the cathedral at Toul in its present Gothic form may go back to a documented tenth-century phase (963–994) and is similar to that of the abbey church at St.-Mihiel, where the thirteenth-century masonry has been found to envelop an eleventh-century (1044–1076) core.[63]

The persistence of this design in the Lorraine throughout the thirteenth century has prompted several scholars to see a regional type at work. Hans Kubach, for example, has gone so far as to define a *Trierer Kunstraum*, following the general boundaries of the Trier diocese, which included the upper Lorraine, and based above all upon a building type composed of a "choir flanked by rectilinear side chapels that are surmounted by towers."[64] The truth may not have been so simple. The two arrangements as exemplified by, and presumably derived from, St. Maximin at Trier and St. Vincent at Metz differ, again owing to the presence or absence of a projecting transept, and may have served as two precedents—alternatives, if you will—the former more popular along the Rhine and Saxony, and the latter favored in the Lorraine.

From the Lorraine the use of bell towers flanking the choir seems to have spread to France. By the middle of the eleventh century, the motif appears in the Ile-de-France between the choir and transept arms of St.-Germain-des-Prés in Paris and at Morienval near Beauvais in Valois.[65] In the Loire and Marne Valleys, stunted bell towers protrude from the otherwise compact ambulatory choirs of the great abbey church of St.-Benoît-sur-Loire (1067–1108) and that of Vignory (mid-eleventh century).[66]

By the second half of the eleventh century, twin bell towers appear in southern Germany above the side chapels of SS. Peter and Paul at Reichenau-Niederzell (ca. 1060).[67] Not unrelated to its appearance in Reichenau is the adoption of twin eastern bell towers for one of the many variants of the churches belonging to the Hirsau monastic reform movement. At the abbey church of SS. Peter and Paul at Hirsau (1083–1091), for example, the outer walls of barrel-vaulted bays have been thickened, in seeming anticipation of bell towers, as at St. Lucius at Werden, but for some reason they were never built (Plate 110C). Nevertheless, twin bell towers are consistently used in churches that follow the sanctuary arrangement established by SS. Peter and Paul, classified by Bernard Hoffmann as "building type II" of the *Hirsauer Bauschule*.[68]

Certain other members of this group of *campanili* and flat-ended chevets display striking analogies to Farfa. Much the closest is the original design of the Hirsau priory of Klosterreichenbach, finished in 1082 and consecrated in 1085 (Plate 110E).[69] The church was originally single-naved, with a timber roof and a square presbytery terminated by a semicircular apse. Between the sanctuary and the nave was a rectangular crossing flanked by bell towers, whose ground floors were open, both to the nave and to the crossing. For Hoffmann, Kloster-reichenbach is at once typical and unique. It is typical by virtue of the two bell towers, though Hoffmann does contend, on the other hand, that the Hirsau school preferred to place such bell towers flush with the flat-ended sanctuary, as at SS. Peter and Paul at Erfurt and the abbey church at Zweifalten. For this development, SS. Peter and Paul at Reichenau may have been an important precedent. Hoffmann considers Klosterreichenbach unique in its melding of his building type II with that of the echelon-apsed east end of St. Aurelius at Hirsau (1059–1071), which he classifies as building type I.[70]

The analogies to Farfa, however, cannot be ignored. In fact, one need only remove the semicircular apses to arrive at a virtually identical plan. There is no documented direct contact between the two great abbeys of Farfa and Hirsau (or Klosterreichenbach in particular). Indeed, construction at Farfa seems to have taken place a full generation before that of SS. Peter and Paul at Hirsau. The most logical solution is that both were developing from a common source: i.e., from monastic architecture of the Holy Roman Empire in general and from that of the Lorraine in particular.

To underscore this point, we need only return to Lotharingia to look at the majestic east end of the abbey church at Murbach in Alsace, deprived of its nave and aisles in the seventeenth century (Plate 116).[71] The design of this church, dedicated in 1134, is now familiar: rectangular crossing flanked by bell towers with vaulted ground floors and a square presbytery. On this basis alone, Mur-bach is usually considered as a Hirsau or pseudo-Hirsau product. There is, however, no evidence of any affiliation with Hirsau. These features of a square presbytery and twin *campanili* were the common property of monastic architec-ture in the Rhine and Mosan Valleys. In short, Murbach should be seen as a summation of a local tradition and development of more than two centuries.

In spite of a separation in building of almost one hundred years, the sim-ilarities between Murbach and Farfa are equally striking, if not more so. True, Murbach has the sophistication of construction and refinement in detailing that belies its substantially later date. Farfa, in turn, lacks the side choirs and stairways to chapels in the second storey of the bell towers. Both have ample precedents from Cluny and the Lorraine. At Farfa, these added features have either been simplified or have been rejected for an Italian ambient. But a common bond seems evident, which would seem to be monastic architecture within the empire and Lotharingia.

Construction

Exterior Pilaster Strips and Blind Arcading.   The exterior of the eastern complex at Farfa is distinguished by a bold articulation of the wall surface by rows of pilaster strips framing tall, slender blind arcades. The most curious feature of this system, though, is the blind gabled arcading—in groups of three and four—marking the second storey of the campanile. Its evocation of the famous *Torhalle* at Lorsch (ca. 774), together with the far cruder decorative niches of the baptistery of St.-Jean at Poitiers (early eighth century), is cited by Serafini as proof of the Carolingian date of the bell-tower base.[72] The gabled arch, however, has a long history and cannot by itself be used to date the entire east end at Farfa, as even Markthaler realized.[73] Although relatively rare, the blind gabled arch is found on a sufficient number of monuments to demonstrate its survival well into the Romanesque period.

For example, a blind gabled arcade with pilaster strips can be seen on the second storey of the north cylindrical stair tower at Gernrode from ca. 960 (Plate 117),[74] and it may have been revived around the year 1000 for the gatehouse at Fulda, if the details of a sixteenth-century woodcut can be trusted.[75] In the late tenth and early eleventh centuries, gabled arches are common in the stripwork characteristic of late Saxon towers in England, such as Earls Barton and Barton-on-Humber.[76] In North Italy, gabled niches are found between the clerestory windows of the church at Galliano, dedicated in 1007,[77] and the baptistery of Lomello (Plate 118), which is usually dated to the early eighth century but seems to have been substantially rebuilt, along with the adjacent basilica, by the middle of the eleventh century.[78] The second storey of the campanile of S. Scolastica at Subiaco also has an inserted gabled brick decoration. In France, gabled arches are found in the Auvergne in the second half of the eleventh century in the crossing of Ste.-Anne at Chappes. At St.-Etienne at Nevers (1066–1099), where gabled arches set on columns alternate with round arches, the motif seems to be a particularly archaizing element. By the twelfth century, gabled arches are reduced to decorative friezes on corbels in the narthex of Ste.-Madelaine at Vézelay and the Chapelle des Templars at Laon (1118–1128).

The use of round-headed blind arcading was far more diffuse. The system seems to have originated in late antiquity as a simple means of reinforcing an otherwise flat wall as it was raised to a greater height, as, for example, in the aisleless *aula regia* of Constantine at Trier (ca. 300). At the end of the fourth century, they are applied in two orders on the aisleless cruciform church of S. Simpliciano in Milan and soon after, in Ravenna, at the Mausoleum of Galla Placidia (ca. 425), which is also aisleless and cruciform but this time vaulted. Thereafter, blind exterior arcading becomes part of the Ravenna building tradition, applied to aisled basilicas such as S. Apollinare Nuovo (490–526) and S. Apollinare in Classe (532/536–549).[79] By the mid-sixth century, they appear on the Istrian coast at the cathedral of Parenzo. Thus, the exterior use of blind arcading seems to have been an old technique that emerged from the capabilities and aesthetic concerns of late antiquity within the political and religious orbits of Trier, Milan, and Ravenna.[80]

It is, therefore, interesting to note the reappearance of this feature within the same general area in the Middle Ages. The use of blind arcading on, for example, the aisled church of S. Salvatore at Brescia (Plate 119) and the central plan of S. Maria in Cividale, both ca. 800, may reflect a conscious revival of late antique models, in much the same manner as the contemporary *aula regia* of Charlemagne in Aachen imitated the audience hall of Constantine in Trier.[81] At the same time, a marked attenuation of the blind arcades appears in the aisleless basilicas of Switzerland, at St. John at Müstair (Plate 120) and St. Martin at Chur,[82] and along the Dalmatian coast in the apses of the towering rotunda of the church of Sv. Donat at Zadar.[83] Coming from either the north or the Adriatic coast, blind arcades were applied to the exterior of the square, centrally planned church of S. Maria delle Cinque Torri at Cassino (788–792), destroyed in the last world war but known through earlier photographs and survey drawings.[84] These Carolingian monuments indicate a process of both imitation and modification, in which they recall the simple local buttressing technique of late antiquity and yet, on occasion, alter the proportions to enhance the decorative quality. The last five churches, being aisleless halls or centralized schemes instead of the normal aisled basilica, should perhaps be seen as special cases, calling for or at least allowing such technical and stylistic change. Nevertheless, it was the decorative potential of blind arcading that seems to have been particularly appreciated by later generations.

Around the year 1000, the motif seems to reappear suddenly with great ferocity throughout North Italy; in Pavia with S. Felice and S. Maria alle Cacce; in the church at Galliano from 1007 (Plate 121); at Gazzo Veronese; in S. Quintino at Signo and S. Pietro at Acqui from ca. 1040 in the Piedmont; and in the façade of the cathedral of S. Maria on the island of Torcello from 1008 (Plate 122).[85] The attenuation of the arcading, begun in the ninth century, has become exaggerated, so that widths and heights vary, depending upon placement, as if they were toying with the plasticity of the wall surface. And in the mid-eleventh century, an echelon of blind niches appears in Provence on the façade of Ste.-Marie in Arles (1046), an arrangement not dissimilar to the campanile base of S. Scolastica at Subiaco.[86]

A parallel development takes place north of the Alps, beginning with the tall pilaster strips and blind arches of the aisleless nave of St. Pantaleon in Cologne (dedicated in 980), which may have used the Constantinian *aula regia* in Trier as its model.[87] Thereafter, blind arcades become a characteristic feature of church building in the first half of the eleventh century along the lower Rhine and Mosan Valleys at St. Vincent, Soignies, Ste.-Gertrude at Nivelles, Hastière-en-Dela, Ostrehem, Zyfflich, Bonn Cathedral, and Celles, to name but a few examples.[88] The proportions of the blind arcades on these monuments tend, for the most part, to follow those of the late antique prototypes more closely than those of contemporary buildings in North Italy. Nevertheless, the blind arch is now considered pliable enough to fit virtually any space, as at Nivelles, where a tall blind arch is squeezed between its neighbor on the transept and the adjoining aisle wall (Plate 123).

Fewer examples of blind arcades may be cited from Burgundy, but they do appear in the early eleventh century on the church of Genouilly and may have been used for the cylindrical stair towers of St.-Benigne at Dijon (1001–1018).[89] A row of blind arches appears on the outer aisle wall—together with Lombard bands in the clerestory—of Romainmôtier (ca. 1030), a dependency of Cluny in what is today western Switzerland (Plate 124).[90] From either Burgundy or the Mosan region, the use of blind arcading may have spread to Normandy, restricted to transitional—and perhaps buttressing—elements in the second storeys of the western towers of the abbey churches of Notre-Dame at Jumièges and St.-Etienne at Caen.

By the second half of the eleventh century, blind arcading can be found, too, in South Italy, where it is particularly marked on the exterior of the cathedral of Gerace in Calabria (Plate 125). This feature, together with aspects of its plan and elevation, points to a direct influence from the north, particularly from the lower Meuse, following the Norman conquest of the area in 1062.[91] In Rome, as was so often the case with "foreign" architectural developments, exterior blind arcading was a late feature, not appearing before the twelfth century. At S. Lorenzo in Lucina (ca. 1130), the arcades of the aisle and clerestory wall follow early Christian proportions, and they may therefore relate to a twelfth-century building revival in Ravenna rather than indicate any influence from the north or the south.[92] On the exterior of the central apse at S. Maria in Trastevere (dedicated in 1143), on the other hand, the arcading is much more narrow and elongated, recalling the apse at Gerace, and it may relate to more direct contact—although seemingly *retardataire*—with the north, whether Italy or the Lorraine.[93]

To sum up, the system of blind arcading as found at Farfa was an important aspect of church building in the first half of the eleventh century, particularly in North Italy and the Lorraine, which is where it first emerged in late antiquity. At the same time, it should be pointed out that at Farfa the blind arcading is applied with singular vigor and variety.

Masonry.   In addition to the pilaster strips and blind arches, another remarkable feature at Farfa is the use of *opus mixtum* masonry found in the exterior lower storeys of the eastern complex. Single rows of rough-hewn tufa blocks alternate with single courses of reused Roman brick, which also outline blind and window arches, with a brick set flat to form a diaper pattern in the spandrels. This colorful masonry has also been cited as evidence for an early dating of the east end at Farfa. Thümmler, for example, compares it to the masonry of the crypt of Einhard's church at Michelstadt, near Steinbach,[94] where thick bricks are occasionally inserted in the stone vaults and arches. The contemporary crypt of

St.-Philibert-de-Grandlieu could also be cited. Far more similar, however, is the *opus mixtum* common in churches in Rome from the sixth to the eighth centuries, among them S. Crisogono, S. Agnese, S. Lorenzo f.l.m., S. Pancrazio, and S. Giovanni a Porta Latina.[95] It is also found in important Lombard buildings of the eighth century, such as S. Sofia in Benevento and S. Salvatore in Spoleto.[96] Nevertheless, several factors show that although related to this development, the masonry at Farfa is clearly distinct from it.

Early medieval *opus mixtum* is, of course, derived from late antique *opus listatum*, used in Rome for foundations and occasionally for rising walls from Constantinian times on.[97] It may have been used for economic reasons, using the local tuff, an igneous rock, as an inexpensive fill within an otherwise brick-faced concrete masonry. Its proliferation in the early Middle Ages may be similarly explained by the economic collapse and disappearance of an organized brick industry, whereas tuff was readily available and easily quarried in and around Rome. Furthermore, the proportion of stone to brick, 1:1, became the rule rather than the exception. Yet *opus mixtum* remained a building technology based upon brick and brick-faced concrete, as shown by the fact that strategic points, such as arches, were always made of pure brick. At Farfa, on the other hand, it is basically a stone masonry that is only outlined or occasionally accented with single brick courses. A view of the exterior north wall of the square presbytery underscores this point and illustrates the erratic nature of the brick striations, which stop and start without apparent logic (Fig. 6). As in the case of the development of pilaster strips and blind arcading, what was originally devised as a structural element has taken on a predominantly decorative quality. At the same time, it may also have been the result of a conscious emulation or study, rather than a continuous tradition, of what must have been considered "ancient" prototypes, early Christian and early medieval—an attitude reminiscent of the desire to build *more romano* in the Carolingian period.

A strikingly similar phenomenon has been demonstrated by Frédéric Lesueur for a small group of churches from the first half of the eleventh century near the mouth of the Loire.[98] As with Farfa, their *opus mixtum* masonry had been taken as an indication of a Carolingian date; Lesueur, however, has shown that in all likelihood they date instead from the first half of the eleventh century and should, therefore, be seen as a revival of an older technique. Foremost among these examples are the crossing piers and arches of St. Martin at Angers (ca. 1040), where double and triple rows of bricks alternate with single rows of ashlars (Plate 126).[99] Equally important are the enigmatic nave piers of St.-Philibert-de-Grandlieu. In the case of St.-Philibert, and perhaps of Angers, it could be argued that there was a conscious emulation of Carolingian masonry.[100] But closest to Farfa from this group would be fragments of a church at Doulon, near Nantes,[101] which has pilaster strips with blind arches and brick courses that are erratic in nature. One need not, of course, establish a direct link between Farfa and the lower Loire. The use of *opus mixtum* can be seen instead as a general movement that arose in certain centers with the availability of brick and late antique prototypes.

A strong indication that this may in fact have been the case is what may be termed the "classroom situation" of the remodeling of Trier Cathedral in the first half of the eleventh century. The core of the Constantinian cathedral was rebuilt ca. 380, under the auspices of the emperor Gratian, with a central square nave, low corner towers, and walls of *opus listatum*. A major transformation of the late antique structure was begun under Archbishop Poppo (1016–1047), when new piers, enveloping the late antique columns, and new arches were constructed using an *opus mixtum* masonry in obvious imitation of its ancient predecessor. Under Bishop Eberhardus (1047–1066), a western extension was built that repeated the basic elements of the late antique plan and elevation (alternating bays, central square space, and corner towers); *opus mixtum* was once again used for arches and piers, but cut stone was used for the walls.[102] Here, thus, is a test case, a conscious revival in both design and construction—a revival of selected elements and not a slavish copying—in a primary imperial and ecclesiastic monument, which may have played a considerable role in the popularization of the technique elsewhere. In sum, the *opus mixtum* masonry at Farfa, while related to pre-Romanesque precedents, is actually part of the building techniques current in the first half of the eleventh century north of the Alps, perhaps centered in Cologne and Trier, but with parallels in the heartland of France as well.

By 1100, Rome had also revived its own rich masonry tradition. *Opus mixtum* is found in parts of S. Bartolomeo all'Isola and S. Clemente, for example. And at S. Giovanni a Porta Latina (before 1191) and in the gatehouse of the monastery of Tre Fontane (ca. 1140), earlier medieval and twelfth-century *opus mixtum* are noticeably juxtaposed.[103] The decorative striking of the mortar, or *falsa cortina*, observed in the interior of the bell-tower base at Farfa is also a characteristic technique in Rome during this period, beginning with renovations of the lower church of S. Clemente from the second half of the eleventh century, probably carried out after the Norman sack of this section of the city in 1084.[104]

The practice of outlining blind arches in brick and setting a tile flat in their spandrels, found at both Farfa and S. Scolastica at Subiaco, followed a similar development. Again precedents may be sought in late antiquity. Brick triangles, for example, were used for the irregular space in the apex of the apse of S. Croce in Gerusalemme in Rome.[105] For the spandrels of arcades, though, bricks were either cut to fit or solid stone spandrels were used to support the intersecting brick arches. By ca. 800, irregularly cut, diamond-shaped bricks are set in the spandrels of the arcades in the brick masonry of important Carolingian-Lombard buildings, such as S. Salvatore at Brescia (all brick) and S. Maria at Cividale (stone with brick arches). Here, in the ninth century, there is still a structural logic, while at Farfa and Subiaco the motivation is purely decorative.

Similar to Farfa, however, are those portions of St. Pantaleon at Cologne that were added to the church at the end of the tenth century after the 980 dedication. As I have already mentioned, both the interior and exterior of the single-naved basilica were articulated by blind arcades. What is less often noted is that the stone voussoirs of the two westernmost interior arcades are outlined by single courses of brick. Furthermore, on the exterior of the westwork, bricks not only outline the arches of Lombard bands, but they have also been set flat to form diamond-shaped patterns in the spandrels. [106] At approximately the same time, bricks at S. Ambrogio in Milan were cut in the shape of elongated pentagons to fit the spandrels of the exterior eave niches (Plate 127). Once established, this practice continued into the eleventh century, as witness the bell tower at Pomposa (Plate 128), near the mouth of the Po just north of Ravenna, which is a particularly important example because it is securely dated by an inscription to 1063. [107] Moreover, Pomposa was an imperial abbey situated along the Adriatic not far from the Marches, where Farfa owned extensive property. Thus, there is again the sense that a decorative sensibility around the year 1000 has both revived and transformed a structural precedent set in late antiquity, which is then taken up by early Romanesque builders.

From a more general point of view, this is not simply a decorative approach to masonry but the important and gradual regularization of the masonry itself during the course of the eleventh century, as has already been well documented for Florence by Walter Horn. [108] It would seem to be equally valid for the rest of Italy as well, if one compares the rough masonry of Galliano, Agliate, and Ferentillo from the beginning of the century, for example, to the finely cut stone of the cathedrals of Pisa and Modena from the end. In fact, this regularization process may be clearly observed by the various masonry breaks in the exterior nave and aisle walls of the Pisan cathedral. For the north, a comparison could be made between the masonry of Ste.-Gertrude at Nivelles, St.-Remi at Reims, Limburg an der Haardt, and Speyer I and that of Cluny III, St.-Etienne at Caen, and Speyer II. Farfa, as one might expect, stands in the middle of this development, with a rough-hewn masonry that achieves a certain amount of regularity.

Interior Wall System of Engaged Columns and Blind Arcading. The use of square corner piers to sustain a groin vault in the interior ground floor of the Farfa bell tower is identical to that of S. Scolastica at Subiaco. The crossing and square presbytery at Farfa, however, exhibit a decidedly different system, employing engaged columns. Those wedged into the corners of the crossing may have supported a vault, groined as at St.-Martin at Aime, from the early eleventh century, or domed as at St.-Martin at Angers, from ca. 1075 (Plate 126), [109] but it seems more likely that they carried a blind arcade and wooden roof similar to that demonstrated for the adjoining square presbytery.

The interior wall system of the presbytery is of particular interest, since it seems to have been designed to serve both a structural and a decorative purpose. On the one hand, the elongated half-columns and blind arches help to sustain the otherwise extremely thin walls of the presbytery, while on the other, they subdivide the tall proportions of the interior through a complex interplay of vertical and horizontal accents. Thus, much like the exterior blind arcading of the presbytery, the interior system tests the plastic potential of the wall surface through an overlay of flat and curved planes. It should come as no surprise, therefore, to find that the same regions cited in my discussion of the exterior blind arcading played a role in the development of the interior wall system as well.

As I indicated earlier, there is a close connection between the development of interior and exterior wall articulation at St. Pantaleon (980), where the blind arcading of the exterior was repeated on the interior of the aisleless nave, albeit with slightly lower and broader proportions. This simple flat wall system of pilasters was taken over and elaborated in the transept and choir of the imperial abbey church of Limburg an der Haardt (1025–1042), where—in the square apse especially—monumental pilasters and blind arcades uniformly frame each window, dividing the elevation into three equal, vertical panels (Plate 129). Such a combination of the square presbytery design with the interior wall articulation may have been an important precedent for Farfa.

The use of applied orders at Limburg certainly served as an important impetus for their use in the twin Salian foundation of nearby Speyer Cathedral, established by Conrad II as the burial place for the new dynasty.[110] The first phase of Speyer Cathedral, generally known as Speyer I, was begun ca. 1030 and was presumably near completion by its consecration in 1061.[111] As reconstructed by Hans Kubach in his detailed monograph of the building, the transept of Speyer I displayed a giant order of pilasters supporting blind arcades, much like the arrangement at Limburg. More important, interior pilasters were carried over into the nave, applied to rectangular piers, and combined with half-columns, creating a scheme that has often been termed a "colossal order" (Plate 130).[112] The resemblance, however, between the nave at Speyer and the Farfa presbytery is more apparent than real. At Speyer there is a sophisticated union of half-column and rectangular pier with an intervening respond linked to the blind arcade, so that each member of the system (pier, respond, and engaged column) is clearly differentiated in function and profile. In this way, the Speyer system reveals its derivation from the tradition of giant pilasters at Limburg and St. Pantaleon at Cologne. Indeed, it is often alleged that the Speyer interior was inspired by the monumental blind arcading on the exterior of Constantine's basilica at Trier.[113] Be that as it may, at Farfa there is the simple union of wall and half-column without the intervening respond to carry the blind arcades, which clearly differentiates it from Speyer I and forces one to look elsewhere for the source of this concept.

Such a use of engaged columns could, of course, have been inspired by the monuments of Roman antiquity; the monumental applied orders of triumphal arches and city gates come first to mind. Also, the interiors of imperial baths and other public buildings, such as the Basilica of Maxentius in Rome (ca. 300), used mammoth columns along the walls of their vaulted halls. Yet in such cases, the diameters of the columns were increased in proportion to their height. In other words, the columns were not stretched over more than one storey; instead, they were simply made larger. Applied orders were also superimposed in late antiquity, as witness the interior of the mausoleum of Diocletian at Split, contemporary with the Basilica of Maxentius. This superimposed system was carried over into early Christian church interiors, especially in North Africa,[114] which may explain its persistence in southern France in the early Middle Ages at such churches as St.-Pierre in Vienne (fifth to seventh centuries) and St.-Laurent at Grenoble (eighth century).[115] Byzantine and Islamic architecture seems to have carried on this tradition. But in each case, the interior applied orders are stacked one above the other, so that they retain the clear demarcation of storeys. The idea of stretching a masonry column bonded with the wall over several storeys seems to have been alien to the classical logic inherent in late antique and Byzantine wall systems.

Regardless of its ultimate origins, the system of engaged columns and blind arcading as I have reconstructed it for Farfa should be distinguished from the "colossal order" of Speyer I by the absence of a respond. It is therefore worth noting that a more flexible approach to the engaged column without an intervening respond or pilaster was current in the middle of the eleventh century in both Burgundy and Italy. At St.-Hymetière in the Jura, for example, one of several churches related to the enigmatic church of St.-Philibert at Tournus, engaged columns that match the giant cylindrical piers of the nave form a blind arcade along the inner curve of the central apse.[116] Similarly, at St.-Hippolyte at Combertault, in the Côte d'Or near Beaune, engaged columns (more accurately described as engaged cylindrical piers) occur not only in the apse but on either side of the choir, forming a triple arcade.[117]

Equally important, by the middle of the eleventh century, the engaged columnar order appeared also in many parts of Italy. In the Piedmont in North Italy, for example, in the abbey church of S. Giusto at Susa, now the cathedral, engaged columns supporting blind arcades were set along the inner nave wall (albeit below the clerestory windows) when side aisles were added to the originally aisleless nave.[118] At Florence in Central Italy, the recently excavated remains of the church of S. Reparata reveal the lower halves of engaged columns without responds preserved along the interior of the apsidioles of two side chapels (Plate 131). Franklin Toker has shown that these side chapels do not belong to the original structure but were added later, most likely in the first half of the eleventh century, perhaps under Cluniac influence. The date of this modification is not certain, but it was presumably complete by 1055, when a synod was held in the church. [119] Influence from Burgundy in both the plan and elevation of the side chapels appears all the more likely when we consider that the reigning bishop, Gerard (1045–1059), later Pope Nicholas II (1059–1061), was himself a Burgundian.

Perhaps the most significant example preserved in Italy is the abbey church of S. Maria, on one of the Tremiti islands off the Gargano peninsula of northern Apulia. The monastery was founded in the early eleventh century while the region was still within the Byzantine political sphere. In 1037, however, the Tremiti islands came under the control of the Holy Roman Emperor Conrad II, and privileges granted to the abbey by him were subsequently renewed by Henry III in 1054. During this period, the abbey church was rebuilt "a novo fundamine," to quote one source, and consecrated in 1045. [120] The centrally planned abbey church at Tremiti may be seen as a synthesis of architectural influences from western Europe and Byzantium, which reflect its geographic location and historical background. [121] Of particular interest to this study is the interior nave elevation, where engaged columns rise from compound piers to support a triple arcade that frames individual clerestory windows (Plate 132), in an arrangement that bears a striking resemblance to the Farfa presbytery.

Although there is, as yet, no evidence to suggest that the abbeys of Farfa and S. Maria di Tremiti were in direct communication with one another, indications of at least indirect contact are not difficult to find. It is well known, for example, that Tremiti was closely associated with the monastery of Montecassino in the eleventh century. [122] Farfa, too, had direct contacts with Montecassino, as shown most obviously by the visit of its abbot, Desiderius, to Farfa in 1059. [123] Another connection comes in the person of Argyros, *catepan* of the Byzantine empire's possessions in South Italy and self-styled *dux Italiae*, who was not only closely associated with the abbey at Tremiti but who also sent gifts to Farfa in 1057, so as to be remembered in the prayers of the brotherhood. [124]

Nevertheless, regardless of whether or not the abbeys of Tremiti and Farfa were in direct contact with one another, a common source presumably lies behind their use of the same interior wall system. At Tremiti, the combination of engaged columns with quadrilobe piers, which are distinctively Lombard in origin, points to North Italy as the primary source of influence. [125] At Farfa, too, as I have shown, elements in the design of the east end—such as the twin bell towers and exterior blind arcading—find close comparisons in North Italy.

In general terms, then, the system of engaged columns and blind arcading at Farfa may be seen to be in keeping with architectural currents in Italy, Burgundy, and the Rhineland in the middle of the eleventh century. More specifically, however, the simple union of the wall and column without an intervening respond at Farfa places it within the development of interior wall systems centered in Burgundy and Italy, a development that may be seen as parallel to, but separate from, the appearance of the so-called colossal order at Speyer I. [126]

Liturgy and the Transmission of Architectural Forms

As I pointed out in the first chapter of this study, the Farfa Customary was taken directly from Cluny as a result of the monastic reform carried out at Farfa under Abbot Hugo (998–1039). Furthermore, the prologue and preface of the text are explicit about the circumstances under which the customary was compiled. Johannes, a monk from nearby Montopoli and a former disciple of Romualdus of Ravenna, went to Cluny "trans Alpium" in order to study ("ad videndum et scribendum") the customs of the monastery, because they were followed "in Gallia" and were renowned "per totum orbem."[127] Although the contact between Farfa and Cluny was initiated by Abbot Hugo, the manuscript of the Customary preserved today was clearly written after his death in 1039, which is mentioned in the necrology. The last historical references in the text date to ca. 1050, and the first marginal note refers to an event in 1087; thus, the manuscript in the Vatican Library was copied sometime during the reign of Abbot Berardus (1047–1089).

What is of interest here, of course, are the architectural implications of the Farfa Customary. First of all, the process of literary transmission involving contact with both Ravenna in North Italy and Cluny in Burgundy coincides with the general direction of influence I have suggested for the design of the east end of the abbey church at Farfa. Second, the insertion in the text of a list of books distributed at Lent and the famous description of the monastery are both considered exceptional for a customary, but their inclusion makes sense when considered from the point of view of Farfa at the time. A list of books would serve as a selected inventory of the Cluny library. Far more information about the monastery of Cluny is provided by the description of its layout, which has often been likened to the Plan of St. Gall in literary form.[128] And like the Plan of St. Gall the description of Cluny may have been composed as much at the instigation of the recipient as of the sender. In other words, the compilation of the Farfa Customary should be seen in the context of a major building campaign at the Italian monastery. Third, the description of Cluny represents one of the many ways in which knowledge of architectural developments north of the Alps could have been transmitted to an abbey in Central Italy.

A primary motivation behind the compilation of monastic customaries was a concern for uniformity in liturgical practice, and the reforms of the tenth and eleventh centuries, emanating from Gorze-Trier in the Lorraine and Cluny in Burgundy, placed ever-increasing emphasis on the liturgical aspect of religious life.[129] The daily horarium of the monk became a busy round of elaborate offices and ceremonials, with little time set aside for manual labor.[130] The abbey church was, of course, the focus of this activity, yet there has been relatively little research into the relationship between architecture and liturgy during this period of monastic reform.[131] Admittedly, this is a difficult area for investigation. While many customaries contain detailed instructions for the celebration of the great feasts of the church calendar, rarely do they mention specific architectural features and even then only in the vaguest terms.

At the beginning of this century, however, Adolf Mettler tried to show that the architectural characteristics of the *Hirsauer Bauschule* could be explained as having been transmitted from Cluny through the adoption of a Cluniac customary.[132] I have already noted certain similarities in plan and elevation between the eleventh-century church at Farfa and the churches of the Hirsau movement. A common link with Cluny could explain these similarities. But Mettler was working at a time when archaeological information about the design of Cluny II was unavailable, and subsequent studies of the architecture of the Cluniac Order, particularly the results of the excavations of the abbey of Cluny directed by Kenneth Conant, demonstrate that Mettler's thesis was over simplistic.[133] This is not to say, however, that Cluniac influence was altogether lacking. The choirs flanking the presbytery of St. Aurelius or SS. Peter and Paul at Hirsau are best explained as coming from Cluny II. Yet the church of SS. Peter and Paul (1083–1091), which was built at the time of the importation of the Cluniac customary to Hirsau by Abbot William between 1085 and 1090, shows little else in common with Cluny II.[134] The obvious conclusion is that liturgical dependency did not necessitate architectural dependency. The reason for this may simply be that the origin of the customs and the origin of the masons did not coincide. I have already demonstrated that the designs of both Hirsau and Farfa seem to be derived instead from a common heritage in the monastic architecture of the empire, emanating most likely from the Lorraine region.

Mettler's pioneering research, recently elaborated upon by Friedrich Möbius, remains of value nonetheless in helping us to understand the function of various parts of the abbey church.[135] In the Farfa Customary and the related, though slightly later, *Ordo Cluniacensis* by Bernhard, distinctions are made between three main divisions of the church: the *presbyterium*, in which stand the main altar or altars and officiants of the mass; the *chorus*, where the monks are seated according to rank to sing the psalms; and the *nave*.[136] The first two divisions relate to the apse and crossing. In the case of Farfa, the main altar stood in the square presbytery, and the *chorus* of monks in the crossing. Furthermore, the nave, choir, and presbytery each seem to have been differentiated progressively by a slightly higher level requiring one or more steps, recalling the changes in floor level I have reconstructed for Farfa based on independent archaeological evidence.[137]

Of particular interest, too, are the frequent references in these texts to the use of bells to announce the masses and to emphasize dramatic moments in the liturgy.[138] It should also be mentioned that the oldest customary associated with St. Maximin at Trier, a Gorze affiliate and dating to the same time as the construction of the church in the mid-tenth century, devotes the first third of its text to instructions for the appropriate times to ring bells.[139] This raises the issue of the placement of these bells. It seems reasonable to suppose that, in order to coordinate the ringing of bells with the liturgy, the bell ringers needed to be aware of the action in the presbytery. At Cluny II and related churches, the bells seem to have been assembled in a central crossing tower. But this arrangement could have proved awkward with bell ringers standing in the midst of the *chorus*. The problem is resolved, however, by placing the bells in towers flanking the choir, as was presumably the case at St. Maximin in Trier. This arrangement can be seen today at S. Abbondio in Como, where one can still see and pull the bell cords in the chapels of the side bell towers. [140] The same was true of the ground floor of the Farfa bell tower until the introduction of an electronic system a few years ago. Thus, liturgical customs explain the need for one or more bell towers, but they do not specify their placement. This was determined presumably by the desires of the monastic community based on a variety of factors, such as local building tradition, outside influences, or purely practical considerations.

Although helpful for understanding the general function of the plan of the east end at Farfa, the Cluniac customary was but one means of influence. As I have indicated, specific details of the design of the church at Farfa are rooted more in the monastic architecture of the center of the empire than in that of Burgundy. [141] In retrospect, this is not surprising, for Farfa was at one and the same time an important imperial abbey and a monastery reformed by Cluny. Farfa was never a Cluniac dependency, however. While Cluny in Burgundy prospered in part because of its independence from secular rule, owing allegiance only to the distant pope, Farfa, in Central Italy, was in the exact opposite position. Farfa could not forsake its alliance with the emperor, as patron and lord, without inviting the encroachment of the papal patrimony into the Sabina.

Summary

No single monument seems to have served as the principal model for the design and construction of the eastern complex at Farfa. I have, therefore, followed the sources and development of important individual features in the hope of determining some common ground. In spite of what may seem at first to be a disparate assemblage of monuments from all parts of medieval Europe, one glance at the map shows a notable concentration of comparative examples in North Italy and in northern Europe within the confines of the Holy Roman Empire (Map 4). That Farfa should have had close ties with these areas should not be surprising. Since it was an imperial abbey, Farfa would have had direct contacts with the major ecclesiastical centers of the Western Empire—we need only recall the numerous journeys made by Abbot Berardus (1048–1089), during whose reign the east end was presumably built, to attend the imperial court.

MAP 4. Western Europe in the eleventh century, with locations of comparative monuments for the early Romanesque abbey church

The immediate source for the design would seem to be in North Italy and the regions of the Alpine passes, for here we find the use of twin eastern bell towers (Aosta, Ivrea, Aime, and Moûtiers), exterior blind arcading (Romainmôtier, Galliano, Pavia, Acqui, and Torcello), decorative use of brick (Milan and Pomposa), and perhaps the colossal order (Susa). Even the triangular capitals or *pulvini* of the bell towers at Farfa find close comparisons to carved capitals in the same area (Plates 68–69, 70a–b, 135).[142] Only the square presbytery finds no counterpart in North Italy. All of these features, however, can be found north of the Alps as well, particularly between the Meuse and Rhine Valleys to the east and west and in parts of Burgundy to the south—in other words, within Lotharingia. Indeed, the dates of the monuments suggest that the arrangement of a square presbytery flanked by chapels surmounted by bell towers may have originated there. The Lombard building tradition, therefore, may have been instrumental in transmitting such new developments from the north into Italy.[143]

The Lorraine, after all, was the center of monastic reform within the empire, and, together with imperial patronage, the reform movement seems to have influenced the design of the great abbey churches of St. Pantaleon in Cologne and Limburg an der Haardt. The city of Trier has appeared prominently in my discussion because that is where monastic reform and imperial patronage converged, at the abbey church of St. Maximin, second in importance only to Gorze itself, and in the remodeling of the early Christian cathedral in the course of the eleventh century. Trier was also the city of Constantine in the north, and the cathedral was considered in the Middle Ages to occupy the site of the house of his mother (*domus Sanctae Helenae*).[144] Furthermore, the upper Lorraine that corresponds to the diocese of the archbishop of Trier has been identified as a *Trierer Kunstraum*,[145] and this concept allows us to delineate the area from which Farfa may ultimately have drawn its inspiration. Our outlook should not be influenced by the confrontation between the empire and the papacy during the Investiture Controversy of the latter part of the eleventh century. In the first half of the same century, we are dealing with a period in medieval history when imperial policy and Church reform were one and the same, as epitomized by the emperor Henry III and his cousin, Bruno, bishop of Toul in the Lorraine, whom he selected to be pope (Leo IX, 1049–1054).

The rebuilding of the abbey church at Farfa in the middle of the eleventh century seems, therefore, to have resulted from a synthesis of architectural currents, emanating from the ecclesiastical centers of the western empire, that were promoted by both monastic reform and imperial patronage. Yet these features were translated at Farfa into a local idiom through the use of tufa, indigenous to the Sabine region, as the primary building material. Thus, if many of the ideas came from the north, they were carried out by local masons. There is no information about the structure of the work force, but it seems likely that the same workmen were active at Subiaco and that they had been trained at the earlier projects of Monte Amiata and Ferentillo; at least, they came out of that tradition. We may further suppose that construction was supervised by one or more master masons from the north, be it North Italy or the heartland of the empire. Abbot Berardus and members of his entourage were undoubtedly well acquainted with many of the monuments I have cited through their extensive travels, during which they may have acquired descriptions of other abbeys, whether written or drawn, like the one of Cluny in the Farfa Customary. While the exact process of the transmission must remain conjectural, it may safely be assumed that there was ample opportunity for knowledge of many of these comparative monuments to have reached Farfa and for their cumulative message to have been translated into stone and mortar.

Interestingly enough, the new building at Farfa seems to have had no immediate following. It may be that the design was too "alien" or too novel to be accepted readily in Central Italy, although it should be pointed out that little is known about contemporary building at the various Farfa dependencies. Nevertheless, Farfa and its neighbor Subiaco may have been influential in other ways, in that their bell towers predate the Romanesque *campanili* of Rome. The bell tower of the church of S. Bartolomeo all'Isola in Rome from ca. 1100, for example, has the same triple-arched openings, brick cornices, and stone corbels as the tower of S. Scolastica at Subiaco, except that these features have been refined and translated into the traditional brick masonry technique of medieval Rome (Plate 133). Once established, this type evolved on its own in the course of the twelfth century, as at S. Maria in Cosmedin and SS. Giovanni e Paolo, becoming one of the most striking features of the urban landscape of the eternal city in the Middle Ages.[146] In this way, Farfa and Subiaco may have served as important links between Rome and the north, due both to their geographic location and to their role as major artistic centers in the middle of the eleventh century.

THE MONASTIC LAYOUT

There is no literary source for the appearance of the abbey in the eleventh century comparable to Abbot Hugo's description of the Carolingian monastery. But there is reliable archaeological evidence for a process of rebuilding after the abbey's abandonment in the late ninth century and reestablishment in the tenth.

A clear horizontal break exists in the masonry of the curved wall (Fig. 12, No. 1, Plate 80) that shows it was heightened ca. 0.50 m. with rubblework far cruder than the masonry below. The central opening in the wall was blocked with the same crude masonry, and the northern end of the wall was extended ca. 2.5. m. The shallow footings of the portico along the south side of the atrium were replaced by a series of rectangular piers of coarse rubble, interspersed at intervals of ca. 3 m. The straight wall projecting from the end of the south arm of the transept (Fig. 12, No. 5, Plate 79) was also patched and heightened by several centimeters. Between the wall and the rectangular piers, fragments of marble paving slabs were found in situ, resting on a fine bed of green clay (Fig. 12). Immediately below one of the slabs was found a silver coin minted during the reign of the emperor Otto III (983–1002), which indicates that the remodeling of this area was undertaken either during the abbacy of John III (963–998) or Hugo (998–1039).[147] The historical background, however, suggests a more precise dating, for the Register tells us that in 999 Otto III issued a *privilegium* in person during a visit to the monastery,[148] and it may well be that the coin, so conspicuously placed directly under the marble paving, was meant to commemorate this event. At some later date, the rectangular piers were themselves replaced by a second set of shallow footings that cut into the westernmost of the preserved piers.

As noted in the last chapter, the remains of the apsed structure or chapel to the south of the atrium were built up against an earlier medieval wall with traces of fresco decoration (Fig. 12, Nos. 9, 10, Fig. 15). There is no specific archaeological evidence to date the chapel, but its masonry, composed of small, roughly hewn tufa and limestone blocks, is identical to that of the interior of the bell tower; there are even traces of the same crude, horizontal pointing (or *falsa cortina*) of the mortar. Similar, too, is the placement of several courses of brick at the springing of the vaults. Today, such bricks can be seen at the top of the respond bonded to the northern half of the apse (Plate 77). A photograph taken in 1935 shows that remains of the chapel were visible above ground (Plate 74), including the springing of the vault in the northwest corner at the back of the chapel. Here the use of bricks wedged between two arches of the vault composed of small limestone voussoirs compares closely to that seen in photographs of the vault of the bell tower taken before the restoration campaign (Plate 33). The chapel may, therefore, be dated to approximately the same time as the bell tower, which would mean the middle of the eleventh century.

The plan of the chapel shows that it was divided into two approximately equal square compartments by projecting stepped piers. This arrangement was dictated in part by the earlier wall, in that the pier along the northern wall is placed so as to envelop the shallow pilaster of the wall it has been built up against (Figs. 12, 15, Plate 76). The chapel was entered through a door, now blocked up, in the south wall of the western bay. To the east, the exterior of the apse seems to have been flat, although the masonry is broken at this point by a later wall set on a north-south axis. Originally, there may have been a splayed window, with a width of ca. 1 m., piercing the apex of the apse slightly off axis (Fig. 12, No. 10). The smooth masonry of the interior facing of the window is preserved on the right (south) side, but it has been broken away on the left; this presumably occurred when the crude set of stairs was inserted during the stable phase.

Patches of painted plaster on the inner surface of the apse show that it was once painted in vivid yellows, reds, and greens with a loose brushstroke reminiscent of the palette and painterly technique of the bell-tower frescoes. Emerging from behind the later stairs are traces of fresco composed of white intonaco bearing black and red diagonal lines, indicating that the lowest zone of the apse was decorated with simulated curtains. Sections of a curved cornice found in the rubble filling the chapel may also have belonged to the structure originally (Plate 86). In short, although small in scale, the chapel was originally vaulted and richly decorated. Aside from the five subsidiary chapels mentioned in the description of the Carolingian abbey, the Register contains documents from the mid-eleventh century that mention two other chapels, one dedicated to St. Benedict and another to the Holy Cross.[149] But no information exists for determining the specific dedication of the excavated chapel.

The chapel was clearly connected to other structures to the east and west. The south wall ends as a spur that was reworked at some later date into a tapering buttress. To the north, two short rubble walls meet at right angles to form a rectangular recess that was used for dumping refuse in the sixteenth through eighteenth centuries (Fig. 12, No. 13). Originally, however, there must have been another vaulted chamber abutting the chapel to the west, as is indicated by the responds wedged into the northeast and southeast corners (Fig. 12, No. 14).

The south wall of the chapel aligns with the series of masonry foundations discovered below the entrance of the Renaissance church by the Superintendency in 1959 and included in the published plan of their excavations (Figs. 15, 17). When first discovered, these walls were interpreted as remains of the fortifications mentioned in Abbot Hugo's description of the Carolingian abbey and believed to have been built during the reign of Abbot Sichardus (ca. 830–842).[150] Several factors bring this assumption into question, however. First of all, the common alignment and similarity in masonry between these remains and the chapel indicate that they are coeval, meaning that these walls were built in the eleventh century rather than the ninth. Second, the walls are too thin to have served as fortification walls by themselves. Third, the spiral staircase and adjoining vaulted spaces, indicated by the presence of corner responds, extend to the south beyond the supposed line of fortifications. A more reasonable solution would be to see these walls as part of a two-storey structure, requiring a staircase, that was set parallel to the abbey church and linked to the chapel. The exact function of this building must remain conjectural, but it may have been a monumental guesthouse or a gateway of some kind.

There is little in the layout of the abbey in the eleventh century that can be compared to the description of Cluny in the Farfa Customary or to the remains of the Burgundian abbey as excavated by Kenneth Conant (Fig. 15, Plate 134).[151] The topography of the two sites is so totally different (Cluny lies on a flat plain, whereas Farfa is set on a narrow terrace of a hillside), that we should not expect the same arrangement of buildings. Nor have the remains of the Farfa cloister yet been found. It presumably lay to the north as it does today rather than along the southern flank of the abbey church, the traditional position for a medieval cloister. Of the few remains of the eleventh-century phase of Cluny that Conant was able to uncover, only the chapel dedicated to the Virgin provides any analogies to the layout at Farfa. The plan of the Lady Chapel is similar to the Farfa chapel, even though it is twice the size; moreover, the remains of internal pilasters indicate that it was vaulted, and there is even evidence to suggest that the apse was flat on the outside as at Farfa.[152] Nevertheless, comparable chapels must have formed part of many, if not all, major monastic complexes. Thus, the excavations have so far provided no direct evidence to link the monastic layout at Farfa to that of Cluny. My analysis of the rebuilding of the abbey church in the eleventh century has produced similar results. Still, one should bear in mind that the reconstruction of Cluny in this early period is highly speculative, since it is based primarily on the description of the monastery in the Farfa Customary.[153] Much more information about both sites is needed before the final word can be said.

In sum, the current excavations, together with those carried out twenty years earlier by the Superintendency, show that the abbey was indeed rebuilt in the eleventh century during the abbacies of Hugo (998–1039) and Berardus (1048–1089) as the historical sources would suggest. But only further excavations can reveal the full extent of this rebuilding.

6

The Later Middle Ages
and Early Renaissance

THE PROJECT FOR A NEW ABBEY

In spite of the building activity of the mid-eleventh century, in 1097 Abbot Berardus II found the monastery to be "decrepit with age" and proclaimed that a new abbey should be built at the summit of Monte Acuziano, now Monte S. Martino.[1] The sorry state of the abbey church and the monastic buildings concurs with my earlier suggestion that only the east end of the church had been rebuilt before the consecration of 1060; the 1978–1983 excavations have revealed a similar piecemeal approach to the remodeling of subsidiary buildings. Berardus's decision was no doubt motivated by strategic considerations as well: a hilltop location would make the monastery more easily defendable. At the end of the eleventh century Farfa was deeply embroiled in the Investiture Controversy, with a tyrannical abbot who inspired open dissent and concern over policy toward the ambitions of the papacy and local nobles. A *milites abbatiae* of vassals was organized to protect the monastery and its land holdings from outside encroachment.[2] Berardus's sponsorship of the Farfa Register with its compilation of *privilegia* and deeds could also be considered a defensive act. From a broader perspective, this project was in keeping with the general tendency in the region during the tenth and eleventh centuries that favored hilltop settlements for defensive purposes, in a process which Pierre Toubert has termed "incastellamento."[3]

Whatever the reason, the scheme of Berardus II seems foolhardy in the extreme, particularly from the point of view of the movement of men and materials. Still, an equally daring feat had been accomplished little more than a generation before in the rebuilding of the abbey church at Montecassino under Desiderius between 1066 and 1071, and Berardus may well have had this precedent in mind. In order to carry out this task, Berardus called upon Farfa's dependencies to provide the revenues and manpower, some four hundred workmen in all.[4] But the project was quickly abandoned following Berardus's death in 1099.[5] It was revived by Abbot Adenolfus in 1142,[6] but he, too, died within two years, and work was again aborted.

The remains of the ill-fated project are still visible today. The church was little more than a hollow shell at Berardus's death; what, if any, part of these ruins should be attributed to the brief revival of the project by Adenolfus cannot be determined. On the southeastern edge of the summit of Monte S. Martino stand the ruins of the unfinished church, its outer walls preserved in some places to a height of more than 12 m. (Plate 87a). The scale of the plan is equally impressive, with an overall length of approximately 70 m. and a width of 25 m. (Fig. 18). The east end is composed of a central apse and a broad, non-projecting transept containing a hall crypt with vaulting sustained by four square piers. The vast main body of the church, separated from the transept by two massive T-shaped piers, was presumably to be divided into a nave and side aisles by two colonnades, although there is no trace of these interior supports. The west end terminates in the square bases of two towers set flush with the exterior façade. (The thickness of the outer walls averages 1.5 m., that of the apse walls increases to 4 m.) The masonry is crude for the most part, a mortared rubble faced with unhewn stones of varying sizes and shapes. Quarried blocks are used only for the piers at the head of the nave and for window surrounds (Plate 87b). The paucity of cut stone may relate to the logistical difficulties of the site; it also suggests the hurried nature of the project.

The most striking elements of the design are the presence of the hall crypt and the two-tower façade. Croquison, who was the first to study the monument, suggested that the idea for the façade came from the abbey church on the hillside below.[7] But as I have shown, the design of the older church was decidedly different, with its towers flanking not the western entrance but the eastern presbytery. Thümmler published a schematic plan of these ruins and compared the design of the west façade to that of S. Salvatore at Monte Amiata, seeing both monuments as the result of influence from northern Europe.[8] Premoli reiterates Thümmler's analysis, and she refers also to the subsequent study of the development of the two-tower façade in Romanesque architecture by Herwin Schaeffer as further evidence that the scheme originated in the Upper Rhineland.[9] The cathedrals at Basel and Strasbourg, together with the abbey church at Limburg an der Haardt, all from the first half of the eleventh century, are among the most important examples that could be cited.

By the middle of the century, the scheme appeared in Normandy at Nôtre-Dame at Jumièges and St.-Etienne at Caen, and from there it was imported to South Italy, first at S. Nicola in Bari (begun 1087), in the wake of Norman conquests.[10] The two-tower façade was never used in Rome, and the hall crypt, present at both Monte Amiata and Bari, did not appear in Rome until after 1100 and is seen first in the early twelfth-century churches of SS. Bonifacio ed Alessio and S. Bartolomeo all'Isola.[11] Thus, the design of the unfinished abbey church on Monte S. Martino, like its predecessor on the hillside below, seems to be the result of continued contact with the architectural currents of northern Europe in general and the Rhineland in particular.

THE TWELFTH CENTURY

With the difficulty of relocating the abbey all too apparent, building activity seems to have focused again on the old abbey church. The four ionic capitals of the left colonnade of the Renaissance church are unquestionably work of the first half of the twelfth century (Plate 88a–b). Rome in this period saw a renaissance in which marble workshops began turning to classical models for many aspects of church decoration. A number of churches, beginning with S. Clemente (ca. 1100–1130) favored the ionic order for interior and exterior colonnades.[12] Indeed, the form and decoration of the capitals at Farfa are less-elaborate versions of the capitals found in the narthex of SS. Giovanni e Paolo in Rome from 1154 (Plate 136).[13] Almost exact duplicates of the capitals at Farfa are found in the nave of the abbey church of S. Andrea in Flumine, near Ponzano Romano in the Sabina, only a few kilometers north of Farfa, a building that has been recently dated to ca. 1140–1150.[14] The original use of the capitals at Farfa, together with their gray granite shafts, is unknown. Again, there is no evidence for aisles in the medieval abbey church; however, their prominent use for narthex porches in Rome (S. Lorenzo in Lucina, SS. Giovanni e Paolo, S. Lorenzo f.l.m., and S. Giorgio in Velabro) suggests that the ionic capitals may have served a similar purpose at Farfa as well, which would also explain why only four capitals were available for reuse in the Renaissance church.[15]

There is additional evidence for the presence of Roman marble workers at Farfa during this period. Before the 1959–1962 restoration campaign, the crossing of the Renaissance church was paved by a number of large plaques, inlaid with colored stone and glass tesserae in roundel and interlace patterns characteristic of the art of the so-called Cosmati, the generic term for craftsmen who produced pavements and church furniture in Rome and Lazio throughout the twelfth and thirteenth centuries (Plate 89).[16] When the cosmatesque plaques were taken up by the Superintendency, the Carolingian *opus sectile* pavement discussed in chapter 4 was found underneath them. Moreover, the back of one of the panels bears the epitaph of Abbot Sichardus, showing that the marble slab of the Carolingian inscription had been reused for the cosmatesque work. Eight panels are preserved in all, varying in size from 0.81 by 1.87 m. to 0.93 by 1.32 m., together with three vertical blocks, averaging 88–89 cm. high, that have deep side grooves (Plate 90). Clearly, the ensemble did not originate as a pavement. Edward Hutton and Dorothy Glass suggest the panels belonged to an ambo,[17] but the rectangular shape of the panels suggests instead that they formed a chancel screen, similar to the kind preserved from the first half of the twelfth century in the church of S. Andrea in Flumine and the cathedral of Ferentino.[18] In addition, the inscription on the border of one of the vertical blocks at Farfa bears the inscription: MAGISTER RAIN. HOC OPUS FECIT (Plate 89), which may allude to Rainerius (also called Ranucius), who was a marble worker active in Rome in the second quarter of the twelfth century and whose descendants constitute a well-known family of cosmatesque artists.[19]

The remains of the second layer of Romanesque frescoes in the square presbytery may also belong to the same restoration campaign. I noted in chapter 3 that in the lower northeast corner of the presbytery two distinct medieval layers are preserved. The first layer is too fragmentary for its subject matter to be identified; only the bright palette of primary colors and loose brushstrokes indicate its contemporaneity with the frescoes of the bell tower. The style of the second layer, on the other hand, as represented by the Assumption of the Virgin and the Last Judgment, exhibits a complex system of drapery folds and geometric highlights that is far more elaborate than anything found in either of the so-called Styles I and II of the tower frescoes. For example, instead of the impressionistic blending of colors that characterizes Style II, the drapery folds of the seated apostles are accented by a network of bright white highlights that form closely nested V-patterns over the forearms, tear drops at the knees, and swirling patterns about the abdomen (Plate 64b). Their complexity and segmentation approximates the cellular highlights of the angels in the apse frescoes of S. Pietro in Tuscania (ca. 1125–1150).[20]

Both the style and iconography of the Last Judgment scene at Farfa find an exact parallel in the middle register of the famous Last Judgment panel in the Vatican Pinacoteca (Plates 64a, 137). Wilhelm Paesler was the first to recognize the innovative quality of the scene, where Christ is represented as a celebrant before an altar rather than as a judge upon a throne. At Farfa, the section representing the altar has been lost, but the gold cross shown against Christ's chest is best understood as the upper portion of a metal cross set on an altar in front of Christ as shown in the Vatican panel (Plates 64a, 137). Thus, in each case Christ has become both *sacerdos et sacrificium*, which formed part of the doctrine of transubstantiation proclaimed at the Fourth Lateran Council of 1215.[21] Paesler therefore concluded that the Vatican panel could not have been executed before that date. E. B. Garrison, on the other hand, points out that while the formal doctrine of transubstantiation may not have become official dogma until the thirteenth century, the concept was current throughout the twelfth.[22] Indeed, early formulations of the concept of transubstantiation may be traced back to the eucharistic controversy of the late eleventh century and the writings of Lanfranc (d. 1089).[23]

In terms of style, Garrison sees the abstract system of highlights on the drapery of the apostles as displaying "a facility, a versatility and a virtuosity far beyond the powers of the S. Elia (near Nepi) frescoists" or the painters of contemporary works in Rome from ca. 1100 or slightly later. Consequently, he concludes that the panel must date to a period between 1140 and 1180. The Vatican panel helps to explain the context of the Farfa fresco as well, because the panel was designed to serve as an altarpiece (Plate 137). At Farfa, the figure of Christ had to be placed to the right of center in order to avoid the engaged column in the middle of the east wall, but its general location on the end wall of the presbytery made the relationship between the image of Christ's sacrifice and mass at the main altar clear to all.

Taken together, the ionic capitals, the cosmatesque panels, and the Last Judgment fresco represent a significant restoration of the abbey church in the middle of the twelfth century. The most likely patron for such an enterprise would have been Abbot Adenolfus (1125–1144), who strengthened Farfa's ties with Rome following the Investiture Controversy and who was named a cardinal of the Church by 1138. We should recall, too, that in 1145 Pope Eugenius III was consecrated at Farfa. In brief, these works may be an expression of the abbey's new and close alliance with the papacy. They also represent the last known restoration campaign of the abbey church in the Middle Ages.

THE FIFTEENTH CENTURY

The presbytery of the medieval abbey church was decorated twice in the fifteenth century. The first campaign involved relining the monumental arch between the square presbytery and the crossing with a new set of limestone voussoirs. The soffit was then painted with busts of Christ and the apostles in a late trecento style that would seem to be in keeping with the consecration of the main altar in 1401 (Plate 62). Under the commendatory Giovanni Orsini (1435–1476), however, the presbytery was entirely repainted, as shown by his stemma that appears on the jambs of one of the windows (Plate 58a). Interestingly enough, the new program closely followed the iconography of the Romanesque Last Judgment, with the fifteenth-century apostles differentiated from their medieval predecessors only by their illusionistic style (Plate 66). Several figures from this zone have been detached from the wall and can be seen in the monastery's museum. Although the remains of these frescoes are extremely fragmentary, we can see that Christ was again represented with his arms outstretched (only the right hand is preserved) to reveal the nail holes in his hands (Plate 91a). Now, though, he seems to be standing in front of an altar rather than behind it. Also, the angels that flanked Christ in the Romanesque representation have been replaced by two very different figures. On Christ's left stood John the Baptist, recognizable by his hair shirt (Plate 91b), while the robed figure on Christ's right is presumably the Virgin Mary (Plate 91a), completing the traditional deesis composition. Thus, the hieratic medieval scene of ritual sacrifice and judgment has been transformed in the quattrocento into a more human and emotional rendering of intercession, on the part of the Virgin Mary and John the Baptist, for the forgiveness of mankind.

The lyric gestures, soft modeling, and crisp outline of these figures resemble the style of followers of the school of Benozzo Gozzoli, such as Lorenzo da Viterbo (ca. 1444–ca. 1476) and Fiorenzo di Lorenzo (ca. 1440–1522), who were both active in Umbria and Lazio in the second half of the fifteenth century.[24] In fact, the three prophets and one evangelist on the soffits of the two lunettes of the west wall of the presbytery (Plate 65), which are among the best-preserved figures in the program, compare closely to the saints and prophets represented in similar architectural frames on the soffit of the entrance archway to the Cappella Mazzatosta of S. Maria della Verità in Viterbo, part of a fresco cycle signed and dated by Lorenzo da Viterbo in 1469 (Plate 138).[25] It seems reasonable to suppose, therefore, that the paintings at Viterbo and Farfa are roughly contemporaneous, if not the products of the same workshop.

These Renaissance modifications represented an act of reverence for the medieval church without altering the fabric of the building. In like manner, the scene of the Last Judgment was retained on the east wall of the presbytery, its style and iconography simply brought up to date. But a new coat of paint could not correct the structural defects of the aging medieval church, nor could the patchwork nature of its design satisfy the architectural ideals of the late quattrocento. In addition, as I indicated in chapter 2, the needs of the abbey had changed. Within a generation of this work, the medieval abbey church was torn down, and the Benedictine abbey of Farfa entered a new era in its architectural development.

7

Conclusion

My analysis has spanned almost a millenium of building activity at Farfa, from the sixth century to the 1490s. It has shown that the architectural remains of the abbey, although fragmentary, have much to tell us when examined with care. Indeed, a convergence of factors—archaeological, historical, and stylistic—has allowed me to reconstruct the major phases in the abbey's physical development and in so doing to provide a rare insight into the formation of one of Europe's most important monastic centers in the early Middle Ages.

The basic sequence of events can be outlined as follows:

1. Scattered Arretine pottery, reused ancient sculpture and building materials, traces of an *opus reticulatum* wall, and a grave containing a coin of the emperor Trajan (98–117) provide evidence of an ancient Roman habitation of the site, presumably in the form of a villa or farmhouse.

2. Tegulated graves and associated artifacts, together with carbon-14 dating, attest to a Christian settlement of the site by the middle of the sixth century.

3. At the end of the seventh century, Thomas of Maurienne came upon the abandoned ruins of a basilica and atrium, in which he established a monastic community. Concomitantly, the nave of the medieval abbey church seems to

have been standing by the late eighth century, if not earlier, and it may have formed an aisleless hall with a funerary chapel along its northern flank.

4. Abbot Sichardus (830–842) extensively refurbished the monastery. Above all, he added an oratory to the west end of the abbey church that took the form of a continuous transept, semicircular apse, and annular crypt that housed relics brought from Rome by Pope Gregory IV (827–844). At the same time, Sichardus remodeled the western atrium, so that its eastern portico circumscribed the new western apse.

5. By the end of the ninth century, the monastery reportedly contained, in addition to the abbey church and atrium, five subsidiary churches, a cloister, workrooms, covered walkways, and a palace for visits by the emperor, all surrounded by massive fortification walls.

6. By the year 1000, following the abbey's abandonment ca. 897 and re-establishment in the early tenth century, the atrium of the abbey church was rebuilt with rectangular piers and marble paving.

7. In the middle of the eleventh century, the east end of the abbey church was rebuilt in the form of a square presbytery flanked by bell towers, presumably complete by the consecration of the two main altars in 1060. At approximately the same time, other subsidiary structures were built, including a small vaulted chapel that was inserted in the remains of an earlier frescoed room.

8. In the middle of the twelfth century, the abbey church was remodeled, with a cosmatesque chancel screen, a new fresco cycle in the presbytery, and ionic capitals that may have belonged to a western narthex.

9. Between 1492 and 1496, the nave and west end of the medieval abbey church were dismantled to make way for a new abbey church that is still in use today.

Farfa's earliest years remain obscure. The final analysis of the artifacts and related archaeological material from the 1978–1983 excavations will undoubtedly provide further information about this period, which may in turn necessitate some revisions to my hypothetical reconstruction of the abbey in its pre-Carolingian phase. Still, the clear evidence for an early Christian settlement of the site has lent new credence to the legendary founding of the monastery by Lawrence of Syria, as recounted in the Farfa Chronicle. Knowledge of the Carolingian and early Romanesque phases of the monastery's development is now far more complete, and it is in these phases that Farfa's place in the history of medieval architecture may be appreciated most fully.

The work sponsored by Abbot Sichardus adds substantially to present knowledge of building in the ninth century. The complex of a projecting transept and annular crypt built at the west end of the abbey church fits in well with the understanding of the Carolingian revival of the plan of Old St. Peter's, both in Rome and north of the Alps. The design of the atrium, on the other hand, with its eastern portico curving about the western apse, has no counterpart in Italy and is known only from ecclesiastical centers in the north, such as the abbey of Fulda, the cathedral of Cologne, and as represented on the Plan of St. Gall. In each case, it served as a simple but ingenious method of accommodating a traditional rectilinear forecourt to the western apse of a double-apse church plan. Seen against this background, Farfa provides a new and fascinating link between the poles of the Carolingian Renaissance.

Beyond the pure analysis of forms, I have also considered aspects of religious life and popular belief that may have motivated the adoption of these features. The annular crypt, for example, was a specifically Roman invention that provided an ideal setting for the veneration of Roman relics. At the same time, the area immediately outside the western apse became a favored place for burial. To be sure, the area had been used for burial before, but the building program of Sichardus seems to have prompted a new hierarchical arrangement based upon the degree of proximity to the relics in the crypt. More specifically, the most elaborately constructed tombs, including at least one reused Roman sarcophagus, were found in and around the curved portico enveloping the western apse, which suggests that this area was reserved for the burial of abbots. In this way, certain details found on the Plan of St. Gall can be said to be "fleshed out" at Farfa, allowing one to see how prevalent architectural motifs could be adapted to the needs of a particular site.

Following the collapse of the Carolingian empire, the history of early medieval Europe is one of destruction and renewal. Farfa, too, participated in this process. Abandoned in 897 in the wake of Saracen raids and reestablished in the early tenth century, by the year 1000 Farfa was on a new spiritual and economic footing, due largely to the leadership of Abbot Hugo (998–1039). The excavations provide clear evidence of this in the rebuilding of the atrium, which, although structurally modest, offers one of the few securely dated construction campaigns in Italy at this time. More specifically, the coin of Otto III found below one of the paving stones of the portico, and perhaps intentionally placed there, symbolizes the abbey's return to imperial patronage.

By the middle of the eleventh century, at the time of the construction of the monumental east end of the abbey church, Farfa was again at its zenith. The Farfa Customary demonstrates that the abbey remained in direct contact with Cluny during the same period that Abbot Berardus I made several journeys to the imperial court in the heartland of the empire. It is, therefore, not surprising to find that the design of the new structure at Farfa should have been derived, at least in part, from architectural developments in Burgundy, the Rhineland, and the Upper Lorraine. But the early Romanesque church at Farfa was not a slavish copy of any particular model; rather, it seems to represent a unique synthesis of many architectural currents of the day.

Again, the implications of this study go beyond the building at Farfa itself. In order to understand the motivating forces behind the church's particular design, I have traced the development of its most important individual features. Pilaster strips, blind arcading, and brick coursing, for example, were part and parcel of the late antique building tradition in both North Italy and the Rhineland. So, it is of interest to observe that, within the areas of their origin, these same building techniques were utilized again in the early eleventh century in order to test the plasticity and decorative potential of the wall surface, thereby playing an integral role in the formulation of the Romanesque architectural aesthetic. On the other hand, the widespread development of bell towers in these same regions, as also in neighboring Burgundy, should be seen as a response to the new liturgical demands of monastic reform. In contrast, the use of the square presbytery seems to have been restricted to the Rhine and Meuse Valleys in the first half of the eleventh century.

In many ways, then, the mid-eleventh-century church at Farfa may be seen as a summation of Romanesque architecture's first phase. This is not to exaggerate Farfa's importance, but rather to emphasize its seemingly eclectic character. In the first half of the eleventh century, in the case of Farfa at least, the currents of architectural influence seem to have flowed from north to south, which suggests that the distinctions usually made between "northern" and "southern" European trends in early Romanesque architecture were, in fact, far more fluid than is generally assumed. Within a few years of the 1060 consecration at Farfa, however, Italian centers began to turn to the rich heritage of the past in a far more emphatic way. The baptistery of Florence, begun soon after 1059, the cathedral of Pisa and the church of San Marco in Venice, both begun in 1063–1064 (although building may not have been carried out in earnest for another decade or two), and the abbey church of St. Benedict at Montecassino (1066–1071) each used specific early Christian building types as their models.[1] Rome, too, had by 1100 experienced an early Christian revival of its own.[2] The international impulses of earlier in the eleventh century were now replaced by more regional developments. In contrast, Farfa, on the brink of the Investiture Controversy, stood architecturally and politically isolated as the product of a bygone "imperial" age. Yet this constitutes the abbey's importance, for it helps to shed light on a particularly obscure yet pivotal moment in the development of medieval architecture.

In spite of the concerted effort at the end of the eleventh century to move the abbey elsewhere, Farfa could not break with its past. The special relationship with the Holy Roman Emperor did of course come to an end in 1122, and the abbey church was remodeled not long after by artisans from Rome, reflecting the abbey's new alliance with the papacy. But the basic structure of the church and monastic buildings remained the products of a century before.

We have seen, then, that the abbey of Farfa has much to tell us about the architectural history of the early Middle Ages. Indeed, it may be seen as a representative monument of its age. In the end, the most fascinating aspect of this study has been the realization of how closely the architecture seems to reflect Farfa's historical position as a major imperial abbey in Italy. That is to say, each major phase in the ninth and the eleventh centuries is in keeping with the latest developments of monastic architecture in centers north of the Alps as well as in Italy.

Much, however, remains to be determined. Did the medieval abbey church ever have side aisles? Did it exhibit a double-apse plan in the ninth century, as it seems to have done in the eleventh? Where was the location of the medieval cloister? And what was the specific nature of the ancient Roman settlement? These and other questions can only be answered with further excavations that, at best, are years in the offing.

It is hoped, nonetheless, that the present study has served to introduce a previously little-known yet significant monument into the discussion of the development of medieval architecture. Thus, while this book is a summation of many years of research, it should also be viewed as a framework for future investigations.

Appendix A:
Abbots

Laurentius, bishop of the Sabina and founder of the monastery, probably in the middle of the sixth century.		Anselmus	881–883
		Teuto	883–888
		Nordebertus	888
Thomas of		Spento	888
Maurienne	ca. 680–ca. 720	Vitalis	889–890
Aunepertus	720–724	Petrus	890–919
Lucerius	724–740	Rimo	919–927?
Fulcoaldus	740–759	Iohannes II	927?–930
Wandelpertus	759–761	Ratfredus	930–936
Alanus	761–769	Campo	936–943
Wigbertus	769–770	Hildebrand	939–d. 970?
Probatus	770–781	Sarilo	943–947?
Ragambaldus	781–786	Dagibertus	947–953
Altbertus	786–790	Adam	953–966
Mauroaldus	790–802	Iohannes III	966–997
Benedictus	802–815	Albericus	997–998
Ingoaldus	815–830	Hugo	998–1039
Sichardus	830–842	Guido I	1009–1014
Hildericus	842–857	Guido II	1027–1036
Perto	857–872	Suppone	1039–1048
Iohannes I	872–881	Almericus	1039–1048

Berardus I	1048–1089	Henricus II	1242–1243
Rainaldus I	1089–1090	Philippus	1243–1245
Berardus II	1090–1099	Stephanus	1245–1247
Odo	1099	Gentilis II	1247–1250
Berardus III	1099–1119	Matthaeus III	1250–1253
Schism: Rainaldus II	1119	Iacobus I	1253–1257
Berardus IV	1119–1123	Nicolaus I	1257–1260
Guido III	1119–1125	Peregrinus	1260–1277
Adenolfus	1125–1144	Moricus	1277–1283
Rainaldus II	1144?–1146	Hugo II	1283–1285
Rolandus	1146–1152	Iacobus II	1285–1295
Berardus V	1152–1154	Iuncta	1295–1296
Rusticus	1154–1163	Iocerandus	1296–1311
Gothifredus	1163–1168	Gregorius	1311–1312
Adenolfus II	1168–1185	Bonus Iohannes	
Pandolfus	1185–1198	(bishop of Veglia)	1312–1332
Gentilis I	1198–1213	Iohannes IV	1332–1350
Matthaeus I	1213–1230	Arnaldus of Moissac	1350–1355
Henricus I	1230–1235	Alardus	1355–1363
Oderisius	1235–1238	Sixtus	1363–1387
Matthaeus II	1238–1242	Nicolaus II	1388–1399

Commendatory Abbots

Cardinal Francesco Carbone Tomacelli	1399–ca. 1406	Napoleone Orsini	1517–1530
		Francesco Orsini	1530–1546
Cardinal Antonio Gaetani	ca. 1406–1411	Ranuccio Farnese	1546–1568
Francesco, abbot of S. Martino in Cimino	1411–1420	Cardinal Alessandro Farnese	1568–1590
Cardinal Giordano Orsini	1420–1437	Cardinal Alessandro Peretti	1590–1622
Cardinal Giovanni Orsini	1437–1476	Francesco Orsini	1622–1627
Cardinal Latino Orsini	1476–1477	Cardinal Francesco Barberini	1627–1682
Cardinal Cosimo Migliorati-Orsini	1477–1482	Cardinal Carlo Barberini	1682–1704
Cardinal Giovanni Battista Orsini	1482–1503	Cardinal Francesco Barberini	1704–1738
Galeotto Franciotti della Rovere	1505–1508	Cardinal Giovanni Antonio Guadagni	1738–1746
Sisto Galla della Rovere	1508–1513	Cardinal Domenico Passionei	1738
Giovanni Giordano Orsini	1513–1517	Cardinal Federico Marcello Lante	1746–1769
		Antonio Lante	1769–1818

Cardinal Luigi Ercolani	1818–1827	*(Following the death of Cardinal*
Stefano Scerra, Vicario		*Lambruschini, the office of commendatory*
Apostolico	1827–1831	*was suppressed by Pope Gregory XVI,*
Cardinal Giacomo		*and the property of the abbey of Farfa*
Giustiniani	1831–1833	*was divided between the dioceses of the*
Cardinal Luigi		*Sabina and of Poggio Mirteto.)*
Lambruschini	1833–1841	

Appendix B:
Documents

Letter of Duke Faroaldus II of Spoleto to Pope John VII, Dated A.D. 705

Domino sancto ac ter beatissimo totoque orbi praedicabili et nobis in christo patri domno iohanni papae, faroald filius vester. Credimus sanctissimae paternitati vestrae non later qualiter, propter dei amorem vel reverentiam sanctae Mariae semper virginis genitricis domini nostri ihesu christi, monasterium in territorio nostro sabinensi consistens, per aliquas donationes nostras in cespitibus vel servis et coloniciis locum ipsum per thomam abbatem et commenditum vestrum restauraverimus. At ubi per praecepti nostri firmitatem locum ipsum venerabilem stabilivimus, unde utile praevidimus praesentem nostram aepistolam ad vestram per eundem virum venerabilem thomam dirigere vestigia. Per quam rogantes, ac si praesentialiter, obsecramus ut pro futuris temporibus vestra beatitudo pro perpetua firmitate privilegium in scriptis eidem loco facere praecipiat. Sub ea scilicet ratione, ut quod nos devotissima voluntate sanctae Mariae monasterio contulimus, vel pro consolatione peregrinorum ibidem deservientium concessimus, inspectas ipsas praeceptiones tali privilegio vestra paterna sanctitas firmare iubeat, ut nullus ullo tempore praesumat aliquas insolentias aut concussionem facere, aut ipsas res de ipso sancto loco, aut de dominatione ipsorum servorum dei auferre. Et qui hoc

praesumpserit sub anathematis vinculo vestra almitas eum alligare iubeat.
Salutantes et commendantes nos sanctitati vestrae petimus ut pro nobis orare
dignemimi. Post autem relecta aepistola petimus ut eorum monasterio reddatur pro
perpetua securitate. [1]

1. *RF*, II, 22–23, doc. 1; *Chronicon farfense*, I, 136.

DOCUMENT II

Letter of Privilege from Pope John VII,
Dated A.D. 705

Iohannes aepiscopus servus servorum dei thomae abbati religioso presbitero, et
congregationi venerabilis monasterii sanctae dei genetricis semperque virginis
Mariae, quod est in fundo acutiano, territorio sabinensi. Salubre nimis est et
complacens deo, pro securitate atque munitate religiose viventium providentiam
facere pastoralem. Presertim autem dum religiosis studiis, pro timore divino, etiam
saecularis potestas se accomodat, et quod pia devotione pro intuitu aeternae
vicissitudinis contulit, cupit, quibus pro servitio dei concessum est, illae sum atque
immutilatum perenniter conservari. Hinc est, quod venerabile monasterium sanctae
dei genitricis semperque virginis Mariae, quod Laurentius quondam aepiscopus
venerandae memoriae, de peregrinis veniens, in fundo qui dicitur acutianus territorii
sabinensis constituit, et propter religiosam eius conversationem, et sedulitatem
divini servitii ibidem secum conversantium, loca quaedam tam emptu, quamque ex
oblatione fidelium acquisivit. Post cuius ad deum excessum, dum tantam religionem
sedule deo deservientium agnosceret gloriosus filius noster Farualdus dux spoletanus,
etiam ipse pro dei amore, et sustentatione ibidem tecum deservientium deo,
habitacula quaedam, et loca, atque cultores, per donationis paginam contulit, et
collaturum se pollicetur, ut sint qui pro eo, eiusque progenie orationum hostias
frequenter offerant deo. Ut qui collaudatur in terris a fidelibus suis, misereatur de
caelis, et parcat excessibus nostris. Cupit autem, et ortatus est idem gloriosus, ut
tam priora, quam ea quae ab eo sunt condonata de iure eiusdem monasterii, nec in
posterum abstrahantur, sed ad sustentationem congregationis proficiant ibidem
conversantium servorum dei, et per eos possit indigentium ac peregrinorum
hospitalis susceptio diligentius procurari. Per quae pietatis officia donantium
animae, de quorum munere caelebrantur, aeternam requiem et receptionem in
sedibus beatis inveniant. Expetitioni itaque gloriosae atque religiosae devotionis
eius, ac postulationi vestrae concedentes effectum, ex auctoritate Beati Petri
apostolorum principis, cui claves regni caelorum a creatore ac redemptore nostro
domino ihesu christo dei filio concessae sunt, ut ligaret in terris quae in caelo
liganda sunt, et in terris solveret quae in caelo solvenda sunt, tanquam vicem eius et
locum, dignatione omnipotentiae eius, implentes, statuimus atque decernimus, ut
quaeque in eodem monasterio usque hactenus conquisita sunt, vel postmodum
conquirentur, sive domicilia, seu loca, colonosue, et mancipia, vel quaeque
animantia, vel mobilia, nullus de eodem monasterio praesumat usurpare, vel
subtrahere, vel per cuiuscumque ingenii circumventionem alienare. Magis autem pro

timore dei eorum studio, atque concursu, ut ibidem indiminuta permaneant, procurare, interdicentes omnibus sive aepiscopi sint, seu praesbiteri, vel diaconi, vel cuiuslibet aecclesiastici ordinis, seu laici cuiuscunque sint dignitatis, atque militiae, vel privati, ut nullus sibi ius aliquod, vel susceptionis usum in eo praesumat defendere, neque dationis, aut munerum consuetudinem, quamlibet ibidem imponere, vel exigere, neque angariis, et quibuscunque condicionibus novis summittere, scientes, quod in districto dei iudicio aeternae se poenae, talia praesumendo, summittant. Quisquis haec, quae auctoritate principis apostolorum statuuntur, tanquam exsors a fide christiana contempserit, praeter si religiositas tua, vel qui post te saepe fatum venerabile monasterium dispensaverit, spontanea voluntate in tempore dedicationis aecclesiae vicinum aepiscopum, vel quemcunque de claero, ad karitatis convivium voluerit convocare, iuxta quod monasterialis mediocritas habet, et victus monachicus consuevit, in abbatis invitandi quem velit, erit arbitrio. Si vaero quoquo tempore religiosum abbatem de hac vita migrare contigerit, quem ibidem posita congregatio, de se ipsis, vel ubi ubi meliorem invenerint, eligentes, ad dandam ei orationem rogatus atque vocatus adveniat reverentissimus aepiscopus, eumque dum ipsi voluerint exortentur, et post huiusmodi orationem, auctoritate principis apostolorum, a pontifice qui pro tempore fuerit, abbatis firmitatem hinc percipiat. Si vaero presbiterum, vel diaconum sibi desiderat eadem religiosa congregatio consecrari, eligentes quem ad hoc aptum de se ipsis vel exteris invenerint, qui primi sunt ad reverentissimum aepiscopum, qui vicinus est, unanimi voto perducant, ut et ille, requisitis regulariter quaeque ad disciplinam sacrorum canonum et aecclesiasticam traditionem in presbitero vel diacono facienda respiciunt, si irreprehensibilem et aptum invenerit, hac auctoritate, invocato dei nomine, solemnem orationem faciens, presbiterum consecret. Nullam tamen ex hoc in eo se dicionem habere cognoscat, neque licentiam habeat ad observationem publicae aecclesiae suae eum compellere, et de monasterii mansione subtrahere. Iccirco vestra religio hanc apostolici privilegii tuitionem indeptam, fructuosum atque laudabile concessum beneficium demonstret. Ante omnia in psalmis et ymnis, et canticis spiritualibus, diebus ac noctibus permanentes, iuxta monachicam disciplinam, et regulam a patribus traditam conversantes sincero proposito, in professione vestra domino servientes, et de monasterii salute portum non relinquentes, karitatem invicem et unanimitatem servantes. Nullus sibi proprium aliquod vendicet in honoribus, vel rebus, vel usibus, sed ut apostolorum christi discipuli omnia habentes communia, non divisa, nichilque vobis proprium defendentes, iuxta quod ab illis est traditum, et a successoribus observatum. Oboedientiam habentes religioso abbati, atque praeposito, et prioribus vestris, quod est sacrificium spirituale. Humilitatem christi demonstrantes in moribus vestris, benevolentiam quoque, atque humanitatem, et compassionem in eis, qui aliquatenus aegrotaverint vel eguerint. Karitatem etiam, et religiosae conversationis studium, ut demonstretur in vobis et floreat piae professionis integritas, familiares vos exhibens deo religiosae vitae sedulitas, et abstinentiae, atque orationis perserverantia fructuosa, ut quantum haec ex puritatis devotione peragitis, tantum deo in vobis operante eius clementiae propinquetis. Orantes etiam pro nobis, et pro stabilitate apostolicae dei aecclesiae, proque pace, atque securitate totius populi christiani, et pro sospitate gloriosi filii nostri, qui pro timore dei, et religiosae conversationis augmento huius apostolici privilegii, utpote ab eo inspiratus, tuitionem vobis nisus est providere, ut et orationes vestras, et aeternam de vobis mercedem acquireret. Quod apostolicum privilegium, quicunque ille est, qui in parte, vel in toto contemnere vel evacuare temptaverit, vel ad resistendum contrariam attulerit voluntatem, noverit se aeternae condemnationi submitti, iudae fieri traditori participem, perpetui anathematis vinculis et alienationis a deo pro suis se illicitis praesumptionibus submisisse. Benedictionem autem et gratiam a deo se percepturum non dubitet, sed confidat, qui fidelis observantiae reverentia haec, quae sub divino conspectu statuuntur, custodit. Bene Valete. Date pridie II kalendas iulii. Imperante domino nostro piissimo perpetuo augusto Tyberio anno VIII., post consulatum eius anno VI., sed et theodosio atque constantino. [1]

1. *RF*, II, 23–25, doc. 2; *Chronicon farfense*, I, 137–139.

DOCUMENT III

Letter of Privilege from Charlemagne, Dated A.D. 775

Karolus gratis dei rex francorum et langobardorum atque patricius romanorum, omnibus aepiscopis, abbatibus, ducibus, comitibus, vicariis, domesticis, centenariis, vel omnibus missis nostris discurrentibus. Quicquid enim ob amorem aecclesiarum, vel quietem servorum dei exercemus, hoc nobis procul dubio, domino adiuvante, ad aeternam beatitudinem pertinere confidimus. Igitur comperiat magnitudo, seu utilitas vestra, qualiter venerabilis vir probatus abbas monasterii quod est constructum in honore beatissimae genitricis dei semperque virginis MARIAE, quod vocatur acutianus, in ducatu spoletano, vel fundato in territorio sabinensi, missa petitione clementiae regni nostri dixit suggerendo, ut pro mercedis nostrae augmento, taliter ei vel ipsi monasterio concedere deberemus, qualiter ipsa casa dei sub tali privilegio esse deberet sicut caetera monasteria lirinensium, agaunensium et luxoviensium, ubi prisca patrum basilii, benedicti, columbani, vel caeterorum patrum regula custodiri videtur, ut nullus aepiscoporum in praelectione abbatis dationem accipere debeat, et potestatem non habeat de ipso monasterio auferre cruces, calices, patenas, codices, vel reliquas quaslibet res de ministerio aecclesiae, nec ipsum monasterium sub tributo ponere principum potestatem minime haberet, nec denuo tributum aut censum in supradicto monasterio eorum exigere debeat. Sed ipsa casa dei, sicut suprascripta monasteria quae infra regna nostra sunt, sub eo privilegio et norma patrum consistat. Cuius petitionem pro divino respectu vel mercedis nostro augmento noluimus denegare, sed ob amorem domini nostri ihesu christi ita confirmasse vel a novo cessisse cognoscite. Praecipientes ergo iubemus ut nullus aepiscopus, abbas, dux, castaldius, vel quislibet de fidelibus nostris, seu iuniores aut successores vestri, praedictum abbatem, nec monachos suos vel agentes ipsius aecclesiae, de rebus praefati monasterii, quae ibidem ex munificentia regum aut reginarum, vel de collatis populi seu pontificum, vel quae ad ipsum monasterium pervenerunt, aut in antea, deo adiuvante, largitae fuerint tam per venditionis, quam et donationis, cessionis, vel reliqua instrumenta cartarum, inquietare aut contra rationis ordinem, vel quoquo tempore generare praesumatis, sed sub nostro privilegio quieto ordine resideant. Et si quandoquidem abbas ipsius monasterii de hac luce migraverit, inter se ipsi monachi, quem digniorem invenerint, secundum regulam sancti benedicti, et sicut eorum ordo edocet et rectum est, vel eis in unum consentientibus, quem unanimiter elegerint licentiam habeant eligendi abbatem. Et neque a nobis, neque a successoribus regibus, ea quae pro mercede nostra indulsimus, irruptum aut confractum aliquando sit. Sed de proprio valeant semper gaudere patrono. Quatinus melius delectet ipsam congrationem sanctae MARIAE, pro nobis, vel stabilitate regni nostri domini misericordiam attentius deprecare. Et ut haec praeceptio nostris et futuris temporibus firmior habeatur, vel per tempora melius conservetur, manu nostra propria supter firmavimus, vel de anulo nostro sigillare iussimus. Signum Karoli invictissimi regis. Guigbald ad vicem hitherii recognovi. Data sub die VIIII. kalendas iunii, anno VII. et I. regni domni nostri Karoli gloriosissimi regis. Actum Karilego palatio publico, in dei nomine. Feliciter. [1]

1. *RF,* II, 108–109, doc. 128; *Chronicon farfense,* I, 161–162.

DOCUMENT IV

Selections from the Constructio Monasterii Farfensis concerning Construction or Decoration of the Abbey Church

Abbot Mauroaldus (A.D. 790–802):

Nam in aecclesia beate Marie multum pretiosum ex auro et argento ornatum fieri iussit. [1]

Abbot Benedictus (A.D. 802–815):

. . . devotus ad suam fratrumque salutem, necnon et in exterioribus ornamentis que ad cultum aecclesie utilia videntur; ita ut in libris et altaris vestibus atque diversis utensilibus construendis nimis sagacissimus esset, ut usque ad presens ex parte apparet. [2]

Abbot Sichardus (A.D. ca. 830–ca. 842):

Ad augmentum quoque huius loci atque habitantium sicut spiritalia studebat edificia construere, ita et temporalia diligenter accommodare non neglegebat. Nam oratorium hoc quod cernimus in honorem Domini Salvatoris, adiunctum aecclesie sancte Marie, ipse construxit cum cripta deorsum ubi corpora sanctorum Valentini et Hylarii martyrum de Tuscie partibus translata, cum corpore sancti Alexandri sancte Felicitatis filii coniuncta, honorifice sepelivit. Multasque alias aecclesias per diversa loca istius monasterii et antiquas studuit reedificare destructas, et noviter plures construere ceu usque hodie apparet. Alia quoque multa bona huic loco acquisivit lucra, scilicet terras, ornamenta diversa aecclesiastica et alia innumerabilia, ita ut pene nullus suorum predecessorum illum in hoc supergrederetur, quemadmodum in epitaphio illius memorie sciri potest. Nam de illius conversatione atque regiminis acceptione necnon et nativitate et transitu ita inibi legitur:

Hoc iacet in tumulo venerabilis abba Sichardus,
Cenobii sacrum qui bene gessit opus.

Hunc Deus adscivit materno viscere septum,
Hieremie consors vatis ut esse quaeat.
Nam genitum mundus necdum cognoverat illum,
Spondet huic templo iam sed uterque parens.
Hec loca prudenti construxit et ordine miro,
Commissumque truci cavit ab hoste gregem.
Pro quo, quisque legis, non cesses mente benigna
Fundere votivas nocte dieque preces,
Angelicas inter mereatur ut esse cohortes,
Morteque devicta regna tenere poli. [3]

1. *Chronicon farfense,* I, 20.
2. *Ibid.,* 21.
3. *Ibid.,* 21–23.

DOCUMENT V

Translation of the Relics of SS. Valentinus, Hilarius, and Alexander to Farfa under Abbot Sichardus (830–842) and Pope Gregory IV (827–844)

Supradicta vero martyrum corpora, Valentini videlicet et Hilarii, de eodem loco in quo usque ad tempora Gregorii quarti Apostolicae Sedis praesulis requieverant, cum debito honore levavit Sichardus abbas venerabilis monasterii sanctae Dei genitricis et semper virginis Marie sito Savinis, et conlocavit in oratorio quem ipse construxit, et coniunxit aulae eiusdem Dei genitricis et semper virginis Mariae, pariter cum corpore sancti Alexandri filii sanctae Felicitatis, quod denique corpus sancti Alexandri, concedente praefato domno Gregorio papa, de Roma adduxerat. Cuius scilicet oratorii dedication ibidem celebratur III. kalendas ianuarias ad laudem et gloriam domini et salvatoris nostri Ihesu Christi cui honor et gloria in saecula saeculorum. Amen. [1]

Nam oratorium hoc, quod cernimus in honorem Domini Salvatoris adiunctum huic aecclesiae Sanctae Mariae, ipse Sichardus construxit cum cripta deorsum, ubi corpora sanctorum Valentini et Hilarii martyrum de Tusciae partibus translata, cum corpore sancti Alexandri, sanctae Felicitatis filii, quod de Roma adduxerat, concedente Gregorio quarto Sedis Apostolicae praesule, honore sepelivit. [2]

1. *Chronicon farfense,* I, 22, n. 1. Taken from a Farfa passionary of the late ninth century now in the Biblioteca Nazionale, Rome, Farfa Ms. 29.
2. *Ibid.,* 198.

DOCUMENT VI

A Description of the Monastery in the Ninth Century as Recounted ca. A.D.1000 by Abbot Hugo in the Destructio Monasterii Farfensis

Ecclesia denique quam mirifice ornata erat et officine cuncte qualiter composite, quis ad plenum valet referre? tamen dicamus pauca ex plurimis. ipsa namque maior ecclesia tota plumbeo tecto cooperiebatur. altare quoque principale ciburium totum ex lapide oniccino habebat. librorum volumina quanta et qualia vel quam diversis aureis argenteisque operibus ac gemmis lapidibusque pretiosis intesta habebantur, longum est enarrare. vestes quoque maioris altaris deaurate atque gemmate tot erant, quot festivitates maiores, id est adnuntiacio, nativitas Domini, circumcisio, ac adventus Spiritus Sancti, necnon assumptio sancte Marie et nativitas eius. diei namque iudicii talis ibi erat vestis terribilis, ut quisquis eam videbat, statim timore incredibili ac pavore graviter replebatur, ita ut sine memoria mortis per plures dies esse non poterat. ornamenta vero alia que ad usum ecclesie pertinent, quam plura et mirifica erant, quis valet comprehendere? basilice alie absque maiore quinque ibi erant, quarum una, que adhuc stat, in honorem santi Petri constructa, in usu canonicorum habebatur, secunda vero et tertia ad opus erant infirmorum monachorum. harum vero duarum una erat pro infirmis qui iam convalescebant, alia vero pro illis qui proximabant morti, simul adiunctis domibus et balneis, que ad utrorum ordinum utilitatem composite habebantur. quarta autem in palatio regali constituta erat, quod ibi honorificum satis edificatum erat, in quo imperatores hospitabantur, quando illus visitandi gratia veniebant. quinta vero ecclesia extra muros ipsius monasterii edificata in honore sancte Marie, parva quidem sed mirifice constructa, ubi mulieres conveniebant orationis causa et visitationis, quia, ut senum refert relatio, antiquitus nulla mulierum intra muros illius ingrediebatur monasterii; sed quotiescumque regine aut alie mulieres causa qua supra diximus illuc properabant, in basilica parvula quam prediximus faciebant ad se venire abbatem ipsius loci aut fratres quos volebant, ut cum eis de spiritualibus agerent que oporterent. officine cuncte laterculis cooperte habebantur, pavimenta vero lapidibus quadratis et septis omnia strata erat, ut usque hodie ex parte apparent. arcus deambulatorii per totum circuitum habebantur intus et foris, quia ut intra erant claustra ad utilitatem monachorum, ita erant extra ad laicorum. foris vero claustrum totius monasterii ex omni parte erat foriter munitum et turritum ad instar fortis civitatis. placita quoque et iudicia nunquam ibi exercebantur; sed habebant unum palatium ultra rivum qui Riana dicitur, ubi hec gerebantur. quid multa? in toto regno Italico non inveniebatur simile illi monasterio in cunctis boni, excepto monasterio quod vocatur Nonantule; sed non ex toto, ut plures fatentur.[1]

1. *Chronicon farfense*, I, 29–31.

DOCUMENT VII

Inventory of Objects Taken from the Monastery by Abbot Hildebrand, Dated A.D. 939

Breve de ipso thesauro huius monasterii sanctae Mariae, quem abstulit et defraudavit hildebrandus presbiter de ipso castello matenano quod est in marchia in comitatu firmano. In primis vestes II altaris de auro brusto cum gemmis. Unam nativitatis domini et resurrectionis atque ascensionis. Aliam diei iudicii cum mirabilibus gemmis. Aliam vestem albam circumornatam auro brusto et in medio crucem auri brusti cum gemmis et margaritis. Calicem de argento maiorem, et unum deauratum tenentem sextarium I cum patena sua. Calices minores XII cum patenis. Coronam de auro I et unam de argento cum dolfinis VIII. Crucem unam purissimi auri longam plus unius brachii ex utraque parte circumdatam gemmis mirabilibus. Alias cruces II de auro cum ligno domini. Aliam de argento. Libros coopertos argento et deauratos IIII. Capsam de auro purissimo cum gemmis mirabilis quam karolus rex pro anima sua dedit in hoc monasterio. Alias capsas II de argento. Sigilla duo de auro quae miserunt karolus et pipinus filius eius in uno praecepto. Alia sigilla de auro, quae guido et lambertus miserunt in alio praecepto quod fecerunt. Dalmaticas II optimas. Turibula II de argento. Paramentum abbatiale I ad missam canendam. Tunicas III de serico. Plauviale I super genesim libros II. Scintillarium I. Super lucam. Super iohannem. Historiam longobardorum. Cena cypriani librum I. De civitate dei. Historiarum librum I. Antiphonarium I. Dicta patrum. Curtem sancti desiderii. Curtem sanctae Mariae de cuperseto. Curtem sanctae Mariae in columnelle. Curtem sancti salvatoris in ophida. Curtem santi angeli in valle veneria. Curtem sancti angeli in villa magna. Curtem sancti sigismundi. Curtem sanctae Mariae matris domini. Curtem sancti marotis. Curtem sanctae Mariae in ortatiano. Curtem sancti salvatoris in vemorie. Curtem sancti benedicti. [1]

1. *RF*, III, 84, doc. 379.

DOCUMENT VIII

Prologue and Preface of the Farfa Customary (1050–1060)

In nomine Sancte Et Individue Trinitatis, Patris Filii Et Spiritus Sancti. Incipit perfectus usus sive ordo ad ornandam ecclesiam catholicam necnon ad conservandam regularis tramitis normam in coenobio beatae Mariae semper virginis in agro Acutiano comptam. Incipit prologus regularis de libro tramitis.

Dum per universam Italiam Christi percepta anullarentur et velut in fastidio versarentur, diabolicae suggestiones caeperunt augumentari et opere compleri, ita ut etiam in sacris constituti ordinibus sicut mos laicorum est uxores acciperent et sine aliqua difficultate heresim exercerent simoniacam. Caelestis tunc clementia favente regis, qui pretioso olim mundum suo redemit cruore suscitatus est quidam decore splendidus monachico Romualdus nomine, qui normam priscae iustitiae in sexu renovavit utroque et ordine. Cuius exampla imitatus venerabilis Hugo abbas renovavit prisca sanctorum patrum eximii benedicti clarissimi et luculenti patris in coenobio beatae Mariae semper virginis in loco qui dicitur Acutianus ubi destructus erat nimis omnis ordo et composito monachorum illorum ulnis imponens usum Cluniaci coenobii in Gallia aedificati ac per totum orbem cuncta ultra monasteria regulari tramite pollentis ipso tempore. Insonante etenim longe lateque fama praelibati coenobii necnon et praedictorum patrum, Romualdi scilicet et domni Hugonis abbatis benignissimi, hi denique patres nimio zelo ferventes et inter se concordantes, domnus Romualdus in theoretica praeclarus effulsit necnon et in aedificatione multorum monasteriorum, pater vero Hugo sequipeda eius effectus in regali coenobio in tantum, ut ad Galliarum studia venerabilium coenobiorum Cluniacensium, ubi venerabilis pater Ocdilo velut lucerna radians adhuc fulget, multa de illorum consuetudine ad utilitatem fratrum illi commissis et in ovile Christi aggregatis imposuerit ad salutem animarum. Ex quibus unus valde inspiratus et accensus in fervore monastico ex discipulis domni Romualdi, nomine Iohannes, cum uno suo socio ad videndum et scribendum properavit apud eundem Cluniacensem coenobium. Et ita exaravit in paginulis, ut oculis vidit, et in codicibus affixit posterisque legenda contradidit. Domnus vero Hugo pater per omnia imitator illorum effectus, haec et multa alia in suo regali et antiquo coenobio advexit, ut ab illorum usu in nullo discreparet cupiens adimplere quod in Actibus apostolorum legitur: *Multitudinis credentium erat cor et anima una.* Quam consuetudinem si quis adimpleverit in praesenti exaltabitur vita et post intra perhennem laetabitur pascuam. Et mavult operibus quam dictis adimpleri. Et sicut quis infra naviculam in medio amne fluminis positus superiora aggredi cupiens, nisi totis viribus certaverit, cito relabitur, ita haec consuetudo, si carnalibus quis assenserit desideriis, in fastidium ei vertitur. Si quis eam imitaverit et secutus fuerit, caeleste illi revelabitur archanum et amabilis deo et dulcis erit hominibus. Si vero preversus fregerit et dereliquaerit eam, relinquetur a deo et odiosus erit in saeculo, et si per multos creverit annos, tempore uno destruetur unusque extraneus centum suorum persequetur, et duo fugabunt decem milia. Et non solum hoc praedictum, sed et cuncta, quae priores nostri bona tenere sancxerunt si derelicta fuerint, non prosperabuntur, sed arcum convertuntur perversum, agentibus sanctis quorum nomina sive reliquiae hic habentur. Facientibus et perseverantibus regnum pateat sempiternum. Explicit prologus.

Incipit praephatio. Summi moderatoris et piis favente religionis insigniti Christi timoris efficatio dum male olita usquequaque sentina emergens efferbuerit, nostri olim sacrati institutio ordinis ita dumtaxat vix uspiam perfectae trames semitae inesse nequiret, commonitus ipse Iohannes trans Alpium huiuscemodi discendi negotium finitima Cluniacum coenobiorum nobilissima expetit gratia, atque quaecumque ibi probatae experientiae didicit, duplici hoc pro diffinitione ad purum contexuit et ad honorem nostri salvatoris intemerataeque eius piisime genitricis in monasterio suo sub religiosissimi abbatis Ioseph sanctorumque piisime monachorum Apuli catervae conspectui, quatinus salutis sit solacium praesentibus haedificatioque profutura succedentibus in Christo Ihesu nostro.

In ordinibus sanctorum coenobiorum threnos. Incipiunt primi libri.

Continet in se usus monachorum iste libellus
Atque alias rerum collectas undique causas
Quae possunt animum titubantem tollere sursum.
Leucasmo pacis sapientia talia nobis
Saepius adponat clarius et pectora pascat
Atque docens animum paulatim ducat in altum.
Vilia sectantes non omnia possumus omnes.
Finis enim mundi noffecibus implicat aevi
Et vetus ecclesiae senium monstratur ubique.
Sed tu natae dei clemens miseres cito nostri
Atque senectutem sponsae non penitus abs te
Prolongare velis sed nunc succurrito lapsis
Illustrans sensum quo te quaeramus amandum
Qui prior has terras humilis intrare volebas
Ut nos ad caelum faceres conscendere sursum
Et tecum regno semper gaudere superno.

Hos frater flores studuit iuxtare Iohannes
Dultia circumiens ut apis per germina pascens.
Haec quicumque legis et sursum gaudia quaeris
Scriptori veniam studiis pro talibus ores.
Si tibi magnarum potis est adtingere rerum
Fercula, delicias quae flagrant undique sanctas
Illic invenies quicquid mare nutrit edendum,
Quicquid terra creat, quicquid ad astra volat.
At nos exiguum scripturae carpsimus horto
Rubra quod adpositum testa ministrat holus
Hos praetermissos pridem nunc scribimus usus.
Primitus adventum domini recolendo beatum
Omnes huc socii mente concurrite sancti.
Praemia nam vitae dantur caelebrantibus ista
Talia nam patribus concessit spiritus almus.
Ipsius et nobis rogitemus munere dari
Quo praecredentium teneamus facta parentum
Ut simil ad requiem, quo iam venire perhennem
Et nos possimus domino donante venire
Ac simul adventum Christi spectare secundum.
Expliciunt versi in laude ordinis compti. [1]

1. *Liber tramitis*, ed. P. Dinter, 1–8; *Consuetudines monasticae*, ed. B. Albers, I, 1–4.

DOCUMENT IX

Letter from Pope Leo IX (1049–1054) to Abbot Berardus, Written ca. 1051

Leo episcopus servus servorum Dei, Berardo abbati Sanctae Mariae de Farfa salutem et apostolicam benedictionem. Petitiones tuas iustas adimplere non denegamus, non solum de coelestibus sed etiam de [terrenis rebus . . . si vero hoc agere nulla ratione . . .][1] cum licentia nostra acquirere episcopum qui tibi tuam consecret ecclesiam undecumque volueris. Cave tamen ne sit symoniacus. [2]

1. For dating see *Chronicon farfense*, II, 202. Words in parentheses are found in a transcription of the same letter in *RF*, V, 284, doc. 1293. Dotted lines indicate erasures in the original manuscript.
2. *Chronicon farfense*, II, 202.

DOCUMENT X

Consecration of the Two Main Altars of the Abbey Church by Pope Nicholas II on July 6, A.D. 1060

Anno dominicae incarnationis millesimo LX, mense iulio, die VI, indictione XIII. Nycolaus sanctissimus papa II invitatus decentissime a domno Berardo venerabili abbate huius farfensis monasterii, omnique fratrum conventu eiusdem coenobii, una cum episcopis romanis et aliquantis cardinalibus ad hoc monasterium libentissime venit ad huius ecclesiae principalia consecranda altaria, hoc est beatae MARIAE dominae nostrae, et domini dei salvatoris mundi. Quo facto honorificentissime, inter sacrae solemnia missae idem pontifex venerabilis omnibus poenitentibus qui ibi convenerant et aderant remissionem trium annorum fecit, et constituit ut haec remissio annualiter fiat omnibus qui in ipsa die cum votis et donis prout potuerint honorifice et honest annue venire studuerint, et pauperibus qui donum non habuerint si religiose properare voluerint. De raptoribus vero ac invasoribus, sive furis aut sacrilegis huius bonorum monasterii excommunicationem anathematis fecit, quam describi et quotiens oportuerit talem legi praecepit. [1]

1. *RF*, V, 291–292.

DOCUMENT XI

Documents concerning the Building of a New Monastery atop Monte Acuziano under Abbot Berardus II (1091–1099)

Post haec cum omnes seniores maiores atque minores huius sancti conventus, de huius monasterii vetustissima defectione causarentur, et de novi monasterii in hoc super nos eminenti monte, constructione assidue ratiocinarentur, plurimi etiam romanorum civium magnates hoc votis omnibus niterentur, tandem vix quasi compunctus et hominum favoribus coactus, hanc fecit constitutionem cum anathemate auctoralique excommunicatione pro novi in monte hoc monasterii constructione:

Notum sit omnibus sub nomine christiano viventibus, suarumque animarum redemptionem in christo habere cupientibus, quod nos scilicet berardus, dei gratia pharphensis abbas, omnisque eiusdem monasterii conventus, divina inspirante gratia et dei genitrice ac semper virgine interveniente beata MARIA. Corde et animo atque irrevocabili voluntate, suam aecclesiam cupimus renovare. Insuper et totum monasterium in monte hoc a fundamento construere. Et hoc beatae MARIAE voluntate, atque quorumdam dei fidelium romanorum, quorum nomina deus scit, iuvamine et exortatione incipimus, ac tantum et tam admirabile opus, dei omnipotentis auxilio atque omnium eius fidelium adiutorio explere confidimus. Quicumque ergo huic sancto operi aliquod adiutorium fecerit, peccatorum suorum remissionem, de quibus vaeram poenitentiam habuit vel habiturus est, per merita sanctae MARIAE, et sibi assidue servientium famulorum orationes, optinebit. Et ut omnes fideles firmissime credant nos tantum opus irrevocabiliter incipere, et inceptum nullo unquam modo usque ad certum finem relinquere, ita placuit nobis sub dei omnipotentis praecepto firmare, ut quicumque nunc vel post nos vivens, cuiuscumque ordinis vel dignitatis, nostram hanc voluntatem et hoc opus studiose voluerit impedire, et suo impedimento, ut non fiat, perturbare, cum traditore iuda et dathan et abiron atque herode, caiphan et pilato participationem habeat, et cum eis in inferno inferiori perpetualiter ardeat atque poenae totius excommunicationis novi ac veteris testamenti, nisi digne satisfecerit, subiaceat. Amen. Hoc actum est in pharphensi claustro anno domini millesimo XCVII. Indictione V. Epacta IIII. Conc. III. IIII kalendas iunii.

Ego Berardus abbas cum omni congregatione pharphensi, hoc fieri iussi atque confirmavi. [Names of members of the monastic community.][1]

In nomine domini nostri Ihesu Christi. Ego Berardus dei omnipotentis nutu pharphensis cenobii humilis abbas, ob meorum et omnium aequo animo adiutorium in hoc ministrantium, scilicet in monasterii huius operis renovatione et in novae aecclesiae in huius cacumine montis constructione, perfectam cunctorum acquirendam peccaminum remissionem, ordinamus atque disponimus, qualiter hoc opus cum dei adiutorio ad perfectum ducatur et nullo modo unquam negligatur nec, quod absit, aliquando relinquatur. In primis concedimus huic magno operi omne servitium, omne debitum, omne obsequium, omne redditum, omne tributum de IIII castellis nostri monasterii. Idest de phara, de postmonte, de arcibus, et de campo sancti benedicti. Exceptis mortuorum oblationibus et manualiis quae solo conventui conservamus, et exceptis equitum fegis sive beneficiis. Ex quibus, videlicet de beneficiis equitum et manualiis conventus, si poterimus, alibi eis concambium dabimus, et ipsa omnia fega et manualia, infra praefata castella ad hoc perficiendum opus constituemus. Similiter de scriptis praecariis sive libellis et pignoribus faciemus. Idest, aut per concambium vel per redemptionem adimplere satagemus. De omnibus etiam mortuorum oblationibus decimam ibidem concedimus, et decimam decimae totius abbatiae. Exceptamus tamin ex eis quae quondam in hospitio nostri monasterii a nostris antecessoribus concessa fuerunt. Item cellam de roma, cum sancto sebastiano in flaiano. Item teloneum mercati. Item molendina XII inter criptulae et pharphae sive currisii flumina posita, praeter illa XXXVI molendina quae conventi in praefatis aquarum vocabulis praediximus danda. Item statuimus de calcariis, ut homines de petradoemone faciant in uno anno calcarias II. De scandrilia II. De ophiano et montaliano II. De caput pharphae I. De cerreto malo I. De salisano et rocca I. De agello I. De caballaria et quinza I. De bucciniano II. De monte operis et tribiliano III. De podio catino et terraniano et limisano II. De tribuco II. Quarum calces factas, idem ipsi qui fecerunt per dominicas dies vel alias festivitates cum asinis suis sursum in montem istum ferant. De omnium hominibus castellorum per omnes ebdomadas XX homines veniant, et huic operi attentius per totam ebdomadam insistant. Qua finita alii XX homines succedant, donec omnes homines uniuscuiusque castelli singulas ebdomadas expleant. Ex quibus exceptamus solummodo bonorum hominum, idest equitum personas. Haec omnia benivola voluntate concedimus. Et si aliquid super his augendum est vel ex eis minuendum, consilio potius nostri conventus augere vel minuere utiliter curabimus. Verumtamen ne ipsum relinquatur opus sub divina institutione stabilimus, et anathema quod exinde concordi fecimus voluntate omnimodis confirmamus. Quod quicumque confirmans custodierit, et adiutorium vel consilium bonum administraverit, perpetuis ut benedictionibus ditetur firmissime optamus, et constantissime rogando domini omnipotentis clementiam flagitamus. Amen.[2]

1. *RF*, V, 156–157, doc. 1153; *Chronicon farfense*, II, 216–218. Dated A.D. 1097.

2. *RF*, V, 158, doc. 1154; *Chronicon farfense*, II, 218–219. Undated, but presumably from the same time as the preceding document.

DOCUMENT XII

Inventory of Precious Objects Left by Abbot Berardus III at His Death, A.D. 1119

Anno igitur dominicae incarnationis millesimo CXVIIII, indictione XII, et XVIII kalendas ianuarii, feria quoque II ebdomadae III adventus dominici, domnus Beraldus nocte obiit famosae memoriae, et huius coenobii farfensis abbas laudabilis. Haec autem sunt ornamenta quae hac in ecclesia ipso die quo migravit certissime reliquit. In primis altare itinerarium quod regina agnes nobis optulit valde optimum. Tabulam quoque ante altare principale maiorem argenteam et deauratam pensantem libras _____. Et altarem minorem super eodem altare simili opere pensantem libras _____ quas ipse fieri fecit, et cruces argenteas II maiores et I minorem. Missalem maiorem cum tabulis argenteis. Missalem domni oddonis, et textum evangelii quem praefata regina huic monasterio dedit cum tabulis eburneis, et alium cum crucifixo argenteo, et alium praedicti oddonis cum tabulis deargentatis, et cottidianum evangelistarium cum tabulis deargentatis, et epistolarium domni oddonis argento ornatum, et alium quem fecit domnus Romanus bonae memoriae, et orationalem cum tabulis eburneis. Item libros IIII opertos pallio, videlicet missales II et textum evangeliorum atque epistolarem. Item calices VII. Turibula argentea tria. Capsulas argenteas IIII cum cocleariis suius. Amulas argenti tres, unam earum opertam auro. Patenas argenti duas, gallum argenteum, scutellam argenteam, situlam argenteam aquae benedictae. Argentum quod remansit a cruce. Nuscam auream foemineam. Stellam argenteam et cristallinam luciferam valde bonam. Item: Vestes IIII altaris principalis. Primam ei dedit domnus Heinricus imperator. Secunda dedit praedicta regina. Tertiam antiquam pentecostis. Quartam fecit domina raimburga filia longini, et mappulam super altare valde bonam quam fecit totadomna ancilla dei. Item: Vestes IIII altaris domini salvatoris: Primam praedicti domini H. regis. Secundam praedictae Reginae. Tertiam pallium rotatum praedicti abbatis Beraldi. Quartam pallium cum leonibus. Item planetas XIII. Pluviales XIII. Dalmaticas II. Tunicas XX. Telam palli I. Brachia pallii III. Crumenam I imperialem quam ei donavit praedictus He. imperator quae fuit optima. Item frigium non modicum vestis praedicti imperatoris et aliud ex diversis vestibus. Item mitram I. Virgas pastorales II. Vexilla II. Offertoria VIII. Camisiales C. Stolas VI cum manipulis suis textas auro. Unam earum cum squillis aureis, et semicintium cum squillis aureis, et manipulum similiter, et alias stolas cum manipulo, exceptis aliis XXIIII. Dorsalia palii II iuxta altare. Tapetia XV. Bullam auream I in praecepto quod fecit huic ecclesiae praedictus H. imperator bonae memoriae. Omnes suprascriptas res et alia plurima ornamenta praelibatus domnus Beraldus abbas in hac reliquit ecclesia, quae nobis non reducuntur ad memoriam. [1]

1. *RF*, V, 310–311.

DOCUMENT XIII

Inventory of Objects Taken from the Monastery by Schismatic Abbot Guido III in A.D. 1121

Qui ornamenta ecclesiae vel quaeque utensilia coepit dispergere absque ulla verecundia, et diversis viris in pignus tribuere. Idest crucem maiorem deauratam cum capulo et pomo eius pro librabus XII. Planetam purpurae nigrae et pluvialem purpurae clavatae quae fuerunt reginae agnetis. Dorsalem leonatum et tunicam reginae et textum evangelii et gausape novum altaris maioris, pro solidis L. Tabulam maiorem, pro librabus LV. Tabulam minorem, pro librabus XIII. Planetam diarodinam et aliam albam, et tunicam I et stellam cristallinam argenti luciferam deauratam, pro librabus tribus et media. Calicem I argenti et stolam maiorem et capsulam argenti et cruciculam auream et nuschas III aureas femineas et planetas II, pro librabus VIIII. Vestem altaris et pluviales II, album diaspidem et aliud nigrae purpurae, pro librabus III et solidis XI. Pluviales II rubeum et viridem, pro ————. Planetam I et psalterium I, pro solidis XXX. Planetam diaspidis albi et tunicam de xamito albo et loricam, pro solidis L. Planetam I et orationalem eburneum, pro solidis L. Turibulum argenteum turritum et candelabrum argenteum pro solidis XXX. Textum evangelii maiorem, pro librabus XX. Turibulum aureum, pro librabus XXII. Sunt autem haec ornamenta ecclesiastica XXXIIII valde praetiosa, ex quibus sola stola maior cum manipulo, nostris temporibus empta fuit librabus XV. De quibus pignoribus tulit libras CLX et eo amplius, quas ut compertum habemus, nec in ecclesiasticos usus, nec in fratrum regimina dedit, nec etiam in guerra expendit. Item haec alia dispersit de quibus ignoramus quid tulerit aut fecerit. Idest turibulum argenteum, dalmaticam optimam, telam I palii, amulam argenteam deauratam, pongam imperatoris, stolam et manipulum cum campanulis aureis, et semicintiam similiter cum campanis aureis. Antiphonarium optimum et priscianum valde bonum, nocturnale perfectum, super isaiam mirificum, mitra I, virgas pastorales II, super hiezechielem, ovidium. . . . De ecclesiasticis quoque ornamentis haec sunt quae distraxit et oppignoravit. Altare reginae praetiosum, missalem maiorem, epistolarem domni romani, calices III, turibulum argenteum I, capsulas argenteas III et coclearium I, amulas argenteas II, patenas argenteas II, gallum argenteum I, scutellam argenteam I, situlam argenteam I, argentum quod remansit a tabula, pallii brachia III et dimidium. Vestem altaris, planetam I, pluviales III, tunicas III, fanones II, dorsalem I, sigilla aurea cum praeceptis VII. . . . [1]

1. *RF*, V, 321–322.

DOCUMENT XIV

Excerpt from a Bull Issued by Pope Sixtus IV in 1477 concerning the Division of Authority within the Monastery

Palatium verò sive Domum Abbatialem dicti Monasterii cum coquina, tinello, cellario, stabuliis et horto, aliisque membris suis extra Claustrum Monasterii et Fratrum habitationem, videlicet à prima Porta usque ad ecclesiam cum turibus [sic], et pertinentiis suis, ac reliqua praesentibus non descripta, eiusdem Monasterii farfen. bona Abbatiali ipsius Monasterii farfens. Mensę assignare, ne Abbas, sivè Commendatarius, et eius Vicesgerentes, conventum, et è contra Conventus, Abbatem, sivè Commendatarium praedictos in bonis huiusmodi molestent, inhibere; Ac pro eiusdem Monasterii farfensis prospero, et felici Regimine, quod in Monasterio praedicto, praeter illius Abbatem, esse debeat Prior Claustralis, per Conventum praefatum assumendus, qui sic electus pari gratia, qua Abbas inibi quo ad Conventum, et illius personas, ac bona Conventualis Menșe, auctoritate fungatur, et unus Cellarius, temporalium bonorum dictae Conventualis Mensa administrationi propositus, qui rationem reddere teneatur, statuere, et ordinare, ac alias super his, et divisionis, ac statuti, et ordinationis huõi observatione, etiam per adiectionem paenarum, et Iuramenti praestationem, opportunè providere de benignitate Apostolica dignaremur. . . .[1]

1. "Catalogus cardinalium abbatuum farfensium," Farfa, 1728, a manuscript in the Farfa Library, AF–291, fol. 4r–5r.

DOCUMENT XV

Records concerning the Construction of the Renaissance Abbey Church

Inscription from the Coffered Ceiling of the Nave, Dated 1494:

Baptista Cardinalis Ursinus Templum Hoc Natali Domine Virginis Patrone Salutis Humane Dicatum A Veteribus Disturbatum A Fundamentis Restituit Anno Salutis MCCCCLXXXXIIII.

Excerpt from the Chronicle of Archangelus De Alexandris:

Sequenti anno [1496] qui fuit decimus regiminis Ill.mi D'Baptisti Commendatorii, mensi Martio, in festo Annuntiationis Sanctissimae Virginis. Consecrata fuit Basilica St'Mariae Farfensis per Venerabilem Patrem D. Antonium de' Sto Miniato Teutonicum, episcopum Balneoregiensem, quae Basilica a fundamentis de' novo, et integraliter reedificata fuit, per prefatum Commendatorium.[1]

1. Archangelus De Alexandris, "Chronicon sacri ac regalis monasterii farfensis ex vetustussimis manuscriptis collectum," 1627, Cod. Vatican Library, Barberini 2350 (XXXII–141), fol. 105r–105v.

DOCUMENT XVI

References to Construction of the Monastic Complex in the Sixteenth and Seventeenth Centuries

A. 1577–1578:

Volendo l'Ill.mo e Reverendissimo Sig. Cardinal Farnese, Abbate e Monaci del Monastero Di Farfa per sicurezza delle Mercanzie che si portano per la fiera di Farfa fare una Dogana . . . consegna una stalla posta avanti la piazza del Palazzo sotto l'ospidale, e fenile delli Monaci, confina con il Giardino della Corte, e Claustra di detto Monastero, e di detti Reverendi Monaci à tale effetto mettono una Lor stalla contigua à detto loco confinante con il Giardino, e Claustro di detto Monastero, quali due stalle habbiano à servire per la detta Dogana, obligandosi detti Monaci à lor spese murare, rassettare, e finire la detta Dogana, e stabilirla commoda ad uso di

Dogana in fra tempo di quattro Mesi, talmente che alla fiera di Marzo prossimo futuro si possi usare. [1]

R. P. D'Honoratus Spinula Ianvensis, et Abbas Claustralis Farfensis, pro maiori Monasterii emolumento, ac mercatorum comoditati, edificavit domum contiguam Monasterio testudinatam, pro conservandis eorundem mercibus exponendis, et Nundinis vendendis. [2]

B. 1585–1590:

Claustrum novum cum cisterna magna. Pars clausurae Muro circondata. [3]

C. 1598–1604:

Anno Domini 1598 . . . Pater Dnus Ambrosius à Puppio Abbas claustralis Farfensis . . . nova iecit fundamenta Refectorii Maioris, eiusque parietes extruxit usque ad altudinem fenestrarum, nec voluit absovere, quia factus fuit Preses, et Abbas Sacri Cassenensis Cenobii. [4]

Anno vero Domini 1601. Pater D'Marcus à Papia Conventualis Abbas Farfensis, satis studuit utilitati huius Cenobii in quantum voluit, posteris egregium relinquens imitandi exemplum: nam infra biennium, quo profuit, ac prefuit, satis strenue se' gessit, inceptam namque Refectorii structuram testudinatam absolvit, et tegulis cooperuit. [5]

1602 . . . Pater D Anastasius à Carpinedulo . . . Refectorium, deinde ab antecessoribus interius incompletum stabilivit, fores seris obseravit, pavimentum lateribus coctis stravit, et fenestris vitreis illuminavit, scamnis, atque mensis adornavit . . . Medietatem quoque Dormitorii, tam inferioris, quam superioris, antiquis loci parientibus demolitis, novum cellae vinariae edificium imposuit. Conquinam, vetusque Refectorium, ac farinarium dextruxit, quarum loco quatuor inferius, pro' hospitibus, atque quatuor superius pro' monachis cellas reedificavit, et absolvit, quas choclea coniunxit, et usque supremum absolvit. . . . [6]

1604 . . . Refectorium magnum, cripta celle vinariae. Clausura circumdata muris quod alteram partem. [7]

D. 1609–1611:

1609 . . . Refectorium parvum, coquina. [8]

. . . anno, qui fuit Dominicae Incarnationis 1611. Abbatum Claustralium cellam vetustati collabentem (quo loci antiquitus extabat Divi Salvatoris sacellum vetustissimum a Sicardo Abbati 13° edificatum) una cum deambulatorio satis deformi, restauravit, et in augustiorem redegit formam: adiunctis a latere cubiculis quatuor quibus, et quintum pro' Priore Claustrali, annexuit: solutis in huiusmodi edificio aureis pené mille. [9]

E. 1622–1624:

. . . sub anno Domini 1622 . . . a fundamentis extruxit, et usque ad culmen perfecit Horreum Monasterii Sacrae turri adherens: deinde Chorum matutinalem ad

conventus comoditatem, interpositum Dormitorio et Ecclesia aptavit; pariter, et
murum Horti superioris collapsum reparavit. . . .[10]

[1624] . . . aquam fontis de' cisternula Plateae nundinarum intra Claustra
Monasterii introduxit. Pretera Ianuam Cenobii antea ad fores Ecclesiae in obscuro,
ac remoto loco sitam, in augustiorem formam, et ad commodiorem ingressum
apervit. Interiorem quoque Monasterii Aream ante introitum Claustri, prius
inequalem, ac macerie repletam adequavit, dilatatisque circumquaque parietibus
ampliavit, quas etiam ad intuentium recreationem, picturis decoravit. Viridarium insuper ei contiguum pene desertum, et neglectum arboribusque malorum citrorum, et
huiusmodi generis, anti quadriennium obscissis deformatii novis arbustis triginta, et
amplius è Roma ollatis, et plantatis, in pulchiorem oreduxit formam, ac ex turpi
delitiosum reddidit, ad solatium sui totiusque Conventus.[11]

1. "Catalogus cardinalium," fol. 9r.
2. De Alexandris, "Chronicon sacri," fol. 116r.
3. "Catalogus cardinalium," fol. 34r.
4. De Alexandris, "Chronicon sacri," fol. 120v.
5. *Ibid.*
6. *Ibid.*, fol. 121r.
7. "Catalogus cardinalium," fol. 53r.
8. *Ibid.*, fol. 57r.
9. De Alexandris, "Chronicon sacri," fol. 121v.
10. *Ibid.*, fol. 123v.
11. *Ibid.*, fol. 124r–124v.

DOCUMENT XVII

Description of the Commendatory's Palace

In Farfa vi è il Palazzo Abbatiale situato dirimpetto ad un angolo della chiesa di
S. Maria Matrice dell'Abb. ad un braccio del Mon.ro de R. R. Monaci dell'Ordine
Cassinese di S. Benedetto, e alla Dogana della fiera e stà diviso dalle Botteghe, e
Case inservienti in tempo di fiera, con un piccolo recinto, che lo forma una casa di
due stanza con il forno à pian terreno della Mensa Abbate, la Dogana, il Monastero,
e la Chiesa; principiando nella parte laterale destra verso detta casa, e respettivam.te
forno al Cantone del Muro del Giardino, che anticam.te era dell'em.o Abbate
Commendat.rio e adesso per ragione di permuta se ne trovano in possesso li R. R.
Monaci, ove per chiuder detto recinto vi è un Portone rotto, et appresso al Cantone
di detto Palazzo ve ne è un altro senza le porte, e caminando avanti al Palazzo
sudetto suolta, e termina infine della parte laterale sinistra verso la facciata della
detta Chiesa, ove stà un Portone in piccolo, parim.te senza Porta, che da una Parte
l'arco del medemo stà appoggiato al Cantone della facciata di detta Chiesa, e
dall'altra al Muro, dove terminano le Stalle, e Stanzione ad uso di fenile della
sudetta Mensa.

Questo Palazzo è di quattro appartam.ti, il primo à pianterreno che da una parte
è diviso in più Stanze per uso di Carceri publiche, sì per gli huomini, che per le
Donne, ed all'altra vi sono le Stalle inservienti in tempo di fiera per rimessa dei
Cavalli, che suol unirsi al Subaffitto dell'osteria, e Gabella del Passo del Ponte

Nuovo di Granica, e stanno sotto all'abitazione del Barigello, e suoi Birri, e respettivam. te allo Stanzione per la rimessa de fieri, venendo divise le d.e Carceri, e Stalle dal Portone dell'ingresso di detto Palazzo. Nel secondo alla Mano dritta vi sono due piccole Stanziole à volta per abitazione del Cane.re Abbate, et à confine di queste vi è la Canc.ria similm. te à volta, e per andare si all'une che all'altra si passa per un altra stanza à volta detta del tormento nella quale corrispondono non solo le porte di dette due Stanze e della Canc.ria; mà anche quelle delle due carceri segrete, ivi stabilite di nuovo alcuni anni sono, entrandosi per andare à d.a. Stanza del tormento per una porta che stà alla detta Mano dritta subito salito il primo capo di scale, avanti della qual Porta vi pende la fune della Campana che stà ad adattata nel suo Campaniletto in un angolo del tetto di detto Palazzo per uso de Ministri della Curia, et alla Mano sinistra vi sono due Stanze, et un Stanziolino à tetto per commodo del Barigello e sua famiglia, come ancora due altre Stanze à tetto rese inabitabili, che si ritengono dal Canc.re per uso di Cantina. Il terzo appartam.to continente in se una gran Sala, e quattro Stanze, serve per abitazione del R.mo Sig. Vicario Generale, et il quarto appartam.to stà à tetto con altra simile Sala, e tre Stanze, che si ritiene dal Sig. Affittuario Generale delle rendite della Mensa Abbatiale, benche frà queste Stanze, la prima più ampla è destinata per abitazione del Sig. Commissario G.nte della Locationi, et Investiture, che sogliono farsi dall'emo, e Rmd Sig. Cardinal Abbate alli Particolari dell'Abbadia di Farfa.[1]

1. "Catalogus cardinalium," fol. 58r–58v.

Abbreviations

AJA	*American Journal of Archaeology*
ASRStP	*Archivio della società romana di storia patria*
BM	*Bulletin Monumental*
DOP	*Dumbarton Oaks Papers*
History of the Church	*History of the Church*, trans. of *Handbuch der Kirchengeschichte*, ed. Hubert Jedin and John Dolan, New York and London, 1969—
IP	*Italia pontificia*, ed. Paul Kehr, Berlin, 1906—
JBAA	*Journal of the British Archaeological Association*
JSAH	*Journal of the Society of Architectural Historians*
Karl der Grosse	*Karl der Grosse*, ed. Wolfgang Braunfels, 4 vols., Düsseldorf, 1965–1967
Krautheimer, *Corpus*	Richard Krautheimer et al., *Corpus basilicarum christianarum Romae*, I–V, Vatican City and New York, 1937–1977
Krautheimer, *Early Christian*	Richard Krautheimer, *Early Christian and Byzantine Architecture*, Pelican History of Art Series, 3rd ed., Harmondsworth, 1979

143

Krautheimer,
Rome   Richard Krautheimer, *Rome, Profile of a City*, 312–1308,
                        Princeton, 1980

Krautheimer,
Studies   Richard Krautheimer, *Studies in Early Christian, Medieval and
                        Renaissance Art*, New York, 1969

LP   *Le liber pontificalis*, ed. Louis Duchesne, 2 vols., Paris, 1886–
                        1892, reprinted 1955–1957

MEFR   *Mélanges d'archéologie et d'histoire de l'école française de Rome*

MGH Ep   *Monumenta germaniae historica, epistolae*

MGH SS   *Monumenta germaniae historica, scriptores*

Partner,
Lands   Peter Partner, *The Lands of Saint Peter*, London and Berkeley,
                        1972.

PBSR   *Papers of the British School at Rome*

PL   *Patrologiae cursus completus, series latina*, ed. J. P. Migne, 221
                        vols., Paris, 1844–1890, suppl. 1958–1974

Porter,
Lombard Architecture Arthur Kingsley Porter, *Lombard Architecture*, 4 vols., New
                        Haven, 1917

QFIAB   *Quellen und Forschungen aus Italienischen Archiven und Bibliotheken*

RAC   *Rivista di archeologia cristiana*

RF   *Il regesto di Farfa*, ed. Ignazio Giorgi and Ugo Balzani,
                        Biblioteca della Società Romana di Storia Patria, Rome,
                        1879–1914

RINASA   *Rivista dell'istituto nazionale d'archeologia e storia dell'arte*

Römisches Jahrbuch   *Römisches Jahrbuch für Kunstgeschichte*

RQ   *Römische Quartalschrift*

Toubert,
Les structures   Pierre Toubert, *Les structures du Latium médiéval*, 2 vols., Rome,
                        1973

Verzone,
L'architettura   Paolo Verzone, *L'architettura religiosa dell'alto medioevo in Italia
                        settentrionale*, Milan, 1942

VK   Friedrich Oswald, Leo Schaeffer, and Hans Sennhauser,
                        Vorromanische Kirchenbauten, Munich, 1966–1971

ZKG   *Zeitschrift für Kunstgeschichte*

ZSRG   *Zeitschrift der Savigny-Stiftung für Rechtsgeschichte, kanonische
                        Abteilung*

Notes

Chapter 1: The Historical
Background and Its Sources

1. Ildefonso Schuster, *L'imperiale abbazia
di Farfa*, Rome, 1921.

2. For a discussion of Gregory of Catino
and his work, with extensive bibliography,
see Herbert Zielinski, *Studien zu den
spolentinischen "Privaturkunden" des* 8.
*Jahrhunderts und ihrer Überlieferung im Regestum
farfense*, Tübingen, 1972, 25–29; *Collectio
canonum regesto farfense inserta*, ed. Theo
Kölzer, *Monumenta iuris canonici*, Corpus
collectionem, V, Vatican City, 1982, 1–29,
esp. 7–8, 26–29. For an overview of the
Farfa scriptorium in the Middle Ages see
Paola Supino Martini, "La produzione
libraria negli *scriptoria* delle abbazie di Farfa
e di S. Eutizio," *Atti del IX congresso
internazionale di studi sull'alto medioevo*, Centro
Italiano di Studi sull'Alto Medioevo,
Spoleto, 1983, 590–607.

3. *Il regesto di Farfa compilato da Gregorio di
Catino*, ed. Ignazio Giorgi and Ugo Balzani,

Biblioteca della Società Romana di Storia
Patria, Rome, 1879–1914.

4. The last entry in the Register by
Gregory is dated May 23, 1099. *RF*, V,
160–161; Zielinski, *Studien*, 27 nn. 11–12;
Collectio canonum, Kölzer, 26.

5. For a philological study of the
Register and a discussion of Gregory of
Catino's working procedure see Zielinski,
Studien, 29–93, and his "Gregor von Catino
und das Regestum farfense," *QFIAB*, LV–
LVI, 1976, 361–404. For a detailed
description of the format and the
palaeography of the Register see *RF*, I,
xxxix–xlvii, and *Collectio canonum*, Kölzer,
9–16.

6. *Il chronicon farfense di Gregorio di Catino*,
ed. Ugo Balzani, Fonti per la storia d'Italia,
Istituto Storico Italiano, XXXIII–XXXIV,
Rome, 1903. For the dating of the
Chronicle see Zielinski, *Studien*, 28 nn.
14–15.

7. The *Registrum Petri Diaconi* from the
early 1130s in the archives of

Montecassino; the *Chronicon vulturnese* (Barb.
lat. 2724) and the *Chronicon S. Sophiae* (Vat.
lat. 4939), both in the Vatican Library and
dating from the early twelfth century. See
Zielinski, *Studien*, 5–6; Ugo Balzani, *Le
cronache italiane nel medio evo*, Milan, 1909, 152
n. 1; O. Bertolini, "La collezione canonica
Beneventana del Vat. lat. 4939," *Collectanea
vaticana in honorem Anselmi M. Card. Albareda*, I,
Studi e testi CCIX, Vatican City, 1962,
119–137; H. Hoffmann, "Chronik und
Urkunde in Montecassino," *QFIAB*, LI,
1971, 93–206. See also Theo Kölzer,
"*Codex libertatis.* Überlegungen zur Funktion
des 'Regestum Farfense' und anderer
Klosterchartulare," *Atti del IX congresso
internazionale di studi sull'alto medioevo*, Centro
Italiano di Studi sull'Alto Medioevo,
Spoleto, 1983, 609–653, esp. 624–625.

8. Balzani, *Chronicon*, I, x.

9. For a description of the manuscript
see *ibid.*, xxxviii–xl.

10. See note 3 above.

11. See note 6 above.

12. *Liber largitorius vel notarius monasterii
pharphensis*, ed. G. Zucchetti, *Regesta
chartarum Italie*, Rome, 1913–1932.

13. Mabillon, *Annales ordinis S. Benedicti*,
IV, 1707, 207ff.

14. *Consuetudines monasticae*, ed. Bruno
Albers, I, Stuttgart and Vienna, 1900.

15. *Liber tramitis aevi odolonis abbatis*, ed.
Peter Dinter, *Corpus consuetudinum
monasticarum*, X, Siegburg, 1980. For a listing
of earlier publications of all or part of the
text see *ibid.*, xxxiii–xxxiv.

16. See, e.g., Julius von Schlosser, *Die
abendländische Klosteranlage des frühen Mittelalters*,
Vienna, 1889, and Georg Hager, "Zur
Geschichte des abendländischen
Klosteranlage," *Zeitschrift für christliche Kunst*,
XIV, 1901, cols. 167–186.

17. Ildefonso Schuster, "L'abbaye de
Farfa et sa restauration au XIe siècle sous
Hugues I," *Revue bénédictine*, XXIV, 1907, 13–
35, 374–402.

18. *Ibid.*, 374–376, and *Liber tramitis*,
Dinter, xxxviii–xliii.

19. See Appendix of Documents, no.
VIII. *Liber tramitis*, Dinter, 3–5 nos. 1, 2.

20. "Ad videndum et scribendum
properavit apud eundem Cluniacensem
coenobium." *Liber tramitis*, Dinter, 4.

21. "Ibi probatae experientiae didicit,
duplici hoc pro diffinitione ad purum
contexuit . . ." *Ibid.*, 5.

22. The term Apuli is not a reference to
a monastery in Apulia, as previously
believed; instead, it has been shown to be a
scribal error for Opuli or Mons Opuli
(Montopoli) near Farfa. See *Liber tramitis*,
Dinter, xliii nos. 100, 105.

23. *Ibid.*, lii, and Schuster, "L'abbaye de
Farfa," 384–385.

24. *Liber tramitis*, Dinter, xlvii–xlviii. See
also Jacques Hourlier, "Sainte Odilon
batisseur," *Revue Mabillon*, LI, 1961, 303–
324; Hourlier, "Le monastère de saint
Odilon," *Studia anselmiana*, L, 1962, 5–21,
reprinted in an English translation in *Cluniac
Monasticism in the Central Middle Ages*, ed.
Noreen Hunt, London, 1971, 56–76.

25. *Liber tramitis*, Dinter, xliv–xlvii. The
significance of the Lenten booklist was first
pointed out by André Wilmart, "Le convent
et la bibliothèque de Cluny vers le milieu du
XIe siècle," *Revue Mabillon*, XI, 1921, 89–
124. However, his terminus ad quem of
1042–1043 must be revised to ca. 1050.
See *Liber tramitis*, Dinter, xlv n. 116.

26. *Liber tramitis*, Dinter, lii–lvi.

27. *Ibid.*, xxxv–xxxviii.

28. As stated above, he began his last
work, the *Liber floriger*, in 1130. The exact
date of Gregory's death is not known. See
Zielinski, *Studien*, 26 n. 5. Schuster,
L'imperiale abbazia, 2, estimates that Gregory
died in 1133.

29. *Chronicon*, II, 319–322, reproduces
the marginal notes in Vat. lat. 6808. See
also P. Kehr, "Urkunden zur Geschichte
von Farfa im XII. Jahrhundert," *QFIAB*, IX,
1906, 170–184; Otto Vehse, "Die
päpstliche Herrschaft in der Sabina bis zur
Mitte des 12. Jahrhundert," *QFIAB*, XXI,
1929–1930, 120–175; I. Guiraud, "La badia
di Farfa alla fine del secolo decimoterzo,"
ASRStP, XV, 1892, 275–288; G. Palmieri,
"Serie degli abbati di Farfa," *Il muratori*, I,
fasc. 1–4, 1892, fasc. 5–6, 1893; II, fasc.

7–10, 1893, fasc. 11–12, 1894; III, fasc. 13, 1894; fasc. 14, 15, 18, 1895. The history of the period is recounted by Schuster, *L'imperiale abbazia*, 272–346.

30. Toubert, *Les structures*, I, 19, calls it a *"médiocre compilation."*

31. The documents in the Archivio di Stato, dating from 1545 to 1860, are listed in catalogue 25: II. They consist of 130 folders containing primarily account books and records of the Farfa fairs.

32. *Aeneid*, VII, 715. *Metamorphoses*, XIV, 328–330. For an etymological discussion of the name Farfarus see A. Ernout, "Farfarus et Marmar," *Studi etruschi*, XXIV, 1955–56, 311–318.

33. See Richard Ring, "The Lands of Farfa: Studies in Lombard and Carolingian Italy," Ph.D. diss., University of Wisconsin, 1972, 9 and nn. 1–2, where the relevant passages in the Farfa Register are cited.

34. See Appendix of Documents, No. II.

35. *Chronicon*, I, 121–132. In the preface to the *Liber floriger*, Gregory suggests that Lawrence founded the monastery at Farfa ca. A.D. 381, during the reign of the emperor Gratian. See *Chronicon*, I, 121 n. 1.

36. *History of the Church*, II, 693; Gregorio Penco, *Storia del monachesimo in Italia dalle origini alla fine del medio evo*, Rome, 1961, 23–24, and his "Il monachesimo in Umbria dalle origini al sec. VII incluso," *Ricerche sull'Umbria tardo-antico e preromanica*, Atti del II convegno di studi umbri, Perugia, 1965, 271. Most recently, Lawrence has been identified with a bishop at Forum Novum, present-day Vescovio, who was active around 554. P. di Manzano and T. Leggio, *La diocesi di Cures Sabini*, Fara Sabina, n.d., 14.

37. *Chronicon*, 3–6.

38. *Ibid.*, 7–8.

39. See Appendix of Documents, Nos. I, II. For the authenticity of these two documents see Carlrichard Brühl, "Chronologie und Urkunden der Herzöge von Spoleto im 8. Jahrhundert," *QFIAB*, LI, 1971, 16–19, and Hans Hubert Anton,

Studien zu den Klosterprivilegien der Päpste im frühen Mittelalter unter besonderer Berücksichtigung der Privilegierung von St. Maurice d'Agaune, Beiträge zur Geschichte und Quellenkunde des Mittelalters, IV, Berlin and New York, 1975, 75–83, 91–92.

40. This collection of homilies was particularly popular in the late eighth and early ninth centuries as one of the first collections of readings and prayers to be arranged according to the ecclesiastical calendar. Max Manitius, *Geschichte der lateinischen Literatur des Mittelalters*, I, Munich, 1911, 266. For a detailed study of the Alanus homiliary see Raymond Etaix, "Le prologue du sermonaire d'Alain de Farfa," *Scriptorium*, XVIII, 1964, 3–10, and Réginald Grégoire, *Homéliaires liturgiques médiévaux: Analyse des manuscrits*, Biblioteca degli Studi Medievali, XXII, Spoleto, 1980, 127–220.

41. *Chronicon*, I, 155, records of the text of an inscription commemorating the completion of the aqueduct: "[Probatus abbas] electus a fratribus et praeordinatus a Domino, in regimine patris elevatus culmine, cooperuit os fontis aquae manantis ab aevo et traxit aquam a pristino cursu suo ab hoc loco miliarios tres. Porro hanc fabricari iussit formam, per montis huius latera haesam. Sub terra decurrens constricta, opitulante Christi gratia, hoc loco honeste fluit aqua. Perfectaque est haec operatio indictione prima, anno vero quinto postquam domnus Carolus excellentissimus rex Italiam coepit." The first indiction, the fifth year of the reign of Charlemagne, corresponds to the year 778. A fragment of this inscription is still preserved at the abbey. See Ildefonso Schuster, "Spigolature farfensi," *Rivista storica benedettina*, II, 1907, 409–410, and Charles B. McClendon, "An Early Funerary Portrait from the Medieval Abbey at Farfa," *Gesta*, XXII, 1983, 18, fig. 8.

42. See Appendix of Documents, No. III. *MGH, Diplomatum Karolinorum*, I, 141–142 n. 98. See also Franz J. Felten, "Zur Geschichte der Kloster Farfa und S. Vincenzo al Volturno im achten Jahrhundert," *QFIAB*, LXII, 1982, 1–58,

and J. Fischer, *Königtum, Adel und Kirche in Königreich Italien,* Bonn, 1965.

43. Carlrichard Brühl, *Fodrum, Gistum und Servitium Regis,* I, Cologne, 1968, 447–448.

44. *Chronicon,* I, 20: "Ragambaldus . . . in Gallia civitate ortus; Altbertus, Parisius civitate exortus Galliarum; Mauroaldus, natione Francus, Wormatia oriundus civitate."

• 45. *Liber tramitis,* Dinter, XXI, and Josef Semmler, "Karl der Grosse und das fränkische Mönchtum," *Karl der Grosse,* II, 274–277.

46. For a letter from Alcuin addressed to Mauroaldus see *Chronicon,* I, 20 n. 3.

47. *RF,* II, 143, 177–175, docs. 216, 217; Schuster, *L'imperiale abbazia,* 61–63.

48. Schuster suggests that Ingoaldus, together with the abbots of Montecassino and S. Vincenzo al Volturno, attended the imperial synod concerned with monastic reform at Aachen in 817. Schuster, *L'imperiale abbazia,* 65.

49. *Ibid.,* 69–71.

50. "Idem dominus apostolicus . . . se recognavit nullum dominium in iure ipsius monasterii se habere, excepta consecratione." *RF,* II, 233–238, doc. 282; *Chronicon,* I, 199; Schuster, *L'imperiale abbazia,* 68–69; and *IP,* II, 61 n. 8. The litigation involving Ingoaldus is recorded in a letter of privilege issued by the emperor Lothar on Dec. 15, 840. It also states: "Quod praedictum monasterium nullatenus sub iure et . . . dominatione praefatae Romanae Ecclesiae vel sub tributo aut pensione esse deberet."

51. Indeed, as Richard Ring points out in his study "The Lands of Farfa," 244–246, the number of donations to the monastery peaked during the reigns of Abbots Benedict and Ingoaldus.

52. Abbot Mauroaldus: "Nam in ecclesia beatae Mariae multum pretiosum ex auro et argento ornatum fieri iussit." Abbot Benedictus is described as "devotus . . . in exterioribus ornamentis que ad cultum ecclesiae utilia videntur, ita ut in libris et altaris vestibus atque diversis utensilibus construendis nimis sagicissimus esset, ut

usque ad presens ex parte apparet." *Chronicon,* I, 20–21.

53. See Appendix of Documents, No. V. Concerning the Farfa Passionary, now in the Biblioteca Nazionale in Rome (Ms. Farf. 29), see Supino Martini, "La produzione," 590–607, and E. B. Garrison, *Studies in the History of Medieval Italian Painting,* II: 3, Florence, 1956, 121–122. Alexander, one of the seven sons of Felicitas, was originally buried in the cemetery of the Giordani on the Via Salaria. For the history of the cult of this St. Alexander, one of several saints by that name, see Serafini Prete, *I Santi martiri Alessandro e Filippo nella chiesa fermana,* Studi di antichità cristiana, XVI, Vatican City, 1941, 82–86. See also Ildefonso Schuster, "Martyrologium pharphense ex apographo cardinalis Fortunati Tamburini O. S. B. codicis saeculi XI," *Revue bénédictine,* XXVII, 1910, 52 n. 1. The report of an eighth-century translation of the relics of St. Alexander to Ottobeuren in Bavaria has been shown to be false: Wilhelm Hotzelt, "Translationen von Martyerreliquien aus Rom nach Bayern im 8. Jahrhundert," *Studien und Mitteilungen aus dem Benediktiner Orden,* LII, 1935, 330–336.

54. *Chronicon,* I, 186–187; and *RF,* II, 221–223, doc. 270. The possible relationship between these two events was suggested to me by Richard Ring in private conversation.

55. See Appendix of Documents, No. IV.

56. For a general discussion of the classical revival in epigraphy of the Carolingian period, especially in Rome, see Nicolette Gray, "The Paleography of Latin Inscriptions in the Eighth, Ninth and Tenth Centuries in Italy," *PBSR,* XVI, 1948, 38–170, esp. 97–105.

57. The *Institutio canonicorum* issued at Aachen in 816, part of the monastic reform legislation sponsored by Louis the Pious, defines the differences between the *vita canonica* and the *vita monastica.* Canons were bound to a cloistral life under the rule of an abbot but were distinguished from monks by the right to own private property, to

wear somewhat finer clothing, and to live on occasion in individual dwellings within the monastery. Canons, unlike most monks in this period, were also generally ordained priests. See *Handbook of Church History*, III, 1969, 330–331, and Fernand Cabrol and Henri Leclercq, *Dictionnaire d'archéologie chrétienne et de liturgie*, III: 1, cols. 236–248.

58. The placement of "palaces" in rural or suburban monasteries was an innovation of the Carolingian period. See Carlrichard Brühl, "Königs-, Bischofs-, und Stadtpfalz in den Städten des 'Regnum Italiae' von 9. bis zum 13. Jahrhundert," *Historische Forschungen für Walter Schlesinger*, ed. Helmut Beumann, Cologne, 1974, 408–410.

59. See Appendix of Documents, No. VI. How well the archaeological evidence agrees with this description is discussed in chapter 4.

60. Fischer, *Königtum*, 142–143; *Chronicon*, I, 207–208.

61. *RF*, III, 11–12, doc. 307; *Chronicon*, I, 221–223; Schuster, *L'imperiale abbazia*, 84–85.

62. For example, in response to a request for military assistance from Abbot Marinus of Farfa in 883, the emperor, Charles the Fat, reconfirmed the abbey's privileges, but no tangible help was forthcoming. *RF*, III, 32–33, doc. 330; Schuster, *L'imperiale abbazia*, 86.

63. S. Prete, *I santi martiri*, 97–98, 118–119, suggests that the cult of St. Alexander and other martyrs, along with their relics, was introduced to Fermo at this time by the monks from Farfa.

64. *Chronicon*, I, 29–32.

65. Schuster, *L'imperiale abbazia*, 96. See *Destructio farfensis*, published in *Chronicon*, I, 32: "[Petrus] sepultus est . . . in oratorio sanctae Mariae quod ipse construxerat."

66. Bernard Hamilton, "The Monastic Revival in Tenth-Century Rome," *Studia monastica*, IV, 1962, 35–68.

67. For a discussion of Alberic's activity in the Sabina see Toubert, *Les structures*, II, 978–998.

68. *Chronicon*, I, 40–41.

69. *RF*, III, 108–114, doc. 404, issued

by Otto I in 967. These privileges were reconfirmed by Otto II in 981, *RF*, III, 114, doc. 406, 116, doc. 407, and again by Otto III, *RF*, III, 122–124, doc. 413, 134–135, doc. 424, 135–137, doc. 425, 143–144, doc. 429, 145, doc. 431, 151, doc. 438. See also Toubert, *Les structures*, II, 985 n. 2.

70. *RF*, IV, 102, doc. 700.

71. Schuster, *Ugo di Farfa*, Perugia, 1911, 193.

72. In the *Destructio farfensis*, *Chronicon*, I, 28, Hugo writes: "Ob memoriam patrum . . . sit restauratio ad spirituales virtutes nostris pectoribus inserendas."

73. "Relatio constitutionis domini Hugonis abbatis," *Chronicon*, I, 56.

74. *Ibid.*, 55–58. Hugo's Constitution may have been confirmed by Pope Silvester II during a visit to Farfa on September 22, 999. See *Liber tramitis*, Dinter, xxii, and *IP*, II, 62 n. 15.

75. *Chronicon*, II, 120–121. Schuster, *L'imperiale abbazia*, 189 n. 3.

76. *RF*, IV, 210–211, doc. 809. See also Toubert, *Les structures*, II, 909 n. 3.

77. Wolfgang Braunfels, *Monasteries of Western Europe*, London, 1972, 51. The number of monks at Cluny in 1063 is reported to have been seventy-three. About seventy monks are recorded in 993 and again in 1042. See A. Wilmart, "Le couvent et la bibliothèque de Cluny vers le milieu du XIe siècle," *Revue Mabillon*, XI, 1921, 117.

78. *RF*, IV, 274–277, doc. 879.

79. See Appendix of Documents, No. X.

80. *RF*, V, 294–295, doc. 130.

81. *RF*, IV, 355–356, doc. 976.

82. These altar cloths are listed in an inventory of the monastery's treasury. See Appendix of Documents, No. XII.

83. *RF*, V, 94.

84. *IP*, II, 68 n. 48, and Partner, *Lands*, 130.

85. See Appendix of Documents, No. XI. *RF*, V, 198, doc. 1154; Toubert, *Les structures*, I, 523 n. 2. The ruins of the unfinished abbey church are discussed in chapter 6.

86. *MGH, Libelli de lite imperatorum et*

pontificum saeculis XI. et XII. conscripti, II, 534–542, and Giorgi, "Il regesto," 460–473. The treatise was written in 1111, on the occasion of the imperial coronation of Henry V. Schuster, *L'imperiale abbazia,* 226. The attribution of the treatise to Gregory of Catino is convincingly disputed by Karl Heinzelmann, *Die Farfenser Streitschriften,* Strasbourg, 1904, 113–120. See also *Collectio canonum,* Kölzer, 8 n. 16, 85 n. 71.

87. See Appendix of Documents, No. XIII.

88. Partner, *Lands,* 163; Schuster, *L'imperiale abbazia,* 270; Vehse, "Die päpstliche Herrschaft," 165.

89. Schuster, *L'imperiale abbazia,* 273, 283. Yet we know very little about the life and work of Adenolfus. Unlike Hugo, he left no writings. More significantly, our main sources for the history of Farfa, the Register and Chronicle, end with the beginning of Adenolfus's reign. The Chronicle was in fact complete before 1119, while the last entry in the Register refers to the election of Adenolfus. Zielinski, *Studien,* 27–28.

90. A marginal note in the Farfa Customary (Vat. lat. 6808) reads: "MCXLII monasterium novum inchoatur in monte." Schuster, *L'imperiale abbazia,* 277 n. 4; *Chronicon,* II, 321.

91. "Anno MCLIIII. Adenolfus abbas obiit." *Chronicon,* II, 321.

92. Schuster, *L'imperiale abbazia,* 283.

93. Kehr, "Urkunden," 177, 184 n. viii.

94. Schuster, *L'imperiale abbazia,* 285, describes Bernard of Pisa as "tutta creatura d'Adenolfo e dei Farfensi."

95. A marginal note in the Farfa Customary, *Chronicon,* II, 321, states: "MCXLV Eugenius III apud Farfense monasterium papa est consecratus." See also *Pontificum Romanorum qui fuerunt ab exeunte saeculo IX usque ad finam saeculi XIII vitae ab aequalibus conscriptae,* ed. J. M. Watterich, II, Leipzig, 1862, rep. Darmstadt, 1966, 282–284, and Schuster, *L'imperiale abbazia,* 286 n. 1.

96. Toubert, *Les structures,* II, 1074–

1081; Partner, *Lands,* 184, 190 n. 1; Daniel Waley, *The Papal State in the Thirteenth Century,* London, 1961, 10–13.

97. "Quod [Farfa] ad ius et defensionem beati Petri et sanctae Romanae pertinet ecclesiae." *IP,* II, 68 n. 52; Kehr, "Urkunden," 172–173; Schuster, *L'imperiale abbazia,* 288; Vehse, "Die päpstliche Herrschaft," 167.

98. Brühl, *Fodrum,* I, 565, 698–702, 737; Partner, *Lands,* 190.

99. *Chronicon,* II, 321.

100. One source (*Chronicon fossae novae*) records that Victor IV was consecrated at Farfa. See *Pontificum romanorum,* II, ed. Watterich, 464. See also Schuster, *L'imperiale abbazia,* 292 n. 3, 293 n. 1, and Paolo Brezzi, *Roma e l'impero medioevale (774–1252),* Bologna, 1947, 351. A marginal note in the Farfa Customary, however, refers to the schism but not to the consecration (*Chronicon,* II, 321).

101. For a general discussion of the shifting political alignments of the period see Partner, *Lands,* 182–205, and Waley, *The Papal State,* 10–16. Evidence for Farfa's political ties during this period is admittedly conflicting. For example, in 1174–1176, after Victor IV's death, Pope Alexander III sent a letter to Abbot Adenolfus II confirming property belonging to the monastery in Ascolano. See *IP,* IV, 153, and Schuster, *L'imperiale abbazia,* 293.

102. Schuster, *L'imperiale abbazia,* 294; I. Giorgi, "Il regesto di Farfa e le altre opere di Gregorio di Catino," *ASRStP,* II, 1879, 452–455. Here the emperor still insists upon the right to collect the *fodrum.* See Brühl, *Fodrum,* I, 737 n. 786.

103. Partner, *Lands,* 229.

104. Palmieri, "Serie degli abbati," *Muratori,* I, 1892, 113–114.

105. Schuster, *L'imperiale abbazia,* 313; Guiraud, "La badia di Farfa," 275–288.

106. Schuster, *L'imperiale abbazia,* 329–346.

107. Commercial enterprises in connection with the abbey are recorded as early as the late ninth century in the

privilegium issued by the emperor Louis II in 872. *RF*, III, 12, doc. 307: "De teloneis verum mercatorum, et pontum, et de decimus ad portam monasterii dandis, sicuti in aliis praeceptis continetur, pariter roboramus."

108. Under the date *Aug. VIII Id.* of the calendar in a fifteenth-century breviary from Farfa (Bib. Naz. Farf. 294) one reads: "Anno Dni. MCCCCII consecratum fuit altare. Dominae Nostrae." Schuster, "De fastorum agiographico ordine imperialis monasterii pharphensis," *Millenaire de Cluny: Congrès d'histoire et d'archéologie tenu à Cluny les 10, 11, 12 septembre, 1910,* I, Macon, 1910, 159, and his *L'imperiale abbazia,* 347–348.

109. See Appendix of Documents, No. XIV.

110. Schuster, *L'imperiale abbazia,* 357 n. 1, erroneously dates the rebuilding to 1444, fifty years too early, after misreading an inscription still extant in the church's coffered ceiling. The date on the ceiling is clearly MCCCCLXXXXIIII and not MCCCCXXXXIIII, as indicated by Schuster. The church was consecrated two years later. See Appendix of Documents, No. XV.

111. The della Rovere family, including Pope Julius II himself, ruled Farfa during 1503–1513; the Farnese ruled during 1546–1590; the Perretti during 1590–1623; and the Barberini during 1628–1738.

112. J. Schmidlin, "Ein Kampf um das Deutschtum in Klosterleben Italiens: Subiaco und Farfa im 16. Jahrhundert," *Historisches Jahrbuch,* XXIV, 1903, 253–282.

113. Schuster, *L'imperiale abbazia,* 390.

114. The property was first purchased by a Scotsman by the name of F. Morgan. *Ricordi dell'imperiale monastero di S. Maria di Farfa 1699 fino al 1882,* in the Farfa library, states: "1878. 19 Ottobre furano posti in vendita tutti i beni di Farfa, e porzione del Monastero. Il Sig. Inglesi [sic] Morgan per il sotto principale offrirano [sic] 215,000 It. L." Subsequently, the property came into the ownership of a lawyer, F. G. Vitale. See Schuster, *L'imperiale abbazia,* 392.

Chapter 2: The State of the Problem

1. For a discussion of the physical geography of the Sabina see Toubert, *Les structures,* I, 135–98, and Ring, "The Lands of Farfa," 9–27. The geomorphology of the central Apennines is analyzed by Jean Demangeot, *Géomorphologie des Abruzzes adriatiques,* Mémoires et Documents, Centre des Recherches et Documentations Cartographiques et Géographiques, Paris, 1965.

2. David Whitehouse, "Farfa Abbey: The Eighth and Ninth Centuries," *Arte medievale,* II, 1985, 245. A full analysis of the excavated material will appear in the final excavation report now in preparation.

3. Krautheimer, *Rome,* 293–294.

4. See Appendix of Documents, No. XV.

5. The design of S. Maria del Popolo, in turn, reflected strong influence from architecture in Lombardy during the second half of the fifteenth century. Gunter Urban, "Der Kirchenbau des Quattrocento in Rome," *Römisches Jahrbuch,* IX, 1963, 75–287; Ludwig H. Heydenreich and Wolfgang Lotz, *Architecture in Italy: 1400 to 1600,* Baltimore, Md., 1974, 55–58; E. Bentivoglio and S. Valtieri, *S. Maria del Popolo a Roma,* Rome, 1976, 15–22.

6. I prefer to use the term presbytery rather than apse or choir, because this corresponds most closely to the medieval term *presbyterium,* which was the area reserved for the main altar and the officiating clergy. As a rule, the "choir" or *chorus,* where the monks were situated, stood in front of the presbytery and usually corresponded to the crossing. For the correspondence between liturgical terminology and architectural design in monastic churches of the early Middle Ages see Friedrich Möbius, "Die Chorpartie der westeuropäischen Klosterkirche zwischen 8. und 11. Jahrhundert," *Architektur des Mittelaters: Funktion und Gestalt,* ed. Friedrich Möbius and Ernst Schubert, Weimar, 1983, 9–41, esp. 32–39.

7. See Appendix of Documents, No. XVI.

8. See Appendix of Documents, Nos. IV–V. In this respect, Schuster was also following the opinion of the seventeenth-century chronicler Archangelus De Alexandris, who states (Appendix of Documents, No. XVI,D) that the abbot's apartments, inserted into the medieval bell tower and square presbytery in 1609, occupied the site of the Sichardan oratory. There is no evidence, however, that Archangelus was any better informed about the architectural history of the medieval abbey than Schuster was. Indeed, in the early 1600s, as in Schuster's day, only the east end of the medieval abbey church was still visible. Moreover, the Sichardan oratory is the sole architectural structure, aside from altar dedications, explicitly mentioned in the medieval sources, which Archangelus knew well. In other words, it is not unreasonable to assume that both men made the same association between the historical record and the fragmentary physical remains of the medieval abbey church that stood before them.

9. Schuster, *L'imperiale abbazia*, 75–80.

10. Alberto Serafini, *Torri campanarie di Roma e del Lazio nel medioevo*, Rome, 1927, 159–162.

11. Paul Markthaler, "Sulle recenti scoperte nell'abbazia imperiale di Farfa," *RAC*, V, 1928, 39–88.

12. *Ibid.*, 67.

13. *Ibid.*, 50–52, 56–57.

14. D. Giuseppe Croquison, "I problemi archeologici farfensi," *RAC*, XV, 1938, 37–71.

15. *Ibid.*, 51–53.

16. *Ibid.*, 64–69.

17. In 1937, Ugo Tarchi published several plans and a reconstruction drawing of the east end of the church, but with no explanatory text. See Ugo Tarchi, *L'arte nell'Umbria and nella Sabina*, II, Milan, 1937, 8, pls. LXXXIV–XCI.

18. *VII Settimana dei musei: Tutela e valorizzazione del patrimonio artistico di Roma e del Lazio*, Rome, Palazzo Venezia, 12–19 April

1964, 122–135. More detailed information appears in an unauthorized report by a journalist, Domenico Pertica, "Recenti scavi all'abbazia di Farfa," *Il cantiere*, IV, 1962, 41–47. The original of the plan published by the Superintendency has, unfortunately, been lost.

19. Nicola Franciosa, *L'abbazia imperiale di Farfa*, Naples, 1964.

20. Carlo Pietrangeli, "L'abbazia di Farfa," *Abbazie del Lazio*, Rome, 1970, 141–175.

21. *Pouchain: 10 anni di attività*, Rome, n. d., 1–15.

22. Adriano Prandi, "Osservazioni sull'abbazia di Farfa," *Roma e l'età carolingia*, Atti delle giornate di studio, 3–8 Maggio 1976, Istituto Nazionale di Archeologia e Storia dell'Arte, Rome, 1976, 357–67.

23. Beatrice Premoli, "La chiesa abbaziale di Farfa," *RINASA*, XXI–XXII, 1974–1975 (1976), 5–77.

Chapter 3: Architectural Analysis and Reconstruction

1. The Markthaler plan is included at the end of the article by Croquison, "I problemi," following p. 70. For the Superintendency plan see *VII Settimana dei musei*, 123, and Franciosa, *L'abbazia imperiale*, 28, fig. 4.

2. Pertica, "Recenti scavi," 42: "Infatti alcuni muri risultavano appartenere ad antichi vani per tombe per cui mancavano d'interesse. Anzi furono proprio questi muri a trarre in inganno alcuni studiosi sulle presunte dimensioni dell'antica basilica di Farfa che si voleva a tre o cinque navate." Unfortunately, there is no other information available about these tombs.

3. For a detailed analysis of this fresco see Charles B. McClendon, "An Early Funerary Portrait from the Medieval Abbey at Farfa," *Gesta*, XXII, 1983, 13–26.

4. Markthaler, "Sulle recenti scoperte," 55.

5. Croquison, "I problemi," 48: "Una testa d'uomo di età avanzata, dalle labbra tu-

mide, postante la tonsura ecclesiastica, è una figura assai espressiva. Le dimensioni di questo frammento sono di ca. m. 0,16×0,115. Il suo colore è rosso mattone."

6. Guglielmo Matthiae, *Pittura romana del medioevo*, I, Rome, 1965, pls. 113, 128, 141–142. See also Pietro Romanelli and Per Jonas Nordhagen, *S. Maria Antiqua*, Rome, 1964, pl. 36A.

7. Croquison, "I problemi," 51–53.

8. Following the excavations by the Superintendency of Monuments in the early 1960s, the outside of the crypt was faced with rubble masonry and capped by asphalt in an attempt to prevent water seepage.

9. May Vieillard-Troiekouroff, "L'architecture en France du temps de Charlemagne," *Karl der Grosse*, III, 336–355, figs. I–II, 7–9; Jules Formigé, *L'abbaye royale de Saint-Denis*, Paris, 1960, 162–163, figs. 142–143; and Sumner McK. Crosby, *L'abbaye royale de Saint-Denis*, Paris, 1953, 14ff.

10. Prandi, "Osservazioni," 360–362, 368. On the other hand, Premoli ("La chiesa abbaziale," 30) believes that the apse and crypt are contemporaneous.

11. B. M. Apollonj-Ghetti, A. Ferrua, E. Josi, and E. Kirschbaum, *Esplorazioni sotto la confessione di San Pietro in Vaticano*, I, Vatican City, 1951, 173–191. See also Jocelyn Toynbee and John Ward Perkins, *The Shrine of St. Peter and the Vatican Excavation*, London, 1956, 211–220, and Krautheimer, *Corpus*, V, 259–61.

12. Krautheimer, *Corpus*, V, 259–61.

13. Krautheimer, *Corpus*, III, 252. Of the two original entrances to the crypt at S. Prassede, only the flight of stairs on the left is preserved, and here the mortar joints between the monolithic steps and the crypt wall are clearly visible.

14. Prandi, "Osservazioni," 367 n. 12. Both mortar samples contained lime, silica, and iron oxide. The amount of lime differed by 4 percent, that of silica or sand by 2 percent, and the amounts of iron oxide were the same.

15. *Ibid.*, 361.

16. Markthaler, "Sulle recenti scoperte,"

49, saw the date of 1732 on the iron railings of the stairway that cuts across the exterior north side of the bell tower. These stairs are recorded as having been built ca. 1730. *Loc. cit.*, n. 22. The room adjoining the bell tower to the south was built as a granary ca. 1622. See Appendix of Documents, No. XVI. At the same time, the corridor which passes across the exterior of the east side of the bell tower base was constructed to link the cloister with the new granary. Markthaler, "Sulle recenti scoperte," 63 and n. 53.

17. Incised in the plaster on a brick coming from the doorway that cut through the east wall of the bell tower giving access to the new second floor was found the inscription, "1592 F[uit] REN[ovata]." *Ibid.*, 63, fig. 24.

18. Since the time this description was written in 1978, this wall of the sacristy has been covered from floor to ceiling by elaborate wooden cupboards.

19. *Ibid.*, 66, fig. 29.

20. *Ibid.*, 62–63, fig. 24.

21. Ildefonso Schuster, "Reliquie d'arte nella badia imperiali di Farfa," *ASRStP*, XXXIV, 1911, 323–332.

22. No report of this work has been issued, but the restorer, Carlo Giantommasi, was kind enough to share his technical findings with me in private conversation.

23. Markthaler, "Sulle recenti scoperte," 77–81, fig. 36.

24. Most of the figures in the group on the right seem to bear a tonsure. Schuster, "Reliquie d'arte," 329.

25. Markthaler, "Sulle recenti scoperte," 74–77.

26. The only other early medieval representation of the Naaman story known to me is found in a ninth-century manuscript, the *Sacra parallela* of John of Damascus, in Paris (Bibliothèque Nationale, Cod. gr. 923, fol. 210v), where three episodes in the story are depicted, none of which compares to the Farfa fresco. See Kurt Weitzmann, "The Illustrations of the Septuagint," *Studies in Classical and Byzantine*

Book Illumination, Chicago, 1971, 56–57, fig. 35.

27. Schuster, "Reliquie d'arte," 327.

28. For Croquison's remarks see "I problemi," 43–44.

29. This type of masonry at Farfa corresponds in general to that found in the monastic churches of Subiaco as classified by G. Giovannoni, "L'architettura dei monasteri sublacensi," *I monasteri di Subiaco,* I, Rome, 1904, 291: "II) Struttura informe eseguita senza cura: sassi di ogni forma e dimensione, frammenti di pietra e di mattoni cementati da abbondante malta e rivestiti di rabboccatura e intonaco: secolo XVI al XVIII."

30. Markthaler, "Recenti scoperte," 40. The architrave of the entrance to the sacristy bears the date 1545.

31. Giovannoni, *loc. cit.,* describes masonry classification no. 1 at Subiaco as: "Strutture con paramento a pietra più o meno accuratamente squadrata (cardellino o calcare), e riempimento a pietra semi squadrata o pietra informe: anteriori alla metà del sec. XV . . . appartiene principalmente al medio evo." This essentially agrees with what one finds at Farfa. For Giovannoni's categorization of 16th- to 18th-century masonry see n. 29 above.

32. A. B. Schuchert, "Eine unbekannte Elfenbeinkassette aus dem 11. Jahrhundert," *RQ,* XL, 1932, 1–11. For the most recent study of the Farfa Casket see Robert Bergman, *The Salerno Ivories,* Cambridge, Mass., 1980, 81–83, 128–130, where it is dated to ca. 1060.

33. According to Croquison, "I problemi," 59 n. 59, the demolition was ordered by the Fondo per il culto in 1889. Records in the archives of the monastery (classified under AF 343) indicate that work may have begun as early as July 24, 1887.

34. Franciosa, *L'abbazia imperiale,* 61–64, fig. 24.

35. Semicircular windows have ample precedent in late antiquity. They appear in the attic of dividing walls in ancient Roman warehouses and seem to have been used for

the clerestory of the inner aisles of Constantine's Lateran basilica from the beginning of the fourth century A.D. See Krautheimer, *Corpus,* V, 1977, 65, 77–78. In the first half of the twelfth century, they appear again in Rome in the nave clerestory of SS. Alessio e Bonifacio and in the inserted cross wall of S. Stefano Rotondo: Krautheimer, *Corpus,* I, 41–42, IV, 198–238. North of the Alps, individual lunettes pierce the east wall of the transept of the abbey church at Hersfeld (1038–1042) to allow light or access into the area of the side aisles above the beam line, depending upon whether or not the side aisle ceilings were coffered or open.

36. See Appendix of Documents, No. XIV.

37. For a similar discussion of building procedures see George H. Forsyth, Jr., "A Problem of Surveying in Medieval Architecture: 'Geometricis et Arithmeticis,'" *Archeology,* III, 1950, 74–79.

38. The zone bears no. 9 in the print, which corresponds to the following label in the index: "Palazzo dell Em.mo Sig.r Card.le Abbate Commend.o con le Carceri, e Piazza avanti le Stalle."

39. *Catalogus cardinalium abbatuum farfensium, 1728–1790,* Farfa Ms. AF 291, fol. 32r. See Appendix of Documents, No. XVII.

40. *Ibid.,* fol. 4v. "Palatium verò sive Domum Abbatialem dicti Monasterii cum Coquina, tinello, cellario, stabulis et Horto, aliisque membris suis extra Claustrum Monasterii et Fratrem habitionem, videlicet à prima Porta usque ad ecclesiam cum turribus. . . ." See Appendix of Documents, No. XIV.

41. Accounts in the Farfa archives (AF 343) record that Cardinal Lambruschini ordered the dismantling of the palace in June, 1836. Receipts for material sold from the palace ruins also date as late as 1893. See also Schuster, *L'imperiale abbazia,* 390–391.

42. Schuster, *L'imperiale abbazia,* 334, and "Reliquie d'arte," 287–288. The records of the *Regestum Alardi abbatis (1355–1363),* Farfa

Ms. AG 311, contain numerous references to a palace, such as: "Actum in palatio dicti monasterii Farfensi" (fol. 113r: dated 1361); "Actum im logia palatii dicti monasterii" (fol. 129r: dated 1361); and "Actum in palatio dicti monasterii in camera dicti domini Abbatis" (fol. 138r: dated 1360).

43. Several books of accounts, entitled "Libri del Stallone," are found in the Archivio di Stato. The complete books for the fairs in March and September are preserved from the year 1700, in which individual entries list the name of the merchant, a brief description of the horse, the day of payment, and the amount. A typical entry reads: "Antonio Amali / un cavallo baio stellato in fronte / Sabato / pagò 1.—." Archivio di Stato, 25/II: n. 37.

Chapter 4: The Pre-Carolingian and Carolingian Phases

1. *Chronicon*, I, 4–6.
2. See Appendix of Documents, No. IV.
3. André Grabar, *Christian Iconography: A Study of Its Origins*, Princeton, 1968, 74–75, fig. 13. See McClendon, "Portrait," 23, n. 10, for further bibliography.
4. Jean Hubert, Jean Porcher, and W. F. Volbach, *Europe of the Invasions*, New York, 1969, 62, fig. 75, 352 n. 75. The inscription refers to the translation of relics.
5. John Osborne, "The Painting of the Anastasis in the Lower Church of San Clemente, Rome: A Re-Examination of the Evidence for the Location of the Tomb of St. Cyril," *Byzantion*, LI, 1981, 255–87.
6. "Arcusque supra tumulum deauratus cum imagine et titulo exstructus." *Vita Karoli Magni*, chapter 31, *MGH SS*, II, ed. G. H. Pertz, 459–60.
7. The *Constructio monasterii farfensis* is published in *Chronicon*, I, 3–23. The pertinent section reads: "Nonus deinceps huius congregationis successit pastor Altbertus, Parisius civitate exortus Galliarum . . . nam quinque annis ac mensibus decem, diebus quindecim huic prefuit congregationi, obiit vero

octavodecimo kal. ianuarias." The abbots in question and the indication of their time of death can be listed as follows: Thomas of Maurienne (died ca. 716): "obiit vero .IV. idus decembris"; Lucerius (died ca. 740): "obiit quoque .XII. kal. iulias"; Fulcoaldus (died ca. 759): "obiit vero in pace .IV. nonas decembris"; Alanus (died ca. 769): "obiit quoque .V. nonas martias"; Probatus (died ca. 781): "obiit namque .IIII. idus augustas"; Ragambaldus (died ca. 786): "obiit quoque .V. nonas martias"; Altbertus (died ca. 790): "obiit vero octavodecimo kal. ianuarias"; Mauroaldus (died ca. 802): "obiit in pace .VIII. namque kal. novembris"; Benedictus (died ca. 815): "obiit in pace .III. idus augusti"; Ingoaldus (died ca. 830): "obiit .VII. kal. aprilis"; Sichardus (died ca. 842): "obiit vero quartodecimo kal. octobris"; Hildericus (died ca. 857): "migravit in pace idus septembris." The specific dates of death are not provided for two early abbots of Farfa, Aunepertus, who died ca. 724, and Wandelbertus, who died ca. 761.

8. Nicolette Gray, "The Filocalian Letter," *PBSR*, XXIV, 1956, 5–13, pls. I–IV. A good example is found in the title page of a manuscript in the Bayerische Staatsbibliothek in Munich (Clm MS 18092) attributed by B. Bischoff and E. A. Lowe to the monastic scriptorium of Tegernsee in southern Bavaria and dated to the late eighth century. Bernhard Bischoff, *Die südostdeutschen Schreibschulen und Bibliotheken der Karolingerzeit*, Leipzig, 1940, 153–156, and E. A. Lowe, *Codices latini antiquiores*, IX, 24. The link between the Tegernsee title page and the Farfa inscription is not solely a matter of style, for the text of the manuscript is one of the earliest preserved copies of the Homilies of Alanus, the abbot of Farfa who died around 770, less than a generation before Altbertus. Gregoire, *Homéliaires liturgiques*, 127–36. It could be that in copying the title page, the scribe followed a model from Farfa. We have no evidence from Farfa to verify this point, but it should be noted that in the *Constructio* Alanus himself is credited with having

produced manuscripts. *Chronicon*, I, 18: "Inter alia bonae operationis exercitia multos etiam mirifice exaravit codices." Still, the elements shared by the inscriptions of the Farfa fresco and the Tegernsee title page could just as well be due to a common Lombard heritage that was still very much alive during the early phases of the Carolingian period, as witness the letter forms of a title page from the Homilies of Egino, bishop of Verona (796–799), now in the Deutsche Staatsbibliothek in Berlin (MS Phillips 1676). Fragments of painted inscriptions in the east end of the abbey church, dating from the Romanesque period, and the letter forms in Farfa manuscripts, none of which dates from before the middle of the ninth century, provide no analogies to our inscription.

9. Paris, Bibl. Nat. Nouv. Acq. Lat. 1203, and Vienna, Österreichische Nationalbibliothek, Cod. 1861. The same could be said of the Gospels in Paris (Bibl. Arsenal Cod. 599). For a detailed description of these manuscripts see Wilhelm Koehler, *Die karolingische Miniaturen*, II, Berlin, 1958, 22–28, 42–46, pls. 18b–19b, 31–32. See also Gray, "Letter," 12, pl. IV, fig. c.

10. Abbot Berardus (or Beraldus) III (1099–1119) also died on the eighteenth. *Chronicon*, I, 291. However, neither the style of the figure in the lunette nor the palaeography of the inscription compares to examples at Farfa from ca. 1100, such as the inscription of a stone altar front now walled up in the courtyard of the sixteenth-century cloister, the frescoes and painted inscriptions in the east end of the abbey church, and the illustrations and letter forms of the Farfa Chronicle and Register. Moreover, the portraits of abbots in the Register show that the monastic habit in the early twelfth century consisted of a long-sleeved cowl instead of the sleeveless form represented in the funerary portrait. Premoli ("La chiesa abbaziale," 32) dates the lunette to the second half of the twelfth century because of the "byzantinizing" style of the figure and the decorative quality of the

letters; she provides no specific comparisons, however, to support this opinion. For a detailed analysis of this fresco see McClendon, "An Early Funerary Portrait."

11. There is evidence to suggest that pagan sarcophagi were reused for the burial of abbots at Farfa. We know this was the case with one ancient sarcophagus, now in the archaeological museum in Perugia, that bears the funerary inscription of Abbot Berardus, who died in 1089. This practice would explain the presence of other Roman sarcophagi still to be seen at the abbey. Charles B. McClendon, "Roman Antiquities from the Medieval Abbey at Farfa," *AJA*, LXXXV, 1981, 206–207. For a general discussion of this practice see I. Ragusa, "The Re-Use and Public Exhibition of Roman Sarcophagi during the Middle Ages and the Early Renaissance," unpublished master's thesis, New York University, 1951, and Claude Fohlen, "Connaissance et utilisation des tombes antiques pendant le haut moyen-age," *Mélanges: Société toulousaine d'études classiques*, II, 1948, 179–93.

12. George M. Forsyth, *The Church of St. Martin at Angers*, Princeton, 1953, 22–65, figs. 183–84. For the church at Müstair see *VK*, 227–228. Hans Rudolf Sennhauser, "Spätantike und frühmittelalterliche Kirchen Churrätiens," *Von der Spätantike zum frühen Mittelalter: Vorträge und Forschungen*, XXV, 1979, 201–206, lists fourteen churches from the sixth to the ninth centuries in Switzerland with side annexes (nine along the north side and four along the south) that opened onto the nave through doorways in a solid wall, rather than through an arcade: Romanshorn; Montlingen; Glarus; Flums, St. Justus; Maienfeld, St. Luzisteig; Schiers, North Cemetery Church; Ramosch; Grepault bei Truns; Sagens; Chur, St. Stephan; Chur, St. Regula; Zillis; Mistail; and Müstair. The function of these annexes remains unclear. Only the annex of the north cemetery church at Schiers is known to have been used for burial. For additional examples of side porches on aisleless churches in the

early Middle Ages and their use for burial see Forsyth, *St. Martin at Angers*, 42 n. 90, fig. 190, and Jean Hubert, *Europe of the Invasions*, 306–307.

13. Markthaler, "Recenti scoperte," 55.

14. Charles B. McClendon, "The Revival of *Opus Sectile* Pavements in Rome and the Vicinity in the Carolingian Period," *PBSR*, XLVIII, 1980, 157–165. See also Federico Guidobaldi and Alessandra Guiglia Guidobaldi, *Pavimenti marmorei di Roma del IV al IX secolo*, Vatican City, 1983, 418–435, 460–485.

15. Apollonj-Ghetti, *Esplorazioni*, 173–191, fig. 141; Toynbee and Ward-Perkins, *The Shrine of St. Peter*, 211–220; Krautheimer, *Corpus*, V, 259–261.

16. Krautheimer, *Corpus*, I, 95–112, 144–164, II, 216–247, IV, 1–36. An annular crypt seems to have been inserted in the apse of S. Crisogono in the first half of the eighth century, but the crypt takes on a stilted, horseshoe shape that finds no comparison at Farfa. An annular crypt from the early seventh century is preserved at S. Pancrazio. See Krautheimer, *Corpus*, I, 144–164, III, 153–174.

17. Krautheimer, *Corpus*, III, 235–262, IV, 179–198. S. Pancrazio, built between 625 and 638, may also have had a continuous transept together with an annular crypt. See *ibid.*, III, 174.

18. Richard Krautheimer, "The Carolingian Revival of Early Christian Architecture," *Studies*, 203–256. See also Bruno M. Apollonj-Ghetti, "La chiesa di S. Maria di Vescovio antica cattedrale di Sabina," *RAC*, XXIII–XXIV, 1947–48, 3–53.

19. Apollonj-Ghetti, "S. Maria di Vescovio," 6–8, and Toubert, *Les structures*, II, 943.

20. The inscription refers to IOHES. D. FOLIANO PRESBYTER, a canon who lived in nearby Gavignano during the papacy of Martin V (1417–1431). Apollonj-Ghetti, "S. Maria di Vescovio," 26.

21. The *Liber pontificalis*, I, 312, states simply that at Old St. Peter's, Pope Gregory the Great "fecit ut super corpus

beati Petri missae celebrantur." See also Krautheimer, *Rome*, 86.

22. Apollonj-Ghetti, "S. Maria di Vescovio," 14–53, esp. 21–33. Claudio Montagne and Loredana Pessa, *Le chiese romaniche della Sabina*, Genoa, 1983, 35–68, provide a more recent, although less critical, discussion of the church at Vescovio with excellent photographs.

23. For the paintings at S. Clemente see G. Matthiae, *Pittura romana*, I, 218–236, fig. 145, and John Osborne, *Early Medieval Wall-Paintings in the Lower Church of San Clemente, Rome*, New York and London, 1984, 24–106, esp. 72–77, for a definition of the "Leo IV" style. The frescoes on the altar at Vescovio represent a very different style and probably date to the tenth century. See Stephan Waetzoldt, "Die Malereien am Hochaltar von S. Maria in Vescovio," *RQ*, LII, 1957, 1–12.

24. References to a church on the site are found already in a letter of Pope Hadrian I (772–795) and in the record of the donation of an altar cloth by Pope Paschal I (817–824). *LP*, II, 63, 68 n. 45.

25. See Appendix of Documents, No. V.

26. For the history and uses of the term "oratory" in the Catholic Church from early Christian times to the present see Aloysius H. Feldhaus, *Oratories*, Catholic University of America, Canon Law Series XLII, Washington, D.C., 1927. See also Charles Du Cange, *Glossarium mediae et infimae latinitatis*, IV, reprinted Graz, 1954, 54–55. For example, the capitularies of Frankfurt from 794 (chapt. 13) explain: "De monasteriis ubi corpora sanctorum sunt, ut habeat oratorium intra claustra, ubi peculiare officium et diuturnum fiat." The Rule of St. Benedict, chapt. 52, simply states: "The oratory should be what its name implies. . . ." (*Oratorium hoc sit quod dicitur. . . .*)

27. Jean Hubert, "'Cryptae inferiores' et 'cryptae superiores' dans l'architecture religieuse de l'époque carolingienne," *Mélanges d'histoire du moyen age dediés à la mémoire de Louis Halphen*, Paris, 1951, 351–357; Du Cange, *Glossarium*, II, 639.

28. Hans Reinhardt and Etienne Fels, "Étude sur les églises-porches carolingiennes et leur survivance dans l'art roman," *BM*, XCII, 1933, 364 n. 1.

29. Alois Fuchs, *Die karolingische Westwerke und andere Fragen der karolingische Baukunst*, Paderborn, 1929, 13–14, and his "Entstehung und Zweckbestimmung der Westwerke," *Westfälische Zeitschrift*, C, 1950, 255; W. Rave, "Die Aufspürung von zwei Westwerke in Italien," *Westfalen*, XXIV, 1939, 149–150; Günter Bandmann, *Mittelalterliche Architektur als Bedeutungsträger*, Berlin, 1951, 207; Friedrich Möbius, *Westwerkstudien*, Jena, 1968, 17.

30. Adolf Ostendorf, "Das Salvator-Patrocinium, seine Anfänge und seine Ausbreitung im mittelalterlichen Deutschland," *Westfälische Zeitschrift*, C, 1950, 357–376.

31. Fuchs, *Westwerke*, 30–31; Reinhardt and Fels, "Étude sur les églises-porches," 331–365; and most recently Carol Heitz, *L'architecture religieuse carolingienne: Les formes et leurs fonctions*, Paris, 1980, esp. 43, 54, 152, and Yves Christe, "'Et super muros eius angelorum custodia,'" *Cahiers de civilisation médiévale*, XXIV, 1981, 173–179.

32. Möbius, *Westwerkstudien*, 9–22, 131–148, provides a useful summary of the various interpretations of the westwork, together with an extensive bibliography on the subject.

33. Krautheimer, *Rome*, 123. See also Nicole Herrmann-Mascard, *Les reliques des saints: Formation coutumière d'un droit*, Paris, 1975, 50–53.

34. Krautheimer, "The Carolingian Revival," *Studies*, 203–256.

35. *Ibid.*, 206–212. Krautheimer, 245 n. 87, questions whether the parallel had been drawn between St. Denis and Dionysius the Areopagite, a disciple of St. Paul, as early as the eighth century. But the fact that Pepin, the king of the Franks, requested a copy of the writings of the Pseudo-Dionysius from Pope Paul I in 758 suggests to me that the triple association (i.e., St. Denis, Dionysius the Areopagite, and the Pseudo-Dionysius) had already been made by that time. See

my review of Carol Heitz, *L'architecture religieuse carolingienne*, in *JSAH*, XLII, 1982, 58–59. Werner Jacobsen, "Saint-Denis in neuen Licht: Konsequenzen der neuentdeckten Baubeschreibung aus dem Jahre 799," *Kunstchronik*, XXXVI, 1983, 301–308, finds the long period (ca. 754–775) usually assigned to the construction of the new church at St.-Denis difficult to explain, and he suggests instead that work did not begin until soon after Pepin's death in 768.

36. Jean Guirand, "Le commerce des reliques au commencement du IXe siècle," *Mélanges G. B. de Rossi*, Paris and Rome, 1892, 73–95; Patrick Geary, *Furta Sacra: The Thefts of Relics in the Central Middle Ages*, Princeton, N. J., 1978.

37. *Translatio et miracula SS. Marcellini et Petri auctore Einhardo*, ed. G. Waitz, *MGH SS*, XV:1, 238–264. Eleanor Shipley Duckett, *Carolingian Portraits: A Study in the Ninth Century*, Ann Arbor, 1962, provides a lively, if not always reliable, summary of these events. See also Josef Fleckenstein, "Einhard, seine Gründung und sein Vermächtnis in Seligenstadt," *Das Einhardkreuz*, ed. Karl Hauck, Abhandlungen der Akademie der Wissenschaften in Göttingen, philologische-historische klasse, LXXXVII, 1974, 96–121.

38. *VK*, 309–11, 320–22; Günther Binding, "Die Kirchen Einharts in Steinbach und Seligenstadt," *Schülerfestgabe für Herbert von Einem*, Bonn, 1965, 12–19. It should also be pointed out that the remains of a pilaster on the southwest crossing pier and foundations below suggest that the transept at Seligenstadt was internally segmented by one or more transverse or diaphragm arches. See *VK*, 309.

39. It has been suggested, for example, that Einhard did not wish to leave the relics at Steinbach, because already in 819 he had willed the property to the abbey of Lorsch. Duckett, *Carolingian Portraits*, 79.

40. In fact Einhard built two successive churches in the area, the second of which, built between 830 and 840, followed the design of Old St. Peter's. Binding, "Die

Kirchen Einharts," 12–14, and Fleckenstein, "Einhard," *Einhardkreuz*, 113–114.

41. *VK*, 298–299.

42. Willy Weyres, "Neue Ergebnisse der Kölner Domgrabung zu Bau VI," *Architectura*, XIII, 1982, 27–30, fig. 1. See also the review of Otto Doppelfeld and Willy Weyres, *Die Ausgrabungen im Dom zu Köln*, Kölner Forschungen, I, Mainz, 1980, by Werner Jacobsen and Friedrich Oswald in *Kunstchronik*, XXXV, 1982, 10–33, esp. 29. For another summary of the excavations see *VK*, 140, with additional bibliography. The church was remodeled under Archbishop Hildebold (787–818).

43. *Catalogus abbatum fuldensium, MGH SS*, XIII, 272: "Ratger, sapiens architectus, occidentale templum . . . mira arte et immensa magnitudine alteri copulans, unam fecit ecclesiam." The abbey church at Fulda was dedicated in 819. *VK*, 85.

44. For the Cathedral of St. Jean at Besançon see René Tournier, *Les églises comtoises: Leur architecture des origines au XVIIIe siècle*, Paris, 1954, 65ff. For St. Salvator at Paderborn see B. Ortmann, *Die karolingischen Bauten unter der Abdinghofkirche zu Paderborn und das Kloster Bischof Meinwerks (1016–1031)*, Ratingen, 1967, who dates the church to ca. 800, whereas in *VK*, 252, it is dated to after 850 on the basis of ceramic finds. For St. Georg at Reichenau-Oberzell see *VK*, 282.

45. Walter Horn and Ernest Born, *The Plan of St. Gall*, Berkeley, California, 1979, provide a detailed study of the Plan. The best reproduction of the Plan in its entirety remains the facsimile edition, *Der St. Galler Klosterplan*, with a commentary by Hans Reinhardt, St. Gall, 1952.

46. For a detailed discussion of the problem, with extensive bibliography, see Albrecht Mann, "Doppelchor und Stiftermemorie: Zum kunst- und kulturgeschichtlichen Problem der Westchöre," *Westfälische Zeitschrift*, CXI, 1961, 149–262. More recently, Carol Heitz has emphasized the impact of the adoption of the *Ordines Romani* in the Carolingian realm, "Nouvelles interprétations de l'art carolingienne," *Revue de l'art*, I–II, 1968, 107, and *idem*, "More romano: Problèmes d'architecture et liturgie carolingiennes," *Roma e l'età carolingia*, 1976, 29.

47. Horn and Born, *St. Gall*, 131–133. For the most complete study of these two Roman basilicas see Krautheimer, *Corpus*, V, 91–285. The direction of the apses in each case was due primarily to topographical considerations.

48. *Chronicon*, I, 9: "Tunc unus . . . respiciens per foramen ianue, vidit ipsum apparatum ante fores ecclesiae depositum. revertensque nuntiavit patri atque sociis, nihil mali adesse, sed e contra largissimis dapibus ciborum atque vini dorsis iumentorum hominumque humeris advectatis atrium esse repletum." Schuster, "Relique d'arte," 281.

49. See, for example, similar graves from the sixth or seventh century at S. Saba in Rome. Krautheimer, *Corpus*, IV, 60, figs. 56–57.

50. The *terra sigillata africana* plate corresponds to type 104A of John Hayes, *Late Roman Pottery*, London, 1972, 160–166. Whitehouse, "Farfa Abbey," 245; *Museo di Farfa: Farfa nella Sabina*, Abbazia di Farfa, 9 Giugno–9 Agosto, 1983, Rome, 1983, 23, 30, fig. 8.

51. Carbon-14 analysis was carried out by James Buckley, Radiocarbon Laboratory, Teledyne Isotopes, Westwood, N. J. Ages were calculated on the Libby half-life of 5568 and then dendrochronologically corrected.

52. For the use of the atrium of a church as a cemetery in the sixth century see Jean-Charles Picard, "La quadriportique de Sant'Agata de Ravenne," *Felix Ravenna*, CXVI, 1978, 31–43.

53. Thomas Hodgkin, *Italy and Her Invaders, 376–814*, IV, 1885, reprinted New York, 1967, 72. The event is recorded in Paul the Deacon's *History of the Lombards*, bk. IV, chapt. 17.

54. For a discussion of the common practice of using the sites of Roman villas for burial in the early Middle Ages, and for

the adaptation of villa structures for the use by monastic communities, see John Percival, *The Roman Villa: An Historical Introduction*, Berkeley and Los Angeles, 1976, 183–199.

55. Current excavations of San Vincenzo al Volturno, under the direction of Richard Hodges, promise to provide a wealth of information about the development of an important early medieval monastery in South Italy with close ties to Farfa. *San Vincenzo al Volturno: The Archaeology, Art and Territory of an Early Medieval Monastery*, ed. Richard Hodges and John Mitchell, British Archaeological Reports, International Series, CCLII, Oxford, 1985, which contains a series of preliminary reports concerning various aspects of this archaeological project, appeared after my study of Farfa was written and in press.

56. The basic studies remain Georges Durand, "Saint-Riquier," *La picardie historique et monumentale*, IV:2, Amiens and Paris, 1907–1911, 133–358, and W. Effmann, *Centula-Saint-Riquier*, Munster, 1912.

57. Jean Hubert, "Saint-Riquier et le monachisme bénédictine en Gaule à l'époque carolingienne," *Il monachismo nel alto medio evo e la formazione della civiltà occidentale*, Settimana di studio di centro italiano di studi sull'alto medio evo, IV, 1957, 293–309.

58. For a critical analysis of the visual and documentary evidence concerning the Carolingian abbey of St.-Riquier see David Parsons, "The Pre-Romanesque Church of St.-Riquier: The Documentary Evidence," *JBAA*, CXXIX, 1976, 21–51.

59. Heitz, *L'architecture religieuse carolingienne*, 238 n. 7. The eleventh-century chronicle and the writings of Angilbertus are published in *Hariulf: Chronique de l'abbaye de Saint-Riquier (Ve siècle–1104)*, ed. F. Lot, Paris, 1894.

60. Heitz, *L'architecture religieuse carolingienne*, 60, fig. 41.

61. Horn and Born, *The Plan of St. Gall*, II, 189–199.

62. Horn and Born, *The Plan of St. Gall*,

I, 51, and Bernhard Bischoff, "Die Entstehung des Klosterplanes in paläographischer Sicht," *Studien zum St. Galler Klosterplan*, ed. Johannes Duft, St. Gall, 1962, 67–68.

63. *Liber tramitis*, Dinter, 203.

64. "Officina vero . . . claustra sunt monasterii et stabilitas in congregatione." *The Rule of St. Benedict*, ed. and trans. Abbot Justin McCann, London, 1972, 32; Horn and Born, *The Plan of St. Gall*, I, 51.

65. Horn and Born, *The Plan of St. Gall*, II, 146–151, 155–165.

66. P. Donaldson, C. McClendon, and D. Whitehouse, "L'abbazia di Farfa: Rapporto preliminare sugli scavi, 1978–80," *ASRStP*, CIII, 1980, 9. For a full report of the ceramic material by David Whitehouse see the final report, now in preparation.

67. *Chronica monasterii casinensis*, ed. Hartmut Hoffmann, *MGH SS*, XXXIV, 1980, 1.17, p. 58, lines 24–27: "Fecit etiam atrium ante eandem ecclesiam longitudine cubitorum quadraginta, latitudine simili et in marmoreis illud columnis numero sedecim undique versus erexit atque in circuitu ipsius lapideos canales iuxta pavimentum, unde semper aqua decurreret, posuit." The English translation was kindly provided by Henry M. Willard. For a study of the building programs of Abbot Gisulf of Montecassino see Armand O. Citarella and Henry M. Willard, *The Ninth-Century Treasure of Monte Cassino in the Context of Political and Economic Developments in South Italy*, Montecassino, 1983.

68. Jean-Charles Picard, "Étude sur l'emplacement des tombes des papes des IIIe au Xe siècle," *MEFR: Moyen Age–Temps Modernes*, LXXXI, 1969, 755–781.

69. Bernhard Kötting, *Der frühchristliche Reliquienkult und die Bestattung im Kirchengebäude*, Cologne and Opladen, 1965, 24–28, and Ejnar Dyggve, "The Origin of the Urban Churchyard," *Classica et mediavalia*, XII, 1951, 147–158.

70. *Homily XXVI on 2 Corinthians*, *Patrologia graeca*, Migne, LXI, 1859, cols. 583–584, and *A Select Library of the Nicene and Post-Nicene Fathers of the Christian Church*,

XII, ed. Philip Schaff, New York, 1889, 403.

71. Kötting, *Der frühchristliche Reliquienkult*, 33–35. The pertinent section from the Synod of Mainz (*MGH*, sectio III, concilia 2, 1, 272) reads: "Nullus mortuus infra ecclesiam sepeliatur, nisi episcopi aut abbates aut digni presbyteri vel fideles laici."

72. Albert Verbeek, "Die Aussenkrypta: Werden einer Bauform des frühen Mittelalters," *ZKG*, XIII, 1950, 7–38.

73. The English translation is taken from Horn and Born, *The Plan of St. Gall*, I, 128.

74. *Ibid.*, 128, fig. 84.

75. *Ibid.*, 155, fig. 150.

76. Reinhod R. Grimm, *Paradisus Caelestis–Paradisus Terrestris: Zur Auslegungsgeschichte des Paradieses im Abendland bis um 1200*, Munich, 1977. The word originated with the Persian *pairidaeza*, used to designate the enclosure around the hunting park of the Persian king. *Paulys Realencyclopädie der klassischen Altertumswissenschaft*, XVIII: 3, ed. Georg Wissowa, Stuttgart, 1949, cols. 1131–1134.

77. Jean-Charles Picard, "Les origines du mot *paradisus*—parvis," *MEFR: Moyen Age–Temps Modernes*, LXXXIII, 1971, 157–186.

78. For a brief discussion of the semicircular atria represented on the Plan of St. Gall see Horn and Born, *The Plan of St. Gall*, I, 204–206, where the exedrae of the Forum of Trajan in Rome are cited as sources for this design. It seems far more likely, however, that such semicircular atria come from late Roman villa architecture. For example, colonnaded hemicycles have been found at the fourth-century villas at Montmauron in southwestern France (G. Fouet, *La villa gallo-romane de Montmauron, Haute-Garonne*, XXe Supplément à *Gallia*, Paris, 1969, 55–98, pls. IV–VI, fig. 23), and at Piazza Armerina in Sicily (J. B. Ward-Perkins, *Roman Imperial Architecture*, Harmondsworth and New York, 1981, 460–463, with bibliography), as well as at the palaces of Antiochos and Lausos in

Constantinople from the fifth century (Richard Krautheimer, *Early Christian*, 74–75). A similar feature stood at the entrance to the Gallo-Roman villa of Teting on the Mosel (Albert Grenier, *Habitations gauloises et villas latines dans la Cité des Médiomatrices*, Paris, 1906, 159–174, plan 11). Nevertheless, in each case the concave arrangement of the colonnade faced outward and served either to funnel movement into a central courtyard or vestibule, as at Montmauron and the Palace of Lausos, or to link a series of separate rooms and building axes along the curvature of the portico, as at Piazza Armerina, the Palace of Antiochos, and the villa at Teting. On the Plan of St. Gall and at the cathedral of Cologne (see below), on the other hand, the convex solid wall of the semicircular atrium faces outward, with the colonnade on the inside. Moreover, the flow of movement is reversed from that of the late antique villas, for here one enters the atrium through a doorway at its apex and is then guided left and right, either to the side aisles of the church or to immediately adjoining buildings. Thus, the late antique precedent seems to have been adapted for a new purpose. A link between the ancient villas and the Carolingian churches is Charlemagne's palace at Ingelheim, built between 788 and 807, where the entrance is a central gateway in a broad curved wall, fortified by towers on the exterior and presumably colonnaded along its concave interior so as to link the east and west ranges of the complex. See Heitz, *L'architecture religieuse carolingienne*, 66, fig. 46, with bibliography, and Uta Wengenrath-Weimann, *Die Grabungen an der Königspflaz zu Nieder-Ingelheim in den Jahren 1960–1970*, *Beiträge zur Ingelheimer Geschichte*, XXIII, Ingelheim, 1973. Jacobsen and Oswald, *Kunstchronik*, XXXVII, 1984, 164, also cite the eighth-century palace at Samoussy as having "eine vergleichbare ringförmige Hofanlage."

79. *VK*, 140; Willy Weyres, "Der karolingische Dom zu Köln," *Karl der Grosse*, III, 384–423, esp. 409; Otto Doppelfeld, "More Romano: Die beiden karolingischen

Domgrundrisse von Köln: VII. Bericht über
die Domgrabung," *Die Ausgrabungen,* 159–
182, esp. 161–162, originally published in
the *Kölner Domblatt,* VIII–IX, 1954, 33–61.

80. "Ne suspiceris autem me haec ideo
elaborasse quod vos putemus n[ost]ris
indigere magisteriis. Sed potius ob amore
dei tibi soli p[er] scrutanda pinxisse
amicabili fr[ater]nitatis intuitu crede." Horn
and Born, *The Plan of St.Gall,* I, 9. For a
somewhat different translation of this
dedicatory legend see the review of the
Horn and Born volumes by Paul Meyvaert
in *University Publishing,* IX, 1980, 18–19.

81. *Vita Eigilis fuldensis, MGH SS,* XVI,
231, cap. 19: "Tamen claustrum monasterii
ex modo construere cogitavit. Vocantur ad
consilium fratres. Quaesitum est, in quo
loco aedificatis claustris congruentes
potuisset aptari. Quidam dederunt
consilium, contra partem meridianam
basilicae iuxta morem prioris, quidam autem
romano more contra plagam occidentalem
satius poni, confirmant, propter vicinitatem
martyris, qui in ea basilicae parte quiescit."

82. Although the term *more romano* is
used to describe the placement of the
cloister at the west end of the abbey church
at Fulda, it remains unclear what Roman
precedent is being cited here. Only the
church of St. Paul's-outside-the-Walls, with
its apse in the east, had its atrium to the
west. St. Peter's, the model for the design
of the abbey church at Fulda, had its apse in
the west and its atrium at the east of the
basilica, adjoining the façade. The small
monastic churches of S. Martino and S.
Stefano degli Abissini stood outside the
western apse of St. Peter's, but we have no
evidence that they possessed either atria or
cloisters. The Lateran basilica may have had
a courtyard, adapted from the remains of an
earlier Roman house, framing or adjoining
its western apse, but its shape and exact
location are uncertain. Nevertheless, it is
interesting to note that in the course of the
early Middle Ages monastic communities
had developed in association with each of
these early Christian basilicas, and although
the origins and function of the early

Christian atrium and the medieval cloister
are decidedly different (see Walter Horn,
"On the Origins of the Medieval Cloister,"
Gesta, XII, 1973, 13–52), the monks at
Fulda may have seen the Roman atria in
general as related to their notions of a
monumental cloister connected to the
church housing the tomb of St. Boniface.
Indeed, the main monastery at the Lateran
is described in the *Liber pontificalis* under the
reign of Pope Leo III (795–817) as having
been located *post basilicam* (Guy Ferrari, *Early
Roman Monasteries,* Vatican City, 1957, 253),
whereas the monastery of St. Stephan
attached to St. Paul's-outside-the-Walls is
described in the eighth century as being
situated *intro atrio beati apostoli Pauli* (Jean-
Charles Picard, "Le quadriportique de Saint-
Paul-hors-les-murs à Rome," *MEFR: Antiquité,*
LXXXVII, 1975, 395). For the Roman
basilicas and their atria in general see
Krautheimer, *Corpus,* V, 1977, and for the
location of monastic communities in Rome
see G. Ferrari, *Early Roman Monasteries.* See
also Heitz, "More Romano," *Roma,* 1976,
30, 35 ns. 20, 21.

83. Joseph Vonderau, "Die
Ausgrabungen am Dome zu Fulda in den
Jahren 1908–1913," *Sechszehnte
Veröffentlichung des Fuldaer Geschichtsvereins,*
1919, 5–36. For a summary of the various
excavations at Fulda see *VK,* 85–87, and
Manfred F. Fischer and Friedrich Oswald,
"Zur Baugeschichte der Fuldaer
Klosterkirchen: Literatur und Ausgrabungen
im Kritischersicht," *Rheinische Ausgrabungen:
Beihefte der Bonner Jahrbücher,* XXVIII, 1968,
268–80.

84. Vonderau, "Die Ausgrabungen," 16.

85. *Catalogus abbatum fuldensium, MGH SS,*
XIII, 273: "Hic [Abbot Thioto] inter cetera
bonitatis suae opera studio . . . sanctos
Antonium et Eonium martires monasterio
gloriose advocavit et porticos inferiores
adornavit ibidemque honorifice requiescere
fecit."

86. It is interesting to note that
Einhard's church at Seligenstadt may have
had a curved wall outside and
circumscribing the apse, for according to

VK, 309, and Georg Dehio, *Handbuch der deutschen Kunstdenkmäler*, III, ed. Magnus Backes, Hessen, 1966, 753, vestiges of a concentric wall were found outside the northern flank of the apse. Could this area have been intended as the site of Einhard's burial? In the past, it has always been assumed that Einhard and his wife were buried in the crypt, but there seems to be no conclusive proof as to the location of their tombs.

87. It has long been suggested that the Plan of St. Gall is in some way derived from the imperial synods at Aachen of 816 and 817 concerned with monastic reform. Indeed, Walter Horn (Horn and Born, *The Plan of St. Gall*, I, 20–33) has gone so far as to suggest that the Plan of St. Gall is a direct copy of a paradigmatic scheme drawn up at Aachen. This theory, however, has many problems, as is pointed out by Paul Meyvaert in his review of the Horn and Born study (*University Publishing*, IX, 1980, 18–19) and more recently by Edward A. Segal, "The Plan of Saint Gall and the Monastic Reform Councils of 816 and 817," *Cuyahoga Review*, I, 1983, 57–71.

88. Meyer Schapiro, "The Frescoes of Castelseprio," *Late Antique, Early Christian and Medieval Art: Selected Papers*, New York, 1980, 106–107, and his "Notes on Castelseprio; II: The Clavus on the Thigh," *ibid.*, 125–142.

89. *MGH Ep*, IV, Karolini aevi, II, 549, XII (dated 812): "Ut aedificia immensa atque superflua et cetera inutilia opera omittantur, quibus fratres utra modum fatigantur et familiae foris dispereunt, sed omnia mensuram et discretionem fiant. . . ." See also Krautheimer, "Carolingian Revival," *Studies*, 209, 243 n. 69.

90. Werner Jacobsen, "Benedikt von Aniane und die Architektur unter Ludwig dem Frommen zwischen 814 und 830," *Riforma religiosa e arti nell'epoca carolingia*, ed. A. Schmidt, Atti del XXIV congresso internazionale di storia dell'arte, I, Bologna, 1979 (1983), 15–22. Indeed, the dimensions (though not the design) of the

abbey church at Farfa are similar to those of the abbey church of Kornelimünster founded by Benedict of Aniane (d. 821), who led the monastic reform movement during the reign of Louis the Pious. Leo Hugo, *Kornelimünster, Rheinische Ausgrabungen*, II, Cologne-Graz, 1968.

Chapter 5: The Early Romanesque Phase

1. Markthaler, "Recenti scoperte," 67.

2. In *Pouchain: 10 anni di attività*, 8, the masonry of the bell tower is described as "le murature, che fra i due paramenti, erano composte da materiale sciolto, polveroso e di scarsa consistenza."

3. Maria Accascina, "Note sul campanile di Santa Scolastica di Subiaco," *Atti del V convegno nazionale di storia dell'architettura* (Perugia, 1948), Florence, 1957, 257–264; Giovannoni, "L'architettura," *I monasteri di Subiaco*, 261–371; Serafini, *Torri*, I, 150–151. For a report of the most recent restoration work and excavations see Raffaele Perrotti, "La chiesa e il campanile di S. Scolastica in Subiaco: Recenti ritrovamenti," *Palladio*, XVI, 1966, 137–147. Claudio Giumelli et al., *I monasteri di Subiaco*, Milan, 1982, 41–52, provides some excellent photographs of the bell tower in its present state. The accompanying text, however, should be treated with caution. Indeed, the author contradicts himself on several major points.

4. Giovannoni, "L'architettura," *Subiaco*, I, 307, suggests that the two top storeys were rebuilt or restored following the earthquake of either 1228 or 1298. The fourth, fifth, and sixth storeys on the east side of the bell tower and the seventh storey on the south side have paired, round-arched windows without intervening colonnettes instead of trifora.

5. Perrotti, "La chiesa," 145–147.

6. For example, the abbot of Subiaco, Johannes Ottonis (1068–1120), originally came from Farfa. See Hans M. Schwarzmaier, "Der Liber Vitae von Subiaco: Die Klöster Farfa und Subiaco in

ihrer geistigen und politischen Umwelt
während der letzten Jahrzehnte des 11.
Jahrhunderts," *QFIAB*, XLVIII, 1968, 80–
147. A continued artistic relationship into
the Renaissance is discussed by Wolfgang
Krönig, "Deutsche spätgotische Architektur
in Farfa und Subiaco," *25 Jahre Kaiser Wilhelm
Gesellschaft*, III, 1937, 57–68.

7. IN NOMINE D[omi]NI N[ost]RI
JHESU / CHR[ist]I ANNO IIII
PONTIFICATUS DOMINI / LEONI
NONI PAPE. HU[m]B[er]TUS
VENERABILIS ABBAS EDIFICAVIT HOC
OPUS / EGREGIE TURRIS AD
ONOR[em] CHR[ist]I / C[on]FESSORIS
BEN[edi]C[ti] EIUSQ[ue] / SORORIS
S[an]C[t]E SCOLASTICE
VI[r]G[inis]. . . . The inscription is now
walled up in an adjoining courtyard.

8. ". . . acquirere episcopum qui tibi
tuam consecret ecclesiam undecumque
volueris." See Appendix of Documents,
No. IX.

9. See Appendix of Documents, No. X.
A Farfa breviary from the late eleventh or
early twelfth century, now in the Vatican
Library (Chigi C. VI. 77), refers to the
relics of several saints (SS. Gethulis,
Amantius, Cerealis, Primitivus, Valentinus,
Hilarius, among others) as being present in
the abbey church, but no indication is given
of their precise location. It should be noted
also that no reference is made to St.
Alexander, who was originally buried
together with Valentine and Hilarius in the
Sichardan crypt. See Garrison, *Studies*, II,
124–129, cited in n. 14 below.

10. These altar cloths are listed in an
inventory of the abbey treasury. See
Appendix of Documents, No. XII.

11. See Appendix of Documents,
No. XI.

12. Premoli, "La chiesa abbaziale,"
states on p. 64, for example, "Tutte queste
considerazioni portano naturalmente a
collocare l'epoca degli affreschi farfensi tra
la fine del X e il primo quarto dell'XI
secolo," whereas on p. 40 she states,
"Ritengo quindi che il complesso farfense sia
stato realizzato entro la prima metà del sec.
XI. . . ."

13. Guglielmo Matthiae, *Pittura romana
del medioevo*, Rome, 1965, I, 237–244, pls.
168–171, II, 12–19, pls. 1–7; Laura Giglio,
S. Sebastiano al Palatino, Le chiese di Roma
illustrate, CXXVIII, Rome, 1975; and Alex
Busuioceanu, "Un ciclo di affreschi del
secolo XI: S. Ubano all Caffarella," *Ephemeris
dacoromana*, II, 1924, 1–65.

14. Matthiae, *Pittura romana*, II, 20–29,
35–38; Otto Demus, *Romanesque Mural
Painting*, New York, 1970, 298–301, pls.
44–52; O. Hjort, "The Frescoes of Castel
Sant'Elia: A Problem of Stylistic
Attribution," *Hafnia*, 1970, 7ff; P. Hoegger,
Die Fresken von S. Elia bei Nepi, Frauenfeld and
Stuttgart, 1975. Basic studies on mural
painting in Rome and Central Italy in the
eleventh and twelfth centuries include: E. B.
Garrison, *Studies in the History of Medieval
Italian Painting*, Florence, 1953–1962; F.
Hermanin, *L'arte in Roma dal secolo VIII al
XIV*, Bologna, 1945, 223–269; and G.
Ladner, "Die italienische Malerei im 11.
Jahrhundert," *Jahrbuch der Wiener
Kunsthistorischen Sammlungen*, n. s. V, 1931,
33ff.

15. C. A. Isermeyer, "Die
mittelalterliche Malerien der Kirche S.
Pietro in Tuscania," *Römisches Jahrbuch*, II,
1938, 291–310.

16. Garrison, *Studies*, II, 1955, 24, III,
1957, 195. Demus, *Romanesque*, 301–302,
pls. 55–58, sees no relation to Farfa.
Matthiae, *La pittura romana*, 30–31, accepts
the late eleventh-century date for Tuscania.

17. Demus, *Romanesque*, XXIII, 79–83,
294–297, pls. 18–37. See also J. Wettstein,
Les fresques de S. Angelo in Formis, Geneva,
1960.

18. Premoli, "La chiesa abbaziale," 62–
66. For the frescoes at Aosta, Galliano, and
Novara see Demus, *Romanesque*, 291–292,
pls. 1–7.

19. For a description of the frescoes and
an analysis of these stylistic differences see
chapter 3 above.

20. Markthaler, "Recenti scoperte," 83–
86, fig. 40. More recently, Percy E.
Schramm has suggested that the portrait
represents Otto II, because the emperor is
shown without a beard. P. E. Schramm,

"Unbeachtete Bilder Kaiser Otto II. und seiner Gemahlin Theophanu in einem mittelitalienischen Kloster," *Homenaje a Jaime Vicens Vives,* I, Barcelona, 1965, 619–623.

21. Garrison, *Studies,* IV: 3, 1962, 235–241, figs. 186–189, and *Collectio canonum,* ed. Kölzer, 52–54, where a date in the third quarter of the eleventh century is proposed. The manuscript seems to have been made for use in the neighboring town of Narni, and it may have been produced at one of Farfa's many dependencies there.

22. Garrsion, *Studies,* IV: 3, 1962, 230, fig. 186b.

23. *Ibid.,* 250–264, figs. 203–215.

24. Schuster, "Reliquie d'arte," 334; Cecilia Davis-Weyer, "Das Traditio-Legis Bild und seine Nachfolge," *Münchener Jahrbuch der bildenen Kunst,* XII, 1965, 7–45; M. Sotomayor, "Über die Herkunft der 'Traditio Legis'," *RQ,* LVI, 1961, 215–230.

25. Kurt Weitzmann, *Late Antique and Early Christian Book Illumination,* New York, 1977, 101–102, pl. 36.

26. I am thinking in particular of the so-called painterly style in Byzantine monumental painting that appeared first in the church of the Nea Moni monastery on Chios (1042–1056). See Doula Mouriki, "Stylistic Trends in Monumental Painting in Greece during the Eleventh and Twelfth Century," *DOP,* XXXIV–XXXV, 1980–81, 89–94.

27. Premoli, "La chiesa abbaziale," 61–62, mentions these illuminated manuscripts, but she fails to recognize their close relationship to the frescoes.

28. Giovannoni, *Subiaco,* I, 265ff; Giumelli, *I monasteri,* 34–41.

29. A similar placement of a bell tower, built in the early eleventh century, is found at the church of St.-Germain-des-Prés in Paris. See Jean Hubert, "Les dates de construction du clocher-porche et de la nef de Saint-Germain-des-Prés," *BM,* CVIII, 1950, 69–84. This comparison becomes all the more intriguing when one notes that Abbot Humbertus, patron of the campanile at S. Scolastica, is described in contemporary sources as having been a Frank (*natione francus*). Excavations carried out from 1962 to 1964 by the Superintendency of the Monuments of Lazio found the footing of a curved wall—perhaps an apse—and of a parapet wall, ca. 0.50 m. high and with crude fresco decoration imitating marble revetment, below the present church. This evidence is, however, insufficient to reconstruct or date the various parts of the early medieval church. See Perrotti, "La chiesa," 137ff.

30. See the fundamental studies of Hans Thümmler, "Die Baukunst des 11. Jahrhunderts in Italien," *Römisches Jahrbuch,* III, 1939, 141–226, and "Die Kirche S. Pietro in Tuscania," *Römisches Jahrbuch,* II, 1938, 263–288.

31. Krautheimer, *Rome,* 142–202.

32. Eduardo Arslan, "L'architettura romanica milanese," *Storia di Milan,* Milan, 1954, III, 397–417; Howard Saalman, *Medieval Architecture,* New York, 1967, 30–34; Porter, *Lombard Architecture,* II, 573 n. 166, 576–584, 595. The complexity of the design of the east end and the hall crypt at Agliate makes Porter's late-ninth-century date unlikely. Moreover, traces of frescoes in the nave clearly date to around A.D. 1000. See now Sandro Chierici, *La Lombardia,* Italia Romanica, I, Milan 1978, 300–305. For a related building in Switzerland see "Amsoldingen, St. Mauritius," *VK,* 24.

33. Thümmler, "Die Baukunst," 204, dates Ferentillo later than Monte Amiata, because he considers the plan of the former more complex. The masonry of Ferentillo, however, is considerably inferior to that of Monte Amiata. Ferentillo was originally founded by Duke Faroaldus II of Spoleto and served as his burial place. The only other documentary evidence before the thirteenth century is a letter of privilege issued by Otto III in 996 for the rebuilding of S. Pietro at Ferentillo. Enzo Borsellino, "L'abbazia di S. Pietro di Ferentillo (Note Storiche)," *Benedictina,* XXI, 1974, 291–299. See also Adriano Prandi, S. Chierici, G. Tamanti and F. Cadei, *L'Umbria,* Italia Romanica, III, Milan, 1979, 108–132, where it is suggested that the church was finished in 1016.

34. Renzo Pardi, *Ricerche di architettura religiosa medioevale in Umbria*, Perugia, 1974, 29–42.

35. Kenneth John Conant, *Cluny: Les églises et la maison du chef d'ordre*, Macon, 1968, 54–59, groupe 3, pl. XXVI, fig. 41; Joan Evans, *The Romanesque Architecture of the Order of Cluny*, Cambridge, 1938, 61ff.

36. Thümmler, "Die Baukunst," 195; Italo Moretti and Renato Stopani, *La Toscana*, Italia Romanica, V, 1982, 376–378.

37. The soundings were made by the Superintendency of the Monuments of Tuscany in the mid-1960s. These findings have never been published, but the remains are still visible in the crypt today, and the curved walls of the apses are unmistakable. Thümmler had already correctly hypothesized the presence of these crypt apsidioles. Notice that his plan (199–200, fig. 193) indicates both a flat and a curved termination for the central sanctuary.

38. Giovanni Volpini, *Storia del monastero e del paese di abbazia di S. Salvatore*, 1966, 23; Moretti, *La Toscana*, 376.

39. Croquison, "I problemi," 64–65.

40. *VK*, 179–181, 282–283.

41. Paolo Verzone, *L'architettura*, 130–131.

42. *VK*, 145–146, and Paul A. Tholen, "Neue baugeschichtliche Ergebnisse in den Kirchen Kölns," *Wallraf-Richartz Jahrbuch*, XII–XIII, 1943, 20–25.

43. Leo Schaeffer, *Der Gründungsbau der Stiftskirche St. Martin in Zyfflich*, Die Kunstdenkmäler des Rheinlandes, Beiheft IX, Essen, 1963, 123–133.

44. *Ibid.*, 136–139; Hans Kubach and Albert Verbeek, *Romanische Baukunst an Rhein und Maas: Katalog der vorromanischen und romanischen Denkmäler*, Berlin, 1976, I, 229–234, II, 728–738, 861–865. See also Paul Rolland, "Un group belge d'églises bicephales à tourelles orientales," *Revue belge d'archéologie et d'histoire de l'art*, XI, 1941, 119–155.

45. W. Zimmermann, "Die Luziuskirche zu Werden," *Die Kirchen zu Werden*, Die Kunstdenkmäler des Rheinlandes, Beiheft VII, Essen, 1959, 160–249.

46. W. Manchot, *Kloster Limburg an der Haardt*, Mannheim, 1912. A more recent monograph on this important Salian abbey church is lacking, except for an unpublished doctoral dissertation: Fritz Wellmann, "Kloster Limburg an der Haardt," diss., Technische Hochschule, Karlsruhe, 1953.

47. Wolfbernhard Hoffmann, *Hirsau und die Hirsauer Bauschule*, Munich, 1950, 16–25.

48. For a discussion of the problem, with detailed bibliography, see *ibid.*, 1–13, 153ff.

49. Franklin Toker, "Excavations below the Cathedral of Florence, 1965–1974," *Gesta*, XIV, 1975, 30.

50. Mariaclotilde Magni, "Un remarquable témoignage du premier art roman en Italie du Nord: La cathédrale d'Aoste," *Cahiers archéologiques*, XXIV, 1975, 163–181, and her *Architettura religiosa e scultura romanica nella valle d'Aosta*, Aosta, 1974, 19–34, 42–45, dates the entire south tower to the early eleventh century and the completion of the north tower several decades later, perhaps as late as the end of the century. Nevertheless, she sees the building as largely complete by ca. 1040. Interestingly enough, Daria De Bernardi Ferrero, "Aoste: La cathédrale Sainte-Marie," *Congrès archéologique de France*, CXXIX, 1971, 157–172, suggests that originally the cathedral may have had a rectangular or flat-ended central apse based upon the preserved plan of the crypt. See also Porter, *Lombard Architecture*, II, 48–54.

51. Hans E. Kubach, *Romanesque Architecture*, New York, 1975, 154, 139, fig. 151; Walter M. Whitehill, *Spanish Romanesque Architecture of the Eleventh Century*, Oxford, 1941 (reprinted 1968), 34–44.

52. J. Puig y Cadafalch, *La géographie et les origines du premier art roman*, Paris, 1935. One need not accept all the premises that are incorporated into Cadafalch's thesis in order to see that a close relationship existed between these regions. To underscore this point, it may be added that the closest parallel to the plan of Aosta Cathedral is the

grand design of S. Maria at Ripoll, which shared the same abbot (Oliba, 1000–1046) with Cuxa in the first half of the eleventh century. See Whitehill, *Spanish Romanesque*, 37.

53. It is generally agreed that the church was begun, if not completed, under Abbot Warmundus (969–1002), as indicated by a preserved inscription. See Daria De Bernardi Ferrero, "Ivrée: Cathédrale Sainte-Marie," *Congrès archéologique de France*, CXXIX, 1971, 185–193; Verzone, *L'architettura*, 147–150; and Porter, *Lombard Architecture*, II, 472–475. The small church of S. Quintino at Spigno, perhaps as early as 991, may have had bell towers flanking the apse, but the building is poorly preserved. See Verzone, *L'architettura*, 153, and Porter, *Lombard Architecture*, III, 431.

54. Thümmler, "Die Baukunst," 169: "Die grosse Betonung der Chorpartie and vor allem die Errichtung von Osttürmen, das alles sind untrügliche Zeichen eines Einflusses von seiten der cluniazensischen Reform."

55. Jean Vallery-Radot, "L'église Saint-Martin à Aime," *Congrès archéologique de France*, CXXIII, 1965, 121–132. Vallery-Radot questions the existence of a tower over the south-side chapel, but an 1869 engraving (*ibid.*, fig. on p. 128) clearly shows the remains of the second storey of a tower. It is also interesting to note that a small round-arched doorway binds the side chapels to the central sanctuary, as at St. Mauritius Amsoldingen (*VK*, 24) and as found later at S. Abbondio at Como.

56. Jean Vallery-Radot, "La cathédrale Saint-Pierre à Moutiers-en-Tarentaise," *Congrès archéologique de France*, CXXIII, 1965, 106–120.

57. *MGH SS*, XIII, 302: "Altare Sti Martini exstat a destris . . . super hoc altare habetur turris continens oratorium Sti Pauli . . . a sinistris . . . altare . . . in honore Sti Andreae apostoli . . . super hoc altare est turris habens." See also H. Bunjes and N. Irsch, "Ehemalige Benediktinerabtei und Kirche St. Maximin," *Die Kirchlichen*

Denkmäler der Stadt Trier, Die Kunstdenkmäler der Rhein Provinz, XIII, 3, Düsseldorf, 1939, 293, and *VK*, 348–349. The towers are represented in an engraving of before 1674 by P. C. Anthony, reproduced in Warren Sanderson, "Monastic Reform in Lorraine and the Architecture of the Outer Crypt, 950–1100," *Transactions of the American Philosophical Society*, n. s., LXI: 6, 1971, 5, fig. 1. Chapels, or *oratorii*, in the second floors of the bell towers of the cathedral at Aosta have been suggested by Magni, "La cathédrale d'Aoste," on purely archaeological grounds.

58. For a detailed archaeological study of the monument see W. Zimmermann, "Die Luciuskirche zu Werden," 160–249, esp. 225–241. However, Zimmermann's 1080–90 date for this rebuilding phase at Werden, based largely on an analysis of architectural sculpture, seems unreasonably late; the bell towers were more likely part of the church consecrated in 1063. The study by W. Effmann, *Die karolingisch-ottonischen Bauten zu Werden*, is now sadly out of date.

59. Zimmermann, "Die Luciuskirche zu Werden," 231–232, fig. 308.

60. Louis Grodecki, *L'architecture ottonienne*, Paris, 1958, 142. A contemporary and perhaps related placement of towers to either side of the chevet is indicated by the foundations of the cathedral of Magdeburg in Saxony, patronized by the emperor Otto the Great and consecrated in 968. The foundations in question, however, are probably from a major building campaign under Archbishop Hunfried (1023–1051); the high altar was consecrated again in 1077 following repairs from a fire. A similar use of towers may have existed at the cathedral of Bamberg, begun shortly before 1007 and sponsored by the emperor Henry II. Traces of massive foundations from this early phase have been found flanking the eastern apse at Bamberg, but the specific design of these proposed towers remains in doubt. Ernst Schubert, *Der Magdeburger Dom*, Cologne and Vienna, 1975, 11–16; Dethard von Winterfeld, *Der Dom in Bamberg*, I, *Die*

Baugeschichte bis zur Vollendung im 13.
Jahrhundert, Berlin, 1979, 16–28, figs. 2–8;
VK, 32, 190–191.

61. *VK*, 212. Metz Cathedral may have
been begun by Archbishop Theodorich I
(964–984), but it was completed by
Archbishop Theodorich II (1005–1046).

62. The general discussion of the
monuments by Grodecki, *L'architecture*, 28,
100, 41 nn. 33, 36, should be updated by
the regional studies of Hans-Günther
Marschall and Rainer Slotta, *Lorraine romane*,
Zodiaque Series, La-Pierre-qui-Vire, 1984,
and Hubert Collin, *Les églises romanes de
Lorraine*, Nancy, 1981, which now supersede
Congrès archéologique de France, XCVI, 1933. In
a recent detailed study of Verdun
Cathedral, Hans-Günther Marschall, *Die
Kathedrale von Verdun: Die romanische Baukunst in
Westlothringen, Teil I*, Veröffentlichungen des
Instituts für Landeskunde im Saarland,
XXXII, Saarbrücken, 1981, assigns the basic
design of the structure and its lower storeys
to the reign of Bishop Haymo (990–1024),
largely on the basis of a dendrochronolog-
ical date of A.D. 998 provided by wood
samples taken from the ground floor of the
northwest stair tower. Heretofore, the
oldest parts of the church had usually been
assigned to a rebuilding following a fire of
ca. 1047. Indeed, Bishop Theoderich
(1047–1089) is reported by contemporary
sources as having rebuilt the church *a
fundamento*, and it may well be that more of
the building resulted from this second
campaign than Marschall suggests. See the
insightful review of Marschall's book by
Jochen Zink in *Kunstchronik*, XXXVI, 1983,
322–339.

63. Rainer Schiffler, *Die Ostteile der
Kathedrale von Toul*, Cologne, 1977, 18–26.

64. *"Chor mit turmüberdeckten rechteckigen
Nebenchören."* Hans Erich Kubach, "Der
Trierer Kunstraum im 11.–13. Jahrhundert,"
Trierer Zeitschrift, XIII, 1937, 81–103. See
also H. Bunjes, "Die Beiträge zur
kunstgeographie des Moselraums in
romanischer Zeit: Trier und Verdun," *Trierer
Jahrbuch*, I, 1939, 1–37. For a recent
discussion of this regional grouping, with

additional bibliography, see H.-G.
Marschall, *Die Kathedrale von Verdun*, 29–34.

65. Pierre Héliot, "Sur les tours
jumelées au chevet des églises du moyen
age," *Arte in Europa: Scritti di storia dell'arte in
onore di Eduardo Arslan*, Milan, 1967, 249–
270; Charles-F. Ricome, "Structure et
fonction du chevet de Morienval," *BM*,
XCVIII, 1939, 299–320.

66. Two bell towers flanked the apse at
St.-Benoît-sur-Loire until 1780. At Vignory,
the towers seem to have been left
unfinished. Jean-Marie Berland, "St.-Benoît-
sur-Loire," *Val de Loire Romans*, Zodiaque
Series, La-Pierre-qui-Vire, 2nd ed., 1965,
1–2, 75–77; F. Deshoulières, "L'église de
Vignory," *BM*, LXXXVIII, 1929, 89–107;
H. Focillon, "L'église St.-Etienne de
Vignory, ses dates de construction," *Revue
archéologique*, 6e serie, IX, 1937, 78 n. 83.

67. W. Erdmann, "Die ehemalige
Stiftskirche St. Peter und Paul, Reichenau-
Niederzell," *RQ*, LXVIII, 1973, 91–103.

68. Hoffman, *Hirsauer Bauschule*, 33–45.

69. *Ibid.*, 36–37.

70. *Loc. cit.*: "Es ist festzustellen dass die
Ostbaulösung von Reichenbach kleinerlei
Nachfloge hat . . . kennen wir keinen Bau,
der diese Gliederung nochmals aufnimmt.
Dagegen findet der Gedanke der Osttürme
sogleich Aufnahme."

71. Robert Will, "Murbach," *Alsace
romane*, Zodiaque Series, La-Pierre-qui-Vire,
1965, 121–140, and Otto Feld, "Zur
Baugeschichte der Klosterkirche Murbach,"
KG, XXIV, 1961, 242ff.

72. Serafini, *Torri*, 159–162. For the
Lorsch gateway see Wolfgang Selzer, "Die
karolingische Königshalle zu Lorsch,"
Laurissa jubilans, Mainz, 1964, 129–130, and
more recently Mario D'Onofrio, "La
Königshalle di Lorsch presso Worms," *Roma
e l'età carolingia*, Rome, 1976, 130–138.

73. Markthaler, "Recenti scoperti," 58–
60.

74. *VK*, 98–100. For the authenticity of
this detail in spite of various restoration
campaigns see Klaus Voigtländer, *Die
Stiftskirche zu Gernrode*, Berlin, 1980, 58–64,
figs. 22, 29, 41, 89–90.

75. Werner Meyer-Barkhausen, "Die frühmittelalterlichen Vorbauten am Atrium von Alt St. Peter im Rom, zweitürmige Atrien, Westwerke und karolingische-ottonische Königshalle," *Wallraf-Richartz Jahrbuch*, XX, 1958, 35, fig. 14.

76. Harold Taylor, *Anglo-Saxon Architecture*, I, Cambridge, 1965, 52–57, 222–226. For a general discussion of pilaster strips and stripwork see *ibid.*, III, 1978, 915–938, where Taylor argues for an indigenous development of the technique.

77. Porter, *Lombard Architecture*, II, 308–310, 439; Thümmler, "Die Baukunst," 157–160; Chierici, *Lombardia*, 269–274.

78. G. Chierici, "Il battistero di Lomello," *Rendiconti della pontificia accademia rom. archeologia*, XVII, 1940–1941, fasc. III–IV, 127–137; Porter, *Lombard Architecture*, II, 500–505, pls. 106–111; Thümmler, "Die Baukunst," 157–160. A rebuilding of the upper storeys of the baptistery in the eleventh century is suggested by Chierici, *Lombardia*, 309.

79. For a detailed study of these monuments see Friedrich W. Deichmann, *Ravenna: Haupstadt des spätantiken Abendlandes*, Wiesbaden, II:1, 1974, 125–190, II:2, 1976, 233–280.

80. Krautheimer, *Early Christian*, 87.

81. Gaetano Panazza and Adriano Peroni, *La chiesa di San Salvatore in Brescia*, Atti dell'ottavo congresso di studi sull'arte dell'alto medioevo, II, Milan, 1962; Hans P. L'Orange and Hjalmar Torp, *Il tempietto longobardo di Cividale*, Acta ad archaeologiam et storiam artium pertinentia, VIII:1–2, 1977; Leo Hugot, "Die Königshalle Karls des Grossen in Aachen," *Aachener Kunstblätter*, XXX, 1965, 38–48, and his "Die Pfalz Karls des Grossen in Aachen," *Karl der Grosse*, III, 546–556.

82. *Die Kunstdenkmäler der Schweiz: Graubünden*, ed. E. Poeschel, VII, Basel, 1948, 233–243, 494ff.

83. Krautheimer, *Early Christian*, 326–327; Vladimir Gvozdonovic, "Pre-Romanesque and Early Romanesque Architecture in Croatia," Ph.D. diss., Cornell University, 1972, 84–87, 187–195.

84. Angelo Pantoni, "Santa Maria delle Cinque Torri di Cassino: Risultati e problemi," *RAC*, LI, 1975, 243–280. See also A. Venditti, *Architettura bizantina nell'Italia meridionale*, I, Naples, 1967, 591–597.

85. Verzone, *L'architettura*, 151–154; Porter, *Lombard Architecture*, III, 406, 431–433, IV, pl. 203, figs. 1–2. Thümmler, "Die Baukunst," 173, realized that the 1008 inscription commemorating a renovation of the cathedral on Torcello by Bishop Ursus refers to the fabric of the church extant today, unlike Bruno Schulz, *Die Kirchenbauten auf der Insel Torcello*, Berlin-Leipzig, 1927, and Raffaele Cattaneo, *L'architecture en Italie du VIe au XIe siècle*, Venice, 1890, who, in order to fit their aesthetic concepts of early Christian and Carolingian architecture, date the church to the ninth century without documentary evidence and therefore explain the 1008 renovation as referring to the replacement of several columns in the nave. The close relationship between the Lombard buildings of the ninth century and those of the late tenth and early eleventh centuries is underscored by the recent, and I think unsuccessful, attempt by Peroni to date S. Felice to the ninth century: A. Peroni, "Per la tipologia architettonico dell'età carolingia nell'area lombarda," *Rome e l'età carolingia*, Rome, 1976, 87–97.

86. J. Puig y Cadafalch et al., *L'arquitectura romanica a Catalunya*, II, Barcelona, 1911, 197, fig. 109.

87. Tholen, "Neue Ergebnisse," 15; Kubach and Verbeek, *Romanische Baukunst*, I, 582–594, esp. 585. For the reconstruction and dating of the various phases of this church see Helmut Fussbroich, *Die Ausgrabungen in St. Pantaleon zu Köln*, Kölner Forschungen, II, Mainz, 1983.

88. Pierre Héliot, "Saint-Etienne de Caen, Saint-Paul d'Issoire, la cathédrale d'Osnabruck et les arcades murales dans l'architecture du Nord-Ouest de l'Europe," *Wallraf-Richartz Jahrbuch*, XXI, 1959, 1ff. See also Schaeffer, *Zyfflich*, 152.

89. See, for example, the famous seventeenth-century engraving by Georges Lallemand representing the remains of the

rotunda and flanking stair towers of St.-
Benigne, reproduced in Jean Hubert, Jean
Porcher, and W. F. Volbach, *The Carolingian
Renaissance*, New York, 1970, 67, fig. 60.

90. H. R. Sennhauser, *Romainmôtier und
Payern: Studien zur Cluniazenerarchitektur des 11.
Jahrhundert in der Westschweiz*, Basel, 1970,
17–48, 77–84.

91. Corrado Bozzoni, *Calabria normana:
Ricerche sull'architettura dei secoli undicesimo e
dodicesimo*, Rome, 1974, esp. 118–151;
Kubach, *Romanesque Architecture*, 73, fig. 71,
77, 87; Heinrich M. Schwarz, "Die
Baukunst Kalabriens und Siziliena im
Zeitalter der Normannen, I: Die
lateinischen Kirchengrundungen des 11.
Jahrhunderts und der Dom in Cefalù,"
Römisches Jahrbuch, IV, 1942–1944, 1–112;
Gisberto Martelli, "La cattedrale di Gerace,"
Palladio, n. s., VI, 1965, 117–126.

92. Krautheimer, *Corpus*, II, 1959, 159–
184, esp. 184.

93. Hermanin, *L'arte in Roma*, 35, pl.
XIV. For the history of the church see Dale
Kinney, "S. Maria in Trastevere from its
Founding to 1215," Ph.D. diss., New York
University, 1975. Krautheimer, *Rome*, 163,
suggests that the church may have been
begun as early as the 1120s.

94. Thümmler, "S. Pietro in Tuscania,"
286, nn. 35, 36.

95. Krautheimer, *Corpus*, I, 19ff, 146ff,
310–317, II, 1–144, esp. 52–54, III, 174,
and G. Bertelli, A. G. Guidobaldi, and P.
R. Spagnoletti, "Strutture murarie degli
edifici religiosi di Roma dal VI al IX secolo,"
RINASA, n. s., XXIII–XXIV, 1976–77, 95–
172.

96. Hans Belting, "Studien zum
beneventanischen Hof im 8. Jahrhundert,"
DOP, XVI, 1962, 141ff; Friedrich W.
Deichmann, "Die Entstehungszeit von
Salvatorkirche und Clitumnustempel bei
Spoleto," *Mitteilungen des Deutschen
Archaeologischen Instituts, Röm. Abt.*, LVIII,
1943, 106–148.

97. Krautheimer, *Early Christian*, 535. B.
M. Apollonj-Ghetti, G. De Angelis d'Ossat,
A. Ferrua, and C. Venanzi, "Le strutture

murarie delle chiese paleocristiane di
Roma," *RAC*, XXI, 1944–1945, 233–248,
esp. 228 n. 2.

98. Frédéric Lesueur, "Saint-Martin
d'Angers: La couture du Mans, Saint-
Philibert de Grandlieu et autres églises à
elements de briques dans la région de la
Loire," *BM*, CXIX, 1961, 211–242, and his
"Appareils décoratifs supposés carolingiens,"
BM, CXXIV, 1966, 167–186.

99. Forsyth, *St. Martin at Angers*, 81–142,
sees three separate phases in the completion
of the crossing tower: the piers and crossing
arches in the late tenth century; the middle
zone of the superstructure in 1029–1040;
and the crossing vault and supporting
columns ca. 1075. Forsyth admits, though,
that the masonry of phases one and two are
distinguishable only by the absence of brick
in the latter; otherwise, "the masonry
technique at St. Martin's shows a
remarkable adherence to the past during the
early eleventh century" (*ibid.*, 115). It seems
more reasonable to assign the entire base of
the tower to ca. 1040 than to relegate part
of it to a hypothetical tenth-century phase.
See also Jacques Mallet, *L'art roman de l'ancien
Anjou*, Paris, 1984, 22–29.

100. Lesueur, "Saint-Martin d'Angers,"
240–241: "Il s'agirant, donc, comme nous
l'avons indiqué, non d'une persistance mais
plutot d'une 'renaissance' d'une imitation
d'une technique déjà fort ancienne. . . . Il
semble que l'on se sait tout d'abord surtout
interesse a l'effet decoratif. . . ." See also
Jean Hubert, "Architecture," *The Carolingian
Renaissance*, 68.

101. Lesueur, "Saint-Martin d'Angers,"
238–239; Gabriel Plat, *L'art de batir en France
des Romains à l'an 1100*, Paris, 1939, 84. Plat
(*ibid.*, 43) states that brick courses cease to
be used in the region by about the first
quarter of the eleventh century; this,
however, is far from an absolute
chronology.

102. Nikolaus Irsch, *Der Dom zu Trier,
Die Kunstdenkmäler der Rheinprovinz*,
XIII:I, Düsseldorf, 1931, 84–86; and
Jochen Zink, "Die Baugeschichte des

Trierer Domes von den Anfängen im 4. Jahrhundert bis zum letzten Restaurierung," *Der Trierer Dom*, ed. Franz Ronig, Neuss, 1980, 17–46.

103. For S. Giovanni a Porta Latina see Krautheimer, *Corpus*, I, 310–317, pl. XL, and Maria E. Avagnina, V. Garibaldi, and C. Salterini, "Strutture murarie degli edifici religiosi di Roma nel XII secolo," *RINASA*, n. s., XIII–XIV, 1976–77, 171–255.

104. Krautheimer, *Corpus*, I, 131; Avagnina et al., "Strutture nel XII secolo," 246. A *falsa cortina* also appears in the Romanesque remodeling of S. Pudenziana that may date from the reign of Pope Gregory VII (1073–1085). See Krautheimer, *Corpus*, III, 291–92, 296–301.

105. Apollonj-Ghetti, "Le strutture," 247, fig. 27.

106. Kubach and Verbeek, *Romanische Baukunst*, II, 587, 590, III, pl. 253(1). For the date of the later westwork and nave extension see Fussbroich, *Die Ausgrabungen*, 238–241, pl. 8.

107. Mario Salmi, *L'abbazia di Pomposa*, Rome, 1936, 250–251, fig. 13.

108. Walter Horn, "Romanesque Churches in Florence: A Study of their Chronology and Stylistic Development," *Art Bulletin*, XXV, 1943, 122ff.

109. Forsyth, *St. Martin at Angers*, 122ff. For a general discussion of this particular method of vaulting see René Chappuis, "Eglises romanes à coupole sortée par deux au trois étages d'arcs," *BM*, CXXIII, 1965, 295–314.

110. Grodecki, *L'architecture ottonienne*, 257.

111. For the chronology of Speyer I see Kubach, *Speyer*, I, 695–697. Wood from a scaffolding hole in the clerestory zone of the nave has provided a date of 1045.

112. See, for example, Louis Grodecki, *L'architecture ottonienne*, Paris, 1958; Hans Reinhardt, "Die deutschen Kaiserdome des elften Jahrhunderts," *Basler Zeitschrift für Geschichte und Altertunskunde*, XXXIII, 1934, 175–194; Pierre Héliot, "L'ordre colossal et les arcades murales dans les églises romanes," *BM*, CXV, 1957, 241–261; and

Héliot, "Encore l'ordre colossal et les arcades murales dans les églises romanes," *BM*, CXVIII, 1960, 31–36.

113. See, for example, Kubach, *Speyer*, I, 792, and Willibald Sauerländer, "Cluny und Speyer," *Vorträge und Forschungen*, XVII, 1973, 22. Elsewhere, Hans Kubach has suggested that the development of the so-called colossal order may be traced within the building sequence of Speyer itself, "Die Wandsysteme des Speyer Domes," *Gedenkschrift Ernst Gall*, ed. Margarete Kühn and Louis Grodecki, Munich and Berlin, 1965, 11–30.

114. See, for example, Jürgen Christern, *Das frühchristliche Pilgerheiligtum von Tebessa*, Wiesbaden, 1976, and Friedrich W. Deichmann, "Wandsysteme," *Byzantinische Zeitschrift*, LIX, 1966, 351.

115. *Congrès archéologique de France*, CXXX, 1972, 243–275, 462–485.

116. See Tournier, *Les églises comtoises*, esp. 48, figs. 17–18, and *Églises de France: Histoire générale et dictionnaire*, V, Paris, 1971, A175. For a summary of the dating controversy surrounding St.-Philibert at Tournus see *Dictionnaire des églises*, II, A165–167, and C. Edson Armi, *Masons and Sculptors in Romanesque Burgundy: The New Aesthetic of Cluny III*, University Park and London, 1983, 131–150. Armi discerns three major campaigns in the construction of the nave and western narthex of the church, but he refrains from assigning dates to these phases.

117. Albert Colombet and Pierre Gras, "L'Église de Combertault," *Mémoires de la commission des antiquités du département de la Côte d'Or*, XXIV, 1959, 141–164.

118. Daria De Bernardi Ferrero, "Saint-Juste de Suse," *Congrès archéologique de France*, CXXIX, 1971, 553–564. Unfortunately, the interior intonaco decoration has prevented a detailed and reliable analysis of this building, so that the dates of construction and remodeling of the church remain uncertain.

119. Franklin Toker, "Excavations," 17–36, esp. 32–34.

120. The major source for the history of the abbey is a thirteenth-century chartulary, *Codice diplomatico del monastero benedettino di S. Maria di Tremiti (1005–1237)*, ed. Armando Petrucci, Istituto Storico Italiano per il Medio Evo, Fonti per la Storia d'Italia, XCVIII, Rome, 1960.

121. See my article "The Church of S. Maria di Tremiti and Its Significance for the History of Romanesque Architecture," *JSAH*, XLIII, 1984, 5–19.

122. *Ibid.*, 6–7, with additional bibliography.

123. *Chronica monasterii casinensis*, Hoffmann, *MGH SS*, I, 17, lib. III, cap. 2; Schuster, *L'abbazia imperiale*, 195.

124. In 1054, Argyros visited the imperial palace at Goslar in northern Germany in the company of monks from Tremiti (Ernst Steindorff, *Jahrbücher des Deutschen Reichs unter Heinrich III*, Leipzig, 1881, II, 264–265). Not long after, in 1057, he gave Farfa six thousand solidi and a mantle of silk and gold valued at one hundred pounds of silver (*Chronicon*, II, 202–203, and *RF*, V, 238–239, doc. 1261).

125. For the origin and development of quadrilobe piers in Italy see my "S. Maria di Tremiti," 15–16.

126. It should be pointed out, however, that Farfa does share with Speyer I the use of carved bases for the engaged columns, a classicizing element that is generally lacking in the examples I have cited in Burgundy and Italy, where the engaged columns tend to have no bases at all. Still, one could cite an Italian precedent in the cathedral at Susa, where the half-columns rest on simple stone blocks of variable height. See De Bernardi Ferrero, "Saint-Juse de Suse," 558.

127. See Appendix of Documents, No. VIII.

128. Hourlier, "Saint Odilon," 316–323; Schlosser, *Die abendländische Klosteranlage*; Hager, "Zum Geschichte"; Braunfels, *Monasteries*, 55–58.

129. For a detailed study of the liturgical traditions and customaries of Gorze and Cluny see Kassius Hallinger, *Gorze-Kluny: Studien zu den monastischen*

Lebensformen und Gegensätzen im Hochmittelalter, II, Studia anselmiana, XXII–XXV, Rome, 1950–1951, 869–983. See also *idem*, "Progressi e problemi della riecerca sulla reforma pre-Gregoriana," *Il monachesimo nell'alto medioevo*, Centro Italiano di Studi sull'Alto Medioevo, Settimane di Studio, V, Spoleto, 1957, 257–291.

130. It has been estimated that by ca. 1050 more than eight hours per day at Cluny were spent in church. David Knowles, *Christian Monasticism*, New York, 1969, repr. 1972, 52–53. For a description of the liturgical horarium see *idem*, *The Monastic Constitutions of Lanfranc*, London, 1951, xv–xviii.

131. Two recent exceptions are the studies by Arnold Klukas, "*Altaria Superioria*: The Function and Significance of the Tribune-Chapel in Anglo-Norman Romanesque: A Problem in the Relationship of Liturgical Requirements and Architectural Form," Ph.D. diss., University of Pittsburgh, 1978, and Sanderson, "Monastic Reform in Lorraine," which is concerned exclusively with the development of the outer crypt. It should be pointed out that neither of these studies deals with features found at Farfa. For a consideration of the implications for architecture of the Gorze and Cluny reform movements see Dieter Grossmann's review of Hallinger's book, *Gorze-Kluny*, in *ZKG*, XX, 1957, 296–302.

132. A. Mettler, "Die zweite Kirche in Cluni und die Kirchen in Hirsau nach den 'Gewohnheiten' des XI. Jahrhunderts," pts. I, II, *Zeitschrift für Geschichte der Architektur*, III, 1909–10, 273–286, IV, 1910–11, 1–16.

133. Summarized in Conant, *Cluny*, 1968.

134. Hoffmann, *Bauschule*, 23–25. For the relation of the Hirsau Customary to those at Cluny see Kassius Hallinger, "Klunys Bräuche zur Zeit Hugos des Grossen (1049–1109)," *ZSRG*, XLV, 1959, 99–140, esp. 120. The Hirsau Customary is published in Migne, *PL*, CL, cols. 997–1146.

135. Friedrich Möbius, "Die Chorpartie der westeuropäschen Klosterkirche

zwischen 8. und 11. Jahrhundert," *Architektur des Mittelalters: Funktion und Gestalt,* ed. Friedrich Möbius and Ernst Schubert, Weimar, 1983, 9–41, esp. 32–39. See also Armand Dehlinger, "Die Ordensgesetzgebung der Benediktiner und ihr Auswerkung auf die Grundrissbestattung des Benediktinischen Klosterbaues in Deutschland unter besonderer Berüchsichtigung der Reform von Hirsau," diss., Dresden, 1936.

136. Mettler, "Die zweite Kirche," pt. I, 277ff, pt. II, 1–4. Mettler, p. 280, suggests that the *chorus maior* is derived from the *chorus psallentium,* as labeled for the crossing on the Plan of St. Gall. Hoffmann, *Bauschule,* 83ff, points out that the oldest of the customaries, the Farfa Customary, mentions only a *chorus maior,* whereas those of Cluny and Hirsau some forty years later distinguish between a *chorus maior* and a *chorus minor,* indicating a further compartmentalization of the eastern half of the church. These divisions of the church are not so explicitly stated in the earliest customaries associated with Gorze, the so-called *Consuetudines Einsidlenses* and those of Sandrat from St. Maximin in Trier, both dating from the middle of the tenth century (published in *Consuetudines monasticae,* V, ed. Bruno Albers, Montecassino, 1912). They refer instead to *altare, chorus,* and *ecclesia.* For the date of the Gorze customaries see Hallinger, *Gorze-Kluny,* esp. 892–897.

137. Mettler, "Die zweite Kirche," pt. I, 281, and Möbius, "Die Chorpartie," 38. The *Ordo Cluniacensis,* ca. 1085, is the more explicit in this regard. It is published by M. Herrgott in *Vetus disciplina monastica,* Paris, 1726, 134–364. See, for example, bk. XLV, 236: the priest stands "super pavimentem ante altare, juxta ultimam stationem chori." For the three divisions of the church see, for example, p. 356: "Dedicatio ecclesiae eveniat tunc, quia tota ecclesia paranda est, tam in navi, quam in choro, et in Presbyterio. . . ."

138. The index of *Liber tramitis,* ed. Dinter, 374, cites under the word *signum* more than eighty references to the use of one or more bells. For the general use of *signum* to mean bell, or *campana,* see Du Cange, *Glossarium,* VII, 483–484.

139. *Consuetudines monasticae,* Albers, V, 73–77.

140. Mettler, "Die zweite Kirche," pt. II, 4–10; Hoffmann, *Baukunst,* 33–45. The practical reasons for placing bells in side towers are amusingly described by Paul Frankl, *Die frühmittelalterliche und romanische Baukunst,* Handbuch der Kunstwissenschaft, Potsdam, 1926, 175: "In Hirsau ist die beabsichtige Verlegung der Glocken in die seitlichen Osttürme wohl damit zu erklären, dass das Ziehen der Glocken an Stricken, die mitten unter die Sänger herabhingen in auffälliger, fast komischer Weise mit der sonstigen Gemessenheit und Würde der Mönche kontrastierte und störte, man muss sich nur die tänzelndzappelige Bewegung vergegenwärtigen, die des Glockenziehen verlangt, dieser Anblick des allzu irdischen Handhabens schädigt das geheimnisvolle Wirken des Getöns!"

141. It should be noted, however, that at Farfa the absence of upper-storey chapels in the bell towers and of a crypt below the presbytery is more in keeping with Cluniac practice, whereas such chapels and crypts are common both in Lotharingia and the Rhineland. Similarly, reference to these features is conspicuously lacking in the Farfa Customary. For a discussion of the architectural implications of the Cluniac and Gorze customaries see A. Klukas, *Altaria Superioria,* 441–451.

142. The capital at Galliano (my Pl. 135) forms part of the entrance to the crypt, and it presumably dates to the time of the consecration of the church in 1007. Comparable capitals are found at Romainmôtier, datable to the mid-eleventh century. Sennhauser, *Romainmôtier,* pls. 44–45. In Central Italy, similar foliate decoration, although somewhat cruder in execution, is found on capitals and other architectural sculpture from the early Romanesque phase (ca. 1028) of the church of S. Rufino in Assisi; the sculpture has been collected in the sacristy. See A. Prandi

et al., *L'Umbria*, 287–293, pls. 138–139. Unfortunately, there is no compendium for sculpture in Italy in the eleventh century comparable to the *Corpus della scultura altomedievale*, Spoleto, 1959–1981, which does not consider works dating later than the tenth century.

143. Premoli, "La chiesa abbaziale," 39–42, and I are in general agreement about the lines of architectural influence.

144. Kempf, "Grundentwicklung Triererdomes," 2ff.

145. Kubach, "Der Trierer Kunstraum."

146. Serafini, *Torri campanarie* I, 162ff; Hermanin, *L'arte in Roma*, 85–94; Krautheimer, *Rome*, 173, 352. One of the first bell towers in Rome may have been that of St. Paul's outside-the-Walls, another Benedictine abbey, added to the church in the eleventh century, as indicated by coins found when the tower was demolished in 1834. See Krautheimer, *Corpus*, V, 101, and A. Armellini, *Le chiese di Roma*, II, Rome, 1942, 1159. For a survey of church towers in Tuscany and related monuments see Marvin Trachtenberg, *The Campanile of Florence Cathedral*, New York, 1971, 151–165.

147. Whitehouse, "Farfa Abbey," 250. The coin was identified by Prof. Finetti of the University of Rome. A detailed analysis of all the numismatic material will appear in the final report of the excavations.

148. "Datum X kalendas Octobris, Anno dominicae incarnationis DCCCCXCVIIII indictione XII . . . Anno tertii Ottonis regnantis XVI, imperii IIII . . . Actum in . . . monasterio sanctae Mariae." *RF*, III, 145, doc. 431. Schuster, "L'abbaye de Farfa," 392.

149. *Regesto*, III, 145, doc. 433, IV, 247, doc. 851, 263, doc. 868. See also Schuster, "L'abbaye de Farfa," 380.

150. *Tutela e valorizzazione*, 122. The attribution to Sichardus is based on the lines of his epitaph that read: HAEC LOCA PRUDENTI CONSTRUXIT ET ORDINE MIRO / COMMISSUMQUE TRUCI CAVIT AB HOSTE GREGEM.

151. Conant, *Cluny*, and his *Carolingian and Romanesque Architecture, 800–1200*, Harmondsworth, 1974, 146–148, fig. 105.

152. A flat exterior wall is clearly indicated for the apse of the Lady Chapel in Conant's excavation drawing published in his *Cluny*, group I, plan II, fig. 2. For reasons that are not altogether clear, Conant chooses to reconstruct the chapel with a curved exterior wall for the apse (see my pl. 134).

153. Conant, *Cluny*, and his *Carolingian and Romanesque Architecture*, 148.

Chapter 6: The Later Middle Ages and Early Renaissance

1. See Appendix of Documents, No. XI.

2. Toubert, *Les structures*, II, 1119–1126.

3. *Ibid.*, I, 303–368, 371–447 (catalogue of sites).

4. See Appendix of Documents, No. XI. See also the analysis by Toubert, *Les structures*, I, 523 n. 2, II, 1166 n. 1.

5. Gregory of Catino does not hide his disdain for either this abbot or his project. *Chronicon*, II, 220: "Praedictus abbas [Berardus II] a plurimus de negligentia correptus, inchoavit in monte ecclesiae magnum opus . . . sed Deus omnipotens . . . praefati abbatis finem imposuit actioni prodigae."

6. A marginal note in the Farfa Customary (Vat. lat. 6808) reads: "MCXLII Monasterium novum inchoatur in monte." *Chronicon*, II, 321.

7. Giuseppe Croquison, "L'abbazia imperiale di Farfa e i suoi problemi archeologici," *L'illustrazione vaticana*, IX, 1938, 864ff, and *idem*, "La basilica carolingia dell'abbazia imperiale di Farfa," *Atti del V congresso nazionale di studi romani*, XVIII, 1940, 12, pl. IV, fig. c.

8. Thümmler, "Die Baukunst," 205–206, 212–213.

9. Beatrice Premoli, "Il S. Martino nuovo di Farfa," *Bolletino della unione storia ed arte*, I–II, 1972 (1973), 21–27, and Herwin Schaeffer, "The Origin of the Two-Tower Façade in Romanesque Architecture," *Art Bulletin*, 27, 1945, 85–108.

10. Richard Krautheimer, "San Nicola in Bari und die apulische Architektur des 12. Jahrhunderts," *Wiener Jahrbuch für Kunstgeschichte,* IX, 1934, 5–42.

11. Krautheimer, *Corpus,* I, 41–42, and his *Rome,* 173.

12. Krautheimer, *Rome,* 161–202; Karl Noehles, "Die Kunst der Cosmaten und die Idee der Renovatio Romae," *Festschrift Werner Hager,* Recklingshausen, 1966, 17–37. Other churches that could be cited are Quattro Coronati (1099–1116), S. Lorenzo in Lucina (ca. 1130), S. Maria in Trastevere (consecrated 1143), SS. Giovanni e Paolo (1145–1159), S. Giovanni a Porta Latina (1180–1190), S. Lorenzo fuori le mura (1216–1227), and S. Giorgio in Velabro (thirteenth century).

13. Krautheimer, *Rome,* 181, 182, fig. 138.

14. Irmgard M. Voss, "Die Benedictinerabtei S. Andrea in Flumine bei Ponzano Romano," Ph.D. diss., Rheinischen Friedrich-Wilhelms Univ., Bonn, 1985. I wish to thank Dr. Voss for sharing the results of her careful research with me. S. Andrea in Flumine was not a Farfa dependency, but contact between the two centers is shown by a document, recorded in the Farfa Register and dated 1052 (*RF,* IV, 234–236, doc. 835), from Abbot Stephanus of S. Andrea to Abbot Berardus I ceding certain lands near Farfa in exchange for property near Ponzano Romano.

15. The fragments of a fifth ionic capital, identical in size and design to the others, is walled up in the courtyard of the sixteenth-century cloister.

16. Edward Hutton, *The Cosmati,* London, 1950, pls. 61–62. The term "Cosmati" is derived from the name of a Cosma(s) or Cosmatus that appears on several works of the thirteenth century. See *ibid.,* 36–37, and Dorothy Glass, *Studies in Cosmatesque Pavements,* British Archeological Reports, International Series, LXXXII, Oxford, 1980, 11.

17. Hutton, *Cosmati,* 41, 54; Glass, *Studies,* 65.

18. Hutton, *Cosmati,* pls. 22–23. The screen at S. Andrea in Flumine, which is reconstructed, is dated by Voss (*S. Andrea in Flumine,* 134) to the mid-twelfth century, while that at Ferentino bears an inscription referring to Pope Paschal II (1100–1118). Hutton, *Cosmati,* 54.

19. *Ibid.,* 6; Glass, *Studies,* 10. The only other work signed by Rainerius was a window, now lost, at S. Silvestro in Capite in Rome. His sons, Petrus and Nicolaus, signed works at S. Maria di Castello in Tarquinia, of which one bears the date 1143. See Hutton, *Cosmati,* 34.

20. Demus, *Romanesque,* 85, pls. 54–55.

21. W. Paesler, "Die römische Weltgerichttafel im Vatican," *Römisches Jahrbuch,* II, 1938, 313–394.

22. Edward B. Garrison, "Dating the Vatican Last Judgment Panel: Monument versus Document," *La bibliofilia,* LXXII, 1970, 121–160, esp. 156–158. He cites Peter Abelard (d. 1142), for example, who wrote: "Christ was made also the priest . . . then was suspended upon the cross as though sacrificed for us upon an altar." *Expositio symboli apostolorum,* Migne, *PL,* CLXXVIII, col. 622.

23. *History of the Church,* III, 468; J. Gieselmann, *Die Eucharistielehre der Vorscholastik,* Paderborn, 1926, 365–375. Lanfranc, *De corpore et sanguine Christi* (Migne, *PL,* CXLIX, cols. 1455ff.) was writing in response to the heretical views of Beregarius (d. 1088).

24. Bernard Berenson, *Italian Pictures of the Renaissance: Central Italian and North Italian Schools,* I, 1897, revised 1968, London, 134–135, 223–224.

25. *Ibid.,* III, 1907, pls. 1083–1084. Italo Faldi, *Pittori viterbesi di cinque secoli,* Rome, 1970, 26–37, pls. 93–125, esp. 126–134. See also Premoli, "Le chiese abbaziale," 67 n. 12.

Chapter 7: Conclusion

1. The most important studies of these individual monuments include: Walter Horn, "Das Florentiner Baptisterium," *Mitteilungen des Kunsthistorischen Instituts zu*

Florenz, V, 1938, 100–151; Piero
Sanpaolesi, *Il duomo di Pisa e l'architettura
romanica toscana delle origini*, Pisa, 1975; Urs
Boeck, "Der Pisaner Dom zwischen 1089
und 1120," *Architectura*, XI, 1981, 1–30; and
Otto Demus, *The Church of San Marco in
Venice*, Washington, D. C., 1960. For
Montecassino and Rome see Krautheimer,
Rome, 178–180. For a recent, and I think
unsuccessful, attempt to date the
construction of the Florence baptistery to
before 1059 see Werner Jacobsen, "Zur
Datierung des Florentiner Baptisteriums S.
Giovanni," *ZKG*, XLIII, 1980,
225–243.

2. Krautheimer, *Rome*, 161–202.

Selected Bibliography

I. *Farfa: Primary Sources and Secondary Studies*

Boccolini, Ippolito, *L'abbazia di Farfa: Descrizione storico-artistico*, Rome, 1932.

"Catalogus cardinalium abbatuum farfensium," Farfa, 1728, Farfa Library, AF-291.

Collectio canonum regesto farfensi inserta, ed. Theo Kölzer, Monumenta iuris canonici, series B: Corpus collectionum, V, Vatican City, 1982.

Consuetudines farfenses, ed. Bruno Albers, Consuetudines monasticae, 5 vols., I, Stuttgart, 1900.

Croquison, Giuseppe, "L'abbazia imperiale di Farfa e i suoi problemi archeologici," *L'illustrazione vaticana*, IX, 1938, 864–867.

———, "La basilica carolingia dell'abbazia di Farfa," *Atti V. congresso nazionale di studi romani*, III, Rome, 1942, 119ff.

———, "I problemi archeologici farfensi," *Rivista di archeologia cristiana*, XV, 1938, 37–71.

De Alexandris, Archangelus, "Chronicon sacri ac regalis monasterii farfensis," 1627, Vatican Library, Cod. Barberini Lat. 2350 (XXXII–141).

Donaldson, P., C. McClendon, and D. Whitehouse, "L'abbazia di Farfa: Rapporto preliminare sugli scave 1978–80," *Archivio della società romana di storia patria*, CIII, 1980, 5–12.

———, "Notizie scavi: Farfa: Nota preliminare," *Archeologia medievale*, VI, 1979, 270–273.

———, "Notizie scavi: Farfa: Seconda nota preliminare," *Archeologia medievale*, VIII, 1981, 566–568.

Etaix, Raymond, "Le prologue du sermonaire d'Alain de Farfa," *Scriptorium*, XVIII, 1964, 3–10.

Felten, Franz J., "Zur Geschichte der Kloster Farfa und S. Vincenzo al Volturno im Achten Jahrhundert," *Quellen und Forschungen aus italienischen Archiven und Bibliotheken*, LXII, 1982, 1–58.

Franciosa, Nicola, *L'abbazia imperiale di Farfa*, Naples, 1964.

Giorgi, Ignazio, "Il regesto di Farfa e le altre opere di Gregorio di Catino," *Archivio della società romana di storia patria*, II, 1879, 452–455.

Guirand, J., "La badia di Farfa alla fine del secolo decimoterzo," *Archivio della società romana di storia patria*, XV, 1892, 275–288.

Heinzelmann, Karl, *Die Farfenser Streitschriften*, Strasbourg, 1904.

Il chronicon farfense di Gregorio di Catino, ed. Ugo Balzani, Fonti per la storia d'Italia, XXXIII–XXXIV, Istituto Storico Italiano, 2 vols., Rome, 1903.

Il regesto di Farfa compilato da Gregorio di Catino, ed. Ignazio Giorgi and Ugo Balzani, Biblioteca della Società Romana di Storia Patria, 5 vols., Rome, 1883–1914.

Kehr, Paul, "Urkunden zur Geschichte von Farfa in XII. Jahrhundert," *Quellen und Forschungen aus italienischen Archiven und Bibliotheken*, IX, 1906, 170–184.

Kölzer, Theo, "*Codex libertatis*. Überlegungen zur Funktion des 'Regestum Farfense' und anderer Klosterchartulare," *Atti del IX congresso internazionale di studi sull'alto medioevo*, Centro Italiano di Studi sull'Alto Medioevo, Spoleto, 1983, 609–653.

Krönig, Wolfgang, "Deutsche spätgotische Architektur in Farfa und Subiaco," *25. Jahre Kaiser Wilhelm Gesellschaft*, III, Berlin, 1937, 57–68.

Liber tramitis aevi odilonis abbatis, ed. Peter Dinter, Corpus consuetudinum monasticarum, 10 vols., X, Siegburg, 1980.

L'Orange, Hans P., "Nuovo materiale per lo studio della scultura altomedievale, I: Sculpture altomedievali dell'abbazia di Farfa," *Acta ad archaeologiam et storiam artium pertinentia*, IV, 1969, 213–214.

Marini, M., *Serie cronologica degli abbati del monastero di Farfa*, Rome, 1836.

Markthaler, Paul, "Sulle recenti scoperte nell'abbazia imperiale di Farfa," *Rivista di archeologia cristiana*, V, 1928, 39–88.

McClendon, Charles, "An Early Funerary Portrait from the Medieval Abbey at Farfa," *Gesta*, XIII, 1983, 13–26.

———, "Discussione," *Roma e l'età carolingia*, Atti delle giornate di studio, 3–8 Maggio 1976, Istituto Nazionale di Archeologia e Storia dell'Arte, Rome, 1976, 368.

———, "Roman Antiquities from the Medieval Abbey at Farfa," *American Journal of Archaeology*, LXXXV, 1981, 206–207.

———, "The Revival of *Opus Sectile* Pavements in Rome and the Vicinity in the Carolingian Period," *Papers of the British School at Rome*, XLVIII, 1980, 157–165.

———, and D. Whitehouse, "Notizie scavi: La badia di Farfa, Fara in Sabina (Rieti): Terza nota preliminare," *Archeologia medievale*, IX, 1982, 323–330.

Notizie degli Scavi, Atti della R. accademia dei lincei, 1888, 292–293.

Palmieri, G., "Serie degli abbati di Farfa," *Il muratori*, I, fasc. 1–4, 1892, fasc. 5–6, 1893; II, fasc. 7–10, 1893, fasc. 11–12, 1894; III, fasc. 13, 1894, fasc. 14, 15, 18, 1895.

Pertica, Domenico, "Recenti scavi all'abbazia di Farfa," *Il cantiere*, IV, 1962, 40–47.

———, "Un pavimento dell'età carolingia scoperta recentemente in una chiesa di Farfa," *Il giornale d'Italia*, 10 April 1962, 11.

Pietrangeli, Carlo, "L'abbazia di Farfa," *Abbazie del Lazio*, Cesare D'Onofrio and Carlo Pietrangeli, Rome, 1970, 141–175.

Prandi, Adriano, "Osservazioni sull'abbazia di Farfa," *Rome e l'età carolingia*, Atti delle giornate di studio, 3–8 Maggio 1976, Istituto Nazionale di Archeologia e Storia dell'Arte, Rome, 1976, 357–367.

Premoli, Beatrice, "Il S. Martino Nuovo di Farfa," *Bolletino dell'unione storia ed arte*, I–II, 1972 (1973), 21–27.

———, "La chiesa abbaziale di Farfa," *Rivista dell'istituto nazionale d'archeologia e storia dell'arte*, XXI–XXII, 1974–1975 (1976), 5–77.

Ring, Richard R., "The Lands of Farfa: Studies in Lombard and Carolingian Italy," Ph.D. diss., University of Wisconsin, 1972–73.

Schuchert, A. B., "Eine unbekannte Elfenbeinkassette aus dem 11.

Jahrhundert," *Römische Quartalschrift*, XL, 1932, 1–11.

Schuster, Ildefonso, "De fastorum agiographico ordine imperialis monasteri pharphensis," *Millenaire de Cluny: Congrès d'histoire et d'archéologie tenu à Cluny les 10, 11, 12 septembre 1910*, Mâcon, 1910, 146–176.

———, "L'abbaye di Farfa et sa restoration au XIe siècle sous Hugues I," *Revue Bénédictine*, XXIV, 1907, 17–35, 374–400.

———, *L'imperiale abbazia di Farfa*, Rome, 1921.

———, "L'oratorio del Salvatore nel monastero imperiale di Farfa," *Nuovo bolletino d'archeologia cristiana*, XVII, 1911, 86–99.

———, "Martyrologium pharphense saeculi XI," *Revue Bénédictine*, XXVI, 1909, 433–463; XXVII, 1910, 75–94, 363–385.

———, "Reliquie d'arte nella badia imperiale di Farfa," *Archivio storico della società romana di storia patria*, XXXIV, 1911, 269–350.

———, "Spigolature farfensi, I: Monumenti epigrafici," *Rivista storica benedettina*, II, 1907, 402–415; IV, 1909, 581–596; V, 1910, 42–88.

———, *Ugo I di Farfa*, Perugia, 1911.

VII Settimana dei Musei: Tutela e valorizzazione del patrimonio artistico di Roma e del Lazio, Palazzo Venezia, 12–19 Aprile 1964, Rome, 1964, 122–135.

Supino Martini, Paola, "La produzione libraria negli *scriptoria* delle abbazie di Farfa e di S. Eutizio," *Atti del IX congresso internazionale di studi sull'alto medioevo*, Centro Italiano di Studi sull'Alto Medioevo, Spoleto, 1983, 581–607.

Tappi-Cesarini, Anselmo, "Note sul reclutamento del 'conventus pharphensis' dal 1048 al 1567," *Benedictina*, III, 1949, 307–330.

Whitehouse, David, "Farfa Abbey: The Eighth and Ninth Centuries," *Arte medievale*, II, 1985, 245–256.

Zielinski, Herbert, "Gregor von Catino und das Regestum Farfense," *Quellen und Forschungen aus italienischen Archiven und Bibliotheken*, LV–LVI, 1976, 361–404.

———, *Studien zu den spoletinischen*
"Privaturkunden" des 8. Jahrhunderts und ihrer Überlieferung im Regestum Farfense, Bibliothek des Deutschen Historischen Instituts Rom, XXXIX, Tübingen, 1972.

Zucchetti, Giuseppe, "Il 'liber largitorius vel notarius monasterii pharphensis,'" *Bulletino dell'istituto storico italiano per il medio evo*, XLIV, 1927, 1–259.

II. *Related Studies*

Accascina, Maria, "Note sul campanile de Santa Scolastica di Subiaco," *Atti del V convegno nazionale di storia dell'architettura* (Perugia, 1948), Florence, 1957, 257–264.

Alle sorgenti del romanico: Puglia XI secolo, ed. Pina Belli D'Elia, Bari, 1975.

Anfray, M., *L'architecture religieuse du Nivernais au moyen age: Les églises romanes*, Paris, 1951.

Anton, Hans Hubert, *Studien zu den Klosterprivilegien der Päpste im frühen Mittelalter unter besonderer Berücksichtigung der Privilegierung von St. Maurice d'Agaune*, Beiträge zur Geschichte und Quellenkunde des Mittelalters, IV, Berlin and New York, 1975.

Apollonj-Ghetti, B. M., "La chiesa di S. Maria in Vescovio," *Rivista di archeologia cristiana*, XXIII–XXIV, 1947–48, 3–53.

———, D. De Angelis d'Ossat, A. Ferrua, and C. Venanzi, "Le strutture murarie delle chiese paleocristiane di Roma," *Rivista di archeologia cristiana*, XXI, 1944–45, 223–248.

———, A. Ferrua, E. Josi, and E. Kirschbaum, *Esplorazioni sotto la confessione di San Pietro in Vaticano*, 2 vols., Vatican City, 1951.

Armi, C. Edson, *Masons and Sculptors in Romanesque Burgundy: The New Aesthetic of Cluny III*, University Park and London, 1983.

Arslan, Eduardo, "L'architettura romanica milanese," *Storia di Milano*, III, Milan, 1954, 397–521.

Avagnina, Maria E., V. Garibaldi, and C. Salterini, "Strutture murarie degli edifici religiosi di Roma nel XII secolo," *Rivista dell'istituto nazionale d'archeologia e storia dell'arte*, n. s. XXIII–XXIV, 1976–77, 171–255.

Babić, Gordana, *Les chapelles annexes des églises byzantines: Fonction liturgique et programmes iconographiques*, Paris, 1969.

Berenson, Bernard, *Italian Pictures of the Renaissance: Central Italian and North Italian Schools*, 3 vols., 1897 and 1907, reprinted London, 1968.

Bergman, Robert, *The Salerno Ivories*, Cambridge, Mass., 1980.

Berland, Jean-Marie, *Val-de-Loire Roman*, Zodiaque Series, La-Pierre-qui-Vire, 2nd ed., 1965.

Bertelli, G., A. G. Guidobaldi, and P. R. Spagnoletti, "Strutture murarie degli edifici religiosi di Roma dal VI al IX secolo," *Rivista dell'istituto nazionale d'archeologia e storia dell'arte*, n. s. XXIII–XXIV, 1976–77, 95–172.

Binding, Günther, "Die Kirchen Einharts in Steinbach und Seligenstadt," *Schülerfestgabe für Herbert von Einem*, Bonn, 1965, 12–19.

Bischoff, Bernard, *Die südostdeutschen Schreibschulen und Bibliotheken der Karolingerzeit*, Leipzig, 1940.

Boeck, Urs, "Der Pisaner Dom zwischen 1089 und 1120," *Architectura*, XI, 1981, 1–30.

Bozzoni, Corrado, *Calabria normana: Ricerche sull'architettura dei secoli undicesimo e dodicesimo*, Rome, 1974.

Brezzi, Paolo, *Roma e l'impero medioevale (774–1252)*, Bologna, 1947.

Brühl, Carlrichard, "Chronologie und Urkunden der Herzöge von Spoleto im 8. Jahrhundert," *Quellen und Forschungen aus italienischen Archiven und Bibliotheken*, LI, 1971, 1–92.

————, *Fodrum, Gistum und Servitium Regis*, 2 vols., Cologne, 1968.

————, "Königs-, Bischofs-, und Stadtpfalz in den Städten des 'Regnum Italiae' von 9. bis zum 13. Jahrhundert," *Historische Forschungen für Walter Schlesinger*, ed. Helmut Beumann, Cologne, 1974, 401–419.

Cabrol, Fernand and Henri Leclerq, *Dictionnaire d'archéologie chrétienne et de liturgie*, 30 vols., Paris, 1907–53.

Cattaneo, Raphael, *L'architecture en Italie du VIe au XIe siècle*, Venice, 1890.

Chierici, Sandro, *La Lombardia*, Italia Romanica, I, Milan, 1978.

Clapham, Alfred and Rose Graham, "The Monastery of Cluny, 910–1155," *Archaeologia*, LXXX, 1930, 143–178.

Collin, Hubert, *Les églises romanes de Lorraine*, Nancy, 1981.

Colombet, Albert, and Pierre Gros, "L'église di Combertault," *Mémoires de la commission des antiquités du départment de la Côte-d'Or*, XXIV, 1959, 144–164.

Conant, Kenneth J., *Carolingian and Romanesque Architecture, 800–1200*, Harmondsworth, 3rd ed. 1974.

————, *Cluny: Les églises et la maison du chef d'ordre*, Mâcon, 1968.

Congrès archéologique de France XCVI, 1933; CXXIII, 1965; CXXIX, 1971; CXXX, 1972.

Constable, Giles, *Medieval Monasticism: A Select Bibliography*, Toronto and Buffalo, 1976.

Consuetudines Monasticae, ed. Bruno Albers, 5 vols., V, Montecassino, 1912.

Crosby, Sumner McK., *L'abbaye royale de Saint-Denis*, Paris, 1953.

Dehio, Georg, *Handbuch der deutschen Kunstdenkmäler*, ed. Magnus Backes, III, Hessen, 1966.

Dehlinger, Armand, "Die Ordensgesetzgebung der Benediktiner und ihr Auswerkung auf die Grundrissbestattung des Benediktinischen Klosterbaues in Deutschland unter Beruchsichtigung der Reform von Hirsau," diss., Dresden, 1936.

Deichmann, Friedrich W., *Ravenna: Hauptstadt des spätantiken Abendlandes*, 4 vols., Wiesbaden, 1958–76.

De Lastyrie, R., *L'architecture religieuse en France à l'époque romane*, Paris, 1912.

Demangeot, Jean, *Géomorphologie des Abruzzes adriatiques*, Mémoires et Documents, Centre des Recherches et Documentations Géographiques, Paris, 1965.

Demus, Otto, *Romanesque Mural Painting*, New York, 1970.

_____, *The Church of San Marco in Venice,* Washington, D.C., 1960.

Der Trierer Dom, ed. Franz Ronig, Neuss, 1980.

Doppelfeld, Otto, and Willy Weyres, *Die Ausgrabungen im Dom zu Köln,* Kölner Forschungen, I, Mainz, 1980.

Deshoulières, Fr., "L'église de Vignory," *Bulletin Monumental,* LXXXVIII, 1929, 93–107.

Du Cange, Charles, *Glossarium mediae et infimae latinitatis,* reprinted Graz, 1954.

Dupont, Jean, *Nivernais-Bourbonais Roman,* Zodiaque Series, La-Pierre-qui-Vire, 1976.

Durand, Georges, *Les églises romanes des Vosges,* Paris, 1913.

_____, "Saint-Riquier," *La Picardie historique et monumentale,* IV:2, Amiens and Paris, 1907–11, 133–358.

Dyggve, Ejnar, "The Origin of the Urban Churchyard," *Classica et medievalia,* XII, 1951, 147–158.

Effmann, W., *Centula-Saint-Riquier,* Münster, 1912.

_____, *Die karolingisch-ottonischen Bauten zu Werden,* I, Strasbourg, 1899.

Églises de France: Histoire générale et dictionnaire, 5 vols., Paris, 1966–71.

Evans, Joan, *The Romanesque Architecture of the Order of Cluny,* Cambridge, 1938.

Eygun, F., "Le baptistère Saint-Jean à Poitiers," *Gallia,* XXII, 1964, 137ff.

Faldi, Italo, *Pittori viterbesi di cinque secoli,* Rome, 1970.

Feld, Otto, "Zur Baugeschichte der Klosterkirche Murbach," *Zeitschrift für Kunstgeschichte,* XXIV, 1961, 242ff.

Feldhaus, Aloysius, *Oratories,* Catholic University of America, Canon Law Series, XLII, Washington, D.C., 1927.

Ferrari, Guy, *Early Roman Monasteries,* Vatican City, 1957.

Fischer, Joachim, *Königtum, Adel und Kirche in Königreich Italien (774–875),* Bonn, 1965.

Fischer, Manfred, and Friedrich Oswald, "Zur Baugeschichte der Fuldaer Klosterkirche: Literatur und Ausgrabungen im Kritischersicht,"

Rheinische Ausgrabungen: Beihefte der Bonner Jahrbücher, XXVIII, 1968, 268–80.

Fleckenstein, Josef, "Einhard, seine Gründung und sein Vermächtnis in Seligenstadt," *Das Einhardkreuz,* ed. Karl Hauck, *Abhandlungen der Akademie der Wissenschaften in Göttingen, philologische-historische Klasse,* LXXVII, 1975, 96–121.

Focillon, Henri, "L'église St.-Etienne de Vignory, ses date de construction," *Revue archéologique,* 6e série, IX, 1937, 78ff.

_____, *The Art of the West, I: Romanesque Art,* New York, 1969.

Fohlen, Claude, "Connaissance et utilization des tombes antiques pendant le haut moyen-age," *Mélanges: Société toulousaine d'études classiques,* II, 1948, 179–93.

Formigé, Jules, *L'abbaye royale de Saint-Denis,* Paris, 1960.

Forsyth, Jr., George H., "A Problem of Surveying in Medieval Architecture: 'Geometricis et Arithmeticis,'" *Archeology,* III, 1950, 74–79.

_____, *The Church of St. Martin at Angers,* Princeton, 1953.

Frankl, Paul, *Die frühmittelalterliche und romanische Baukunst,* Handbuch der Kunstwissenschaft, Potsdam, 1926.

Fuchs, Alois, *Die karolingischen Westwerke und andere Fragen der karolingischen Baukunst,* Paderborn, 1929.

Fussbroich, Helmut, *Die Ausgrabungen in St. Pantaleon zu Köln,* Kölner Forschungen, II, Mainz, 1983.

Garrison, Edward B., "Dating the Vatican Last Judgment Panel: Monument versus Document," *La bibliofilia,* LXXII, 1970, 121–160.

_____, *Studies in the History of Medieval Italian Painting,* 4 vols., Florence, 1953–62.

Geary, Patrick, *Furta Sacra: The Theft of Relics in the Central Middle Ages,* Princeton, 1978.

Genicot, Luc-Fr., *Les églises mosanes du XIe siècle,* Louvain, 1972.

Giovannoni, Giuseppe, "L'architettura dei monasteri sublacensi," *I monasteri di Subiaco,* with P. Egidi and F. Hermanin, 2 vols., Rome, 1904, 261–371.

Giumelli, Claudio, et al., *I monasteri benedettini di Subiaco*, Milan, 1982.

Glass, Dorothy, *Studies in Cosmatesque Pavements*, British Archaeological Reports, International Series, LXXXII, Oxford, 1980.

Gray, Nicolette, "The Filocalian Letter," *Papers of the British School at Rome*, XXIV, 1956, 5–13.

———, "The Paleography of Latin Inscriptions in the Eighth, Ninth and Tenth Centuries in Italy," *Papers of the British School at Rome*, XVI, 1948, 38–170.

Grégoire, Réginald, *Homéliaires liturgiques médiévaux: Analyse de manuscrits*, Biblioteca sugli studi medievali, XII, Spoleto, 1980, 127–220.

Grimm, Reinhod, *Paradisus Caelestis–Paradisus Terrestris: Zur Auslegungsgeschichte des Paradieses im Abendland bis um 1200*, Munich, 1977.

Grodecki, Louis, *L'architecture ottonienne*, Paris, 1958.

———, Florentine Mütherich, Jean Taralon, and Francis Wormald, *Le siècle de l'an mil*, Paris, 1973.

Grossmann, Dieter, Review of Kassius Hallinger, *Gorze-Kluny*, *Zeitschrift für Kunstgeschichte*, XX, 1957, 296–302.

Guidobaldi, Federico, and Alessandra Guiglia Guidobaldi, *Pavimenti marmorei di Roma dal IV al IX secolo*, Vatican City, 1983.

Guirand, Jean, "Le commerce des reliques au commencement du IXe siècle," *Mélanges G. B. de Rossi*, Paris and Rome, 1892, 73–95.

Gvozdonovic, Vladimir, "Pre-Romanesque and Early Romanesque Architecture in Croatia," Ph.D. diss., Cornell University, 1972.

Hager, Georg, "Zur Geschichte der abendländischen Klosteranlage," *Zeitschrift für christliche Kunst*, XIV, 1901, cols. 167–186.

Hallinger, Kassius, *Gorze-Kluny: Studien zu den monastischen Lebensraum und Gegensätzen im Hochmittelalter*, 2 vols., Rome, 1950–51.

———, "Kluny Bräuche zu Zeit Hugos des Grossen (1049–1109)," *Zeitschrift der Savigny-Stiftung für Rechtsgeschichte: Kanonistische Abteilung*, XLV, 1959, 99–140.

———, "Progressi e problemi della ricerca sulla riforma pre-Gregoriana," *Il monachesimo nell'alto medioevo e la formazione della civiltà occidentale*, Centro italiano di studi sull' alto medioevo, Settimane di studio, V, Spoleto, 1957, 257–291.

Hamilton, Bernard, "The Monastic Revival in Tenth-Century Rome," *Studia monastica*, IV, 1962, 35–68.

Handbook of Church History, ed. Hubert Jedin and John Dolan, trans. Anselm Biggs, New York and London, 1969–1981.

Hariulf: Chronique de l'abbaye de Saint-Riquier (Ve siècle–1104), ed. F. Lot, Paris, 1894.

Heitz, Carol, *L'architecture religieuse carolingienne: Les formes et leurs fonctions*, Paris, 1980.

———, *Recherches sur les rapports entre architecture et liturgie à l'époque carolingienne*, Paris, 1963.

———, "Nouvelles interprétations de l'art carolingienne," *Revue de l'art*, I–II, 1968, 107ff.

Héliot, Pierre, "Encore l'ordre colossal et les arcades murales dans les églises romanes," *Bulletin Monumental*, CXVIII, 1960, 31–36.

———, "L'ordre colossal et les arcades murales dans les églises romanes," *Bulletin Monumental*, CXV, 1957, 241–261.

———, "Saint-Etienne de Caen, Saint-Paul d'Issoire, la cathédrale d'Osnabruck et les arcades murales dans l'architecture du Nord-Ouest de l'Europe (Xe–XIIIe siècles)," *Wallraf-Richartz Jahrbuch*, XXI, 1959, 41–74.

———, "Sur les tours jumelées au chevet des églises du moyen-âge," *Arte in Europa: Scritti di storia dell'arte in onore di Eduardo Arslan*, Milan, 1967, 249–270.

Hermanin, F., *L'arte in Roma dal secolo VIII al XIV*, Bologna, 1945.

Herrgott, M., *Vetus disciplina monastica*, Paris, 1726.

Herrmann-Mascard, Nicole, *Les reliques des saints: Formation coutumière d'un droit*, Paris, 1975.

Heydenreich, Ludwig, and Wolfgang Lotz,

Architecture in Italy: 1400 to 1600, Baltimore, Md., 1974.

Hodges, Richard, and John Mitchell, eds., *San Vincenzo al Volturno: The Archaeology, Art and Territory of an Early Medieval Monastery*, British Archaeological Reports, International Series, CCLII, Oxford, 1985.

Hoffmann, H., "Chronik und Urkunden in Montecassino," *Quellen und Forschungen aus italienischen Archiven und Bibliotheken*, LI, 1971, 93–206.

Hoffmann, Wolfbernhard, *Hirsau und die Hirsauer Bauschule*, Munich, 1950.

Hodgkin, Thomas, *Italy and Her Invaders*, 8 vols., 1880–89, reprinted New York, 1967.

Horn, Walter, "Das Florentiner Baptisterium," *Mitteilungen des kunsthistorischen Instituts zu Florenz*, V, 1938, 100–151.

———, "Romanesque Churches in Florence," *Art Bulletin*, XXV, 1943, 112ff.

———, and Ernest Born, *The Plan of St. Gall: A Study of the Architecture and Economy of, and Life in, a Paradigmatic Carolingian Monastery*, 3 vols., Berkeley, Los Angeles and London, 1979.

Hotzelt, W., "Translationen von Martyrreliquien aus Rom nach Bayern im 8. Jahrhundert," *Studien und Mitteilungen zur Geschichte des Benediktinerordens*, LIII, 1935, 286ff.

Hourlier, Dom Jacques, "Saint Odilon bâtisseur," *Revue Mabillon*, LI, 1961, 303–324.

Hubert, Jean, "'Cryptae inferiores' et 'cryptae superiores' dans l'architecture religieuse de l'époque carolingienne," *Mélanges d'histoire du moyen age dediés à la mémoire de Louis Halphen*, Paris, 1951, 351–357.

———, "Les dates de construction du clocher-porche et de la nef de Saint-Germain-des-Prés," *Bulletin Monumental*, CVIII, 1950, 69–84.

———, "Saint-Riquier et le monachisme bénédictine en Gaule à l'époque carolingienne," *Il monachesimo nel alto medio evo e la formazione della civiltà occidentale*,

Centro Italiano di Studi sull'Alto Medioevo, Settimana di studio, V, 1957, 293–309.

———, Jean Porcher, and W. F. Volbach, *Europe of the Invasions*, New York, 1969.

———, *The Carolingian Renaissance*, New York, 1970.

Hugo, Leo, *Kornelimünster*, Rheinische Ausgrabungen, II, Cologne and Graz, 1968.

Hutton, Edward, *The Cosmati*, London, 1950.

Irsch, Nikolaus, *Der Dom zu Trier*, Die Kunstdenkmäler der Rheinprovinz, XIII:1, Düsseldorf, 1931.

Isermeyer, Christian-Adolf, "Die mittelalterlichen Malerien der Kirche S. Pietro in Tuscania," *Römisches Jahrbuch für Kunstgeschichte*, II, 1938, 291–310.

Italia pontificia, ed. Paul Kehr, Rome, 1906–.

Jacobsen, Werner, "Benedikt von Aniane und die Architektur unter Ludwig dem Frommen zwischen 814 und 830," *Riforma religiosa e arti nell'epoca carolingia*, ed. A. Schmidt, Atti del XXIV congresso internazionale di storia dell'arte, I, Bologna, 1979 (1983), 15–22.

———, Review of Otto Doppelfeld and Willy Weyres, *Die Ausgrabungen im Dom zu Köln*, *Kunstchronik*, XXXV, 1982, 10–33.

———, "Saint-Denis in neuen Licht: Konsequenzen der neuentdeckten Baubeschreibung aus dem Jahre 799," *Kunstchronik*, XXXVI, 1983, 301–308.

———, "Zur Datierung des Florentiner Baptisteriums S. Giovanni," *Zeitschrift für Kunstgeschichte*, XLIII, 1980, 225–243.

Karl der Grosse, ed. W. Braunfels, 4 vols., Düsseldorf, 1965–67.

Kempf, Theodor, "Grundentwicklung und Baugeschichte des Trierer Domes," *Das Münster*, XXI, 1968, 1–32.

Kier, Hiltrud, *Der mittelalterliche Schmuckfussboden*, Düsseldorf, 1970.

Klukas, Arnold, "*Altaria Superiora*: The Function and Significance of the Tribune-Chapel in Anglo-Norman Romanesque: A Problem in the Relationship of Liturgical Requirements and Architectural Form,"

Ph.D. diss., University of Pittsburgh, 1978.

Knowles, David, *Christian Monasticism*, New York, 1969.

——, *The Monastic Constitution of Lanfranc*, London, 1951.

Koehler, Wilhelm, *Die karolingische Miniaturen*, 4 vols., Berlin, 1930–71.

Kötting, Bernhard, *Der frühchristliche Reliquienkult und die Bestattung im Kirchengebäude*, Cologne and Opladen, 1965.

Krautheimer, Richard, *Early Christian and Byzantine Architecture*, 3rd edition, Harmondsworth, 1979.

——, *Rome: Profile of a City, 312–1308*, Princeton, 1980.

——, "The Carolingian Revival of Early Christian Architecture," *Studies in Early Christian, Medieval and Renaissance Art*, New York, 1969, 203–256.

—— et al., *Corpus basilicarum christianarum Romae*, 5 vols., Vatican City, 1937–77.

Krusch, Bruno, "Die Übertragung des H. Alexander von Rom nach Wildeshausen durch den Enkel Widukinds 851," *Nachrichten von der Gesellschaft der Wissenschaften zu Göttingen*, IV, 1933, 405–436.

Kubach, Hans Erich, *Das frühmittelalterliche Imperium*, Baden-Baden, 1968.

——, "Der Trierer Kunstraum im 11.–13. Jahrhundert," *Trierer Zeitschrift*, XII, 1937, 81–103.

——, "Die Wandsysteme des Speyer Domes," *Gedenkschrift Ernst Gall*, ed. Margarete Kühn and Louis Grodecki, Munich and Berlin, 1965, 11–30.

——, *Romanesque Architecture*, New York, 1975.

——, and Walter Haas, *Der Dom zu Speyer*, Kunstdenkmäler von Rheinland-Pfalz, V, 3 vols., Berlin, 1972.

——, and Albert Verbeek, *Romanische Baukunst an Rhein und Maas: Katalog der vorromanischen und romanischen Denkmäler*, 3 vols., Berlin, 1976.

——, *Romanische Kirchen an Rhein und Maas*, Neuss, 1972.

Ladner, G., "Die italienische Malerien im 11. Jahrhundert," *Jahrbuch der Wiener Kunsthistorischen Sammlungen*, n. s., V, 1931, 33ff.

Lanzoni, Francesco, *Le diocesi d'Italia*, 2 vols., Faenza, 1927.

Lehmann, Edgar, *Der frühe deutsche Kirchenbau*, Berlin, 1938.

Le liber pontificalis, ed. Louis Duchesne, 2 vols., Paris, 1886–92, reprinted 1955–57.

Lesueur, Frédéric, "Appareils décoratifs supposés carolingiens," *Bulletin Monumental*, CXXIV, 1966, 167–186.

——, "Saint-Martin d'Angers: La coutoure du Mans, Saint-Philibert de Grandlieu et autres églises à éléments de briques dans la région de la Loire," *Bulletin Monumental*, CXIX, 1961, 211–242.

Llewellyn, Peter, *Rome in the Dark Ages*, New York and Washington, 1970.

McClendon, Charles B., "The Church of S. Maria di Tremiti and Its Significance for the History of Romanesque Architecture," *Journal of the Society of Architectural Historians*, XLIII, 1984, 5–19.

Magni, Mariaclotilde, *Architettura religiosa e scultura nella valle d'Aosta*, Aosta, 1974.

——, *Architettura romanica comasca*, Milan, 1960.

——, "Un remarquable témoignage du premier art roman en Italie du Nord: La cathédrale d'Aoste," *Cahiers archéologiques*, XXIV, 1975, 163–181.

Mallet, Jacques, *L'art roman de l'ancien Anjou*, Paris, 1984.

Manchot, W., *Kloster Limburg an der Haardt*, Mannheim, 1912.

Manitius, Max, *Geschichte der lateinischen Literatur des Mittelalters*, 3 vols., Munich, 1911–31.

Mann, Albrecht, "Doppelchor und Stiftmemorie. Zum kunst- und kultgeschichtlichen Problem der Westchöre," *Westfälische Zeitschrift*, CXI, 1961, 149ff.

Marschall, Hans-Günther, *Die Kathedrale von Verdun: Die romanische Baukunst in Westlothringen*, I, Veröffentlichungen des Instituts für Landeskunde im Saarland, XXXII, Saarbrücken, 1981.

———, and Rainer Slotta, *Lorraine romane*, Zodiaque Series, La-Pierre-qui-Vire, 1984.

Matthiae, Guglielmo, *Pittura romana nel medioevo*, 2 vols., Rome, 1965.

Mettler, Adolf, "Die zweite Kirche in Cluny und die Kirche in Hirsau nach den 'Gewohnheiten' des 11. Jahrhunderts," *Zeitschrift für Geschichte der Architektur*, III, 1909–10, 273–286, IV, 1910–11, 1–16.

Meyer-Barkhausen, Werner, "Die frühmittelalterlichen Vorbauten am Atrium von Alt St. Peter in Rom, zweitürmige Atrien, Westwerke und karolingisch-ottonische Königskapelle," *Wallraf-Richartz Jahrbuch*, XX, 1958, 7–40.

Meyvaert, Paul, Review of Walter Horn and Ernest Born, *The Plan of St. Gall*, University Publishing, IX, 1980, 18–19.

Möbius, Friedrich, "Die Chorpartie der westeuropäischen Klosterkirche zwischen 8. und 11. Jahrhundert," *Architektur des Mittelalters: Funktion und Gestalt*, ed. F. Möbius and E. Schubert, Weimar, 1983, 9–41.

———, *Westwerkstudien*, Jena, 1968.

Montagne, Claudio and Loredana Pessa, *Le chiese romaniche della Sabina*, Genoa, 1983.

Moretti, Italo, and Renato Stopani, *La Toscana*, Italia Romanica, V, 1982.

Müller, Otto, *Die Einhards-Basiliken in Steinbach bei Michelstadt*, Mainz, 1965.

Noehles, Karl, "Die Kunst der Cosmaten und die Idee der Renovatio Romae," *Festschrift Werner Hager*, Recklingshausen, 1966, 17–37.

Ortmann, B., *Die karolingischen Bauten unter der Abdinghofkirche zu Paderborn und das Kloster Bischof Meinwerks, 1016–1031*, Ratingen, 1967.

Osborne, John, *Early Medieval Wall-Paintings in the Lower Church of San Clemente*, Rome, New York and London, 1984.

———, "The Painting of the Anastasis in the Lower Church of San Clemente, Rome: A Re-Examination of the Evidence for the Location of the Tomb of St. Cyril," *Byzantion*, LI, 1981, 255–287.

Ostendorf, Adolf, "Das Salvator-Patrocinium, seine Anfänge und seine Ausbreitung im mittelalterlichen Deutschland," *Westfälische Zeitschrift*, C, 1950, 357–376.

Oswald, F., L. Schaeffer, and H. R. Sennhauser, *Vorromanische Kirchenbauten: Katalog der Denkmäler bis zum Ausgang der Ottonen*, Munich, 1966–71.

Paesler, W., "Die römische Weltgerichttafel im Vatican," *Römisches Jahrbuch für Kunstgeschichte*, II, 1938, 313–394.

Panazza, Gaetano and Adriano Peroni, *La chiesa di San Salvatore in Brescia*, Atti dell'ottavo congresso di studi sull'arte dell'alto medioevo, II, Milan, 1962.

Pantoni, A., "Santa Maria delle Cinque Torri di Cassino: Risultati e problemi," *Rivista di archeologia cristiana*, LI, 1975, 243–280.

Parsons, David, "The Pre-Romanesque Church of St.-Riquier: The Documentary Evidence," *Journal of the British Archaeological Association*, CXXIX, 1976, 21–51.

Partner, Peter, *The Lands of St. Peter*, Berkeley and Los Angeles, 1972.

Penco, Gregorio, "Il monachesimo in Umbria dalle origini al secolo VII incluso," *Ricerche sull'Umbria tardo-antico e preromanico*, Atti del II convegno di studi umbri, Perugia, 1965, 257–276.

Percival, John, *The Roman Villa: An Historical Introduction*, Berkeley and Los Angeles, 1976.

Peroni, Adriano, "Per la tipologia architettonica dell'età carolingia nell'area lombarda," *Roma e l'età carolingia*, Atti delle giornate di studio 3–8 Maggio 1976, Istituto Nazionale di Archeologia e Storia dell'Arte, Rome, 1976, 87–97.

Picard, Jean-Charles, "Étude sur l'emplacement des tombes des Papes des III au Xe siècle," *Mélanges de l'école française de Rome: Moyen-Age–Temps Modernes*, LXXXI, 1969, 755–781.

———, "Le quadriportique de Sant'Agata de Ravenna," *Felix Ravenna*, CXVI, 1978, 31–43.

———, "Les origines du mot *paradisus—parvis*," *Mélanges de l'école française de Rome:*

Moyen-Age–Temps Modernes, LXXXIII, 1971, 158–186.

Plat, Gabriel, *L'art de bâtir en France des Romains à l'an 1100*, Paris, 1939.

Pontificium Romanorum qui fuerunt ab exeunte saeculo IX usque ad finem saeculi XIII vitae ab aequalibus conscriptae, ed. Johann M. Watterich, 2 vols., Leipzig, 1862, reprinted Darmstadt, 1966.

Porter, Arthur Kingsley, *Lombard Architecture*, 3 vols., New Haven, 1917.

Prandi, Adriano, S. Chierici, G. Tomanti, and F. Cadei, *L'Umbria*, Italia Romanica, III, Milan, 1979.

Prete, Serafino, *I Santi Martiri Alessandro e Filippo nella chiesa Fermana*, Vatican City, 1941.

Prinz, Friedrich, *Frühes Mönchtum im Frankenreich*, Munich and Vienna, 1965.

Puig y Cadafalch, J., *La géographie et les origines du premier art roman*, Paris, 1935.

————, A. Falguera, and G. Godey y Casals, *L'arquitectura románica a Catalunya*, 3 vols., Barcelona, 1909–18.

Ragusa, Isa, "The Re-Use and Public Exhibition of Roman Sarcophagi during the Middle Ages and Early Renaissance," unpublished master's thesis, New York University, 1951.

Rave, W., "Die Aufspürung von zwei Westwerke in Italien," *Westfalen*, XXIV, 1939, 149–150.

Reinhardt, Hans and Etienne Fels, "Étude sur les églises-porches carolingiennes et leur survivance dans l'art roman," *Bulletin Monumental*, XCII, 1933, 331–365.

Rivoira, G. T., *Le origine della architettura lombarda*, Milan, 1908.

Roma e l'età carolingia, Atti delle giornate di studio, 3–8 Maggio 1976, Istituto Nazionale di Archeologia e Storia dell'Arte, Rome, 1976.

Romanelli, Pietro and Per Jonas Nordhagen, *S. Maria Antiqua*, Rome, 1964.

Saalman, Howard, *Medieval Architecture*, New York, 1967.

Salmi, Mario, *L'abbazia di Pomposa*, Rome, 1936.

Sanderson, Warren, "Monastic Reform in Lorraine and the Architecture of the Outer Crypt, 950–1100," *Transactions of the American Philosophical Society*, n. s., LXI:6, 1971.

Scarafoni, E. Scaccia, "La chiesa cassinese detta 'Santa Maria delle Cinque Torri,'" *Rivista di archeologia cristiana*, XXII, 1946, 139–189.

Schaefer, Herwin, "The Origin of the Two-Tower Façade in Romanesque Architecture," *Art Bulletin*, XXVII, 1945, 85–108.

Schaeffer, Leo, *Der Gründungsbau der Stiftkirche St. Martin in Zyfflich*, Die Kunstdenkmäler des Rheinlandes, Beih. 9, Essen, 1963.

Schapiro, Meyer, "The Frescoes of Castelseprio," and "Notes on Castelseprio, II: The Clavus on the Thigh," *Late Antique, Early Christian and Mediaeval Art: Selected Papers*, New York, 1980, 67–114, 125–142.

Schiffer, Rainer, *Die Ostteile der Kathedrale von Toul*, Cologne, 1977.

Schlosser, Julius, *Die abendländische Klosteranlage des früheren Mittelalters*, Vienna, 1889.

Schmidlin, L., "Ein Kampf um das Deutschtum im Klosterlebens Italiens: Subiaco und Farfa im 16. Jahrhunderts," *Historisches Jahrbuch*, XXIV, 2903, 253–282.

Schramm, Percy E., "Unbeachtete Bilder Kaiser Ottos II. und seiner Gemahlin Theophanu in einem mittelitalienischen Kloster," *Homenaje a Jaime Vicens Vives*, I, Barcelona, 1965, 619–623.

Schubert, Ernst, *Der Magdeburger Dom*, Cologne and Vienna, 1975.

Schwarz, Heinrich M., "Die Baukunst Kalabriens und Siziliens im Zeitalter der Normannen, I: Die lateinischen Kirchengrundungen des 11. Jahrhunderts und der Dom in Cefalù," *Römisches Jahrbuch für Kunstgeschichte*, VI, 1942–44, 1–112.

Schwarzmaier, M., "Der Liber Vitae von Subiaco: Die Klöster Farfa und Subiaco in ihrer geistigen und politischen Umwelt während der letzten Jahrzehn des 11. Jahrhunderts," *Quellen und Forschungen aus italienischen Bibliotheken u. Archiven*, XLVIII, 1968, 80–147.

Segal, Edward A., "The Plan of Saint Gall and the Monastic Reform Councils of 816 and 817," *Cuyahoga Review*, I, 1983, 57–71.

Selzer, Wolfgang, "Die karolingische Königshalle zu Lorsch," *Laurissa jubilans*, Mainz, 1964, 129–134.

Sennhauser, H. R., *Romainmôtier und Payerne: Studien zur Cluniazenserarchitektur des 11. Jh. in der Westschweiz*, Basel, 1970.

———, "Spätantike und frühmittelalterliche Kirchen Churrätiens," *Von der Spätantike zum frühen Mittelalter: Vorträge und Forschungen*, XXV, 1979, 201–206.

Serafini, Alberto, *Torri campanarie di Roma e del Lazio nel medioevo*, 2 vols., Rome, 1927.

Studien zum St. Galler Klosterplan, ed. Johannes Duft, St. Gall, 1962.

Tarchi, Ugo, *L'arte nell'Umbria e nella Sabina*, II, Milan, 1937.

Tholen, Paul A., "Neue baugeschichtliche Ergebnisse in den Kirchen Kölns," *Wallraf-Richartz Jahrbuch*, XI–XII, 1943, 1ff.

Thümmler, Hans, "Die Baukunst des 11. Jahrhunderts in Italien," *Römisches Jahrbuch für Kunstgeschichte*, III, 1939, 196–203.

———, "Die Kirche S. Pietro in Tuscania," *Römisches Jahrbuch für Kunstgeschichte*, II, 1938, 265–288.

Toker, Franklin, "Excavations below the Cathedral of Florence, 1965–1974," *Gesta*, XIV, 1975, 17–36.

Toubert, Pierre, *Les structures du Latium médiéval: Le Latium méridional et la Sabine du IXe siècle à la fin du XIIe siècle*, 2 vols., Rome, 1973.

Tournier, René, *Les églises comtoises: leur architecture des origines au XVIIIe siècle*, Paris, 1954.

Toynbee, Jocelyn and John Ward-Perkins, *The Shrine of St. Peter and the Vatican Excavation*, London, 1956.

Trachtenberg, Marvin, *The Campanile of Florence Cathedral*, New York, 1971.

Vehse, Otto, "Die päpstliche Herrschaft in der Sabina bis zur Mitte des 12. Jahrhunderts," *Quellen und Forschungen aus italienischen Archiven und Bibliotheken*, XXI, 1929–30, 120–175.

Urban, Günther, "Der Kirchenbau des Quattrocento in Rom," *Römisches Jahrbuch für Kunstgeschichte*, IX, 1963, 75–287.

Valtieri, S., *S. Maria del Popolo a Roma*, Rome, 1976.

Venditti, Arnaldo, *Architettura bizantina nell'Italia meridionale*, 2 vols., Naples, 1967.

Verbeek, Albert, "Die Aussenkrypta: Werden einer Bauform des frühen Mittelalters," *Zeitschrift für Kunstgeschichte*, XIII, 1950, 7–38.

Verzone, Paolo, *L'architettura religiosa dell'alto medioevo in Italia settentrionale*, Milan, 1942.

Voigtländer, Klaus, *Die Stiftskirche zu Gernrode*, Berlin, 1980.

Vonderau, Joseph, "Die Ausgrabungen am Dome zu Fulda in den Jahren 1908–1913," *Sechzehnte Veröffentlichung des Fuldaer Geschichts-Vereins*, 1919, 5–36.

von Winterfeld, Dethard, *Der Dom in Bamberg, I: Die Baugeschichte bis zur Vollendung im 13. Jahrhundert*, Berlin, 1979.

Voss, Irmgard M., "Die Benedictinerabtei S. Andrea in Flumine bei Ponzano Romano," Ph.D. diss., Rheinischen Friedrich-Wilhelms Universität, Bonn, 1985.

Waetzoldt, Stephan, "Die Malereien am Hochalter von S. Maria in Vescovio," *Römische Quartalschrift*, LII, 1957, 1–12.

Waley, Daniel, *The Papal State in the Thirteenth Century*, London, 1961.

Weitzmann, Kurt, *Late Antique and Early Christian Book Illumination*, New York, 1977.

———, "The Illustrations of the Septuagint," *Studies in Classical and Byzantine Book Illumination*, Chicago, 1971, 45–75.

Wellmann, Fritz, "Kloster Limburg an der Haardt," diss., Technische Hochschule Karlsruhe, 1953.

Wettstein, J., *Les fresques de S. Angelo in Formis*, Geneva, 1960.

Weyres, Willy, "Neue Ergebnisse der Kölner Domgrabung zu Bau VI," *Architectura*, XIII, 1982, 27–30.

Whitehill, Walter M., *Spanish Romanesque Architecture of the Eleventh Century*, 1941, reprinted Oxford, 1968.

Will, Robert, *Alsace romane*, Zodiaque Series, La-Pierre-qui-Vire, 1965.

Wilmart, Dom André, "Le couvent et la bibliothèque de Cluny vers le milieu du XIe siècle," *Revue Mabillon*, XI, 1921, 89–124.

Zimmermann, W., "Die Luziuskirche zu Werden," *Die Kirchen zu Werden*, Die Kunstdenkmälern des Rheinlandes, Beih. 7, Essen, 1959, 160–249.

Index

Illustrations

All illustrations, unless otherwise noted, are of the Benedictine abbey of Farfa and are the author's. All drawings, unless otherwise noted, are by Daniel Cecil. Figures 1–18 are plans, sections, elevations, and reconstruction drawings of Farfa Abbey and the medieval abbey church; unless otherwise noted, the scale is 1:50. Plates 1–91 are of buildings and material of Farfa Abbey; plates 92–138 are of comparative material.

Illustration Credits

Other credits appear in the captions to the illustrations.

Plates 2, 3, 13, 34, 40–44, 61, 84, 88a, 89. Courtesy of the Istituto Centrale per il Catalogo e la Documentazione, Rome, with the following negative numbers: C6678, E58524, E58564, E73172, E73208, E73184, E73154, E73168, E73202, M1608, E58557, E58522, E104499.

Plate 92. George H. Forsyth, Jr., *The Church of St. Martin at Angers: The Architectural History of the Site from the Roman Empire to the French Revolution.* Copyright 1953, (c) 1981 renewed by Princeton University Press. Fig. 183c redrawn with permission of Princeton University Press.

Plate 94. Reproduced with permission of the Biblioteca Vaticana.

Plate 95. Drawing by Spencer Corbett. Courtesy of Richard Krautheimer.

Plate 103. From J. Vonderau, "Die Ausgrabungen am Dome zu Fulda in den Jahren 1908–1913," Verlag Parzeller, Fulda, West Germany.

Plate 105b. Reproduced with permission of De Luca Editore, Rome.

Plate 111B. Courtesy of Harry N. Abrams, Inc., redrawn with permission from Kubach, *Romanesque Architecture,* 139, fig. 151, after Studio Enzo Di Grazia.

Plate 116. Marburg/Art Resource, New York.

Plate 134. Kenneth John Conant, *Carolingian and Romanesque Architecture 800–1200,* 1966, 83, fig. 26, copyright (c) Kenneth John Conant, 1959, 1966, 1974, 1978. Reprinted by permission of Penguin Books Ltd.

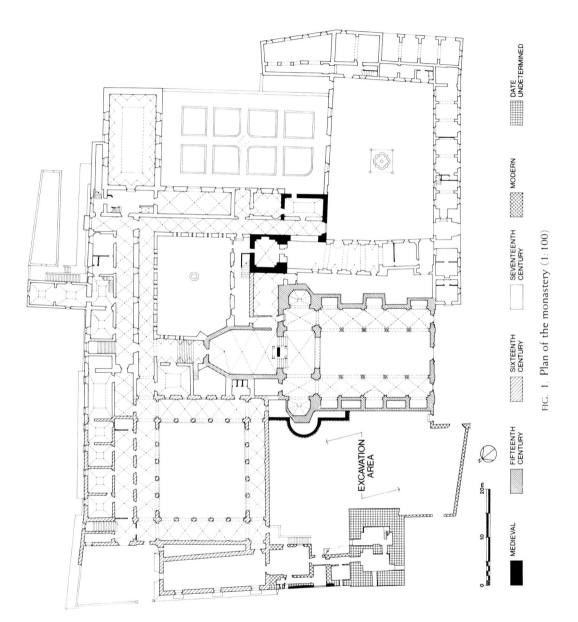

EXCAVATION
AREA

MEDIEVAL   FIFTEENTH   SIXTEENTH   SEVENTEENTH   MODERN   DATE
            CENTURY   CENTURY   CENTURY   UNDETERMINED

0   10   20m

FIG. 1. Plan of the monastery (1:100)

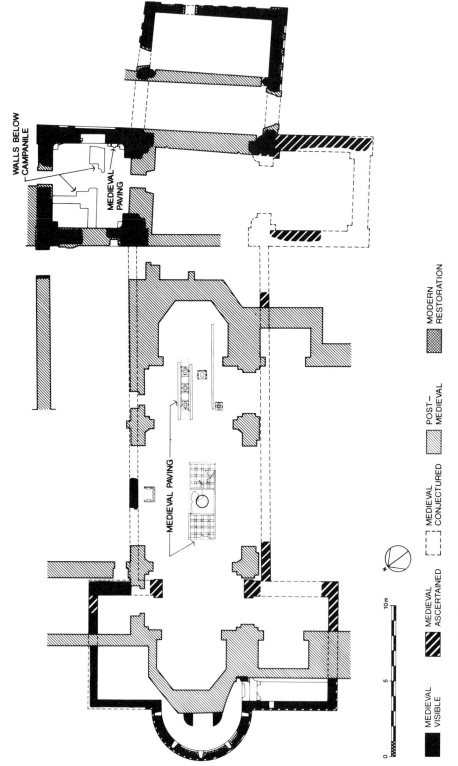

WALLS BELOW
CAMPANILE

MEDIEVAL
PAVING

MEDIEVAL PAVING

MEDIEVAL
VISIBLE

MEDIEVAL
ASCERTAINED

MEDIEVAL
CONJECTURED

POST–
MEDIEVAL

MODERN
RESTORATION

0   5   10m

FIG. 2. Plan of the remains of the medieval abbey church at various levels; east end at 0.00 m. and west end at −1.75 m.

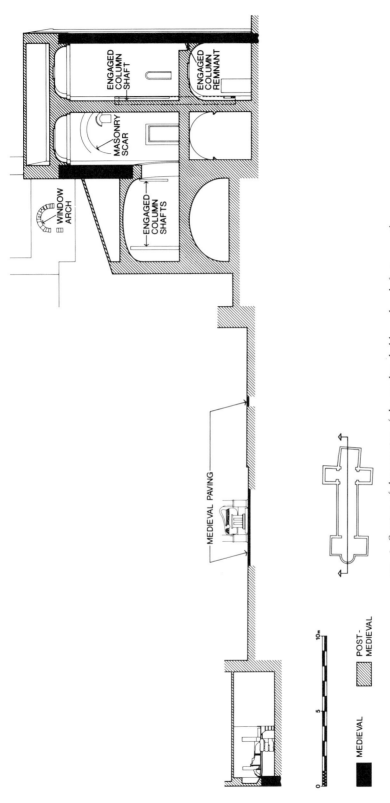

WINDOW ARCH

ENGAGED COLUMN SHAFT

ENGAGED COLUMN REMNANT

MASONRY SCAR

ENGAGED COLUMN SHAFTS

MEDIEVAL PAVING

MEDIEVAL

POST-MEDIEVAL

0   5   10m

FIG. 3. Section of the remains of the medieval abbey church facing north

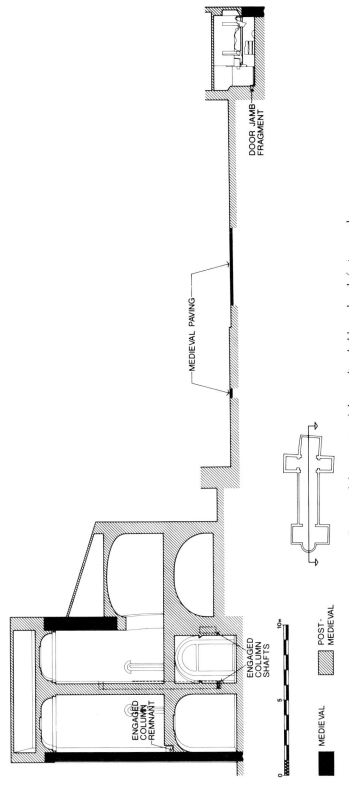

DOOR JAMB
FRAGMENT

MEDIEVAL PAVING

ENGAGED
COLUMN
SHAFTS

ENGAGED
COLUMN
REMNANT

0   5   10m

MEDIEVAL

POST-
MEDIEVAL

FIG. 4. Section of the remains of the medieval abbey church facing south

0   5   10m

■ MEDIEVAL   ▨ POST-
                MEDIEVAL

ENGAGED
COLUMN SHAFT

FIG. 5. Medieval abbey church, east end, section of presbytery facing west, and
east elevation of bell tower

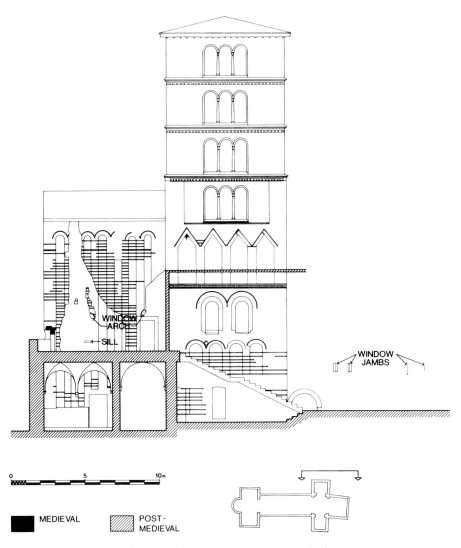

WINDOW
ARCH

SILL

WINDOW
JAMBS

0   5   10 m

■ MEDIEVAL   ▨ POST-
                        MEDIEVAL

FIG. 6. Medieval abbey church, east end, north elevation

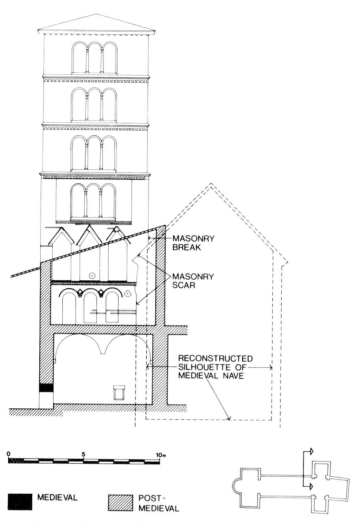

MASONRY
BREAK

MASONRY
SCAR

RECONSTRUCTED
SILHOUETTE OF
MEDIEVAL NAVE

0   5   10 m

MEDIEVAL   POST-
                  MEDIEVAL

FIG. 7. Medieval abbey church, east end, west elevation of bell tower, and
reconstruction of nave silhouette

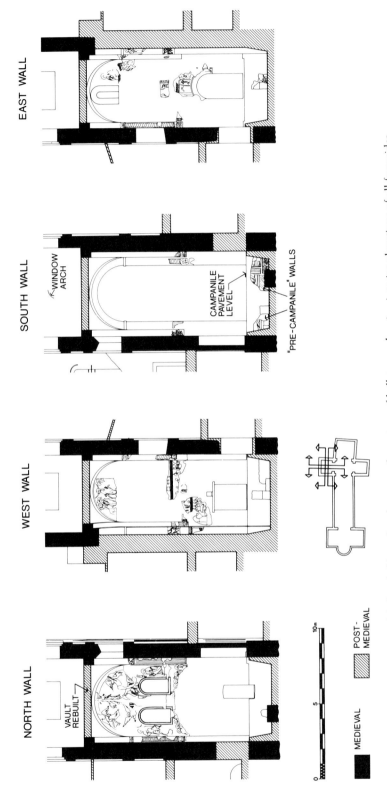

NORTH WALL

VAULT REBUILT

WEST WALL

SOUTH WALL

WINDOW ARCH

CAMPANILE PAVEMENT LEVEL

"PRE-CAMPANILE" WALLS

EAST WALL

MEDIEVAL

POST-MEDIEVAL

10 m

5

0

FIG. 8 Medieval abbey church, east end, sections of bell tower showing interior elevations of all four sides

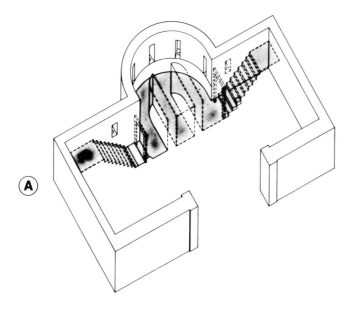

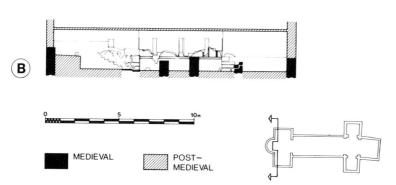

FIG. 9. Medieval abbey church, west end: A. reconstruction of transept and annular crypt; B. section of transept and annular crypt facing west

FIG. 10. Medieval abbey church, east end, axonometric reconstruction of the
exterior ca. 1060

0   5   10m

FIG. 11. Medieval abbey church, east end, axonometric reconstruction of the
interior ca. 1060

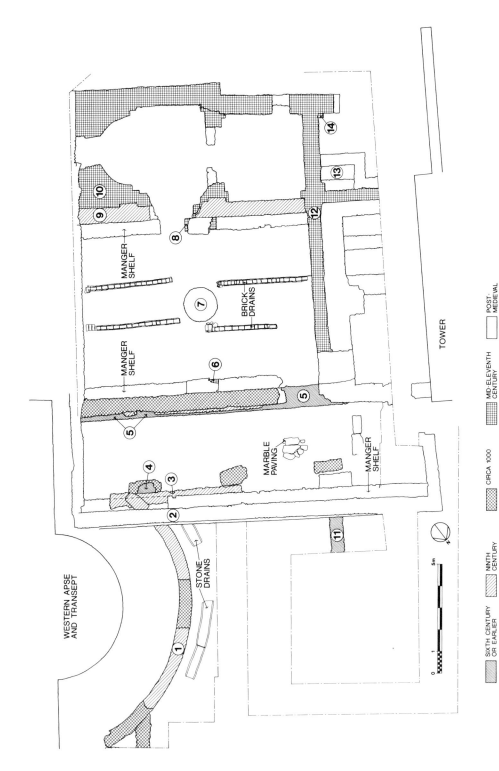

WESTERN APSE
AND TRANSEPT

STONE
DRAINS

MANGER
SHELF

MANGER
SHELF

BRICK
DRAINS

MARBLE
PAVING

MANGER
SHELF

TOWER

SIXTH CENTURY
OR EARLIER

NINTH
CENTURY

CIRCA 1000

MID-ELEVENTH
CENTURY

POST-
MEDIEVAL

0   1   5m

N

FIG. 12 Plan of excavations, 1978–1983 (1:20): numbers 1–14 indicate features referred to in the text

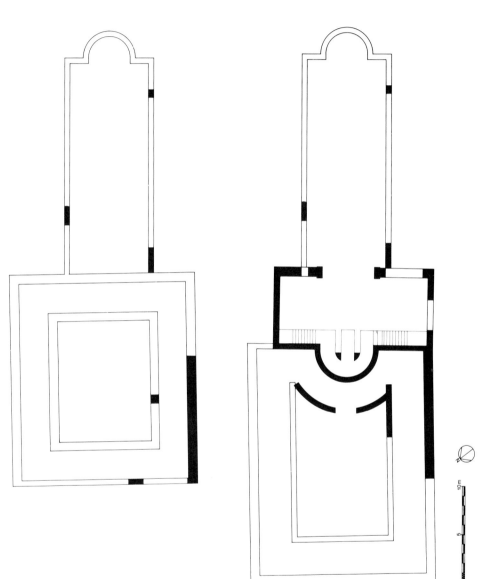

FIG. 13. Reconstructions of the plans of the abbey church and atrium: (*above*) under Thomas of Maurienne (680–720); (*below*) under Abbot Sichardus (830–842)

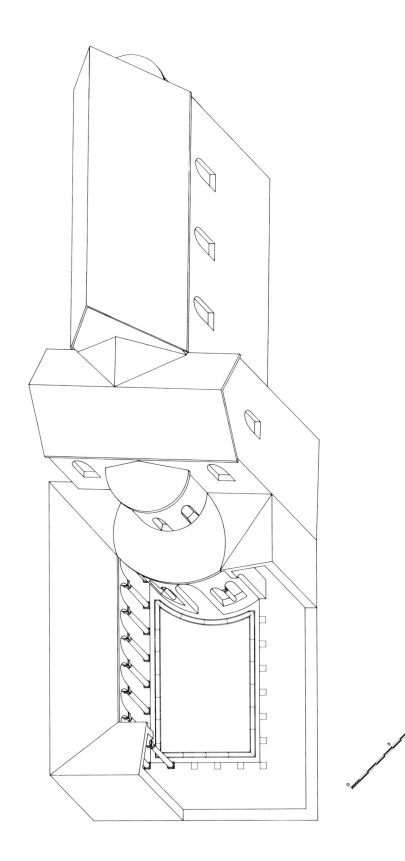

FIG. 14. Axonometric reconstruction of the abbey church and atrium under Abbot Sichardus (830–842)

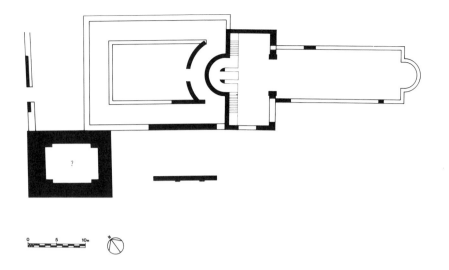

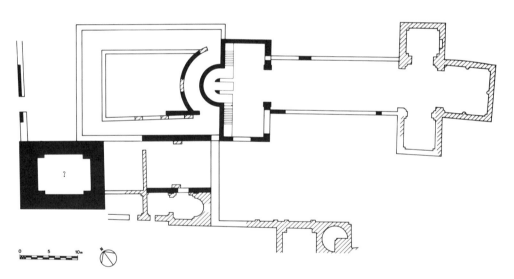

FIG. 15. Reconstructions of the layout of the medieval abbey: (*above*) mid-ninth century; (*below*) mid-eleventh century (black: Carolingian and pre-Carolingian; hatching: early Romanesque) (1:100)

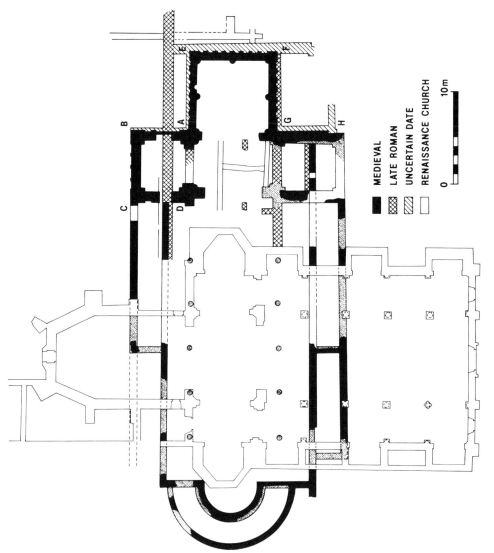

FIG. 16. Plan of Markthaler's investigations of the medieval abbey (after Croquison, "I problemi," facing p. 71)

MEDIEVAL

LATE ROMAN

UNCERTAIN DATE

RENAISSANCE CHURCH

0   10m

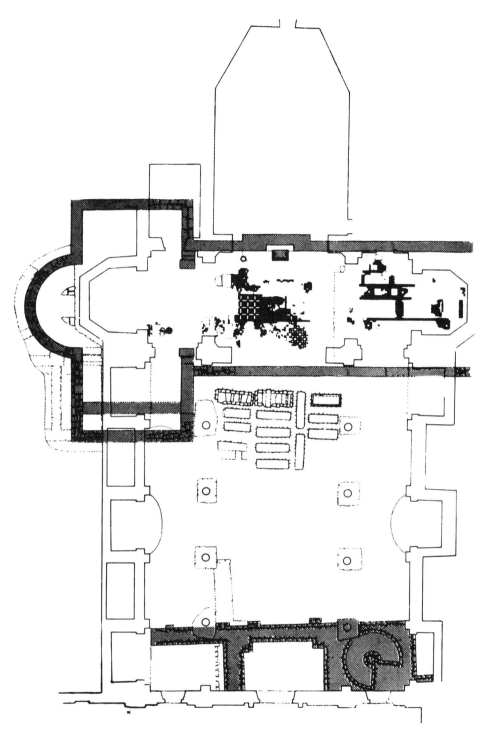

FIG. 17. Plan of 1959–1962 excavations by the Superintendency of the
Monuments of Lazio (from Franciosa, *L'abbazia*, fig. 4)

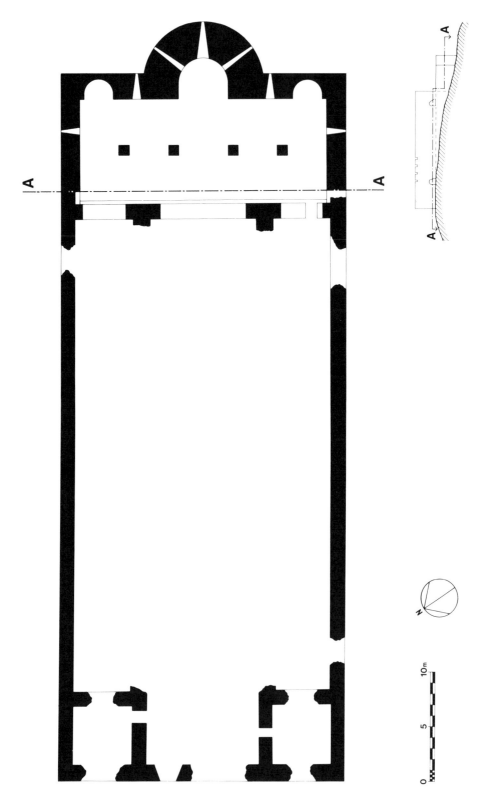

FIG. 18 Plan of ruins of church atop Monte S. Martino (1:100) (redrawn from a plan provided by the British School at Rome)

PLATE 1. Barberini map of Farfa dated 1686 (Library of Farfa Abbey)

PLATE 2. Medieval abbey church, east end, bell tower before restoration (Istituto Centrale per il Catalogo e la Documentazione, Rome)

PLATE 3. Abbey church, modern main altar (Istituto Centrale per il Catalogo e la Documentazione, Rome)

PLATE 4. Abbey church, wall fragment discovered within main altar during 1959–1962 restoration and excavations, south side (Istituto Centrale per il Catalogo e la Documentazione, Rome)

PLATE 5. Abbey church, wall fragment, discovered within main altar during 1959–1962 restoration and excavations, north side (Istituto Centrale per il Catalogo e la Documentazione, Rome)

PLATE 6a–b. Abbey church, medieval pavement upon discovery
in 1959 (Soprintendenza per i Beni Ambientali ed Architettonici
del Lazio, Rome)

PLATE 7. Medieval abbey church, foundations of west end uncovered in 1959, triumphal arch (Soprintendenza per i Beni Ambientali ed Architettonici del Lazio, Rome)

PLATE 8. Medieval abbey church, foundations of west end uncovered in 1959, southeast corner of south transept arm (Soprintendenza per i Beni Ambientali ed Architettonici del Lazio, Rome)

PLATE 9. Medieval abbey church, foundations of west end uncovered in 1959, northeast corner of north transept arm (Soprintendenza per i Beni Ambientali ed Architettonici del Lazio, Rome)

PLATE 10. Medieval abbey church, west end, foundations, south transept arm,
view of west wall facing south

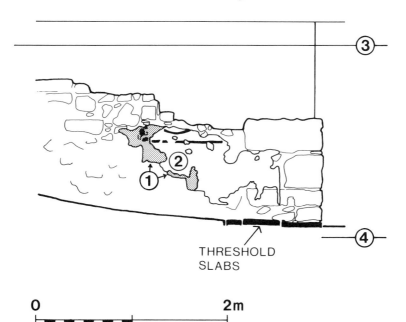

THRESHOLD
SLABS

0   2m

PLATE 11. Medieval abbey church, west end, foundations, south transept
arm, drawing of west wall showing profile of stairs; 1: first plaster layer; 2:
second plaster layer; 3: floor level of medieval nave; 4: original floor level
of crypt (author, redrawn by D. Cecil)

PLATE 12. Medieval abbey church, west end, annular crypt, view during excavations in 1959 (Soprintendenza per i Beni Ambientali ed Architettonici del Lazio, Rome)

PLATE 13. Medieval abbey church, west end, annular crypt, view after restoration (Istituto Centrale per il Catalogo e la Documentazione, Rome)

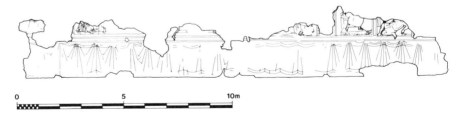

PLATE 14. Medieval abbey church, west end, annular crypt, remains of fresco decoration (author, redrawn by D. Cecil)

PLATE 15. Medieval abbey church, west end, annular crypt, view
from above during excavations in 1959 (Soprintendenza per i
Beni Ambientali ed Architettonici del Lazio, Rome)

PLATE 16. Medieval abbey church, west end, annular crypt, detail
of lamp niche during excavations in 1959 (Soprintendenza per i
Beni Ambientali ed Architettonici del Lazio, Rome)

PLATE 17. Medieval abbey church, west end, annular crypt, threshold
of south entrance

PLATE 18. Medieval abbey church, west end, annular crypt, south entrance,
remains of door jamb in situ

PLATE 19. Medieval abbey church, east end, exterior, facing west (Bibliotheca
Hertziana, Rome)

PLATE 20. Medieval abbey church, east end, exterior, bell tower, detail of east wall, upper half of ground floor (Bibliotheca Hertziana, Rome)

PLATE 21. Medieval abbey church, east end, exterior, bell tower, detail of east wall, lower half of ground floor (Bibliotheca Hertziana, Rome)

PLATE 22. Medieval abbey church, east end, exterior, bell tower, detail of north wall, ground floor

PLATE 23. Medieval abbey church, east end, exterior, bell tower, north wall, upper storeys

PLATE 24. Medieval abbey church, east end, exterior, bell tower, west wall, detail
of upper portion of ground floor

PLATE 25. Medieval abbey church, east end, exterior, bell tower, west wall, detail
of middle zone of ground floor (Bibliotheca Hertziana, Rome)

PLATE 26. Medieval abbey church, east end, exterior, bell tower, west wall, detail of ground floor showing masonry break indicating profile of nave

PLATE 27. Medieval abbey church, east end, exterior, bell tower, west wall, base of ground floor with niche bearing date 1546

PLATE 28. Medieval abbey church, east end, exterior, bell tower, south wall, detail of second storey showing blocked window

PLATE 29. Medieval abbey church, east end, interior, bell tower, south wall, second storey, detail of blocked window arch

PLATE 30. Medieval abbey church, east end, exterior, bell tower, east wall, base
of ground floor, detail of blocked archway

PLATE 31. Medieval abbey church, east end, exterior, bell tower, east wall, detail of ground floor showing decorative brickwork

PLATE 32. Medieval abbey church, east end, exterior, bell tower, west wall, detail of ground floor showing decorative brickwork and inlaid porphyry strips

PLATE 33. Medieval abbey church, east end, interior, bell tower, west wall and remains of vault of ground floor ca. 1927 before restoration (Soprintendenza per i Beni Ambientali ed Architettonici del Lazio, Rome)

PLATE 34. Medieval abbey church, east end, interior, bell tower, east wall,
lunette immediately below vault (Istituto Centrale per il Catalogo e la
Documentazione, Rome)

PLATE 35. Medieval abbey church, east end, interior,
bell tower, east wall, base of wall with arched recess
(Bibliotheca Hertziana, Rome)

PLATE 36. Medieval abbey church, east end,
interior, bell tower, west wall, base of wall showing
blocked doorway (Bibliotheca Hertziana, Rome)

PLATE 37. Medieval abbey church, east end,
interior, bell tower, ground floor, view of south wall
showing blocked archway (Bibliotheca
Hertziana, Rome)

PLATE 38. Medieval abbey church, east end,
interior, bell tower, remains of medieval paving

PLATES 39a (*top right*) and 39b (*below*). Medieval abbey church, east end,
interior, bell tower, mortar striking or *falsa cortina* below remains of
medieval wall painting

PLATE 40. Medieval abbey church, east end, interior, bell tower, north wall,
lunette immediately below vault with remains of fresco decoration representing
the Ascension of Christ (Istituto Centrale per il Catalogo e
la Documentazione, Rome)

PLATE 41. Medieval abbey church, east end, interior, bell tower, north wall, detail of the Ascension of Christ, window zone showing angels and SS. Peter (right) and Paul (left) (Istituto Centrale per il Catalogo e la Documentazione, Rome)

PLATE 42. Medieval abbey church, east end, interior, bell tower, north wall, detail of the Ascension of Christ, apostles in lowest zone (Istituto Centrale per il Catalogo e la Documentazione, Rome)

PLATE 43. Medieval abbey church, east end, interior, bell tower, west wall, lunette immediately below vault with remains of fresco decoration representing Christ in Majesty (Istituto Centrale per il Catalogo e la Documentazione, Rome)

PLATE 44. Medieval abbey church, east end, interior, bell tower, west wall, middle zone with remains of fresco decoration representing the Story of Naaman (upper right) and the Sacrifice of Noah (lower left) (Istituto Centrale per il Catalogo e la Documentazione, Rome)

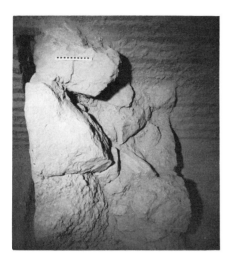

PLATES 45a (*top left*), 45b (*top right*), and 45c (*above*). Medieval abbey church, east end, interior, bell tower, vestige of wall below the bell tower: a. view from above; b. north face with first fresco layer; c. north face with second fresco layer upon discovery in 1925–1928 (Pontificio Istituto di Archeologia Cristiana, Rome)

PLATE 46. Medieval abbey church, east end, remains of arch adjoining the bell tower at the northwest corner

PLATE 47. Medieval abbey church, east end, exterior, square presbytery, south wall, general view during restoration, date not specified (Soprintendenza per i Beni Ambientali ed Architettonici del Lazio, Rome)

PLATE 48. Medieval abbey church, east end, exterior, square presbytery, south wall after restoration (Bibliotheca Hertziana, Rome)

PLATE 49. Medieval abbey church, east end, exterior, square presbytery, north wall, upper portion after restoration

PLATE 50. Medieval abbey church, east end,
exterior, square presbytery, north wall, remains
of window arch and sill

PLATE 51. Medieval abbey church, east end, exterior, square presbytery, north wall, detail of cornice

PLATE 52. Medieval abbey church, east end, exterior, square presbytery, base of north wall

PLATE 53. Medieval abbey church, east end, exterior, square presbytery, east wall after restoration (Bibliotheca Hertziana, Rome)

PLATE 54. Medieval abbey church, east end, exterior, square presbytery, east wall, detail of base of wall

PLATE 55. Medieval abbey church, east end, interior, square presbytery, south wall, detail of upper southeast corner (Bibliotheca Hertziana, Rome)

PLATE 56. Medieval abbey church, east end, interior, square presbytery, north wall, upper northwest corner (Bibliotheca Hertziana, Rome)

PLATES 57a (*left*) and 57b (*right*). Medieval abbey church, east end, interior, square presbytery, middle of south wall, detail of engaged column: a. shaft; b. base

PLATES 58a (*left*) and 58b (*right*). Medieval abbey church, east end, interior, square presbytery, middle of north wall: a. view of blocked window and engaged column shaft (Library of Farfa Abbey); b. detail of engaged column base

PLATES 59a (*top left*), 59b (*top right*), and 59c (*above*).
Medieval abbey church, east end, interior, square
presbytery, east wall, remains of engaged column
shafts: a. northeast corner; b. middle;
c. southeast corner

PLATE 60. Medieval abbey church, east end, interior, square presbytery, west wall, remains of archway and lunettes originally opening onto crossing (Bibliotheca Hertziana, Rome)

PLATE 61. Medieval abbey church, east end, interior, square presbytery, west wall, detail of meander border of medieval fresco decoration on soffit of archway originally leading to crossing (Istituto Centrale per il Catalogo e la Documentazione, Rome)

PLATE 62. Medieval abbey church, east end, interior, square presbytery, west wall, detail of soffit of second lining of archway leading to crossing showing two layers of Renaissance fresco decoration (Library of Farfa Abbey)

PLATE 63. Medieval abbey church, east end, interior, crossing, remains of engaged column shaft in northwest corner

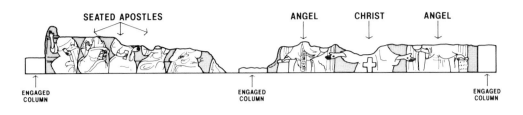

PLATES 64a (*top*) and 64b (*bottom*). Medieval abbey church, east end, interior,
square presbytery, east wall, middle zone with remains of fresco decoration
representing the Last Judgment: a. drawing showing remains of seated apostles,
Christ, and attendant angels (author, redrawn by D. Cecil); b. detail
of seated apostles

PLATE 65. Medieval abbey church, east end, interior, square presbytery, soffit of lunette in west wall, detail of Renaissance fresco decoration representing the prophet Habakkuk

PLATE 66. Medieval abbey church, east end, interior, square presbytery, south
wall, middle zone, southeast corner, remains of two distinct fresco layers—the
lower medieval, the upper Renaissance—both representing seated apostles

PLATE 67. Abbey museum, detached painted lunette, detail, Thomas of Maurienne holding model of the medieval abbey church, late fifteenth century

PLATE 68. Medieval abbey church, east end, bell tower, upper storey, walled up medieval colonnette and capital upon discovery ca. 1925–1928 (Pontificio Istituto di Archeologia Cristiana, Rome)

PLATE 69. Medieval capital used as corbel for vault of seventeenth-century corridor

PLATES 70a (*above*) and 70b (*right*). Abbey museum: a. medieval capital, presumably from destroyed medieval bell tower (Bibliotheca Hertziana, Rome); b. ends of medieval capitals, presumably from destroyed medieval bell tower

PLATE 71. Excavation zone, view of tower, after restoration, facing west

BADIA di FARFA

RUDERI DEL PALAZZO ABBAZIALE

PLATE 72. Excavation zone, view of tower and surrounding area, 1935, before restoration, facing west (Library of Farfa Abbey)

PLATE 73. Blocked arch and surrounding medieval masonry in wall bordering excavation zone to the west

PLATE 74. Excavation zone, vestige of wall standing ca. 1935 (Soprintendenza per i Beni Ambientali ed Architettonici del Lazio, Rome)

PLATE 75 Excavation zone, view from above, facing east, 1982

PLATE 76. Excavation zone, view from above, facing east, 1982

PLATE 77. Excavation zone, detail of apse of medieval chapel, northeast corner

PLATE 78. Excavation zone, wall behind apse of medieval chapel, fresco fragment
showing draped right thigh of a standing figure

PLATE 79. Excavation zone, wall extending from end of south arm of medieval transept, north side

PLATE 80. Excavation zone, view of curved wall outside western medieval apse, west side

PLATE 81. Excavation zone, medieval tombs and rectangular piers found below
cobblestone floor of Renaissance stables

PLATE 82. Excavation zone, view of curved wall and stone drains outside western apse of medieval abbey church, facing south

PLATE 83a. Abbey church, interior, medieval walls discovered below Renaissance nave immediately inside west façade in 1959–1962: wall with pilasters, facing south (Soprintendenza per i Beni Ambientali ed Architettonici del Lazio, Rome)

PLATE 83b. Abbey church, interior, medieval walls discovered below Renaissance
nave immediately inside west façade in 1959–1962: foundations of spiral staircase
(Soprintendenza per i Beni Ambientali ed Architettonici del Lazio, Rome)

PLATE 84. Epitaph of Abbot Sichardus (830–842) discovered by the Superintendency of Monuments of Lazio in 1959 (Istituto Centrale per il Catalogo e la Documentazione, Rome)

PLATE 85. Excavation zone, ancient Roman battle sarcophagus upon discovery in 1959 outside the medieval western apse at juncture with north transept arm (Soprintendenza per i Beni Ambientali ed Architettonici del Lazio, Rome)

PLATE 86. Excavation zone, fragments of stone cornice

PLATES 87a (*top*) and 87b (*bottom*). Ruins of church atop Monte S. Martino,
exterior, west end: a. remains of south wall and west façade; b. detail of window
and surrounding masonry in west façade

PLATE 88a Abbey church, interior, view of nave, facing northwest (Istituto Centrale per il Catalogo e la Documentazione, Rome)

PLATE 88b. Abbey church, interior, detail of ionic capital, mid-twelfth century

PLATE 89. Abbey church, Cosmatesque panels set in floor of crossing, before
restoration of 1959–1962 (Istituto Centrale per il Catalogo e
la Documentazione, Rome)

PLATE 90. Abbey museum, fragments of Cosmatesque chancel screen,
mid-twelfth century

PLATES 91a (*top*) and 91b (*bottom*). Abbey museum, Renaissance fresco fragments
detached from interior east wall of square presbytery of medieval abbey church:
a. torso of the Virgin Mary and pierced right hand of Christ; b. torso of John the
Baptist with hair shirt

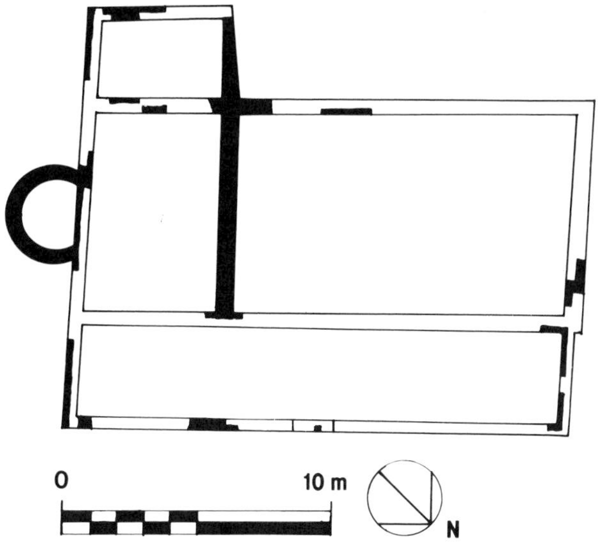

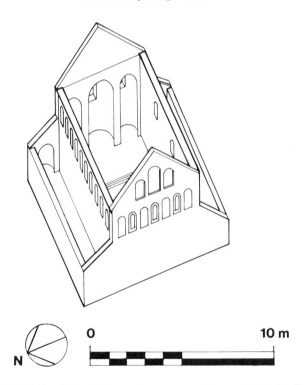

PLATE 92. St. Martin at Angers, plan, early eighth century (after Forsyth, *St. Martin at Angers*, fig. 183c)

PLATE 93. St. John, Müstair, isometric reconstruction, ca. 800 (after Frankl, *Baukunst*, 23, fig. 32)

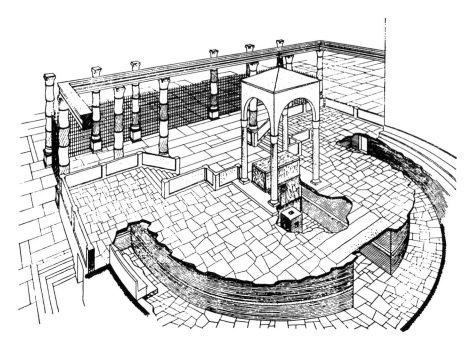

PLATE 94. Old St. Peter's, Rome, reconstruction of annular crypt, ca. 600, outer row of columns early eighth century (from Apollonj-Ghetti, *Esplorazioni*, fig. 141)

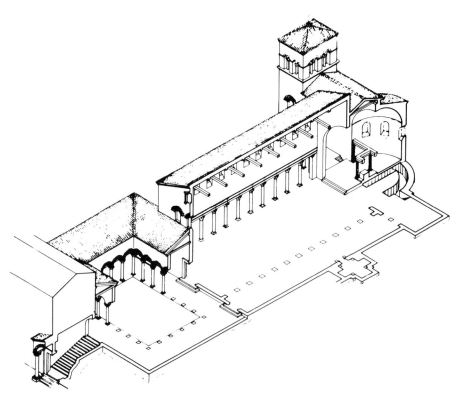

PLATE 95. S. Prassede, Rome, 817–824, isometric reconstruction (from Krautheimer, *Corpus*, III, 256, fig. 226)

PLATE 96. S. Maria in *Vescovio*, exterior, transept and apse, mid-ninth century

PLATE 97. S. Maria in Vescovio, interior, annular crypt, end of perpendicular
corridor, mid-ninth century

PLATE 98. S. Maria in Vescovio, interior, confessio and main altar, ninth and
tenth centuries

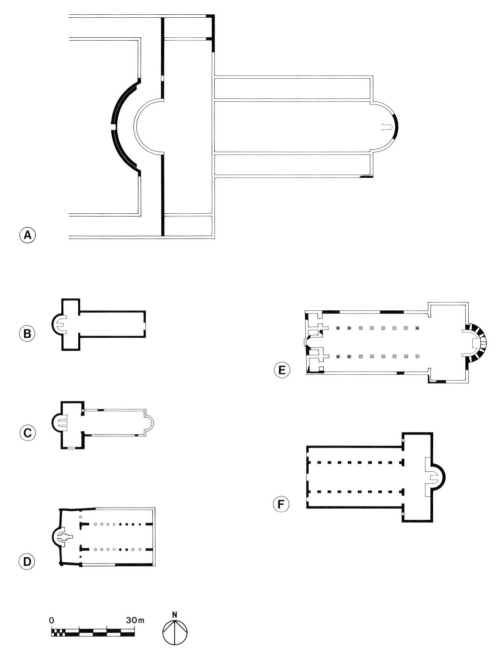

PLATE 99. Comparative plans of Carolingian churches with transepts: A. Abbey church at Fulda, dedicated 819 (after Fischer and Oswald, "Zur Baugeschichte," fig. 1); B. S. Maria in Vescovio, mid-ninth century (after Tarchi, *L'arte*, II, pl. XCII); C. Abbey church of Farfa, mid-ninth century; D. S. Stefano degli Abissini, 847–855 (after Krautheimer, *Corpus*, IV, pl. XI); E. Abbey church of St.-Denis, 754–775 (after Heitz, *L'architecture*, 23, fig. 10); F. SS. Peter and Marcellinus, Seligenstadt, 830–840 (after Binding, "Kirchen," fig. III)

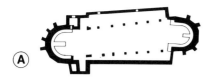

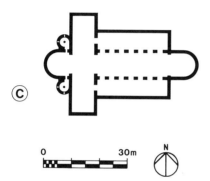

PLATE 100. Comparative plans of Carolingian churches with double apses: A. St.-Maurice d'Agaune, late eighth century (after *VK*, 297); B. Cologne cathedral, ca. 800 (after Weyres, "Neue Ergebnisse," 28, fig. 1); C. St. Salvator, Paderborn, ca. 875 (after Ortmann, *Die karolingische Bauten*, 66, fig. 102)

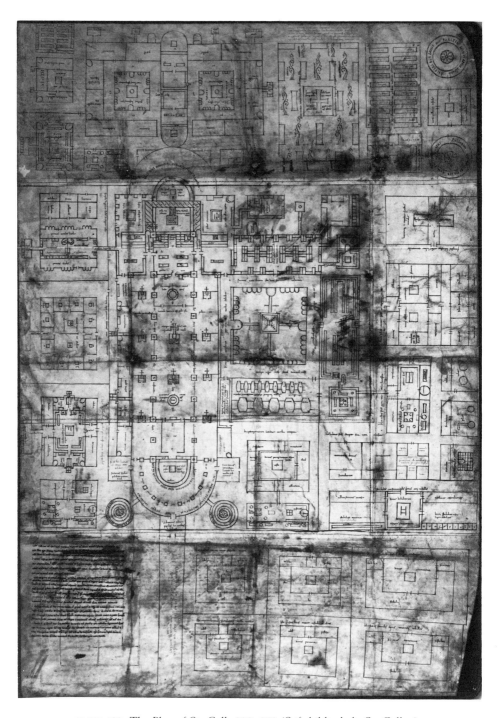

PLATE 101. The Plan of St. Gall, 820–830 (Stiftsbibliothek, St. Gallen)

PLATE 102. Abbey of St.-Riquier, engraving, 1612 (Biblioteca Apostolica Vaticana)

PLATE 103. Abbey church at Fulda, excavations 1908–1913, remains of curved walls outside western apse, ca. 822 (from Vonderau, "Die Ausgrabungen, 1908–1913," pl. II)

PLATE 104. Abbey church of S. Scolastica, Subiaco, exterior, bell tower, dedicated 1053

PLATE 105a. Abbey church of S. Scolastica, Subiaco, exterior, bell tower, ded.
1053, south wall, during restoration 1962–1964 (Soprintendenza per i Beni
Ambientali ed Architettonici del Lazio, Rome)

PLATE 105b. Abbey church of S. Scolastica, Subiaco, exterior, bell tower, ded.
1053, south wall, ground floor, detail of blind arcading and decorative brickwork
(from Perrotti, 146, fig. 13)

PLATE 106. Evangelistary from Farfa, fol. 7r, the Ascension of Christ, third
quarter of the eleventh century, Madrid, Biblioteca Nacional, Vitr. 20–6
(Biblioteca Nacional, Madrid)

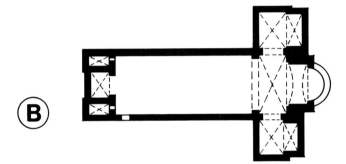

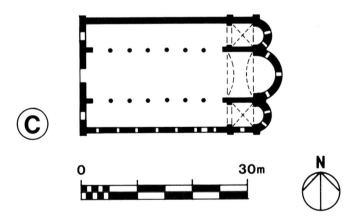

PLATE 107. Comparative plans of early Romanesque churches in Central and North Italy: A. S. Pietro at Ferentillo, first half of the eleventh century (after Thümmler, "Die Baukunst," 145, fig. 133); B. S. Salvatore at Monte Amiata, ca. 1036 (after Thümmler, "Die Baukunst," 195, fig. 193); C. S. Pietro at Agliate, ca. 1000 (after Thümmler, "Die Baukunst," 202, fig. 204)

PLATE 108. S. Pietro at Ferentillo, east end, exterior, first half of
the eleventh century

PLATE 109. S. Salvatore at Monte Amiata, west façade, ca. 1036

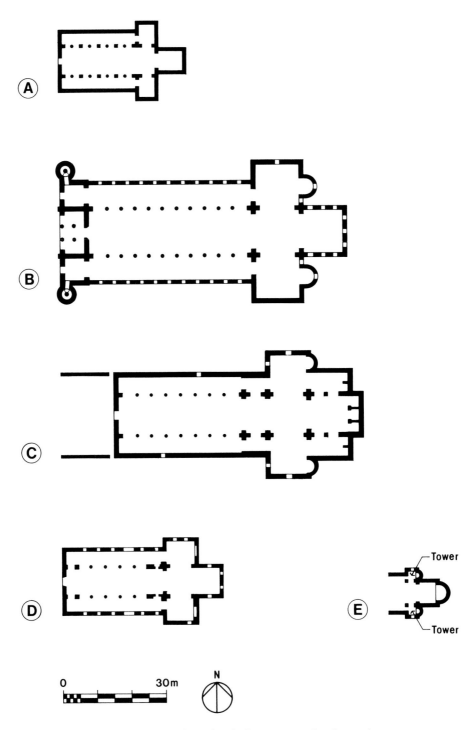

Ⓐ

Ⓑ

Ⓒ

Ⓓ

Ⓔ ┌─Tower

└─Tower

0   30m   N

PLATE 110. Comparative plans of early Romanesque churches with square or
rectangular presbyteries: A. St. Martin, Zyfflich, ca. 1020 (after Schaeffer,
Zyfflich, fig. 187); B. Abbey church, Limburg an der Haardt, 1025–1042 (after
Wellmann, "Kloster Limburg," pl. 1); C. Abbey church of SS. Peter and Paul,
Hirsau, 1083–1091, (after Hoffmann, *Hirsau*, 17); D. Abbey church, Wiblingen,
ca. 1093 (after Hoffmann, *Hirsau*, 32); E. Klosterreichenbach, ded. 1085 (after
Mettler, "Die zweite Kirche," *Zeitschrift für Geschichte*, IV, 6)

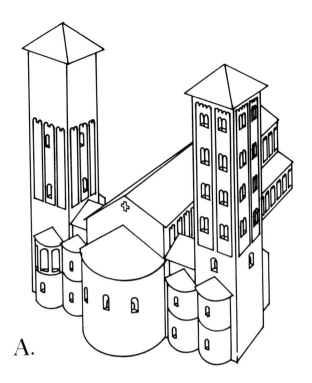

A.

B.

PLATE 111. Comparative exterior elevations of churches with towers over eastern transepts: A. Cathedral of Aosta, reconstruction, ca. 1020–1040 (after Magni, "Cathédrale d'Aoste," 178, fig. 22); B. St.-Michel, Cuxa, reconstruction of phase II, by 1040 (after Kubach, *Romanesque*, 139, fig. 151)

PLATE 112. Cathedral of Ivrea, exterior, early eleventh century

PLATE 113. S. Abbondio, Como, east end, exterior,
consecrated 1095

PLATE 114. S. Abbondio, Como, interior, base of south bell tower,
consecrated 1095

PLATE 115. St. Lucius, Werden, reconstruction of exterior elevation, consecrated 1063 (from Effmann, *Werden*, fig. 3)

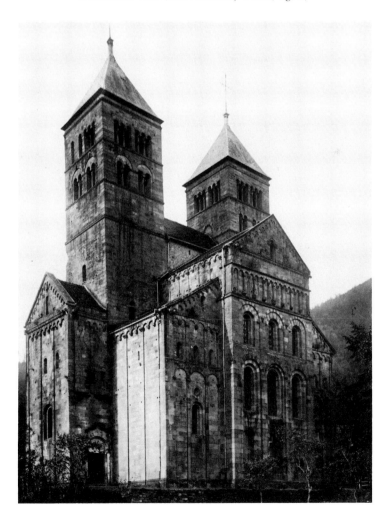

PLATE 116. Remains of the abbey church at Murbach, view of the east end, ded. 1134 (Bildarchiv Foto Marburg)

PLATE 117. St. Cyriacus, Gernrode, view of west end, ca. 960
(Slides and Photographs Collection, Yale University)

PLATE 118. Baptistery at Lomello, detail of attic storey, rebuilt in
early eleventh century

PLATE 119. S. Salvatore, Brescia, south side, exterior, ca. 800

PLATE 120. St. John, Müstair, east end, exterior, ca. 800

PLATE 121. S. Vincenzo, Galliano, eastern apse, exterior, consecrated 1007

PLATE 122. Cathedral of Torcello, west façade, exterior, consecrated 1008

PLATE 123. Ste.-Gertrude, Nivelles, north transept arm, exterior,
consecrated 1046

PLATE 124. Abbey church, Romainmôtier, south side, exterior,
consecrated 1040

PLATE 125. Cathedral of Gerace, northern side apse, exterior, second half of the
eleventh century

PLATE 126. St. Martin at Angers, east end, interior, crossing piers and
arches, ca. 1040

PLATE 127. S. Ambrogio, Milan, east end, exterior, detail of main apse,
late tenth century

PLATE 128. Pomposa, bell tower, exterior, detail of brickwork, 1063

PLATE 129. Abbey church, Limburg an der Haardt, east end, interior of presbytery, 1025–1042

PLATE 130. Speyer Cathedral, reconstruction of interior nave elevation, ca. 1060
(from Lehmann, *Kirchenbau*, pl. 17, fig. 37)

PLATE 131. Florence, S. Reparata, east end, interior, detail of apse of north side chapel, mid-eleventh century

PLATE 132. Abbey church of S. Maria di Tremiti, nave, interior elevation, south side, consecrated 1045

PLATE 133. S. Bartolomeo all'Isola, Rome, bell tower, exterior, ca. 1100

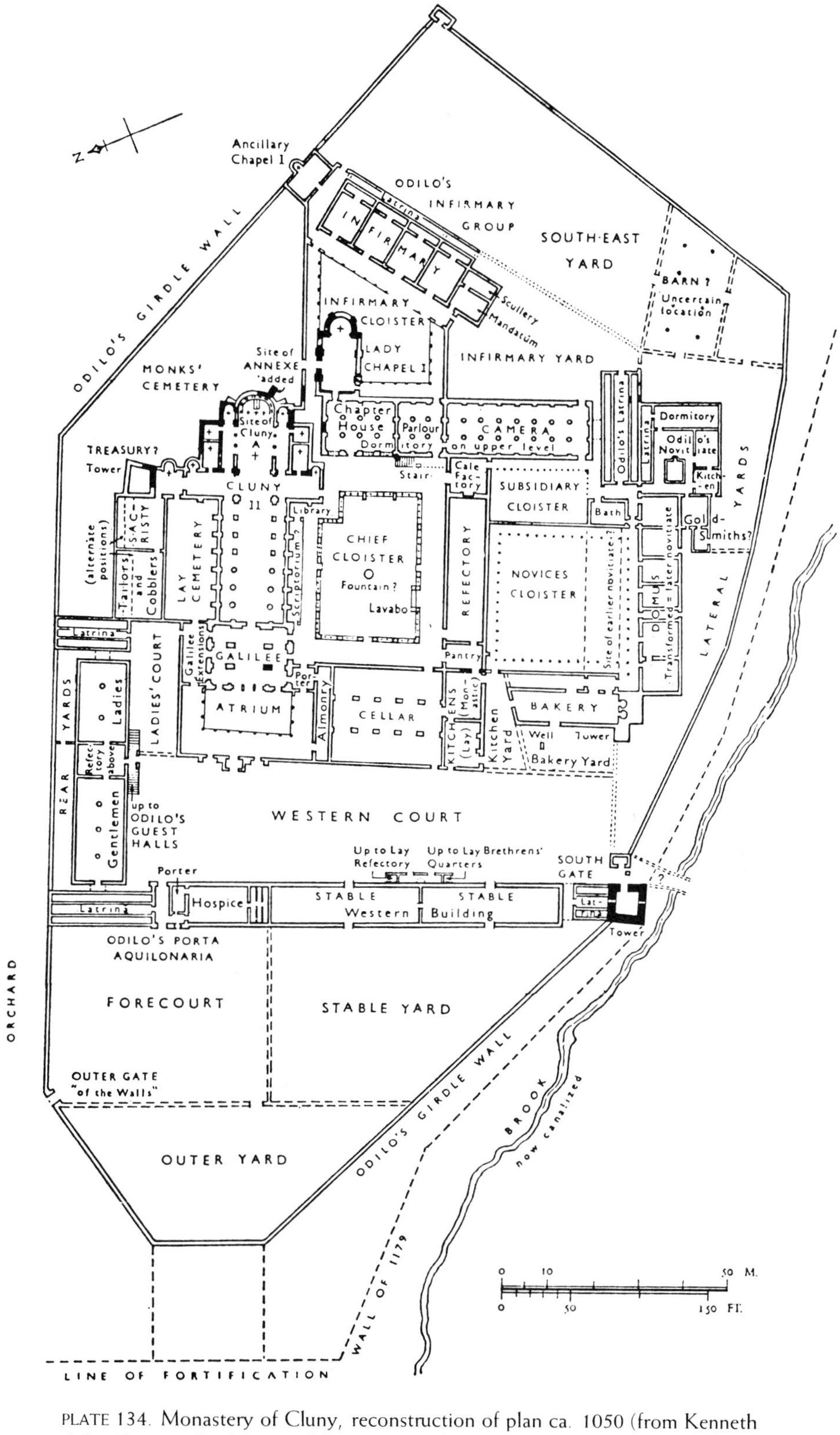

N

Ancillary
Chapel 1

ODILO'S
INFIRMARY
GROUP

SOUTH-EAST
YARD

BARN ?
Uncertain
location

Latrina

ODILO'S GIRDLE WALL

INFIRMARY

INFIRMARY
CLOISTER

Scullery
Mandatum

INFIRMARY YARD

MONKS'
CEMETERY

Site of
ANNEXE
'added

LADY
CHAPEL 1

Dormitory

ODILO'S Latrina

ODILO'S
Novitiate

Site of
Cluny

Chapter
House

Parlour

CAMERA

on upper level

LATERAL YARDS

Dormitory
Kitch-
en

TREASURY ?
Tower

CLUNY
II

Stair

Cale-
fac-
tory

SUBSIDIARY
CLOISTER

Bath

Gold-
Smiths ?

(alternate positions)

Library

Scriptorium

CHIEF
CLOISTER

Fountain ?

Lavabo

REFECTORY

NOVICES
CLOISTER

DOMUS

Site of earlier novitiate

Transformed = later novitiate

Tailors'
and
Cobblers'

SAC-
RISTY

LAY
CEMETERY

Galilee extensions

GALILEE

Por-
ter

ATRIUM

Almonry

CELLAR

Pantry

(Mon-
astic)

BAKERY

REAR YARDS

Refec-
tory
above

LADIES' COURT

Ladies

KITCHENS
(Lay)

Kitchen
Yard

Well

Tower

Bakery Yard

Gentlemen

up to
ODILO'S
GUEST
HALLS

WESTERN COURT

Up to Lay
Refectory

Up to Lay Brethrens'
Quarters

SOUTH
GATE

Porter

Hospice

STABLE
Western

STABLE
Building

Lat-
rina

Latrina

Tower

ODILO'S PORTA
AQUILONARIA

FORECOURT

STABLE YARD

BROOK
now canalized

ORCHARD

OUTER GATE
"of the Walls"

OUTER YARD

ODILO'S GIRDLE WALL

WALL OF 1179

LINE OF FORTIFICATION

0   10   50 M.

0   50   150 FT.

PLATE 134. Monastery of Cluny, reconstruction of plan ca. 1050 (from Kenneth
John Conant, *Carolingian and Romanesque Architecture 800–1200*, 1966, 83, fig. 26)

PLATE 135. S. Vincenzo, Galliano, interior, crypt entrance, capital, early
eleventh century

PLATE 136. SS. Giovanni e Paolo, Rome, narthex, exterior, detail of ionic
capital, 1154

PLATE 137. Last Judgment Panel, Pinacoteca Vaticana, mid-twelfth century
(Archivio Fotografico, Musei Vaticani)

PLATE 138. S. Maria della Verità, Cappella Mazzatosta, Viterbo, detail of fresco decoration of arch soffit representing Old Testament prophets, by Lorenzo da Viterbo, 1469